"Every invention in communication technology—the printing press, photography, motion pictures, videotape, the Internet—was quickly co-opted to produce and disseminate erotica. Just as the microscope and the telescope illuminated for the first time the very small and the very large, *A Billion Wicked Thoughts* uses the power of the Internet to illuminate, with unprecedented wattage, human male and female desires. Ogas and Gaddam analyzed a mountain of Internet data to produce a breakthrough in the study of human sexuality."

—Donald Symons, professor emeritus, University of California, Santa Barbara; author of *The Evolution of Human Sexuality*

"*A Billion Wicked Thoughts* provides a brilliant, thoroughly researched, and totally engaging analysis of human sexuality using vast and original analyses of the Internet. It furnishes an X-ray of male and female sexual minds and explains why they differ so profoundly. The insights it yields are often surprising, sometimes shocking, and never boring. I couldn't put the book down."

—David M. Buss, author of *Evolutionary Psychology: The New Science of the Mind* and *The Evolution of Desire: Strategies of Human Mating*

"On the Internet, the evolutionary past meets futuristic technology, enabling the blossoming of all manner of sexual tastes, fantasies, and desires. Ogas and Gaddam have mined these new sources of information—arguably the world's largest experiment on human behavior—to produce a fascinating and terrific book on human sexuality, in all its timeless mysteries and ultramodern manifestations. This well-written, entertaining book is packed with information, ideas, and insights. There is no better way to understanding your desires, your partner's, or anyone else's."

—Roy Baumeister, professor of psychology, Florida State University

"A brilliant romp through the darkest recesses of our sexual minds, based on the unwitting confessions of millions of anonymous Internet users."

—Simon LeVay, author of *The Sexual Brain* and *Gay, Straight, and the Reason Why*

"Ogas and Gaddam mine the power of the Internet for expressions of male and female mating psychology that are unfiltered by social expectations. In the process, they unearth A Billion Wicked Thoughts, many of which depart radically from our standard script for human mating psychology. These counterintuitive insights into the sexual psyche of our species should provide much fodder for discussion among sex researchers."

—Paul Vasey, professor of behavioral science, University of Lethbridge

A BILLION

WICKED THOUGHTS

What the World's Largest Experiment
Reveals About Human Desire

OGI OGAS AND **SAI GADDAM**

DUTTON

DUTTON
Published by Penguin Group (USA) Inc.
375 Hudson Street, New York, New York 10014, U.S.A.
Penguin Group (Canada), 90 Eglinton Avenue East, Suite 700, Toronto,
Ontario M4P 2Y3, Canada (a division of Pearson Penguin Canada Inc.);
Penguin Books Ltd, 80 Strand, London WC2R 0RL, England; Penguin Ireland,
25 St Stephen's Green, Dublin 2, Ireland (a division of Penguin Books Ltd);
Penguin Group (Australia), 250 Camberwell Road, Camberwell, Victoria 3124,
Australia (a division of Pearson Australia Group Pty Ltd); Penguin Books India Pvt Ltd,
11 Community Centre, Panchsheel Park, New Delhi – 110 017, India; Penguin Group
(NZ), 67 Apollo Drive, Rosedale, North Shore 0632, New Zealand (a division of
Pearson New Zealand Ltd); Penguin Books (South Africa) (Pty) Ltd, 24 Sturdee
Avenue, Rosebank, Johannesburg 2196, South Africa

Penguin Books Ltd, Registered Offices: 80 Strand, London WC2R 0RL, England

Published by Dutton, a member of Penguin Group (USA) Inc.

First printing, May 2011
1   3   5   7   9   10   8   6   4   2

LIBRARY OF CONGRESS CATALOGING-IN-PUBLICATION DATA
has been applied for

ISBN 978-0-525-95209-1

Printed in the United States of America
Set in Janson Text
Designed by Spring Hoteling

CONTENTS

FOREWORD

My first encounter with one of the authors of this book, Ogi Ogas, was about a year ago. True to the online nature of the research he was doing for this book, I heard from him via e-mail.

Ogi had read a book on sexuality called *Warrior Lovers* that I wrote a few years ago, along with Don Symons. In it we used "slash"—stories about heterosexual male fictional characters who fall in love, such as Captain Kirk and Mr. Spock or Clark Kent and Lex Luthor—revealing an unexpected yet telling aspect of female desire.

Slash is, in a sense, the ultimate romance for its female readers: one in which there is no doubt at the end of the tale that these heroes have found their soul mates. Ogi wanted to know if I had any new work to tell him about. To be honest, I was a bit surprised by the initial e-mail—most conversations I have about slash are with other women—but it soon became clear that Ogi was interested not only in slash but in the bigger picture of human sexuality that can be found in the vast world of the Internet. There is a lot of truth to the belief that if you can imagine it, you can find it as

Internet porn. That initial e-mail was the beginning of a long and lively conversation about the nature of sexual desire.

But this book does far more than just show how wild and wooly online porn can be. It opens your eyes to the sexual desires of millions of people and it does so in a unique and valuable way. So much research on sexuality relies on surveys and questionnaires that ask people to reveal secrets they aren't comfortable sharing (least of all with a researcher who will do who-knows-what with the information). There is a real advantage in finding other methods of insight into our desires—unobtrusive measures that don't require people to actively participate in the process of data collection. Just as Don and I demonstrated with commercial erotica and slash in *Warrior Lovers*, Ogi Ogas and Sai Gaddam study digital footprints on the Internet to illuminate our understanding of the stark differences between the desires of males and females.

The most startling insights often come from the most unexpected sources. The authors' academic background, for instance, is hardly typical for the authors of a book on sex. Ogi and Sai were classmates in graduate school and their PhDs are from the Department of Cognitive and Neural Systems at Boston University. Most cognitive neuroscience researchers, if you hadn't already guessed, aren't doing research on porn. But Ogi and Sai's computational neuroscience background led them to ask novel questions such as "how does the brain software that generates sexual desire and arousal actually work?" No one else in their field was thinking that way. It led them to not only use the Internet as a source of data (their data-mining approach was one their mathematical background made them uniquely suited to) but also to an adaptationist approach to human sexual behavior. This approach views male and female sexuality through a functional lens, as the products of differing selection pressures (or problems) that males and females had to face (or solve) over evolutionary time.

The adaptationist perspective has been incredibly fruitful, particularly in the area of female sexuality. Historically, there have been a number of challenges to studying female desire and sexual behavior. There have been times when it wasn't considered appropriate for a doctor to even look at his female patients' genitals. For male researchers to ask women about their sexual desires and behavior was simply not acceptable. Even today, a female sex researcher will have a much easier time in terms of how both participants and others view her and her work. So the study of female sexuality has languished behind that of males, especially back in the day when most scientists and researchers were male. It was often only considered legitimate to study female sexuality if you were trying to help women become pregnant. But the rise of the adaptationist perspective (led by both male and female researchers) has focused attention on questions surrounding the female choice of partners and how such choices would have resulted in greater reproductive success in the past. This research has led to discoveries about female mate preferences, the role of hormones and the ovulatory cycle in female sexuality, and the function of female orgasm.

Without an adaptationist perspective, it's unlikely anyone would have designed a study to look at how well exotic dancers are tipped according to their ovulatory cycle. The fact that tips are higher when dancers are more fertile tells us something about both female desirability and behavior during ovulation and how attractive this is to males.

The adaptationist approach was also the critical tool Ogi and Sai used to unlock their exhaustive Internet data.

And they did so elegantly and eloquently. This book provides a refreshing look at the big picture of human sexuality, informed by the ultimate unobtrusive source of data, the Internet. And regardless of your background, you're in for a treat. You will learn about the endless variety of kinks and squicks (kinks that you find gross as opposed to a turn on) that people have. You will also learn about the essential male and female sexual psychologies, as illustrated by Elmer Fudd (the trigger-happy hunter who sees what he wants, aims and fires, and then does it all over again) and the Miss Marple Detective Agency (the female software for figuring out if this guy is the right one). If that hasn't convinced you that you need the insights these authors have to offer, there is also the importance of the Magic Hoo Hoo, critical to all romance novels . . . part of the female desire to be sexually irresistible, and all that we can learn from watching gay porn (which is amazingly different from slash, considering both are about guy on guy action).

If you want answers to pretty much anything you need to know about sexual desire, this is the book for you.

Catherine Salmon
Coauthor of Warrior Lovers: Erotic Fantasies, Evolution and
Female Sexuality and The Secret Power of Middle Children

PREFACE

The World's Largest Behavioral Experiment

> While the individual man is an insoluble puzzle,
> in the aggregate he becomes a mathematical
> certainty.
>
> — Sherlock Holmes, *Sign of the Four*

There's one special challenge that every behavioral scientist must eventually confront. A challenge that sets all behavioral scientists apart from physicists, biologists, and engineers. It's the reason most students of behavioral science are drawn to the field, and one reason most behavioral scientists are women. It's also the reason it's the only discipline requiring all its practitioners to have their ethics evaluated by committee. What is this unique challenge? The subjects of behavioral science: people.

And people are a problem.

Most people aren't particularly interested in contributing to scientific progress. Who wants to keep a daily journal recording every time she yawns? Who wants to get injected with radioactive cobalt before sticking his head into a hole the size of a water bucket? There are groceries to shop for, customers to sell to, kids to pick up. What kind of person wants to do boring tasks with no personal benefit and for trivial money? Fortunately for science, there is such a person.

The undergraduate.

Many sciences have a standard test subject, used over and

over by its practitioners. Geneticists use fruit flies, endocrinologists use guinea pigs, molecular biologists use mice. For behavioral scientists, it's the college freshman. It's easy to understand why: they're cheap, in plentiful supply, easy to motivate through course requirements, and willing to endure even the most unusual experimental methods. Much of our contemporary understanding of ethics, aggression, and sexuality is based upon the behavior of adolescent psych majors. But recently, researchers have begun to wonder just how valid this understanding really is. After all, don't undergrads—jobless, childless, and marinating in sex hormones—represent a unique specimen of *Homo sapiens*?

Surely there are behavioral experiments that don't use college students? There are indeed studies that use adults, children, and retirees. But almost all of these people are still "WEIRD": Western, Educated, Industrialized, Rich, and Democratic. A stunning 96 percent of subjects in psychology experiments from 2003 to 2007 have been WEIRD, according to Joseph Henrich, an evolutionary anthropologist at the University of British Columbia, and his coauthors. But the real trouble, says Henrich, is that WEIRD people are different from the other 88 percent of the world's population. He compared the result of studies on cooperation, learning, decision-making, and even basic perception that used both WEIRD and non-WEIRD subjects. Henrich found striking differences. "The fact that WEIRD people are the outliers in so many key domains of the behavioral sciences renders them—perhaps—one of the worst subpopulations one could study for generalizing about *Homo sapiens*."

But if people are such a problem, how can we possibly observe the behavior of the full spectrum of humankind? Fortunately—amazingly—there is an unprecedented new source of behavioral data, one that reveals the unfiltered activities of a stunning diversity of people. This is the world's largest experiment on human behavior: the Internet.

The Internet records the activities of more than a billion people from every country on the planet. This online data offers the opportunity to view even the most fundamental human behaviors in a brand-new light. In this book, we use data from the world's largest behavioral experiment to reexamine one of the most important and intimate of all behaviors: sexual desire. In the pages that follow, you'll learn the truth about what men and women secretly desire—and why.

Everyone has strong feelings about sexual behavior, and that's a problem for the researchers who study it. We all have our favorite theories that fit our experiences and prejudices. We all tend to think our own desires are pretty natural and normal. But other people's desires? They're gross, immoral, or downright dangerous. Sometimes, though, we hide desires we don't want to talk about, don't understand, and maybe don't want to understand. As a result of all these intense feelings and prejudices, many twenty-first-century convictions about desire are still imbued with superstition. By analyzing the intimate desires of tens of millions of men and women and explaining the mechanisms that produce them, we hope this book might shine some light into the darkness.

We need to warn you up front. In the pages that follow, you're going to peer into other people's minds without filters or cushions. The sexual brain is guaranteed to upset the politically correct, the socially conservative, and just about everyone in between. This book is not an expanded issue of *Cosmopolitan* or *Maxim*, and it's definitely not for children. You're certain to be challenged and occasionally dumbfounded.

We also want to emphasize that this book is not intended as a complete catalog of the diversity of human desire; far from it. We've omitted many important sexual interests because of space limitations, and sometimes because we felt we simply didn't have enough data to do justice to a particular topic. Instead, we've strived to convey the most defining and illuminating features of our sexual desires.

Our lawyers instructed us to add another cautionary warning. Throughout this book, we describe many adult Web sites that depict various sexual situations. Often, these situations are depicted as genuine, even though they involve actors in scripted scenarios. Sometimes these situations involve nonprofessional performers and unscripted acts. However, much of the time it is not possible to determine whether a sexual situation depicted as genuine on a Web site is, in fact, fictional or authentic.

Finally—and most important—we can't emphasize enough that when it comes to understanding human desire, scientists focus on statistics rather than individuals. We might say that men are taller than women because the average height of the human male is taller than the average height of the human female. But perhaps you yourself are a tall woman or a short man, defying the averages and exposing the limitations of such generalizations. Nevertheless, by identifying a real difference in the average heights of men and women, scientists can then look for reasons why—such as the discovery that the pituitary gland releases more growth hormones in men than in women.

We can understand how the sexual brain works using statistics and large sample sizes. But you—you are a wholly unique combination of desires and experiences that almost certainly exists nowhere else. No matter how unique your own tastes, we hope this book might help you understand why you like the things you do—and why your partner's tastes can seem so different.

A BILLION
WICKED THOUGHTS

To encounter erotica designed to appeal to the other is to gaze into the psychological abyss that separates the sexes.

—Donald Symons

CHAPTER 1
What Do We *Really* Like?
Sexual Cues

The study of desire has never been for the faint of heart.
—Marta Meana, professor of clinical psychology

The year 1886 witnessed the birth of two remarkable scientific disciplines, each founded by a German. One scientist gazed outward at the hidden patterns of the physical universe. The other peered inward at the secret workings of the mind. One discipline has achieved stunning progress. The other, perhaps surprisingly, lags far behind.

Heinrich Hertz built the very first radio antenna in 1886. He wanted to test for the existence of electromagnetic waves as predicted by Scottish theoretical physicist James Clerk Maxwell. Hertz became the first person to successfully transmit and receive a radio signal, simultaneously proving Maxwell correct and inaugurating the field of *radiophysics*. The subject of this new field was a strange, invisible "wave" that no philosopher or priest had ever dreamed of in their most extravagant fantasies. Yet over the ensuing century, radiophysicists developed the lasers used in DVD players and eye surgery. They figured out how to scan the brain for tumors. They even listened to the lingering sounds of the big bang, the event marking the origin of the known universe.

We all have a more intimate and personal relationship with the subject studied by Richard von Krafft-Ebing, a subject scrutinized by humankind since we yawped our first words in the valleys of Africa. In 1886, Krafft-Ebing published a landmark book. He deliberately wrote sections in Latin and chose a Latin title in order to discourage laypeople from reading it. The book was *Psychopathia Sexualis*. It addresses such arcane topics as clitoral stimulation, reduced libido, and homosexuality. The discipline Krafft-Ebing founded is known as *sexology*.

So in the 125 years since *Psychopathia Sexualis* initiated the scientific study of a very familiar activity, how do the field's achievements match up to those of radiophysics? It's rather like comparing the Olympics gold medal tallies of the United States and Fiji. Unlike the origins of electromagnetic energy, the origins of desire remain mysterious and controversial. There's no consensus on which sexual interests are normal, abnormal, or pathological. Scientists can't even agree on the purpose of female orgasm, whether there is such a thing as having too much sex, or whether sexual fantasies are innocent or dangerous.

Today, a wide variety of scientists study desire, including neuroscientists, psychologists, anthropologists, biologists, and pharmacologists. One of their most basic questions is: why do we like the things we like? This question has never been adequately answered, because we must first determine *what* people like. To steal an expression from American writer William S. Burroughs, we need to "see what's on the end of everyone's fork." But stealing a look at men and women's true interests has been far from easy.

While modern radiophysicists have discovered black holes and developed the means for communicating with extraterrestrials, scientists studying desire still struggle to identify basic differences between the sexual interests of men and women. Why is there such a gap between the achievements of the fields founded by Heinrich Hertz and Richard von Krafft-Ebing? One big reason is *data acquisition*.

The best method for acquiring scientific data is direct observation. Nothing beats watching a subject in action. But scientists have an easier time gazing at intergalactic quasars than peeking into someone's bedroom. Quasars don't close the curtains out of modesty or suspicion. In contrast, most of us are unwilling to let curious scientists photograph us as we tumble between the sheets. Radio waves may be invisible, but they don't try to deceive curious physicists and they're incapable of self-deception. Humans are guilty of both.

Since direct observation of sexual behavior is so challenging, most scientists acquire sexual data using self-report surveys. But are *you* willing to jot down answers to questions like "Have you ever felt attracted to your pet schnauzer?"—even if the unshaven young grad student surveying you insists, "Trust me—your answers are completely anonymous."

The difficulties associated with acquiring sexual data are not limited to skittish subjects who don't want to be studied. Many social institutions don't want sex to be studied, either. Federal funding agencies, advocacy groups, ethics review boards, even fellow scientists all bring powerful social politics to bear on those researchers brave enough to investigate human desire. For example, in 2003, congressmen led by Pennyslvania representative Pat Toomey sought to block federal funding of four sexual research projects, including a study of the sexual habits of older men in New England and a study of homosexual and bisexual Native Americans. "To obtain grant money, my colleagues in mainstream psychology are free to invoke 'basic research' or say they want to 'expand our understanding of human behavior," laments Marta Meana, a clinical psychologist and sex researcher at the University of Nevada, Las Vegas, and one of the world's leading authorities on female sexuality. "But if you're studying sex and want to get significant funding, you have to link your work to 'health' or 'human rights.'"

Institutional sex taboos have stymied efforts to uncover the true patterns of human desire. In fact, since the publication of Krafft-Ebing's book, only one scientist has managed to survey a large number of people on a broad range of sexual interests: Alfred

Kinsey. Kinsey was an entomologist who spent his career studying the gall wasp. He collected more than 1 million of the tiny, reddish insects, pinning and labeling each one by hand. Mrs. Kinsey surely expected a life of placid stability, where the most exciting event might be an occasional wasp sting. But in 1940, Kinsey abruptly exchanged his wasps for the birds and the bees. He had become fed up with the moralizing and superstitions that abounded in sex education in the 1930s. But what really motivated him was his frustration with the complete absence of scientific data on what people were actually *doing*.

Kinsey and a small group of research assistants interviewed thousands of subjects in person, asking 521 questions about a tremendous variety of sexual interests, including bondage, bestiality, and silk stockings. Even by today's standards, the results were shocking. Before Kinsey, homosexuality was believed to be exceedingly rare, yet more than one-third of the men reported having a homosexual experience. Women were believed to possess a very low sex drive, yet more than half of the women reported masturbating. Premarital sex, extramarital affairs, and oral sex all occurred far more frequently than anyone had guessed.

"Too darn hot" croons Paul in Cole Porter's Broadway musical *Kiss Me, Kate*, after singing about the findings in the Kinsey Reports. He wasn't the only one feeling that way. After the publication of Kinsey's landmark book on female desire, *Sexual Behavior in the Human Female*, the Rockefeller Center dropped his funding. Kinsey was denounced as a Communist and savaged by conservative and religious organizations. He became addicted to sleeping pills and developed heart trouble, dying at age sixty-two from pneumonia and heart complications.

The eighteen thousand men and women interviewed by Kinsey represent the most comprehensive scientific attempt at determining ordinary people's true sexual interests. But the Kinsey surveys are now more than a half century old. Subsequent researchers, constrained by politics and social pressures, never followed up with large-scale replications of Kinsey's inquiry into the variety of desire. Even Kinsey's own data was limited in several respects. The subjects were primarily educated, middle-class Caucasians. The subjects were chosen opportunistically according to who was available, rather than being selected randomly or systematically. The survey data consisted of recollections the subjects chose to share, rather than verifiable information or direct observation.

The intellectual heirs of Heinrich Hertz have quietly studied radar and X-rays without encountering push-back from society. In contrast, many intellectual heirs of Richard von Krafft-Ebing have been pilloried in the media, faced criminal prosecution, or been fired from their jobs. Physicists can observe subatomic particles and galactic superclusters. But human desire? What does desire truly look like? Science hasn't been able to answer this question, because there just hasn't been a way to observe the natural sexual behavior of large numbers of women and men.

Until now.

A BILLION WICKED THOUGHTS

The 1960s and '70s were the heyday of bold and slightly reckless social psychology experiments, which often resembled episodes of MTV's prank show *Jackass*. The 1971 Stanford prison experiment divided subjects into prisoners and guards and forced them to live in a makeshift prison, resulting in degrading abuse by the guards and a riot by the prisoners. The 1960s Milgram obedience experiments required subjects to shock a man with increasing levels of electricity until the man appeared to die. In 1973, psychologist Kenneth Gergen of Swarthmore College conducted another social psychology experiment that would probably fail to get approved by today's ethics boards. His research asked, "What do people do under conditions of extreme anonymity?"

In Gergen's experiment, five young men and five young women entered a small room one at a time. They did not know one another before the experiment, and they were kept isolated before they entered the room. Once they entered, they were free to do whatever they liked. At the end of the experiment, the subjects left the room one at a time. But what made this experiment so interesting was the room itself. It was pitch-dark.

The subjects couldn't see one another, they didn't know one another, and they knew they would not learn one another's identities after the experiment. In other words, they experienced complete and total anonymity. So what did these anonymous strangers do? At first they talked, but conversation soon slacked off. Then the touching began. Almost 90 percent of subjects touched someone else on purpose. More than half of the subjects hugged someone. A third of the subjects ended up kissing. One young man kissed five different girls. "As I was sitting Beth came up and we started to play touchy face and touchy body and started to neck. We expressed it as showing love to each other. We decided to pass our love on and share it with other people. So we split up and Laurie took her place." Hidden by anonymity, the participants freely expressed their desires. One man even offered to pay Gergen to be let back into the room. Almost 80 percent of the men and women reported feeling sexual excitement.

The Internet is like a much, much, much larger version of the Gergen experiment. Put a billion anonymous people in a virtually darkened room. See what they do when their desires are unleashed.

When he was younger, Peter Morley-Souter enjoyed writing comics. He was influenced by *Calvin and Hobbes*, the family-friendly syndicated strip following the adventures of the mischievous six-year-old Calvin and his stuffed tiger Hobbes. Peter would come up with a humorous idea for a comic drawn from his everyday experience. His younger sister, Rose, would draw it. The audience consisted mainly of Peter's friends, though sometimes he would post his work on the Web. Today, Peter is training to be a secondary schoolteacher in Britain. He considers his comic writing a discarded hobby from his youth. He has trouble recalling much of his work—with one notable exception.

In 2003, Peter was a shy sixteen-year-old when a friend e-mailed him a "reimagining" of a *Calvin and Hobbes* comic. In it, Calvin and Hobbes were having enthusiastic sex with Calvin's mother. Peter felt "pretty traumatized."

"I knew there was a lot of sex on the Internet. But Calvin and Hobbes?" bemoans Peter, explaining why he decided to come up with his own single-panel comic in response. "If there was porn of Calvin and Hobbes, I figured there must be porn of anything and everything."

Peter's anguished comic portrays himself, gaping at his computer screen in shock. The black-and-white drawing is amateurish and not very memorable. But Peter seemed to tap into something in the zeitgeist with the comic's caption: *Internet Rule #34: There is porn of it.*

Peter posted his comic on an image-sharing Web site. The comic itself quickly disappeared from view, but the caption went viral. Peter's words ricocheted across online communities, where they were modified into their more common phrasing: *Rule 34: If you can imagine it, it exists as Internet porn.* Today, Rule 34 thrives as sacred lore on blogs, YouTube videos, Twitter feeds, and social networking sites. It's frequently used as a verb, as in "I Rule 34'ed Paula Abdul and Simon Cowell on the judging table." Tech blog Boing Boing even hosts the "Rule 34 Challenge," in which contestants race to find outrageous erotic combinations on the Web, like Ludwig van Beethoven fornicating with Britney Spears.

Why did Rule 34 resonate with so many people? Because for anybody who has spent time surfing the Web, Peter's maxim certainly seems true. EroticFalconry.com features photos of predatory birds with nude women, Snarry.net contains erotic stories about Harry Potter and Professor Severus Snape, and LoonerVision.com consists of videos for people who get sexually aroused by popping balloons. "The Web brings people together," offered comedian Richard Jeni, "because no matter what kind of a twisted sexual mutant you happen to be, you've got millions of pals out there. Type in 'Find people that have sex with goats that are on fire' and the computer will say, 'Specify type of goat.'"

In 1991, the year the World Wide Web went online, there were fewer than ninety different adult magazines published in America, and you'd have been hard-pressed to find a newsstand that carried more than a dozen. Just six years later, in 1997, there were about nine hundred pornography sites on the Web. Today, the filtering software CYBERsitter blocks 2.5 *million* adult Web sites. As the puppets in the Broadway musical *Avenue Q* sing, "The Internet is for porn."

It's true that visual pornography is mostly a male interest. But surging numbers of women are also using the Internet to satisfy their own erotic tastes. For large segments of the world, both Western and Eastern, sex-related online activities have become routine, with large majorities of both men and women using the Internet for sexual purposes. It's hard to imagine a more revolutionary development in the history of human sexuality. With a visit to an adult video site like PornHub, you can see more naked bodies in a single minute than the most promiscuous Victorian would have seen in an entire lifetime. But there's an even more dramatic change. We no longer have to interact with *anyone* to obtain erotica.

Women who previously felt too mortified to be seen in the back room of the local video rental store are finally empowered to explore their erotic interests in privacy and comfort. Gay men who were previously isolated in suburban neighborhoods can now surf an endless variety of exciting content without leaving their chair. Anyone can view porn on a smart phone while riding the subway or sneaking off to the office bathroom. Billions of people around the planet are free to satisfy their most secret erotic desires by thinking, clicking, and typing—all while remaining cloaked by the anonymity of the Internet.

Kenneth Gergen was able to watch his subjects' behavior in the darkened room using infrared cameras. But how do we observe people's sexual activities on the Web if they are indeed anonymous? For better or worse, our online behavior is rarely traceless. We leave behind a trail of digital footprints. For example, if you use a search engine like Google, Yahoo!, or Bing, the text of your search is recorded and stored in a variety of places. The search engine companies certainly retain data about your search, and a few companies have even released semi-anonymized collections of individuals' search histories. There are also third-party software tools that monitor, record, and sell search data. By examining this raw search data, we can finally see what's on the end of everyone's fork.

Take a look at this list. Each phrase represents an actual search someone entered on the Dogpile search engine in May 2010. Dogpile.com is a popular "meta-engine" that combines results from Google, Yahoo!, Bing, and other major search engines. This list is an unfiltered snapshot of human desire.

shemales in prom dresses

Twilight slash Edward and Jacob

black meat on white street

wives caught cheating on cam

best romance novels with alpha heroes

kendra wilkinson sex tape

spanking stories

free gay video tube

Jake Gyllenhaal without shirt

girls gone wild orgies

jersey shore sex cartoons

There's a popular term for unusual sexual interests: *kinks*. There's also a popular term for those kinks that gross you out: *squicks*. Many people's natural reaction is to feel squicked out by some of the things on this list. You may instinctively feel that whoever is searching for this stuff must be an absolute weirdo. But one thing that immediately jumps out from this list is the remarkable diversity of people's sexual interests. It's like staring at a restaurant menu that contains Big Macs, sea slugs, Rocky Road ice cream, fried grasshoppers, and organic tofu. *Do human beings really eat all of this stuff?*

Where does this diversity come from? Why does one person seek out "spanking stories" and someone else seek out "shemales in prom dresses"? Why are your own erotic preferences different from your partner's? These questions are at the very heart of our investigation.

We're going to combine Internet data with the latest findings from neuroscience and sex research to make sense of the diversity of human desire. We're going to explain why you or your partner might like things in private that you would never share in public—or with each other. This explanation will come in the form of surprising new ideas about the mind software governing our desires. We'll start with a seemingly simple question. What is the original source of our sexual interests? How does the initial impulse to seek out "best romance novels" or "free gay video" get into our brain in the first place?

One possibility is that our desire software is influenced by social stimuli. Maybe our brains are designed to sample our cultural environment—including messages communicated by our parents, our peers, and the media—then set our desires according to the examples dictated by these social inputs. How could we test this "social inputs" hypothesis? Here's one possible experiment: we could try to use social inputs to intentionally engineer a person's most fundamental sexual desires.

If we could take a newborn infant and control everything in his social environment—including the way everyone interacted with him—could we dictate the kind of person that infant will find sexually desirable when he grows up?

THE UNANTICIPATED CONSEQUENCES OF BRAINWASHING

While circumcising two-week-old David Reimer with an electrocautery needle in Manitoba in 1965, the attending urologist accidentally burned off David's entire penis. Confronting this horrific tragedy, the Reimers consulted the most famous sexologist of the time, Dr. John Money of Johns Hopkins University. Dr. Money believed that sexuality was entirely the product of social inputs. He assured the Reimer family they had nothing to worry about. Just dust off the name Mrs. Reimer had intended to use if she had given birth to a girl, have David undergo surgery to give him a vagina, and raise their emasculated son as a daughter.

Brenda Reimer's parents never told her she was born male, initiating one of the most delicate family secrets imaginable. They gave her dolls and dresses and hormone treatments, and regularly schlepped her to Dr. Money's Baltimore office for therapy. What kind of therapy does one provide to a young girl if one believes that sexual desire is dictated by social inputs? Dr. Money showed little Brenda pictures of nude adult men and said, "This is what grown-up girls like." Money was pleased with Brenda's development. For more than a decade, he reported to the scientific community that the first-ever experiment in neonatal gender bending was an "unqualified success."

But if you spoke with Brenda, she would have described the experiment quite differently. As early as age three, she angrily tore off her dresses. She refused to play with dolls, preferring cars and guns. Instead of using her jump rope for skipping, she used it to whip her brother and tie people up. Brenda's earliest memory was asking her father if she could shave like him. At school, she became an outcast, teased and rejected for her strange, boyish behavior. The Reimers enrolled Brenda in the Girl Scouts. "I remember making daisy chains and thinking, 'If this is the most exciting thing in Girl Scouts, forget it!' I kept thinking of the fun stuff my brother was doing in Cub Scouts."

And what about her sexual desire, the main focus of Dr. Money's vigorous therapy? When Brenda hit puberty, she felt no attraction to boys at all. Money asked her distraught parents, "How do you feel about your daughter being a lesbian?" Overwhelmed by Brenda's conspicuous psychological agony, her parents finally revealed the truth when she was fourteen. "Suddenly it all made sense why

I felt the way I did," explained Brenda, who quickly changed his name back to David. "I wasn't some sort of weirdo."

He had a mastectomy to remove his hormone-induced breasts and a phalloplasty to provide him with a nonfunctional penis. He started dating girls, to whom he felt a strong attraction. Eventually he got married. But he certainly never visited Dr. Money again. "It was like brainwashing," David reminisced a decade later. "What they did to you in the body is sometimes not near as bad as what they did to you in the *mind*—with the psychological warfare in your head."

David's failed experiment was the first of its kind, but unfortunately not the last. In the wake of Dr. Money's buoyant reports of the successful experiment on Brenda, thousands of genetically male infants with various anatomical disruptions were raised as girls. In 2004, one urologist compiled a report on fourteen genetic males who underwent neonatal sex reassignment. Seven had switched back to living as males, six were still living as females, and one refused to declare a sexual identity. Only those living as men had dated and were able to live independently. Today, the medical profession discourages surgical sex reassignment in newborns, and one reason is because of the tragic experiment on David Reimer. In 2004, at age thirty-eight, David permanently ended his psychological warfare by firing a shotgun into his brain.

David Reimer's story suggests that the social environment has very little influence on the male brain's attraction to women. But Reimer was a single person. Let's try another experiment testing the effects of social inputs on desire, using many more subjects. What happens if mainstream society exposes *all* of its boys to the same sexual stimuli? How many of these boys will feel an attraction to these stimuli as adults?

For example, imagine a culture in which every prepubescent boy is encouraged to perform fellatio on an older teenager several times a week for three or four years, as part of a ritualistic initiation into adulthood. If social inputs determine whether the male brain finds men or women to be sexually attractive, then we might expect this would result in a society dominated by adult homosexuality, or at least bisexuality.

In fact, a society with such practices actually exists: the Sambia. These Papua New Guinea people are jungle horticulturalists who live in mountain hamlets. The Sambia believe that semen is the essence of manhood (sort of like Austin Powers's mojo) and all Sambian boys must ingest quite a bit of it to become strong, masculine men. When the boys hit puberty and start to develop a manly physique, their elders say, "See? It's working!" Now the adolescent boys get fellated by a new crop of prepubescent boys.

So what is the rate of homosexuality among adult Sambian men? Roughly 5 percent, about the same level of homosexuality found in Western societies. By the time a Sambian man reaches his twenties, he usually marries a Sambian woman. "They have pleasant memories of their youth," reports the anthropologist Gilbert Herdt, who lived among the Sambia. "But their real lust is for women."

What do these two "natural experiments" teach us? They point to the same conclusion: some things we *instinctively* find arousing. Even if society urges us to participate in a specific sexual practice during our formative years, this does not necessarily determine our adult desires. Of course, we haven't learned anything yet about female desire, which may operate quite differently from male desire. There may also be important social inputs that influence a man's other desires. But his fundamental attraction to men or women does not appear to be one of them. To fully understand human desire, we must consider the specific design of our brain's software.

THE GENIE OF A MILLION SQUICKS

The Internet search engine is a marvelous digital genie. It grants us not just one, but an infinite number of erotic wishes. Ordinary folks can sit at their keyboards, liberated from any need for modesty, and express precisely what they would like to pop up on their computer screen. *I wish for . . . Zac Efron in his bathing suit.* If we want to make sense of the diversity of the sexual interests expressed on the Internet—and the mind software responsible for these interests—we should start by looking for patterns in these wishes.

We collected about 400 million different searches that were entered into the Dogpile search engine from July 2009 to July 2010. We collected these searches through a process called *scraping*: we wrote a program to capture the searches listed on Search-Spy, a Dogpile-run Web site that displays in real time the actual searches people entered into the Dogpile search engine. If you visit SearchSpy, it's like looking through a window into a planetary stream of human consciousness—and you won't have to wait more than a few seconds to see its sexual side. Of the 400 million searches we collected, about 55 million (roughly 13 percent) were searches for some kind of erotic content. These sexual searches represent the desires of roughly 2 million people. Two-thirds are from the United States, though some users are from India, Nigeria, Canada, and the United Kingdom.

Next, we categorized all of these sexual searches by interest. For example, we categorized "hot Latino ass," "bootylicious babes," and "sexy guys with bubble butts" as examples of the interest *butts*. (These categories do not distinguish between male and female searchers, or between gay and straight searchers.) Some searches we categorized into multiple interests. For example, "Asian sailor orgy" was counted as *Asians, sailors,* and *group sex*. It's important to note that these searches reflect what people *desired* to find at a given point in time, not what they actually found. It's the wishes, not what the genie actually produced.

Sometimes it was difficult to immediately know whether a particular search expressed an erotic urge, such as "college cheerleaders." Perhaps this search reflects the innocent interest of someone on the varsity squad scoping out the competition for the National Cheerleading Championship. In such uncertain cases, we turned to other data sets for guidance, including the AOL (America Online) data set.

In 2006, AOL released a data set containing the search histories for 657,426 different people. Each search history contains all the searches made by a particular AOL user over three months, from March 1, 2006, to May 31, 2006. For example, here's the abbreviated search history for "Mr. Bikinis," our name for user #2027268:

college cheerleaders

cheerleaders in Hawaii

pics of bikinis and girls

the sin of masturbation

pretty girls in bikinis

girls suntanning in bikinis

college cheerleader pics in bikinis

noooooooo

christian advice on lust

The release of this data set was a public relations disaster for AOL and was named one of the "101 Dumbest Moments in Business." Even though users' names were not included, the data was widely viewed as an egregious violation of user privacy. The person responsible for the release of the data, the head of AOL Research, was fired. But the data has proven to be an unparalleled gold mine for researchers investigating online behavior—though, surprisingly, not by researchers studying desire.

Using the AOL data (and other data sets), we determined whether an ambiguous Dogpile search phrase was likely a sexual search, by analyzing what other searches occurred most frequently with the ambiguous search phrase in the AOL data. This allowed us to see, for example, that the search phrase "college cheerleaders" occurs most frequently with "naked cheerleaders," "busty cheerleaders," and "free cheerleader porn." If an ambiguous search phrase was highly correlated with sexual searches, then we counted the search in the appropriate category—in this case, *cheerleaders*.

Take a look at the following list, which shows the most popular sexual interests on Dogpile. But before you do, take a guess. What do you think is searched for the most: *cheerleaders, cheating wives,* or *butts?*

% of all Sexual Searches	Popularity Ranking	Category	Example Search
13.5	1	Youth	free non-nude teen videos
4.7	2	Gay	straight guys paid to have gay sex
4.3	3	MILFs	MILFs in bikinis
4.0	4	Breasts	huge tits
3.4	5	Cheating wives	cuckold porn
2.8	6	Vaginas	shaved pussies
2.4	7	Penises	giant cocks
.9	21	Butts	hot Latino ass
.1	79	Cheerleaders	free cheerleader porn

What are we to make of the fact that *cheating wives* (#5) are more popular than *butts* (#21) or *cheerleaders* (#79)? Why is *youth* (#1) so much more popular than anything else? We saw that culture did not influence whether male brains prefer men or women. But could social inputs influence some of the other interests people search for on the Internet?

One fact argues against a cultural influence on certain sexual interests: some of the most popular sexual interests are commonly held to be squicks. For example, *transsexuals* (#17) are more popular than *celebrities* (#23) or *Asians* (#29). "Shemale porn," as it is known in the adult industry, is internationally popular and profitable, despite the fact that mainstream society finds it pretty strange. You certainly won't see any Hollywood blockbusters or CNN reports touting the pleasures of transsexual erotica. Yet behind the veil of anonymity, millions of people actively seek it out.

It's certainly possible that people are more likely to use a search engine to locate rare interests that are not well represented on popular adult sites. Perhaps most people have no need to use a search engine to locate the "vanilla" porn they can easily find on mainstream, high-traffic sites. Consequently, we might hypothesize that the popularity of squicky interests is overstated on the Dogpile list. But this seems unlikely for a number of reasons. For one thing, many of these seemingly unusual interests *are* well represented in mainstream porn sites—including transsexual pornography, which is often featured on the front page of PornHub, the world's most popular adult video site.

Moreover, the most popular sexual search category by far is *youth*, which is exceedingly well represented in mainstream porn sites. It appears people are using search engines like Dogpile even when they want to locate sexual interests that are very easy to find. Finally, the relative popularity of the interests expressed in sexual searches—including both squicky and familiar interests—is confirmed using a variety of other online data, such as Web site traffic, porn site subscriptions, and porn video downloads.

So now that we've categorized all 55 million Dogpile sexual searches, just how diverse is the full list of *Homo sapiens*' sexual interests as expressed on the Internet? Not very diverse, it turns out. Just twenty different interests account for 80 percent of all searches. That's rather remarkable. With less than two dozen interests, you can satisfy the desires of almost everyone who uses a search engine to find erotic content. In fact, the thirty-five top interests account for 90 percent of all searches. This doesn't even include *cheerleaders* (#79), *massage* (#51), or *virgins* (#61). This means that most people's desires are clustered together into a relatively small set of common interests. When it comes to our kinks, we all have a lot more in common than you might think.

Strictly speaking, Rule 34 may be true. If you can imagine it, there is almost certainly porn of it on the Internet. If you Google "skeleton porn" or "sexy funeral director" or "erotic stories about lumpy potatoes" you will find results. But most of us aren't spending our time looking for this stuff. Instead, the vast majority of our desires are shared by crowds of other people.

But some of you are probably thinking, hang on. There's something pretty glaring about this list of sexual searches. It sure seems to reflect the tastes of *men*. Certainly *breasts*, *cheerleaders*, and *gay* are predominantly male interests. Does this mean that women don't use the Internet to satisfy their own desires?

The following tables list the most popular "erotic" Web sites, though it would be more accurate to say these Web sites reflect the interests of men and women's sexual brains. The first table shows the five most popular Web sites among men. The second table shows five Web sites popular among women, including the most popular fan fiction Web site, the most popular romance author Web site, the most popular romance novel Web site, and the most popular porn site for women.

Millions of Visitors per month	Web Sites Popular with Men	Type of Site
16.0	Pornhub.com	Adult video site
9.9	RedTube.com	Adult video site
9.8	XHamster.com	Adult video site
8.3	YouPorn.com	Adult video site
7.4	XNXX.com	Adult video site

Millions of Visitors per month	Web Sites Popular with Women	Type of Site
1.8	FanFiction.net	Story site
.6	StephenieMyers.com	Romance author fan site
.2	eHarlequin.com	Romance novel fan site
.2	AdultFanFiction.net	Adult story site
.1	ForTheGirls.com	Adult video site

On the Web, men prefer images. Women prefer stories. Men prefer graphic sex. Women prefer relationships and romance. This is also reflected in the divergent responses of men and women when asked what sexual activities they perform on the Internet.

Preferred Online Sexual Activity	% of Men	% of Women
Viewing erotic pictures and movies	37	6
Staying in contact with love/sex partners	8	21
Reading erotic stories	6	9

When men and women are free to search for anything they want behind the anonymity of their computer screen, they don't just seek out different interests. They seek out different modes of stimulation. Men prefer to watch, women prefer to read and discuss. This fundamental dichotomy in sexual interests confirms the predictions of one of the most influential sex scientists, Donald Symons.

"In the male fantasy realm of pornotopia, sex is sheer lust and physical gratification, devoid of courtship, commitment, durable relationships, or mating effort. Porn videos contain minimal plot development, focusing instead on the sex acts themselves and emphasizing the display of female bodies, especially close-ups of faces, breasts, and genitals," explains Symons and psychologist Catherine Salmon in their book, *Warrior Lovers*. "The female fantasy realm of romantopia is quite different. The goal of a romance novel's heroine is never sex for its own sake, much less impersonal sex with strangers. The core of a romance novel's plot is a love story in the course of which the heroine overcomes obstacles to identify, win the heart of, and ultimately marry the one man who is right for her."

Biological anthropologist Donald Symons is a professor emeritus at the University of California, Santa Barbara. Symons is retired from research, living with his wife in a canyon looking up at the chaparral-covered Santa Ynez Mountains. He's a vegetarian and an ardent fan of comedian Richard Pryor. He is also the most cited living researcher in the contemporary science of sex. His pioneering work is referenced by scientists investigating an astonishingly diverse range of phenomena, including gay relationships, female fantasies of coercion, incest avoidance, anal sex, and porn star hip size.

Richard von Krafft-Ebing established the science of human desire with *Psychopathia Sexualis* in 1886. But the establishment of the "hard science" of human desire waited nearly another century for the publication of Symons's 1979 book *The Evolution of Human Sexuality*. Many prominent scientists have been influenced by this book, including Harvard psychologist Steven Pinker: "*The Evolution of Human Sexuality* was a landmark in its synthesis of evolutionary biology, anthropology, physiology, psychology, fiction, and cultural analysis, written with a combination of rigor and wit. It was a model for all subsequent books that apply evolution to human affairs, particularly mine." For the first time, human desire was integrated within the theoretical framework of evolutionary biology. This theory-based approach to desire was something quite different from Alfred Kinsey's observational approach.

Whereas Kinsey and most previous sexual research described *what* men and women liked, Symons attempted to explain *why* men and women liked such different things.

THE DELICIOUS ELEMENTS OF DESIRE

Humans find a tremendous variety of food to be delicious: bananas, oysters, milk, bacon, peanuts, anchovies, zucchini. And that's just the natural goodies. The aisles of modern supermarkets are overflowing with a cornucopia of manufactured edibility, including Tater Tots and bagel pizzas. Confronted with such an astounding diversity of culinary desires, one might be tempted to argue that they can't possibly be reduced to a tiny set of hardwired tastes.

But in fact, our mind's taste software responds to just five perceptual inputs: sweet, salty, sour, savory, and bitter. (Some researchers also suggest fatty and metallic.) Each of these taste cues is processed by a cue-specific neural pathway, elicits a cue-specific subjective experience, and fulfills a cue-specific evolutionary function. For example, our taste for sweetness detects sugar, which we need for energy. Consequently, our taste software has evolved so that we find sweetness desirable and rewarding. Our bitterness taste detects alkaloid substances, which are often associated with toxic plants. Thus, our taste software has evolved to find bitterness unpleasant.

Of course, our taste software is also designed to be highly adaptive. Even though all foods can be reduced to a handful of taste cues, the taste combinations we prefer are influenced by both culture and experience. We like pork chops or curry because that's what Mom made. Most Americans don't like braised cow tongues because they were never exposed to them growing up, though they are a common Filipino dish. College students eat a lot of Hot Pockets because they're cheap and easy to prepare. We can learn to appreciate food that is bitter, like coffee or olives. But no culture enjoys cinnamon-sprinkled feces.

Food is a wonderful example of how our brains appreciate an infinite variety of stimuli using a limited set of perceptual cues. This is possible because taste cues combine together to form different amalgams of taste. A chocolate-covered almond consists of sweet and bitter cues, while a dill pickle consists of sour and salty cues. People learn to love highly complex taste combinations, like wine or caviar.

We believe that our sexual desire software works in a similar fashion. Just as all food can be broken down into a finite set of taste cues that activate our taste software, our sexual interests can be broken down into a finite set of sexual cues that activate our desire software. The idea that our brains contain innate mechanisms designed to detect specific sexual cues originated with Donald Symons. "It is clear that human beings evolved psychological mechanisms for detecting and assessing cues of mate value that are independent of other people's preferences and are highly resistant to cultural modification. These mechanisms account for a very large proportion of individual variability in attractiveness."

But there is one crucial difference between taste cues and sexual cues—a gender difference. Though the brains of both men and women are wired to detect the same taste cues, when it comes to sexual cues, things are different. It's as if men were born with detectors for salty and sour taste cues, and women were born with detectors for sweet and bitter taste cues. We could both eat the same peanut brittle but experience different flavors: a man would report a salty taste, a woman would describe its sweetness.

We opened this chapter by describing the historical difficulties in determining what people desire. Symons knew enough about people's desires to craft a theory of male and female sexual cues that remains a cornerstone of the science of desire. But the Internet expands our knowledge of what people desire as never before. When we are first confronted with this awesome diversity—as expressed in the Dogpile sexual searches—we might believe it cannot be reduced to a simple set of elements. But our brain's taste software shows how an apparent infinitude of appealing stimuli can be reduced to a finite set of cues.

We sifted through a billion different Web searches, including a half million personal search histories. We analyzed hundreds of thousands of online erotic stories and thousands of romance e-novels. We looked at the forty thousand most trafficked adult Web sites. We examined more than 5 million sexual solicitations posted on online classifieds. We listened to thousands of people discussing their desires on online message boards.

The goal? To understand the specific innate cues that trigger desire in women and men.

CHAPTER 2

Monkey Pay-Per-View

Male Visual Cues

A large penis is always welcome.
—Atia of the Julii, *Rome*, season 1

Wolfgang likes to look at images of female derrieres. He prefers certain poses: bent over, legs splayed, leaning on her knuckles. He likes these images so much that he is willing to pay for the privilege of looking at them. Sometimes he pays several times a day. This might seem excessive, though not exactly remarkable, except for one fact: Wolfgang is a monkey.

Rhesus macaques at Duke University Medical Center's monkey colony are able to trade fruit juice for peeks at photos of female perinea (the scientific term for "bright pink monkey butts"). Researchers led by neurobiologist Michael Platt have consistently found that males are willing to trade juice to view these images and will trade more juice to look at monkey erotica than any other image, including powerful males or friendly female faces.

Men aren't the only primates willing to spend money just to *look* at females, but they're the only ones to develop it into an industry. The most popular paysites featuring adult videos, including Brazzers, Bang Bros, and Reality Kings, typically attract an audience that is around 75 percent men. Of course, that does mean that one out of four visitors is a woman—a minority, though a significant minority. But when it comes to actually *paying* for porn, the gender gap widens into an abyss. According to CCBill, the billing service most commonly used by the online adult industry, only 2 percent of all subscriptions to pornography sites are made on credit cards with women's names. In fact, CCBill even flags female names as potential fraud, since so many of these charges result in an angry wife or mother demanding a refund for the misuse of her card.

A willingness to drop cold hard cash on porn is certainly the best indication that men's motivation to ogle images is stronger than women's. But there are plenty of other indicators. Consider one surprising investigation sponsored by the National Science Foundation.

The National Science Foundation (NSF) is a federal government agency that funds approximately 20 percent of all basic research in American universities in every field of science and engineering, including the mapping of the genome and the construction of radio telescopes. Its board of directors is appointed by the president of the United States and confirmed by the Senate. No other institution has a greater influence on American science. But in 2009, a certain activity was stealing so many hours from employees at the NSF headquarters in Washington, D.C., that the agency's inspector general launched a formal inquiry. The activity? Surfing Internet porn.

More than two dozen employees at all levels of management were spending thousands of work hours watching pornography on taxpayer-purchased computers. These were smart, educated people used to interacting with America's intellectual elite. But these white-collar executives couldn't resist the temptations of online erotica. One senior executive spent 331 days viewing naked girls on his office computer, though he insisted his activities were a charitable contribution: "These young women are from poor countries and need to make money to help their parents." The NSF porn-viewing employees had one thing in common: they were all men.

Over the past three years, the Securities and Exchange Commission (SEC), the Department of Defense at the Pentagon, and the Minerals Management Service (responsible for monitoring the BP oil spill) all held internal investigations to deal with numerous male employees watching porn on government computers. Men are so highly motivated to look at graphic sex that they're willing to risk public shame and even their jobs just to visit porn sites.

So what exactly are all these men so driven to look at?

GIRL METROPOLIS AND *COUGAR TOWN*

In this chapter, we're going to review some of the main visual cues that activate male desire. Of course, men are also aroused by psychological cues. But the Internet demonstrates quite convincingly that most men prefer visuals to stories or discussion. Some of men's visual cues will probably come as no surprise. Others are quite unexpected. Strictly speaking though, the most influential male cue of all is not visual, but chronological.

Age dominates sexual searches, adult Web site content, and pornographic videos. On Dogpile, terms describing age are the most frequent type of adjective in sexual searches, appearing in one out of every six sexual searches. When the male desire software evaluates a woman's visual appearance, one of the most prominent criteria is age—and not just youth, either.

Take a look at the graph on the next page. It shows the frequency of sexual searches on Dogpile that contain *specific* ages, such as "naked 25-year-olds" or "sexy 40-year–olds." The higher the bar, the more popular the age. Notice there are two separate peaks, marked in dark gray.

The first peak is on the left, in a narrow cluster of searches

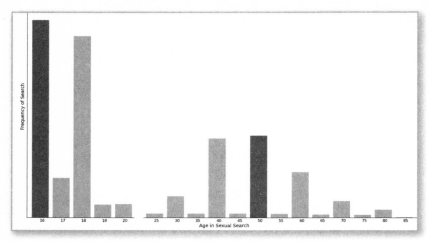

Frequency of age-related sexual searches on the Dogpile search engine

for teens. But there's a broader cluster of searches on the right, with a peak at age fifty. Though the popularity of adult women doesn't quite reach the stratospheric heights of teens, it's worth observing that more men search for fifty-year-olds than search for nineteen-year-olds. There is a rather shocking number of searches for underage women, but you may be equally surprised to discover there is significant erotic interest in sixty- and seventy-year-olds.

The adult industry recognizes there are distinct audiences for women of different ages. "A MILF falls into the 35-50-year-old category (50+ is 'mature'). 'Teens' can be 18–20. The 21–35s are just plain porn," explains Stephen Yagielowicz, senior editor for Xbiz, the leading source of news and business information for the adult industry. "Anecdotally, much of the mature content that I'm seeing on [nontube sites] today is vintage content from Eastern Europe, showing the widespread and perennial appeal of this material. You gotta love dirty old ladies!"

....

In the late 2000s, the online adult industry went through a dramatic change. This change was made possible by new technological developments, but was ultimately driven by male desire—namely, the desire to look at things. The Web site that epitomizes this change is known as PornHub.

Following the explosive success of YouTube—a Web site that allows users to upload and share their videos—a number of Web sites began to emulate YouTube, but with adult content. These sites are known as *tubes*. Dozens of tubes sprung up in 2007, including RedTube, XTube, YouPorn, and XNXX. Each offered thousands of video clips. The tubes quickly incited the wrath of the rest of the online adult industry. The reason for this animosity is perfectly understandable: many tube sites gave away content for free that they acquired for free. Instead of earning money from subscriptions—the previous business model for adult Web sites— the tubes earn money from advertisements.

In 2007, the Montreal-based PornHub came online. Their three floors of sedate offices, just across the street from a Walmart, resemble the sterile corporate cubicles of any high-tech startup. In just two years, PornHub became the most heavily trafficked adult video site in the world, attracting more than 10 million visitors each day. Though it had an "anything goes" attitude in its earliest days, the now caution-minded PornHub offloads squickier content (such as fisting and golden showers) onto its sister tube sites, and completely prohibits videos depicting rape, incest, or bestiality. Their success is partially predicated on an interface that makes it easy for users to locate appealing visual content. Videos are searchable by tags, categories, and a search engine. So what is the single most popular search term users enter into the PornHub search engine?

"Mom."

We can get a clearer perspective on the popularity of age-related genres (such as "Mom") by considering the frequency of specific age-related *adjectives* used in sexual searches.

% of All Sexual Searches on Dogpile	Adjective	Example Search
5.8	Teen	free non-nude teen videos
2.0	Young	young naked waitresses
1.4	Mom	my friend's hot mom
1.3	MILF	MILF next door
.5	Grannies	hot nude grannies
.3	Old	free porn of old women
.2	Older	busty older women
.1	Cougar	cougar seductions
.1	Mature	mature women in bikinis

This table mirrors the previous figure: youth dominates male desire, but there is also significant interest in older women, including MILFs. What's a MILF? A "Mother I'd Like to Fuck." This term was popularized in the 1999 teen comedy *American Pie*. MILFs became a profitable online niche in the early 2000s with the rise of Internet video, led by Web sites like MILF Hunter. Today, MILFs is one of the most popular and profitable genres of male-targeted pornography. Even socially conservative India has its own homegrown version of the MILF genre.

An erotic online comic titled *Savita Bhabhi* gained a massive following in India soon after its initial publication in 2009. The comic strip, published in English, Hindi, and several other Indian languages, details the adventures of lusty buxom housewife Savita, who seduces salesmen, milkmen, neighborhood youth, and other assorted characters while her husband is away at work. The *bhabhi*—a Hindi word that literally means "sister-in-law" but is used to address married women in general—is a staple of erotic Indian tales as an aggressively amorous woman. Savita Bhabhi's adventures, tame as they were by Western standards, did not go unnoticed by Indian authorities and the comic strip was banned within a few months.

The male desire for older women is also reflected in the

popularity of "mom" searches on PornHub (since teen content is highly visible and easily accessible on PornHub, users may be more likely to manually type in searches for content they don't immediately see).

More than a quarter of all men report that their first sexual fantasy was triggered by a sexy older person. There is a popular notion that older women, colloquially referred to as *cougars*, are more aggressive at pursuing sex than younger women. The tagline for ABC's television show *Cougar Town* asks, "Can a woman of a certain age be a mom, a successful career woman, and still be on the prowl?" The answer seems to be yes. A 2010 study found that women age twenty-seven to forty-five have more sexual fantasies, a greater willingness to have one-night stands, and a greater willingness to have casual sex than women in other age ranges.

"The main reason I like MILFs is because they're more experienced and mature. They know exactly what they want, so there's none of the awkwardness," explains Brad Fowler, a twenty-one-year-old college student from Boston. "You feel like you can learn something from them, and there's also an aspect of desiring something that you seemingly can't have. . . . It's easier to hook up with a hot college freshman than a hot forty-year-old with a kid and a minivan, so there's a sense of accomplishment involved. It's not Moms I *Can* Fuck, it's Moms I'd *Like* to Fuck—it makes all the difference."

Almost no academic research has been done investigating the appeal of MILFs. But it's reasonable to presume that at least some of the interest in MILFs depends on psychological cues. The terms "aggressive" and "seduction" appear on the vast majority of MILF sites, including My Friend's Mom and Mommy Got Boobs. The "MILF-lovers" Facebook group asserts in its mission statement, "We love the experience and confidence of the older woman. How she is comfortable seducing a young guy, then fucking him with abandon and no romantic complications." MILF sites typically feature innocent young men who are seduced by aggressive older women. The self-assured Mrs. Robinson, who seduces a very young Dustin Hoffman in *The Graduate*, is perhaps the most famous MILF in cinema.

Though the self-confidence of the MILF appears to be essential to her appeal to the male brain, she also seems to present a number of visual cues that activate male desire. Most MILFs in online porn are busty, curvy, with large, round butts. This is often reflected in the titles of Web sites: My Busty MILF, MILF Ass, Busty Moms Videos, Sexy Ass MILF, Busty MILF Pics.

Many men find both young and adult women to be appealing. On AOL, one out of four people who searched for MILFS also searched for teens. Intriguingly, there is a similar level of overlap between searches for teens and searches for another age-related sexual interest known as GILFs. About one out of four GILF searchers also searched for teens. So what does GILF stand for? Granny I'd Like to Fuck.

Here is the abbreviated AOL search history of one granny fan, Mr. Playstation:

mature deepthroat movies

old lady oral movies

granny cum swallowing movies

what is the optimum humidity for a home

grandma anal movies

star wars lego game cheats for playstation 2

teen deepthroat movies

mature oral movies

Many people find GILFs to be squicky. After all, if men are free to search for any porn they desire, surely they'll avoid post-menopausal women? Such thinking, apparently, is uninformed ageism. Though it's true that the total number of *granny* searches amounts to less than 8 percent of the total *youth* searches, there are more sexual searches for *grannies* (#19) than for *spanking* (#25). But are GILFs truly that popular? Perhaps it's simply some particular eccentricity of Dogpile users?

Alexa is a company that measures traffic to different Web sites through the use of its Alexa toolbar. Alexa publishes a list of the million most popular Web sites in the world. According to our analysis, 42,337 of these Web sites were adult sites in March 2010, or about 4 percent of all sites. We'll call this set of the most popular adult sites in the world the *Alexa Adult List*.

Out of the 42,337 sites on the Alexa Adult List, 313 are *granny* sites. In fact, there's an active and well-defined community of granny porn enthusiasts, with sites such as GILF Porn, Tube Granny, and Granny Rides Again. The popularity of GILFs presents a serious challenge for evolutionary science. A broad body of research has demonstrated that men prefer smooth skin to wrinkles and long, lustrous hair to short, gray frizz. What might be going on with all these searches for sexy women of a certain age?

Two countries boasting the highest interest in granny porn are Kenya and England. In Kenya, the "rules of sexual shame" encourage young people to discuss sexual matters with grandparents. Among the Kisii, the grandmother is often the confidante of her grandchildren regarding sexual experiences and sexual technique. In fact, for many Kisii boys, their first acquisition of sexual knowledge from a woman comes from an older woman.

Following a somewhat different pattern, the United Kingdom features a widespread boarding school culture involving strict rules, corporal punishment, and severe, elderly matrons. "There's a lot of interest in older ladies from the Brits because when a lot of them were schoolboys they were spanked or slapped or pinched by a schoolmarm," explains a longtime adult industry veteran. "It might have been their first intimate contact with a woman." We'll explore these cultural possibilities further in the next chapter.

Some of the interest in older women may simply be due to their greater availability. On the Web site Granny Sex Forum, a user named LoveSelsie describes where he goes to pick up GILFs: "Wal-Mart is very close to my home so it is common for me to visit the store almost daily. Some time ago, I noticed a new greeter at the door. She was about 5 foot 5 inches tall and just a little fluffy. Her hair was gray, short and straight. She was a very appealing lady and I wanted to get to meet her." It's worth observing that LoveSelsie focuses on the *visual* attractiveness of GILFs, as do many other granny fans.

Even though there are sizable male audiences for both moms and grannies, youth remains the empress of the Internet. *Youth* is the number one sexual interest by a wide margin on search engines in Russia, Japan, Europe, and India. On the Alexa Adult List, there are 2,462 adult sites that feature youth, compared to 1,237 sites that feature MILFs or mature women. In Web site names, "Teen" is a prefix or suffix applied to just about every interest imaginable: CandyCoatedTeens.com, TeenSnow.com, FineArtTeens .com, DrunkTeenParty.com, DoctorTeen.com.

"Legal teen content has been a consistent earner in the adult industry," observes Stephen Yagielowicz. "It's the most competitive niche, with the lowest conversion [to paid subscription] rates. But it's also got the highest traffic. If you throw up a site with young women, you're guaranteed plenty of eyeballs. But with so much competition, you certainly aren't guaranteed profit."

THE MYTHIC APPEAL OF SKINNY

"Essentially the fashion world sees toothpicks toppling under the weight of their false lashes as attractive," blogs Claire L on the fbomb Web site. "Arms must be willowy, stomachs trim and God forbid your thighs touch . . . and all for the convenience and pleasure of the male population."

A recent Girl Scouts survey found that almost nine out of ten girls between thirteen and seventeen say they feel pressured by the fashion and media industries to be skinny. It's true that many magazines often feature women with a lower-than-average body mass index (BMI), but these magazines—such as *Cosmopolitan*, *Vogue*, and *InStyle*—target *women*, not men. The porn that men seek out in the privacy of their laptops tells a different story—one supported by male visual cues rather than women's fashion.

Like youth, a woman's body size is another cue that appears to be an innate trigger of male arousal. Adjectives describing body size (such as "chubby" and "thin") are the third most frequent category of adjectives appearing in Dogpile searches. Are most of these searches seeking the slender bodies of cover models? For every search for a "skinny" girl, there are almost three searches for a "fat" girl.

On the Web, many men are fans of BBW, which stands for Big, Beautiful Women. On the Alexa Adult List, there are more than 504 adult sites explicitly dedicated to heavy ladies (such as Fat Tube, Sugar Fat Girls, and Hippo Girls), and only 182 explicitly dedicated to skinny ones (such as Skinny Teens Naked). There are also more than 150 nonerotic BBW dating networks, such as Large and Lovely, Large Passions, and Chubby Fishing.

The women on adult BBW sites have very large and round breasts, large and curvy hips, and large and round butts. Indeed, the overall impression is one of supersized visual cues of femininity. "It's simply better when there's more," explains a thirty-one-year-old natural gas engineer and BBW fan from central Pennsylvania. "Tits are great, why wouldn't I want more? An ass is great, why wouldn't I want more? It's just nice to be able to really feel a woman there with you instead of trying to search for even a bit of some skeletal girl's arm or leg to hold on to when you're having sex. Bigger girls will have more fun, and will work twice as hard to meet the standards of the skinny girls most people find attractive."

Nevertheless, though the popularity of chubby sites is indisputable, it's true that the majority of women in mainstream porn are skinnier than average. We analyzed the average BMI and weight of 202 popular American porn actresses under age thirty. In addition, psychologists Martin Voracek and Maryanne Fisher analyzed the bodies of mainstream European porn actresses. The following table compares the BMI and weights of these porn stars with other women.

Woman	BMI	Weight in Pounds
Paris Hilton	16	115 (52kg)
Angelina Jolie	17.9	120 (55kg)
European Porn Actresses	18.4	115 (52kg)
Healthy Women	18.5–24.9	
American Porn Actresses	18.8	115 (52kg)
Average American Woman, ages 20–29	26.8	156 (71kg)

American porn actresses have an average weight and BMI that is below the average for all American women ages 20–29, but still remain within the Centers for Disease Control and Prevention's healthy range. European porn actresses dip just below healthy.

Many sex scientists believe that women's waist-to-hip ratios are a visual cue for men. Some research suggests that men around the world find a specific waist-to-hip ratio (.7) to be most arousing. This is the same average waist-to-hip ratio Voracek and Fisher found among European porn actresses. A particular part of the male brain associated with reward processing, the anterior cingulate gyrus, even appears to be activated when a man views an ideal waist-to-hip ratio. However, it's worth observing that "hips" and "waists" themselves rarely appear in sexual searches. There are no Web sites on the Alexa Adult List devoted to hips or waists, nor could we find any online list of "Top 10 Hips" (though there are plenty of such amateur lists of "best" breasts and butts). None of the major adult tube sites have a hips or waist category, and there are no hip fetishes reported in the clinical literature.

If the male desire software does target a particular waist-to-hip ratio, this must operate using a different neural mechanism from the desire software used to process other visual cues, since men do not search for hips, use "hips" as a tag when labeling videos, or fetishize hips the way they do breasts, butts, vaginas, feet, and penises. However, if men do prefer a low waist-to-hip ratio, this may be one reason why some men prefer heavy women, since many of the models featured in BBW porn have a low ratio due to their excessive hip size.

But one thing is clear: willowy, toothpick-thin women are a rarity in male-targeted pornography.

GIANT, HUGE, AND JUMBO

There is an anatomical mystery taking place all around the world. Women's breasts are getting larger. And not just because women are getting heavier.

"In a country [Britain] where one in three women is overweight, you'd think there was a simple, fat-related reason for this, but obesity alone doesn't explain the jump in cup size, nor the biggest growth area in bra sales: smaller back size and bigger cup size," ponders *Guardian* journalist Alice Fisher. "Judging by recent underwear figures, there are more slimmer women with larger boobs than ever before. Women are happy about this. Men are happy about this. But no one seems happy to explain why this is happening."

Breasts, no matter what size, are the most popular body part in sexual searches in every country we looked at, including the United States, Russia, India, Germany, Japan, and Saudi Arabia. *Breasts* is the third most popular category of sexual search—and the *most* popular category exclusive to heterosexual men. Large breasts are extraordinarily popular in Internet porn, dominating images, stories, videos, and most international variations of animated erotica. Their popularity was confirmed in an experiment conducted by psychologist Nicolas Gueguen, who used padding to vary a female confederate's breast size from A-cup to C-cup, then counted the number of times she was approached by men at a nightclub and bar in France.

Bra cup size	A	B	C
# of Times Woman was Approached by Men	18	28	60

There are more than 1,672 large breast Web sites in the Alexa Adult List, making them one of the most popular categories of sexual sites. Dozens of synonyms for "large" appear in sexual searches for breasts—busty, big, gigantic, monster, huge, massive, ginormous—while there are only three common synonyms for small breasts—small, tiny, petite. As Alice Fisher observed, there does seem to be an intriguing coincidence between men's preference for large breasts and the increase in women's actual breast sizes. Of course, not all men are fans of busty.

"I like small breasts. They're like, *Hi! How can I help you!*" muses comedian Mitch Fatel. "Large breasts are like, *I'm sorry, we're closing in 5 minutes.*"

Flat-chested women have enthusiastic fans. The Web sites Flat Chested Coeds, Sexy Small Boobs, and I Love Small Tits all celebrate women who are less endowed. In Japan, a woman with small breasts is called "Delicious Flat Chest" or DFC, and there are many popular animated DFC characters, such as Sailor Moon, Lina Inverse, Konata from *Lucky Star*, and Nagi from *Kannagi: Crazy Shrine Maidens*. Keira Knightley and Kate Hudson are both A-list and A-cup movie stars with devoted male followings.

But it's the big ones that dominate Internet porn. Just like "Teen," "Busty" is a common prefix used in a variety of porn site names: Busty Island, Busty and Dusty, Busty Elders, Busty at Work, Busty Party. "It's just nice to have something big right there . . . and you can do way more with them. When they're bigger, right?" asserts Lee Malden, a twenty-two-year-old music producer. "Grab 'em, hold on to 'em, fuck 'em if you'd like! Bigger tits are better tits, man."

The significant historical and cross-cultural popularity of breasts supports the notion that they are an innate visual cue triggering male desire. However, one possible challenge to this notion is the fact that breasts are rarely fetishized in primitive hunter-gatherer cultures—the type of cultures that may be most similar to our Stone Age ancestors. But it's worth observing that in these cultures, such as the Amazonian Yanomamo, a twenty-two-year-old's breasts often resemble a Western forty-year-old woman's breasts. In modern societies, dramatically improved nutrition, health, and fitness mean that women can maintain firm, youthful breasts well into adulthood—or MILFhood.

Though there seems to be a cross-cultural preference for larger breasts, the preferred size of a woman's areola seems to be highly variable. There are no nipple-size-specific Web sites on the Alexa Adult List, but there are many large-nipple sites, and many small-nipple sites. One cross-cultural study found that men in Papua New Guinea preferred large areolae, Samoan men preferred slightly smaller areolae, and New Zealand men preferred medium-sized areolae. The color of a woman's nipples is an even less influential visual cue. There are no adult sites dedicated to dark-colored nipples or light-colored nipples, and out of the 55 million Dogpile sexual searches, fewer than two thousand specified the coloration of the nipple.

Butts are almost as popular as breasts in sexual searches, and there are almost as many porn sites dedicated to butts as breasts, hinting that men may also have an innate sensitivity to buttocks cues. Regarding butts and breasts, bigger is usually better. Not so for another male visual cue.

AN EXQUISITE PAIR OF JIMMY CHOOS

"I do have a bit of a foot fetish, yes," affirms comic actor Jack Black. "I find myself staring at feet. I like a heel. If she's wearing clogs, that does something for me. Flip-flops. Sandals. Bare feet are the best."

Scientific attempts at explaining the widespread male interest in feet have been quite varied. Richard von Krafft-Ebing believed such an interest could develop when "emotional and visual impressions are brought into associative connection." Freud thought a foot fetish reflected a submissive, immature personality. Social scientists have speculated that they form because of the strong odor of feet or because fancy women's shoes draw heightened attention to ladies' feet. But another possibility is that men's brains are *designed* to respond to women's feet. The biggest piece of evidence supporting this possibility is men's preferred foot size.

The anthropologist Daniel Fessler found that men from a broad variety of societies (including Iran, Brazil, Tanzania, and Papua New Guinea) rate small female feet as more attractive than large feet. In contrast, women rated an average male foot size as most attractive. Moreover, on sexual foot Web sites, small feet are represented almost exclusively. If an interest in feet was purely cultural, we might expect to see at least one society or Web site celebrating large female feet.

"In the Cinderella folktales the prince is never canvassing his kingdom in search of a girl whose feet will fill out a gravy boat of a shoe," observes Donald Symons, who also points out some additional clues supporting an innate male interest in foot cues. Women's feet typically grow during pregnancy, sometimes a half or even a full shoe size, and pregnant women should be less attractive from an evolutionary perspective since further reproduction is not possible during pregnancy. Several cultures, such as the Chinese and Persians, historically practiced foot binding in an effort to make the feet physically smaller. Many American women habitually wear shoes that are too small for their feet. Women themselves often seem to eroticize their feet, as epitomized by Carrie Bradshaw on *Sex and the City*, indicating an awareness (even if unconscious) that men are paying attention.

Another challenge for cultural theories of the male sexual interest in feet: why feet and not hands? Hands are more visible in all cultures, and the general shape and detail of the hand is quite similar to the foot. Women's hands are often decorated with bright, manicured fingernails, drawing attention to them. In online porn, women's hands are frequently portrayed as actively participating in sexual acts: there are far more handjobs than footjobs. So hands are highly visible, attractively adorned, and presented as sexual instruments. Yet in the Dogpile data there were 93,885 sexual searches for feet and only 5,831 sexual searches for hands. There are 276 different foot sites in the Alexa Adult List, but we could only find one Web site that could be construed as hand-focused: Glove Mansion.

So if men are attracted to feet because of an innate receptivity to foot cues, was Freud mistaken in his belief that a foot obsession is related to submissiveness? Perhaps not. According to the AOL search data, searches for foot erotica are highly correlated with searches for bondage and submission porn. Many webmasters cross-link their foot sites to submission sites to capture cross traffic from each. One popular type of foot porn consists of a man being stepped on by a domineering woman or being forced to lick a woman's feet. It's not clear whether these submissive interests arise as a way of simply engaging the foot in a more intimate way, whether an interest in feet may drive an interest in submission, or whether feet and submission are both related to some other unknown factor.

Searches for women's shoes, pantyhose, and stockings are also highly correlated with sexual searches for feet. There are many Web sites and online forums that cater to an erotic interest in women's footwear, such as Pretty High Heels, Cute Pantyhose, and Teens' Pantyhose. "I definitely love girls with beautiful feet," admits rap star Ludacris. "Sometimes she can trick me and just wear boots and not even show her feet. But when I see the feet, it's a wrap."

Men's interest in breasts, butts, and feet are well known and well documented. The next anatomical cue, however, may come as something of a surprise.

HOSTING A SPECIAL EXHIBITION

Comedian Ron White describes a conversation with his cousin Ray.

"I told him we're all gay, buddy. And Ray goes, *That's bullshit, man*. Do you like porn? *Yeah, I love porn*. Oh, and do you only watch scenes with two women? *No, I'll watch a man and a woman makin' love.* Do you like the guy to have a half-flaccid penis? *No, I like big, hard, throbbing cock.* . . . See? You like looking at a big cock."

The fact of the matter is that men are more interested in penises than women are—and men are *much* more interested in *large* penises than women are. In a recent academic survey of more than fifty thousand respondents between the ages of eighteen and fifty, just 15 percent of women reported dissatisfaction with their partner's penis size, while 45 percent of men wanted a larger penis. But it's not just their own penis that men are concerned with.

An eye-tracking study recorded what men and women looked at as they viewed different (nonerotic) images. They found that men consistently direct their gaze to the male crotch, though women rarely do so. In romance novels, even ones that include explicit descriptions of sex, visual details about a man's penis, including size, are seldom offered. But in porn, the penis is always under the spotlight. The Web site Fantasti.cc is a community-based adult content aggregator, a social networking site where the predominantly male users rate and comment on more than 1 million images and videos. Out of the hundred top-rated images on Fantasti.cc, twenty-one feature close-up shots of a penis. The number of Dogpile searches for "pussy" just barely beats out searches for "dick," 1,096,614 to 938,134. *Big Dick* is a popular category of porn on all of the major adult tube sites, including PornHub.

For men, the penis can never be too big, apparently. Just .2 percent of men wish they had a smaller penis, compared to 9 percent of women who wish they had smaller breasts. Indeed, there are more than six times the number of searches for "big dick" than "small dick." There are 1,072 Web sites in the Alexa Adult List that feature heterosexual porn with large penises such as Monsters of Cock, Mr.Biggz, and Teens Like It Big. The number of Alexa sites devoted to small penises? Just three: PinkyDick, Little-Cock, and My Tiny Dick.

Here's the AOL search history of one fan of oversized organs, Mr. Amish:

big cocks

big dicks

monster cocks

tight pussy big dicks

long dong sex

big texas cocks

enormous cocks

gigantic cocks

big white dick sex

horny Amish women

So far, all of the visual cues we've encountered draw a man's attention to the female body. But not the penis. So why might the male organ captivate men's attention? One possible explanation may lie with our primate cousins. Among New World monkeys, Old World monkeys, and the apes, the penis is a prominent and versatile social tool. The erect primate penis is used as a sign of male-male aggression, to mark territory, and as a sexual invitation to females. If the invitation is witnessed by a competing male, the erect penis can provoke hostility and attacks. It may also be a visual cue that motivates males to copulate with a female shortly after she has mated with a competing male. Biologist Richard Dawkins even suggests that an erection may be a visible sign of a male's general health. But some primates go further than simply inspecting each other's phalli.

When male savanna baboons meet, they frequently perform an intense greeting that scientists have endowed with the technical term *diddling*—"the fondling of the penis and scrotum." Similarly, among the Australian Walbiri and Aranda people, when grievances need to be settled, the men participate in what is known as the penis-offering rite, which is said to represent "paying with one's life." Each man presents his semierect penis to all the others, pressing it into each man's palm and drawing it along the length of the upturned hand. Anyone who has seen a *koteka*, the colorful two-foot-long penis cap worn by men in Papua New Guinea, can easily believe that men have inherited our primate cousins' attentiveness to the penis.

But men aren't satisfied by checking out other men's penises. They also like to flaunt their own. Historically, male exhibitionism has been considered a mental disorder. If that is the case, the Internet suggests we are a planet of mentally deranged men. Chat Roulette is a Web site that allows users with a webcam to randomly connect to other people around the world. Once you enter Chat Roulette, you see whatever the other person has chosen to place in front of their webcam. It might be a party, a cute kitten, an old man with a beard, or—very rarely—a bored teenage girl. One blogger recorded what he saw on 1,276 consecutive Chat Roulette sessions: 298 webcams (about one in four) were aimed at a penis. Another blogger created software to track the global locations of penis sightings on Chat Roulette: ChatRouletteCockMap.com reveals that Europe, Brazil, and the American east coast are dense with Internet exhibitionism.

On Fantasti.cc, 23 percent of the male users use an image of their penis as their avatar, while another 13 percent used a penis from a porn clip. In comparison, 5 percent of the female users use an image of a vagina. On reddit's heterosexual Gone Wild forum, where users are free to post NC-17 pictures of themselves, 123 of the 345 self-posted male images (about 35 percent) consist of close-ups of penises.

Though encountering a male exhibitionist on the subway or in the city park can be frightening and unsettling, clinical psychiatrists do not consider them dangerous. Exhibitionists rarely follow up their lewd displays with any attempt at contacting the women they've exposed themselves to. Often, the urge to exhibit oneself manifests as an inexplicable compulsion, rather than a conscious intention to dominate or scare a woman. "The act was more magical than sexual, a ritual to restore that all-important sense of power that the defeats of life had temporarily destroyed," explained Lance Rentzel, former wide receiver for the Dallas Cowboys, recounting the incident that got him arrested. "On this day, for some reason, I needed someone to play with me in a childish game I was making up. Look at me, look at me. Look at what I've got. I sat in the car and they came over and I exposed myself. It took maybe 10 seconds, then I drove off, strangely relieved."

Perhaps men are tapping into an ancient display mechanism we share with other primates, similar to the way girls' enjoyment of brushing other girls' hair may reflect our primate grooming mechanisms. It's true that some women are enchanted by a substantial phallus. But for men, a large penis is always welcome.

AN ANIMATED LADY

One way to get a better sense of the visual cues that trigger male desire is to consider erotic art designed for men. An artist is not constrained by gravity or biology but is free to fashion impossible bodies limited only by his imagination. If a particular style of erotic art becomes popular across diverse cultures, this may be a good indication that it is activating men's innate desire software. With the growth of the Internet, one type of erotic art has risen to unchallenged dominance across all wired nations: *Japanese anime.*

A more relaxed judicial reinterpretation of obscenity laws in the 1990s released the floodgates on Japanese animated erotica, an art form that traces its roots back to nineteenth-century woodblock printings. With the advent of the Internet, Japanese anime quickly spread throughout the world. Japanese anime (sometimes known as *hentai*) is the most searched for type of erotic animation or erotic art on search engines in the United States, Russia, France, Thailand, Brazil, and Australia, suggesting that it is highly effective in exploiting men's visual cues. (*Animation,* including non-Japanese cartoons, is the ninth most popular category of sexual searches on Dogpile.) So what do the women in Japanese anime look like? The typical anime female is a high school teenager.

She has large, baby-like eyes, emulated by Lady Gaga in her "Bad Romance" video. Her voice is extremely high-pitched. She frequently wears school uniforms, complete with pleated skirts, vests, and saddle shoes. She is often sexually inexperienced and reacts with embarassment at the mention of sex (indicated by reddening cheeks). Yet, despite all these vivid cues of youth, she is drawn with impossibly large breasts, a perfectly round and firm butt, a low waist-to-hip ratio, and small feet. It's also worth noting that Japanese animation frequently contains men with gargantuan penises, sometimes longer than a girl's arm.

In other words, the Internet's most popular visual erotic art contains supercharged versions of all the male visual cues. This probably explains why many men are *schediaphiliacs*—sexually attracted to animated characters.

Now that we have a better understanding of *what* men like to look at, we can ask—*why?*

CHAPTER 3

Elmer Fudd, Wabbit Hunter

Male Desire

> If you put little, warm holes in the wall of my house—given enough time, I'm going to have sex with it.
>
> —Comedian Joe Rogan

What does a hen need to turn a rooster on? A sultry clucking, a tail-swinging sashay, a thickly feathered breast? When it comes to sex appeal, the white leghorn rooster has simple tastes. All a hen needs to get a rooster crowing is a red comb. Head and body optional.

When biologists tried to figure out which visual cues evoked sexual behavior in male fowl, they found that roosters would exhibit mating behaviors even when exposed to an *artificial* hen's comb. About half of all roosters attempted copulation with an artificial chicken head mounted on a feather-covered board. Turkeys are even less discriminating: male gobblers will try to mate with a rubber ball, as long as it's the size and height of a female head.

The objectification of female anatomy is not limited to farm birds. Male chacma baboons find the bright red rumps of ovulating females to be particularly arousing. Using an ingenious experiment, one scientist attempted to determine whether a female's scarlet derriere was the actual cue exciting males, rather than her odor or behavior. A nonovulating female baboon was fitted with a "thermoplastic perineum swelling"—a fake baboon butt. The artificially enhanced female was kept in a separate cage where she was visible to the males, but could not be touched by them. The experimenters then counted the number of times the males masturbated. The bigger and brighter the fake butt, the more the male baboons pleasured themselves.

The butt fixation of male baboons would probably come as no surprise to clinical psychologists, who encounter far more men than women obsessed with body parts. Men's sexual fantasies are more visually explicit than women's and men remember more visual details from sexual encounters than women do. Erotic stories written by men use more visual descriptions than stories written by women. In the AOL search data, almost no one who searched for "Martha Stewart" searched for "porn," though "Martha Stewart" searchers were four times more likely than chance to search for erotic stories.

The male brain is designed to be more visually responsive to sexual stimuli than the female brain. Male arousal itself relies on two structures located in the subcortex: the amygdala and the hypothalamus. These are tiny structures that operate without conscious awareness. The amygdala is responsible for emotional responses. The hypothalamus is the engine of sexual arousal. In studies where both men and women viewed pornography, the amygdala and the hypothalamus were activated more strongly in men. This is the case even when women report stronger arousal than men (which happens infrequently). Together, the amygdala and the hypothalamus urge a man to pay attention: *wow, look at those curves!*

Visual cues trigger desire in men. If a man's brain decides a picture is arousing, he swiftly experiences physical and psychological arousal. Immediately following exposure to erotic visual stimuli, the brain areas responsible for the generation of an erection are activated. Men's greater sex drive may be partially due to the fact that their sexual motivation pathways have more connections to the subcortical reward system than in women.

In other words, what you may have long suspected is true: men's brains are designed to objectify females. This objectification of women extends deep into the mists of prehistory. The famous 26,000-year-old Venus of Willendorf statuette, hand-carved by a Cro-Magnon in Paleolithic Germany, features GG-cup breasts and a hippopotamal butt, but no face. The 40,000-year-old Venus of Hohle Fels boasts even more prodigious hips and mammaries—and titanic labia.

Out of the one hundred highest-rated images on Fantasti.cc, twenty-three feature close-ups of female anatomy without a face. One close-up of a woman's bare bottom generated hundreds of enthusiastic comments, including, "Delicious!", "This is what I call a MASTER PIECE," and "Great hindquarters. Now saddle up!" One imagines that if male baboons could speak, they'd shout similar cat calls over baboon booty.

Many adult sites targeting men focus on body parts. Daily Basis features a gallery of glossy bits of female anatomy—lips, toes, butts, eyelashes, bellies, breasts. The site looks like a Victoria's Secret catalog passed through a paper shredder. Boobpedia is an online "Encyclopedia of Big Boobs," containing detailed information on almost ten thousand pairs of breasts—and a few notes on the models, celebrities, and porn stars who own them. Mighty Fine Ass rates "amateur submitted nice asses and sexy round butts," while Foot Fap displays hundreds of images of women's feet.

Most women find such clinical portrayals of anatomy to be unappealing. But men's brains scrutinize the details of arousing visuals with the kind of concentration jewelers apply to the cut of a diamond. Consider one of the most popular sexual visual interests in Japan, *zettai ryouiki*, translated as "the absolute territory."

The absolute territory is the band of skin visible between a woman's skirt and the top of her socks—or, even more tantalizing, between a miniskirt and thigh-high stockings. "The socks and skirt are usually darker shades than the skin," explains one fan on the blog Anime Desho Desho. "Therefore the skin is the light at the end of a dark tunnel, gleaming in an aura of brilliance. Always seek the light!"

The anatomical fixations of men are often subject to intense analytical and mathematical scrutiny. Women are "Perfect 10s." Baby Boomers described girls as 36-24-36. Fans of *zettai ryouiki* categorize the bewitching strip of skin into six different types, ranging from Grade E (too much skin and too much skirt) to A (very thin strip of skin and very short skirt). Fans spend hours measuring the ratio of skirt to skin to sock length on a wide variety of *zettai ryouiki* images in order to derive a "golden mean." According to one blogger's laborious calculations, the most sublime ratio for [skirt length]:[skin length]:[length of socks above knees] is 4:1:2.5. Another fan adds, "memorizing this formula is as important as knowing the first 30 digits of pi."

The interest in the absolute territory is almost exclusive to Japanese men. In India, the belly is a common male obsession. In Victorian times, ankles were considered highly erotic. Salvador Dalí claimed to be aroused by a woman's earlobe. Thus, culture does seem to play some role in determining what part of a body the male brain targets. Nevertheless, internationally, three of the most consistently popular sexual searches on the Web are parts of the female body: *breasts*, *butts*, and *feet*. So how does the male brain guide some men to ankles and others to bellies—and most men to breasts and butts?

A SULTRY JAR OF PENNIES

Gentlemen, if you decided to participate in an intriguing experiment run by psychologists Joseph Plaud and James Martini, here's how it would go down. First, you look through a collection of slides of women. Some are nude, some partially nude, but you select five that you find arousing. Next, you sit down in a comfortable reclining chair, remove your pants, and slip a loop of wire around your penis. This device, known as a *plethysmograph*, measures blood flow to your private parts. After relaxing as best you can for five minutes, a slide show begins.

A rather boring picture appears on the screen for fifteen seconds: a jar of pennies. Then, one of your personally selected erotic slides appears, this one for thirty seconds. Then it vanishes and you wait two minutes. If you were especially aroused by the pictures, you'd wait even longer, since the researcher would wait for you to return to "baseline detumescence." Then the slide show repeats itself fourteen more times: pennies, porn, wait. That's it! You'd collect your $20 for your contribution to science, drop the plethysmograph in a bowl of sanitizing fluid, and head home.

Plaud and Martini's experiment tested the hypothesis that specific male desires are formed through a process known as *conditioning*. Famously associated with Ivan Pavlov's salivating dogs, conditioning exposes a subject to a neutral stimulus (such as a ringing bell), followed immediately by an arousing stimulus (such as tasty dog food). According to the science of conditioning, if the neutral and arousing stimuli are paired enough times, then eventually the neutral stimulus should acquire the same properties of the arousing stimulus; the dog salivates at the mere sound of the bell.

So what did Plaud and Martini find? By the end of the experiment, two out of three subjects became aroused by the jar of pennies. This demonstrated in a very limited fashion that visual conditioning can influence arousal in men. So could *social* conditioning be responsible for men's interest in specific parts of the female anatomy? Most of the time, the answer is probably no.

First of all, the jar of pennies did not make any of the men become erect. There was only a slight increase in blood flow to some of their penises. But more important, after a few weeks the men in the Plaud and Martini experiment were no longer aroused at all by the jar of pennies. In contrast, for virtually all men, a sexual interest in breasts, butts, or feet is sustained for life, and may even get more intense with age. In conditioning, if the neutral stimulus (e.g., the jar of pennies) is repeatedly shown to a subject without the arousing stimulus (e.g., naked woman), the neutral stimulus will eventually lose its power—a process known as *extinction*. But men spend their lives looking at presumably neutral stimuli (such as breasts or butts) without ever experiencing extinction. Moreover, few men are sexually aroused by the sight of a flat-screen monitor or a box of Kleenex, though both are frequently associated with arousing stimuli. Something else must be happening in the male brain to maintain a lifelong interest in specific female anatomy.

There are several interesting clues regarding how male visual interests form. First, many male sexual obsessions appear to form after a single exposure, rather than after repeated pairings of a neutral stimulus and an arousing stimulus. Second, almost all life-long sexual interests in men first form during adolescence. Clinicians report that it is very rare for an adult man to form a new sexual obsession with a visual object. If the male desire software was operating solely according to the principles of conditioning, then age should not be a significant factor. Instead, there appears to be a special window of time when visual sexual interests can form—what neuroscientists call a *critical period*.

In studies where male sheep were raised by goats, the young sheep sexually imprinted upon goats during the sheep's critical period. Afterward, the male sheep would only try to mate with goats. Other sheep were not sexually desirable. In contrast, when female sheep were raised by goats, their imprinting was reversible. The female sheep could become willing to mate with other sheep. This same pattern of irreversible male sexual imprinting and weak female imprinting was observed when young goats were raised by sheep.

A critical period for sexual imprinting is also supported by research on zebra finches. A male finch's ideas about what a sexy partner looks like are strongly influenced by how its mother looks. However, this influence only operates during a few months when the bird is about a year old. During this critical period, a visual representation of the ideal female is burned into the male finch brain and will guide its sexual behavior for life. (Intriguingly, female finches are more likely than males to form "visual fetishes," such as preferring a single brightly colored feather, if their father possessed such a cue. But, unlike humans, the male finch is more colorful and ornamented than the female.) When researchers prevented a male finch from seeing its mother during the critical period, it never developed a visual attraction to female finches.

A male finch's sexual interest in mother-like visual qualities is an example of what we might call a *cued interest*. A cued interest develops when the brain's natural responsiveness to a particular kind of cue causes the brain to sexually imprint upon a target that exhibits that cue. An innate visual cue guides the male zebra finch to imprint upon the physical appearance of its mother, creating a cued interest in mother-like finches. In Chapter 1, David Reimer developed a cued interest in girls, even though Dr. Money attempted to condition him to like boys. Breasts, butts, and feet are most likely cued interests.

If men's brains instinctively target visual foot cues, then a sexual interest in stockings or stiletto heels would also be a cued interest, since they both "match" the male brain's innate sensitivity to foot cues. Though men are not instinctively responsive to female footwear, the male desire software guiding a man to look at a woman's feet may lead him to imprint on a cute pair of open-toed Jimmy Choos.

During adolescence and early adulthood, perhaps the male desire software targets specific parts of female anatomy. "I can actually recall when my appreciation for breasts first started," confesses one forty-two-year-old accountant. "I was fourteen and watching the soft-core video *Taking It Off*. It was the first time I ever saw naked breasts. It was also the first time I ever got an erection. The star of the movie was this actress with a huge chest, Kitten Natividad. Before that, breasts were like elbows or anything else. But watching those huge jugs, it was like putting on an enchanted necklace. I was bewitched."

Cued interests don't always have a distinct moment when they form. Many men report that their interest in a particular body part developed over several years without a defining moment, though almost always forming during adolescence or their early twenties. Often, men characterize their cued interests as inexplicable. "I don't know why I like breasts," offers comedian Mitch Fatel. "They just sit there and make me happy." This may be because a cue is unconsciously steering a man's attention to a particular target. Things are different with *uncued interests*. Uncued sexual interests almost always seem to have a distinct, memorable beginning—an "origin story."

"When I was nineteen, I had a hydrocele, which is the accumulation of fluid around the testicle. The doctor needed to check how it was doing using ultrasound. So I was in the doctor's office lying on the cot with my pants down, and the female technician rubbed this warm gel on my testicles. That got my attention, certainly," explains Billy Chou, a forty-three-year-old Massachusetts government employee. "But then she took the ultrasound tool and began to roll it around my testicles. Instant hard-on. Like a block of iron. Ever since then, I get intensely turned on by doctor's offices. The moment I get on the crinkly paper of the cot, I get stiff. I love to role-play doctor and patient with my wife. I'm not gay, but once I'm on the exam table I even get hard around a male doctor."

Uncued interests are rarer than cued interests. The top fifty most popular sexual search categories on Dogpile are all cued interests, according to our reasoning. By definition, uncued interests are much more variable than cued interests, since just about anything can become an uncued interest if it presents itself in the right circumstances.

In our opinion, an uncued interest forms when an unexpected event interferes with the natural sexual imprinting process. Often, uncued interests involve the senses of touch or smell, like the doctor pressing the ultrasound paddle into Billy Chou's testicles. There may be another factor that strongly influences the formation of uncued interests in men: ejaculation. Most male turkeys initiate sexual behavior the first time they encounter an artificial female turkey, but fewer than half initiate sexual behavior a second time. Which males *do* repeat their amorous attention? Only those who ejaculated the first time.

Unfortunately, there is no research on the formation of uncued interests in humans. It's difficult to imagine any ethics review board would approve an experiment that required adolescent men to masturbate while probing their testicles with paddles in the hope of instilling a permanent erotic fixation. However, one case from the medical literature supports the importance of ejaculation in forming an uncued interest.

Chaminda was a young Buddhist Sri Lankan living in a town outside of the capital of Colombo. His father was an engineer and his mother died from cancer when Chaminda was very young. As a child, he gathered up brown ants from his garden and kept them in a cupboard in his bedroom, where he fed and took care of them. He called them his "little zoo." One of his favorite activities was to lie down naked on the floor and let the little ants crawl on his legs, giving him a pleasant tingly sensation.

When he was fourteen, he locked the door to his room and was playing with his little zoo. He tried a new solo activity common to boys around the world: masturbation—or what Sri Lankans call *athe gahanawa*. As he ejaculated, the ants tickled his thighs and testicles. A lifelong interest was forged. Several times a week for the next decade, he would let various insects and creatures crawl upon his naked body while he masturbated furiously, sometimes four or five times in an hour. Sexologists dubbed his erotic passion *formicophilia*—a love of crawling things.

Chaminda's formicophilia is a perfect example of an uncued interest. Innate cues did not guide the young Buddhist to find ants sexually appealing. Rather, he experienced a special tactile event during his sexual critical period, accompanied by ejaculation. Most of the time, a young man's brain could expect that the source of a tactile sensation on the penis producing ejaculation was a woman—an appropriate target to imprint upon. But fortune provided Chaminda and Billy Chou—and millions of other men—with a different experience.

Though Chaminda's formicophilia and Billy Chou's medical fetish suggest that male sexual imprinting may be flexible, the relative popularity of the various categories of online erotica reveals that uncued interests are quite rare compared to the overwhelming prevalence of cued interests in breasts, butts, feet, penises, and vaginas.

But why are men predisposed toward these body parts in the first place?

THE SEXY FAT

Breasts, hips, butts. Biologists have a name for the oversized parts of female anatomy that men find so enchanting: *ornamentation*. You might think that ornamentation is appealing because it signals a woman's current fertility. But according to many scientists, that's not quite right. Instead, the shapely curves of female ornamentation indicate how many years of healthy childbearing remain across a woman's entire lifetime. The difference between current fertility and future fertility is crucial: current fertility offers a man benefits from a short-term sexual encounter, while future fertility offers benefits from a long-term relationship, such as marriage.

Donald Symons was the first scientist to fully develop the idea that men should find visual cues associated with *youth* to be most attractive. "A nubile woman [i.e., one who is just beginning ovulation and has never been pregnant] would not have been investing her time and energy in other men's children, would have had more living relatives to invest in her and her children, and would have been more likely to survive until a newly conceived child was old enough to survive on its own," explains Symons. His ideas are well supported by the Internet, where searches for adolescent women are the most common sexual search around the world by a large margin.

If Symons is correct and the male desire software is designed to prefer adolescent ornamentation over adult ornamentation, this would suggest that men evolved to generally prefer long-term child-rearing relationships over short-term sexual liaisons. If male desire software was designed to prefer one-night stands, men should prefer sex with adult women over adolescents, since adolescents have relatively low fertility. (Most women don't attain regular ovulation until many years after menarche; over the past century, the age of first menstruation is happening earlier and the onset of regular ovulation is happening later.) Indeed, in most primate species, including chimpanzees, males *do* prefer fertility cues over youth cues. Male chimps do not find adolescents sexually attractive. They prefer mature females. Revealingly, chimpanzees do not form long-term relationships, but instead engage in frequent short-term liaisons.

Though men exhibit a general preference for youth and long-term relationships, the male brain is designed to flexibly pursue both long-term and short-term relationships—what psychologist David Buss calls *mixed mating strategies*. This might be one of the main reasons for the appeal of MILFs. As we saw in the previous chapter, most fans of MILFs emphasize older women's wishes to avoid romantic complications. MILF fans fantasize about getting seduced by a MILF for a one-night stand rather than wooing her as a girlfriend.

The red rump of the baboon, the orange throat patch of the striped plateau lizard, and the dangly combs of hens are all examples of female ornamentation. But throughout the animal kingdom, male ornamentation, such as the lion's mane and the peacock's tail, is far more common. Female ornamentation is found in species where females vary in quality and a female can obtain nongenetic benefits from males, such as food, shelter, or the protection of her offspring. Females compete with other females for these male-provided resources, with the most attractively ornamented females usually obtaining the most benefits. Dozens of young women flaunted their bodies on the adult image site Lightspeed, but the most attractive ones received jewelry, electronics, and cash from male admirers.

Ornamentation evolved as a result of this female competition—through an endless series of beauty pageants where the judges were the most desirable men. As men became more interested in female body parts, women developed bigger and better parts. The women with the best parts attracted the men with brains that targeted these parts. These couples then passed on genes for better parts to their daughters and genes for desiring these parts to their sons.

Across species, more attractive female ornamentation is associated with greater health, fertility, and offspring survival. This is definitely true with regard to human ornamentation. The anatomy that men find attractive—breasts, hips, butts, feet, as well as feminine facial features—are all influenced by the same molecule: *estrogen*. Estrogen is sensitive to a woman's energy and health. Unhealthy and underfed women produce less estrogen and therefore may not be able to bear children, or may bear unhealthy children. A woman's estrogen level indicates if she is getting enough to eat, if she's infested with parasites, and how much stress she's experiencing. The same way that our taste for sweetness guides us to sugar, which in turn provides us with energy, male visual cues guide men to estrogen, which in turn provides men with improved chances of healthy offspring.

Female ornamentation consists of a specific kind of female-only fat called *gynoid* fat. Gynoid fat supports the energy demands of pregnancy and lactation. Like men, women also possess *android* fat. Gynoid fat is only used during childbearing, whereas android fat is used for everyday energy needs. Android fat accumulates in the trunk and abdomen, and internally. Gynoid fat is stored in the breasts, hips, butt, and thighs.

A woman's body accumulates its maximum percentage of gynoid fat during adolescence. This accounts for teenage girls' shapely bodies. Since these estrogen-fueled, gynoid fat–based ornaments are the best indicators of a woman's long-term reproductive value, youthful forms of these ornaments evolved to become the most potent visual cues for men. There is even evidence that estrogen limits the growth of foot bones. Thus, small foot size might be another indirect indicator of a woman's health and long-term childbearing prospects.

Supersized signals of estrogen may be one source of BBW porn's popularity. These heavy women have large amounts of android fat, but they have very large amounts of sexy gynoid fat, too. The Venus of Willendorf is likely the creation of a prehistoric fan of BBW—and a lover of gynoid fat.

Donald Symons believes the preference for heavier-than-average women over skinnier-than-average women may be due to a concept known as *asymmetrical fitness*. Evolutionary theory predicts that men will prefer women who weigh a pound more than the optimum weight for reproduction over women who weigh a pound less, if there is a penalty associated with mating with a skinnier woman. In fact, low female weight is associated with infertility and poor health. If a woman's weight drops below a certain level, she will even stop ovulating. Women with weights somewhat higher than optimum do not suffer much of a drop in fertility or health, leading to evolutionary pressure for a man to prefer heavier-than-average women over lighter-than-average women.

This also applies to breasts: breasts that are slightly larger than average are more likely to reflect health and fertility than ones slightly smaller than average. Levels of gynoid fat in breasts positively predict all aspects of female lifetime reproductive capacity, including conception probability, probability of successful pregnancy, and offspring quality. Breast size is not correlated with milk production, though gynoid fat is correlated with lactation quality.

But even though men generally prefer large breasts over small breasts, the Internet demonstrates quite clearly that there's significant interest in a wide range of cup sizes. If the male brain responds instinctively to a visual breast cue, why do some men prefer double-D's while others prefer Delicious Flat Chests?

TAKING A CUE FROM MOTHER NATURE

Polish breasts are different from Vietnamese breasts, which are different from Zulu breasts. And breasts are always changing. The average Japanese bra size went from 34A in the 1980s to 34C in the 1990s. The average British bra size went from 36B in 1997 to 34D today. The male brain is designed to be sensitive to this variation. A visual cue guides a man's attention to a suitable erotic target, then the imprinting process establishes a cued interest using the specific details of the actual visual stimulus. This stimulus-sensitive imprinting process is not limited to sexual interests—or humans.

Famously, goslings (baby geese) imprint upon the first large, moving object they see. Most of the time when a gosling hatches, that large, moving object is the mother goose. But if a sneaky scientist intervenes, removing the mother goose and placing her own human body in view of newly hatched goslings, the baby geese will imprint upon the scientist instead. After that, the goslings will follow the scientist wherever she goes. For the baby geese, the scientist has become a cued interest.

The "mother cue" for the gosling brain (large, moving objects) is rather simple and nonspecific. There are two reasons for this. First, this simple design is pretty effective, since the first big, moving object a gosling sees is usually its mother. But just as important, the cue is simple and general because the gosling brain doesn't know ahead of time exactly what its mother will look like. Perhaps mom will be an unusual color, or smaller than average, or sport an injured wing. The geese "mother imprinting" brain software is designed to adapt to variable mother stimuli—though it can also be tricked by unusual interventions, such as sneaky scientists.

Men's desire software is also designed to adapt to variable visual cues. The same way that our taste for sugar may cause us to develop a taste for Snickers or Ben and Jerry's Karamel Sutra, men appear to imprint upon the specific female body parts that are available in a young man's environment. In other words, men aren't born with a "visual template" for the ideal breast, any more than they are born with a notion of the ideal candy bar. Instead, the male brain flexibly responds to a wide range of stimuli that contain a visual cue of "breastness," just as many candies contain a taste cue of sweetness. Thus, early exposure to anatomical stimuli that match a man's innate visual cues can result in a wide variety of anatomical preferences.

"I have been crazy for small breasted women since my first girlfriend when we were both 13. She was a very small A cup, and her nipples were very sensitive," relates one man online. "Just sucking them would make her come. When I later dated other larger breasted women, it seemed like the larger the breast, the less sensitive they were. Plus, a downblouse [looking down a woman's shirt] of a small breasted woman makes it easy to see her nipples, whereas a large breast makes it much more difficult. Smaller breasted women just look better to me!!!"

This cue-driven imprinting process in men may help explain some of the interest in mature women and GILFs, while also accounting for the fact that the fellatio-performing Sambia boys end up still liking women. Older women still present feminine visual and psychological cues that may (or may not) trigger sexual imprinting in the male brain. The odds of imprinting may go up if these cues are paired with physical contact or a sexual context—such as Kenyan boys learning about sex from grandma, or British boys getting paddled by a matron. The Sambia boys, on the other hand, don't experience any feminine cues during their rituals, so sexual imprinting may be less likely to be triggered, or imprinting may be weaker.

It appears that for a man, youthful sexual experiences are crucial for forming lifelong sexual interests—both common cued interests like big butts, and accidental uncued interests like ants in your pants. The enduring potency of interests forged in adolescence may explain the popularity of "vintage porn" on the Internet; *vintage* is the 57th most popular category of sexual search on Dogpile and numerous well-trafficked Web sites—such as the Classic Porn and My Retro Tube—that feature movie clips from the '70s and '80s.

Men are wired for blasts from the past.

ELMER FUDD, WABBIT HUNTER

In many ways, tube sites like PornHub are technological innovations that are perfectly designed to appeal to the male sexual brain. They offer unlimited visual stimuli that can be easily searched by body part, age, and weight. Video streaming technology allows viewers to instantly jump ahead to the good stuff—or pause to examine some especially enticing visual. Many men spend hours online each week hunting for images that perfectly match their own personal set of cued and uncued interests.

Male desire is instantly activated by visual cues and is directed toward immediate action—in particular, behavior leading toward orgasm. Once male desire is triggered, it does not easily subside. As comedian Louis C.K. put it, "If you showed me my mother's decapitated head while I was fucking, I would tell you: 'We're going to have to talk about this just as soon as I'm done.'"

On the Internet, male desire is a solitary affair. Men sit alone clicking on videos and images, rarely seeking to share their tastes and experiences with other men. Other men's opinions about what is sexy are irrelevant or distracting. Men don't require any information about a woman other than what they can see with their own eyes. They're also quite happy to masturbate in the airplane bathroom or at the back of a university classroom—or in their office at the Pentagon.

Solitary, quick to arouse, goal-targeted, driven to hunt . . . and a little foolish. In other words, the male brain's desire software is like Elmer Fudd. Fudd, the comic foil of Bugs Bunny in the Loony Tunes cartoons, is always on the hunt for a specific target: rabbits. Or as Fudd says it, *wabbits*. Fudd is a solitary hunter who likes to work alone. Fudd is trigger-happy. The moment he sees a wabbit—or thinks he sees a wabbit—he squeezes the trigger and fires. Fudd is easily fooled by ducks dressed up as rabbits and other tricks played on him by Bugs Bunny. But even when Fudd shoots his gun at a phony rabbit, he never gets discouraged. He reloads and gets back out there. Tomorrow's another day for the hunt. Another chance to bag a wabbit.

But if male desire software is like Elmer Fudd, what about female desire?

CHAPTER 4
The Miss Marple Detective Agency
Female Desire

> The best way to a man's heart is to saw through his ribs.
>
> —Sai's ex-girlfriend

Though social psychologist Elaine Hatfield is one of the nicest people you could ever meet, her life has been filled with controversy, mostly because of her independent streak. When she was a young professor at the University of Minnesota in 1963, there were two rules. Women were not allowed to hang their coats in the faculty cloak room. Women were not allowed to dine at the Faculty Club. One Monday evening, Hatfield decided to challenge the rules.

She and fellow psychologist Ellen Berscheid approached the table where their male colleagues were sitting.

> When we walked into the Faculty Club and chorused: "May we sit down?" our six colleagues couldn't have been more courtly. "Of course! Do sit down." But, Colleague #1 glanced at his watch and declared, "Oh, do excuse me I have to run." Colleague #2 shifted uneasily, then remembered that his wife was picking him up. Colleague #3 snatched up a dinner roll and said that he better walk out with his

friend. The remaining men realized that they'd better be going, too. Within minutes Ellen and I were sitting alone at the elegant table, surrounded by six heaping plates.

Shamed but undeterred, they kept returning to the Faculty Club until they finally obtained their own table. Eventually, Hatfield became a full professor at the University of Wisconsin, where she pioneered research into the psychology of falling in love. The National Science Foundation awarded her a grant for her research; ironically, this grant led to a much bigger setback than she experienced that Monday evening at the Faculty Club.

In 1975, she was awarded the Golden Fleece Award, which was no award at all. This notorious "honor" was bestowed by Wisconsin senator William Proxmire on federally funded research projects that didn't meet his notions of "good science." He launched his well-publicized smear campaign against Elaine Hatfield's research with a press release:

> I object to this not only because no one—not even the National Science Foundation—can argue that falling in love is a science; not only because I'm sure that even if they spend $84 million or $84 billion they wouldn't get an answer that anyone would believe. I'm also against it because I don't want the answer.

After newspapers published accounts suggesting that her research was silly and perhaps immoral, she lost her research funding. But even worse was the public shame—even her neighbors believed she had fleeced the government for bogus research.

She didn't give up. In 1978, she wrote a book called *A New Look at Love*, summarizing what was known about the psychology of passionate and companionate love. It won the American Psychological Association's National Media Award. She went on to author more than one hundred academic papers on desire and romance. She's published other well-received science books, like *Love, Sex, and Intimacy,* and applied her knowledge of human psychology in several detective novels, such as *Vengeance Is Mine.* But the publication that generated the most lasting controversy for Hatfield was also one of her shortest—a psychology research paper focused on the differences between the desires of women and men.

One sunny afternoon, Hatfield and fellow psychologist Russell Clark sent nine research assistants onto the college campus of Florida State University: four young men and five young women from an undergraduate psychology class, all neatly dressed in casual attire. The male confederates were instructed to approach female students. The female confederates were instructed to approach male students. Each confederate asked his or her target one of three questions:

1. Would you go out with me tonight?
2. Would you come over to my apartment tonight?
3. Would you go to bed with me tonight?

How do you think the *male* students responded? The results are on the next page, but before you look, try to guess. What percentage of men do you think would say *yes* to a sexual solicitation from an attractive but completely unknown stranger?

	Date me?	Go home with me?	Go to bed with me?
Men who said yes	50%	69%	75%

Men were apparently more motivated to sleep with a woman than to date her. But what about women? What percentage of college women do you think would say yes to an invitation to go home with an attractive college guy who just walked up to her on campus?

	Date me?	Go home with me?	Go to bed with me?
Women who said yes	56%	6%	0%

For almost a decade, Hatfield and Clark couldn't get these dramatic results published. Some journal editors suggested that it must be something unique to Florida State—perhaps the torrid weather. Journal editors expressed disbelief, denigrating the research as unscientific, naive, or simply too provocative. One editor wrote, "This paper should be rejected without possibility of being submitted to any scholarly journal. If *Cosmopolitan* won't print it then *Penthouse Forum* might like it."

But by now, Hatfield was used to such setbacks. She and Clark repeated the same study at Florida State. They obtained near-identical results: this time, no women agreed to go home with the male research confederate. The results were finally published in the *Journal of Psychology and Human Sexuality* in 1989. Today, the paper is considered a social psychology classic.

In the 2000s, the Hatfield and Clark study was replicated in Belgium, Denmark, and Germany with similar results. The results were also reinforced by the responses of more than 6 million users on the online dating site OkCupid. One primary feature of OkCupid is member answers to member-created questions. One such question asked, "How would you react if someone sent you a text message and quickly started talking about sex?" There was an enormous gender difference in the responses: only 15 percent of women said they would react positively, compared to 60 percent of men. Another question asked, "Would you consider sleeping with someone on a first date?" Most women said no. Most men said yes.

These fascinating results suggest that the desires of men and women are *different*. But what is the source of this difference? Maybe it's culture. Perhaps men and women possess fundamentally similar desire software, it's just that Western society encourages us to express our desires differently. How much would you be willing to bet that the brain software for female desire is the same as the brain software for male desire?

The pharmaceutical companies bet millions.

A SEXIST DRUG

Angina pectoris is a medical condition that causes severe chest pain due to the obstruction of the heart's blood vessels. Drugmakers are interested in this condition because of its prevalence: roughly 6.5 million Americans experience angina, mostly in middle age. In 1996, researchers at Pfizer's Kent facility in England developed a test compound known as 5 cyclic GMP-specific phosphodiesterase inhibitor. The Kent researchers were one of many teams at Big Pharma companies battling to reach the holy grail of drug discovery: a successful Phase III treatment of human subjects. Success would mean hundreds of millions of dollars of annual drug profits. Unfortunately for Pfizer, Phase III was a failure.

The phosphodiesterase inhibitor had no significant effect on unblocking the heart's blood vessels. But the researchers did notice something quite interesting. Even though the male subjects' angina did not improve, many of them asked for more of the test drug. When the researchers asked why, the men rather shyly explained it was helping their marriage. The researchers took a closer look at the drug's effects. What they found would revolutionize male desire. The drug did facilitate blood flow after all—just not where they expected. They published their findings in an impotence research journal as "Sildenafil: An Orally Active Type 5 Cyclic GMP-Specific Phosphodiesterase Inhibitor for the Treatment of Penile Erectile Dysfunction."

Viagra was born.

When Pfizer launched Viagra in 1998, its share price doubled within days. Since then, the little blue pill has been a multibillion-dollar cash cow and transformed the sexual lives of millions of middle-age men. But what was good for the gander was surely good for the goose. Almost immediately, Pfizer and other Big Pharma multinationals turned their attention to developing "pink Viagra"—a pill to treat female sexual dysfunction. Around the world, state-of-the-art biotech labs became focused on developing an effective female aphrodisiac—what in previous eras had been an urban myth known as the "Spanish fly." The prize for this research? With twice as many women as men suffering from "sexual desire disorders," the profits from pink Viagra could be astronomical.

Vivus, a California-based biopharmaceutical company that designed drugs to restore male sexual function, joined the quest. It started testing a Viagra-like drug that widened blood vessels and increased blood flow, known as a *vasodilator*. It reasoned that increasing blood flow to the vagina would increase women's feeling of arousal, just as it does for men. It even hired a documentarian to shoot pornographic movies to test female subjects' arousal. But after dozens of trials and $10 million of costs, the Vivus vasodilator failed to boost female desire.

Pfizer itself encountered similar problems. It tested Viagra itself on more than seven hundred women, including two hundred estrogen-deficient women. None of the women felt more aroused, though many reported headaches. Next, Pfizer tried Vasoactive intestinal peptide (VIP) a compound that is believed to control vaginal blood flow. This also failed to show any improvement in female libido. In fact, almost every attempt at stimulating female desire through "peripherally acting agents" was a failure. Though the male brain responds to the physical changes wrought by Viagra, Cela, and Levitin with increased sexual interest, the female brain does not.

It wasn't just the *behaviors* of men and women that seemed different—their *brains* seemed different, too. Why did so many Big Pharma and biotech companies fail to find female Viagra? The answer also explains Hatfield and Clark's dramatic results.

THE MIND-BODY PROBLEM

Meredith Chivers is an assistant professor of psychology at Queen's University in Canada. As the director of the Sexuality and Gender Laboratory at the university, she is one of the world's leading researchers on the neuropsychology of female desire. In 2004, Chivers conducted an ingenious experiment to find out what turns women on.

She invited women to her lab and showed them a variety of erotic pictures. Chivers measured their arousal from viewing the pictures in two different ways. First, she asked them how they felt—a measure of conscious, *psychological* arousal. Second, she inserted a plethysmograph into their vaginas—the female version of the device used to measure erections in the jar of pennies experiment. The plethysmograph measured blood flow in women's vaginal walls—a measure of *physical* arousal. But the most interesting part of Chivers's experiment was the pictures themselves.

They consisted of photographs depicting exercising men, exercising women, gay sex, lesbian sex, straight sex—and monkey sex. One of the images showed copulating bonobos, a type of primate also known as the pygmy chimpanzee.

So which images elicited *physical* arousal in the women? *All* the images, even the monkey porn. Women's vaginal blood flow increased after viewing each erotic picture. Which images elicited *psychological* arousal—which caused the women to *say* they were turned on? Heterosexual sex generated the greatest psychological arousal, followed by lesbian sex. Watching people exercise wasn't much of a turn-on. The reported amount of psychological arousal from watching monkey porn? A very emphatic zero.

In other words, there was a dissociation between the conscious arousal of the mind and the unconscious (or semiconscious) arousal of the body. When the exact same experiment was conducted with male subjects, there was virtually no dissociation between the two types of arousal. If a man was *physically* turned on, he was also *psychologically* turned on. And none of the men got turned on by monkey sex.

This intriguing dissociation between the mind and body in women seems to reflect a common experience among women that is frequently unvoiced. "Thanks to you women who wrote about the dichotomy between getting turned on and (intellectually) being turned off," writes one woman on Salon.com, in response to an article addressing why women don't watch porn. "Just last night my husband was asking me to watch porn with him and I was try-ing to explain that after about 10 minutes of it I'm more turned off than on (even if I'm turned on too—the other part won't let me enjoy it). I think it would be easier to be a guy when it comes to porn—having all this conflicting stuff flying around my brain and body makes me crazy."

In the same online discussion, when several men expressed dis-belief that it's possible to be physically aroused and psychologically grossed out, another woman responded: "It's hard not to notice when your panties are soaking wet. It's just that being aroused by something that *disgusts* you is very, very unpleasant."

After obtaining her provocative results, Chivers reviewed 132 different laboratory studies published between 1969 and 2007 that simultaneously investigated physical and psychological arousal. The results were very clear. Men experienced a strong correlation between the arousal of mind and body. Women did not. In fact, the correlation between physical and psychological arousal in women was so low that it's safe to say a woman's vaginal lubrication is a poor predictor of what she is actually feeling. In fact, many women report lubrication and even orgasm during unwanted and coercive sex: a woman's body responds, even as her mind rebels. In contrast, if a man is erect, you can make a very reasonable guess about what's going on in his mind.

The conclusions from Meredith Chivers's groundbreaking research are inescapable: psychological and physical arousal are usually linked in men, but in women there's a disconnect. It's as if the carnal signals from a woman's body somehow get cut off before they enter her conscious awareness. Male sexuality, in contrast, is like the knee-jerk reflex: a message of arousal from the body triggers instant mental desire. Elmer Fudd readies, aims, fires at the slightest hint of a wabbit.

This is a profound difference in the brain software of men and women. It explains why the pharmaceutical industry's quest for female Viagra kept running into dead ends. Stimulating the vagina or the spine does not automatically fire up desire in the conscious mind. Instead, women need to feel *psychologically* aroused. This dichotomy was even present in a rare sex survey in the 1920s that found that the most frequent complaint among a thousand married women was a failure to reach orgasm—and that their obstacles to sexual pleasure were primarily psychological rather than biological. The drug companies might have garnered better results if they had first considered the wild popularity of romance novels, which stimulate women's minds without ever touching their bodies.

In the past few years, Big Pharma have changed their tactics. Now they realize that any pharmaceutical solution to desire disorders will have to act on the brain itself, and likely involve conscious mechanisms. Ironically, the drug with the greatest promise for improving libido resulted from a botched attempt at solving a different problem, just like the discovery of Viagra. The German drugmaker Boehringer Ingelheim was trying to develop a fast-acting antidepressant. Though the drug, known as Flibanserin, failed in its Phase III trials, researchers found that it resulted in a surging libido for the female subjects. What part of the brain does

Flibanserin target? Regions involved in the *conscious* processing of emotion. It operates by stimulating the conscious mind, not the body.

In men, the sexual body and the sexual mind are united. So why are they separated in women?

THE MISS MARPLE DETECTIVE AGENCY

When it comes to the design of our sexual brain, women appear to possess the same basic components as men: circuits to handle physical arousal, circuits to handle psychological arousal, circuits to reward sexual thoughts and behavior, circuits to control motivation, and circuits to respond to sexual cues. However, there are dramatic differences in how these components operate in the minds of men and women.

"Booty is so strong there are dudes willing to blow themselves up for the highly unlikely possibility of booty in another dimension," observes comedian Joe Rogan. "There are no chicks alive willing to blow themselves up for a penis." Women masturbate less, fantasize about sex less frequently, and initiate sex less often than men. Women report low sexual desire much more often than men. In fact, among medical professionals who treat sexual disorders, low female desire is the single most common complaint. In women, desire is much less likely to initiate orgasm-seeking behavior. Women are much more likely than men to pursue sex for reasons other than sexual pleasure. Women are more likely to report low desire as resulting from relationship difficulties and high desire as resulting from relationship harmony. According to Marta Meana, such findings "have contributed to the development of a theory of women's desire as being substantially different from that of men."

But why? In women, why is there such a distinct separation of the physical from the psychological?

When contemplating sex with a man, a woman has to consider the long term. This consideration may not even be conscious, but rather is part of unconscious software that has evolved to protect women over hundreds of thousands of years. Sex could commit a woman to a substantial, life-altering investment: pregnancy, nursing, and more than a decade of child raising. These commitments require enormous time, resources, and energy. Sex with the wrong guy could lead to many unpleasant outcomes. If a man abandons her, she would face the challenges of single motherhood. If the man turns out to be cruel, he might injure her or her children. If the man turns out to be weak or incompetent, he might fail to protect her from threats.

A woman's sexual desire must be filtered through a careful appraisal of these potential risks. During human prehistory, women who blindly gave in to every sexual urge likely faced a host of daunting challenges, including—in the most extreme cases—death. Most important, from an evolutionary point of view, her children would have a harder time surviving than the children of a woman who limited the expression of her sexual urges to a strong and decent man willing to invest in a stable, long-term, child-rearing relationship. All modern women are the fruit of feminine caution. The result of this whittling away of the impulsive branches of our ancestral maternal tree is a female brain equipped with the most sophisticated neural software on Earth. A system designed to uncover, scrutinize, and evaluate a dazzling range of informative clues. We've dubbed this female neural system the *Miss Marple Detective Agency.*

Agatha Christie's fictional detective Miss Marple is an independent, neatly dressed elderly lady who appears to be sweet and frail. She lives alone and enjoys knitting and weeding her garden. Others dismiss her as scatterbrained or erratic. However, she is actually a shrewd judge of human character and harbors deep knowledge of the dark side of human nature. Though others underestimate her mental powers, she frequently solves mysteries that have stumped the police.

The unique detective skills of the female sexual brain were honed over hundreds of thousands of years of amateur sleuthing, investigating the character of sneaky and aggressive men in an extraordinary variety of contexts. Like the fictional Miss Marple, a woman's Detective Agency mulls over a variety of evidence concerning a potential partner's character, weighs clues from the physical and social environment, and examines her own experiences and feelings before permitting—or pursuing—sex.

The range of clues Miss Marple gathers is extensive, as captured in a scene from the movie *Up in the Air*, in which Natalie, an earnest businesswoman fresh out of college, describes "her type" of man: "You know, white collar. College grad. Loves dogs. Likes funny movies. Six foot one. Brown hair. Kind eyes. Works in finance but is outdoorsy, you know, on the weekends. I always imagined he'd have a single syllable name like Matt or John or . . . Dave. In a perfect world, he drives a Four Runner and the only thing he loves more than me is his golden lab. Oh . . . and a nice smile."

The Detective Agency's focus on intimate, detailed clues can be seen in consumer choices. Many women are willing to pay money for celebrity biographies in order to read about the private life of Leonardo DiCaprio or Johnny Depp, but they won't pay money to see photos of them nude. Men whip out the credit card to see a naked Angelina Jolie or Scarlett Johannsen, though it would never occur to them to shell out cash for their biographies.

Craigslist, the largest online classifieds Web site, contains a section called Missed Connections. In this section, men and women leave messages for others they encountered and were attracted to, but for some reason lost contact with. Are there any patterns in the half million Missed Connections postings we scraped in the spring of 2010? For men, the single most common phrase is "looking for." For women, it's "miss you." Elmer Fudd is hunting for wabbits, searching for his lost partner. In contrast, Miss Marple reviews the details of a shared moment. Women fondly recall the place, weather, food, wardrobes, and conversation of an intimate encounter.

The Miss Marple Detective Agency is responsible for the separation of a woman's sexual mind from her sexual body. Miss

Marple inhabits a woman's conscious mind and intercepts signals coming from her body, preventing them from triggering conscious, psychological arousal. *Wait*, says Miss Marple, *let's think this over.*

The Detective Agency consists of four different types of mind software—four detectives—that seek out and evaluate different types of clues:

An emotional detective

A social detective

A cultural detective

A physical detective

The physical detective evaluates things like nutrition, stress, shelter, and safety. A woman's ovulation cycle and estrogen production are sensitive to changes in the physical environment. Women are much more likely than men to report a decrease in sexual desire due to physical illness, hunger, or anxiety about physical security. Indeed, the male sexual brain is just the opposite: heightened physical threats—such as impending warfare—tend to enhance male desire.

Overseeing these four software detectives is Miss Marple herself: a master sleuth who sifts through all the accumulated clues in order to make one all-important decision: *should I or shouldn't I?*

THE EMOTIONAL DETECTIVE

The dating advice book for women *He's Just Not That Into You* opens with a group of young, professional women sitting around a table. They're all writers for the show *Sex and the City*. They are carefully analyzing the ambiguous behavior of a guy dating one of the women in order to determine how he *really* feels. They weigh one clue after another, offering elaborate and divergent interpretations of the guy's recent silence. Finally, they solicit the advice of comedian Greg Behrendt, who succinctly tells the women, "He's just not that into you."

Though Behrendt cuts through the convoluted analysis of the table full of Detective Agencies, there are very good reasons for Miss Marple to spend so much effort evaluating a man's heart. When it comes to sex, men are enterprising and devious. Google "men will say anything" to see a list of fifty thousand cautionary tales. Here are two: "He saw I had a cat and he told me he loved cats and then later after I slept with him I learned he is allergic to them and hates them. I should've known he was lying cuz he started sneezing when we were in bed." "He told me he worked in the front office of the Yankees and was friends with Derek Jeter. Turns out he was just the friggin' bat boy."

A man's true character cannot be evaluated as swiftly or as easily as a woman's bust size. Since the inner life of a man is so elusive, the Detective Agency has developed sophisticated instruments for appraising his personality. Is he honest? Sincere? Considerate? Loyal? Generous? Does he love his mama? She must also evaluate her own feelings. Do I feel appreciated and adored? Do I feel attractive? Am I nervous? Embarrassed? Guilty?

Studies show that women ruminate over emotional situations more than men, and reflect more often on negative feelings and on memories of negative life experiences. Women recall emotional memories more quickly than men and report emotions as more vivid and intense. Women have superior autobiographical memory: compared to men, they remember more details and their narratives of recollection are longer. Women recall their first life event more quickly, recall more life events, date life events more accurately, and recall earlier events than men. Their superior memory for life experiences does not depend on socialization, since this advantage is evident in girls as young as three. Interestingly, though women are more emotionally expressive than men, they also possess greater ability to control their facial and body expressions of emotions. Similarly, even though women ruminate more than men, some studies show that they are better at suppressing unwanted thoughts. Most relevant for the study of desire, women's sexual fantasies haves higher romantic and emotional content than men's fantasies.

These mental differences are reflected in neural differences. There is a flood of evidence pointing to physical differences between the male brain and the female brain. Some scientists even suggest that "sex differences in the human brain may be the norm rather than the exception." Though some of these differences are present at birth, many don't form until puberty, when the release of sex hormones initiates changes in neural structures and connections. In fact, the peak age of onset for mental health disorders is age fourteen, the age when gender differences in biologically based mental disorders first manifest themselves. Women are more likely to suffer from anxiety, depression, and eating disorders. Men are more likely to suffer from schizophrenia and autistic spectrum disorders. Later in life, women are more likely to suffer from Alzheimer's, while men are more likely to suffer from Parkinson's.

Before puberty, boys and girls suffer from anxiety, depression, and panic disorders equally. But after the adolescent brain starts to change, women are twice as likely to suffer from mood disorders as men. Scientists speculate this may be because of the greater changes occurring in the female emotional software. Perhaps greater susceptibility to mood disorders is one of the costs of the emotionally shrewd Detective Agency.

The emotional software of the Detective Agency runs mostly on three brain structures. Two of the structures are in the cortex, where conscious thinking occurs: the anterior cingulate cortex and the insular cortex. These are both involved in the appraisal of emotions of self and others. These structures are slightly larger in women and also more active in women during social processing. When women are processing sexual stimuli, the anterior cingulate cortex tends to react by inhibiting emotion, perhaps one way the Detective Agency prevents a woman from reacting to an arousing stimulus until it has been properly evaluated. The insular cortex and the hippocampus are both involved in the storage and retrieval of emotional memories, and are both larger and more active in women than in men.

The other emotional structure is the amygdala, located in the unconscious subcortex. Women code emotions through the left amygdala, while men process emotions through the right amygdala. In men, the activation of the right amygdala and right cortical hemisphere enhance memory for the "big picture" or the gist of an experience. In women, activation of the left amygdala and left cortical hemisphere enhance memory for peripheral details. Interestingly, though the right amygdala is active in men while viewing pornography, it isn't in women. However, the left amygdala is active in women while processing erotic narratives.

It's often difficult to acquire enough clues about a potential lover by relying on your own investigation. For one thing, even Miss Marple has trouble being objective sometimes. In addition, there are a number of important clues that can only be verified by others, such as a man's reputation or social status. It's also worth knowing if other women are eyeing the same guy.

Sometimes Miss Marple needs to outsource her sleuthing to other Detective Agencies.

THE SOCIAL DETECTIVE

Miss Marple knows that the best way to gather and analyze clues is often to ask for help. Women solicit the opinions of other women on almost every aspect of a potential partner. They also rely on others for ideas about topics indirectly related to love and sex, such as beauty tips, health, child rearing, fashion, dieting, and myriad other factors that generate additional information analyzed by the Detective Agency. In other words, Miss Marple relies on her social network.

The social software of the Detective Agency is one of the biggest reasons that women are more verbal than men. Women begin communicating earlier in life than men, and spend more time communicating as both adolescents and adults. This verbal superiority appears as early as age five and does not appear to be controlled by hormones, since women performed better than men on verbal tasks even when they were matched on their levels of the hormone estradiol. This suggests the verbal differences are due to differences in mind software.

On average, girls age twelve to seventeen send and receive eighty texts a day; boys send and receive thirty. More women than men use social networking sites like Facebook, Classmates, Twitter, and MySpace. Women also have more friends on these sites. (Digg, a Web site where users rate news stories, is the rare exception of a social network with more male users.) Fifty-nine percent of teenage girls call friends on their cell phone every day, while only 42 percent of boys do. The social detective appears to be located mainly within the frontal cortex, including the prefrontal cortex. The areas of the frontal cortex devoted to language are larger in women and develop more rapidly during puberty in girls than in boys. There are also more connections between the female language centers and the subcortical reward systems, suggesting that talking is more rewarding for women than for men. Female brains also have greater connectivity between the two cortical hemispheres, leading some neuroscientists to speculate that the female brain is designed for more effective processing and production of language.

Men are more likely to suffer from autism, which is frequently characterized as a social disorder based on an inability to take in the point of view of others. One prominent researcher characterizes autism as a consequence of the "hypermasculinization" of the brain, emphasizing the fact that social software is less developed in the male brain.

In addition to communicating with others, Miss Marple also pays attention to the rules, expectations, and attitudes of the society she finds herself in.

THE CULTURAL DETECTIVE

One of the more noticeable differences between male-targeted and female-targeted porn on the Web is the presence of political messages. On men's porn sites—including gay porn sites—there is a complete absence of any kind of explicit politics. The only exception is the rare imploration to support free speech. Though there are far, far fewer numbers of female-targeted porn sites, those that do exist contain a relative abundance of political messages. "We do what we can to support the activists who fight for awareness of cultural appropriation," proclaims graphic porn site NoFauxxx, adding, "We follow an all-inclusive casting attitude: we do not take gender, size, race, or any other consideration into consideration when choosing our models." The Web site Crash Pad Series says the actress and director Shawn "can be found in front of the computer designing digital landscapes of desire as well as in front of the camera sharing her passion for the 'personal as political' lifestyle." The East Van Porn Collective calls itself an "anarcho-feminist porn collective." Especially common are female-targeted adult sites promoting "empowerment" and "positivity," concepts men do not associate with erotica.

Social psychologist Roy Baumeister suggests that women's greater sensitivity to cultural influences is rooted in brain mechanisms. "Women's sexuality appears to be more plastic than men's, relying on social framing and cultural conditions when making decisions regarding relationships. Men's sexuality seems far more driven by simple physiological mechanisms." Keenly attuned to cultural values and social rules, the Detective Agency asks: Which behaviors and relationships are celebrated—and which are frowned upon? What values should I endorse when it comes to sex and relationships? Women are sensitive to messages on magazines and television shows, even indirect messages, such as a model's body weight, the car a politician is driving, or a celebrity's views on mental health—subjects that elicit more online comments from women than men. Many more women than men report feeling social pressure on how to behave, dress, and look. Women are also much more likely to attribute sexual anxiety to social pressures.

Women's cultural evaluation mechanisms appear to be especially concentrated in the middle prefrontal and inferior prefrontal cortex and the middle temporal cortex. These parts of the brain are social evaluation centers, considering what behaviors are appropriate and inappropriate in a given situation. They handle moral cognition (is this right or wrong?) and social judgment (what will other people think of me?).

Cultural information helps Miss Marple play it safe: Who does society value more, doctors or software programmers? Can I get away with wearing a tattoo on my back or will people think it's a "tramp stamp"? Can I post photos on Facebook of me in my bathing suit or will guys think I look fat? Since women must always consider the long-term consequences of their sexual decisions, a woman's brain is designed to evaluate the particular cultural conditions in which she finds herself.

Why is the female brain designed to play it safe? Because historically, the odds of a woman reproducing are very good. In fact, today's human population is descended from twice as many women as men. According to recent DNA analysis, through the history of the human race about 80 percent of the women reproduced. Only 40 percent of men reproduced. This means that plenty of men were able to have children with multiple women—but the majority of men never had *any* kids. Roy Baumeister observes the psychological consequences for a man:

> If you go along with the crowd and play it safe, the odds are you won't have children. Most men who ever lived did not have descendants who are alive today. Their lines were dead ends. Hence it was necessary to take chances . . . Sailing off into the unknown may be risky, and you might drown or be killed, but if you stay home you won't reproduce anyway. We're descended from men who took chances (and were lucky).
>
> For women throughout history, the odds of reproducing have been pretty good. Taking chances like [sailing off into the unknown] would be stupid, from the perspective

of a biological organism seeking to reproduce. Women might drown or be killed by savages or catch a disease. For women, the optimal thing to do is go along with the crowd, be nice, play it safe. The odds are good that men will come along and offer sex and you'll be able to have babies. All that matters is choosing the best offer. We're descended from women who played it safe.

A woman's social environment is also crucial. Does a woman have a network of family and friends who can help provide emotional support and assist with child care? Does this social network approve of her partner? Is a woman in a position in her career where she can take time out for a relationship and to possibly raise children? Are there any other decent men available?

For a woman, context is everything.

MISS MARPLE'S FEMININE INTUITION

The Detective Agency's decision-making process is often experienced as "female intuition"—a gut sense that a particular guy is Mr. Right or Mr. Wrong. This is the subjective outcome of Miss Marple's evaluation of the complex array of clues gathered by the emotional, social, and cultural detectives—combined with an evaluation of a potential mate's physical attractiveness—to produce a simple answer to the profoundly complex question: should I or shouldn't I?

Should I marry Tom, or wait until he gets a better job? Should I sleep with this hot guy I just met at the club, or will my friends think I'm a slut? Should I use one of my last contraceptive sponges on Enrique, or is he not really sponge-worthy? A woman's mind is filled with difficult choices, the result of Miss Marple's endless sleuthing. In India, women even outsource this sleuthing to a booming business of "wedding detectives" who track down hidden information about prospective husbands.

Miss Marple's cautious detective work is responsible for the dramatic results in Hatfield and Clark's study. Women don't want to go to bed with a complete stranger, even if he's attractive, because there are not enough clues to determine what he's *really* like. The Detective Agency is responsible for Meredith Chivers's findings that physical arousal is separate from psychological arousal, since Miss Marple won't permit psychological arousal unless enough of her criteria are met, regardless of what a woman feels down below. This is also why there can be no female Viagra. Simply increasing heat and blood flow between a woman's legs won't sway the discerning Miss Marple.

Most of the software of the Detective Agency software is located in the conscious parts of the brain, in the cortex. This is also the part of the brain that gets inhibited by alcohol and many recreational drugs. Perhaps drinking is a fast-acting substitute for what author Lori Gottlieb calls "The Case for Settling for Mr. Good Enough" in her book *Marry Him*. Gottlieb argues that women set the bar too high and urges them to settle, to not try and check off every requirement on Miss Marple's exacting list. And this list often seems endless, as captured in a cottage industry of books for women. Leslie Parrott talks about *Saving Your Marriage Before It Starts*. Helen Norman Wright identifies *101 Questions to Ask Before You Get Engaged*. Monica Leahy makes sure the Detective Agency leaves no stone unturned by presenting *1,001 Questions to Ask Before You Get Married*.

The constant, conscious swirl of thoughts in the offices of the Detective Agency is the result of wisdom inherited from millions of sexual transactions conducted by women over a period of a few hundred thousand years. The result is the most sophisticated neural structure on Earth. How can we make such a grand claim? Because the Detective Agency is nature's most successful long-term investment planner.

As any portfolio manager can tell you, long-term investment planning is tough. The most important requirement for long-term investment success is information, especially inside information.

Mutual fund managers are absolute data hounds, voraciously gathering and analyzing oceans of economic and financial data. They're also among the most highly paid people in America.

The second most important requirement for long-term investment planning is an effective analysis of the probability of various outcomes. Mutual fund managers employ teams of mathematical PhDs, macroeconomic wizards, and number-crunching supercomputers to predict the financial future. Long-term investing is expensive, difficult stuff. But this is precisely what Miss Marple excels at.

What is the payoff for spending my precious time with this guy? Will investing in a sexual relationship with this man give me the greatest chance of success to raise healthy, happy children in the future? The Detective Agency is ultimately a highly adaptive, highly intelligent system for successful long-term investment planning in a dynamic environment, which is why it represents the pinnacle of brain evolution. The male brain solves a man's investment planning problem using simple, quick shortcuts: go after youth and gynoid fat. The female brain is more like Warren Buffett, always taking the long-term view and adjusting to changing circumstances. The male brain is like a stockbroker who gives all his clients the same advice whether the market is up or down: invest in Google, you can't go wrong.

This fundamental difference in desire software is reflected in the type of erotic obsessions that men and women develop. As we saw in the previous chapter, men are quite prone to developing sexual obsessions with objects, which they frequently use for masturbation. Some male fetishists require the object to be present in order to ejaculate. Women, however, rarely develop sexual fetishes for objects. They do, however, develop *emotional* fetishes, a condition known as *objectum sexualis.*

Women who suffer from objectum sexualis usually claim that they are in love with an inanimate object, such as fences, a roller coaster, or a Ferris wheel. Though they sometimes have sex with the objects, their interest usually expresses itself as a powerful emotional connection and a desire for intimacy. Sometimes these feelings culminate in a romantic ceremony. One objectum sufferer named Eija-Riitta Berliner-Mauer married the Berlin Wall. Another objectum sufferer, Erika Naisho, married the Eiffel Tower. After the ceremony, she changed her name to Erika Eiffel. "There is a huge problem with being in love with a public object," she reported sadly, "the issue of intimacy—or rather lack of it—is forever present."

It was relatively easy to summarize the main sexual cues used by Elmer Fudd. The male brain relies on a few effective visual shortcuts. But we need two chapters for the most basic sampling of the psychological cues used by the female brain.

CHAPTER 5

Ladies Prefer Alphas

Female Psychological Cues I: The Hero

A porn video has almost as many climaxes as it
does scenes, but a romance novel has only one
climax: the moment when the hero and heroine
declare their mutual love for each other.
                    —Catherine Salmon and Donald Symons,
                    Warrior Lovers

When looking for clues, Miss Marple prefers stories over
visuals. As we saw in the previous chapter, the Detective
Agency brain software is designed to process psychological, social,
and contextual information. This kind of information is transmitted more effectively through narratives and verbal exchanges
than imagery. Consequently, whereas men are more aroused by
visual cues, women are more aroused by psychological cues. Visual
cues convey information about a woman's health, fertility, and
youth—data important to Elmer Fudd. Psychological cues convey information about a man's stability, commitment, social status, competence, and kindness—data important to the Detective
Agency. One particular kind of story packs the densest compilation of psychological cues into a single Miss Marple–thrilling
fantasy: the *romance*.

The romance novel has long been described as "pornography

for women." This is a somewhat unfair and misleading comparison. After all, would we characterize gang bang porn as "romance for men"? However, the comparison is apt in one respect. As we've seen in previous chapters, porn reveals the sexual cues that activate male desire. Similarly, romance reveals the sexual cues that activate female desire. "The romance novel is a chronicle of female mate choice," assert Catherine Salmon and Donald Symons in their book, *Warrior Lovers*, "in which the heroine overcomes obstacles to identify, win, and marry the hero, who embodies the physical, psychological, and social characteristics that constituted high male mate value during the course of human evolutionary history."

The basic elements of the romance novel can be traced back to the 1740 book *Pamela, or Virtue Rewarded*. The story is told through a series of letters. *Pamela* follows the courtship of a fifteen-year-old servant-maid by her master, Mr. B, a nobleman. Mr. B repeatedly tries to seduce and ravish Pamela, but she refuses his advances. Eventually, she realizes she loves him. When he realizes he feels the same way, he marries her. *Pamela* was one of the earliest bestsellers in the English language, though it was criticized for its perceived lewdness. For the second edition, the author relied on women's reading groups for editorial advice.

In the nineteenth century, Jane Austen took the romance to its greatest literary heights. Best-selling romance authors today include Nora Roberts, Jackie Collins, and Stephenie Meyer. But the modern structure of the romance is often attributed to the 1972 novel *The Flame and the Flower* by Kathleen Woodiwiss. This classic romance has been through forty-two printings and is still in print today. Here's the summary of the book from its back cover:

> *The Flower*: Doomed to a life of unending toil, Heather Simmons fears for her innocence—until a shocking, desperate act forces her to flee . . . and to seek refuge in the arms of a virile and dangerous stranger.

The Flame: A lusty adventurer married to the sea, Captain Brandon Birmingham courts scorn and peril when he abducts the beautiful fugitive from the tumultuous London dockside. But no power on Earth can compel him to relinquish his exquisite prize. For he is determined to make the sapphire-eyed lovely his woman . . . and to carry her off to far, uncharted realms of sensuous, passionate love.

There are two necessary and sufficient characters in every romance novel from *Pamela* to *Pride and Prejudice* to *Twilight*: the hero (the "Flame") and the heroine (the "Flower"). The hero and his romantic journey represent Miss Marple's fantasy of an ideal partner. The romantic hero is constructed from female psychological cues, in the same way that young, busty porn stars are built from male visual cues. In this chapter, we examine the virile, dangerous, and lusty adventurers that make Miss Marple swoon. We will introduce you to the psychology of the innocent, lovely Flower in the next chapter.

But first, let's guide you through some of these "uncharted realms of love" by reviewing the different kinds of romance stories in the Internet age.

AN EFFLORESCENT GARDEN OF ROMANCE

If you don't read romances yourself, you probably don't realize just how astonishingly popular they really are. According to the Romance Writers of America, romance fiction generated $1.37 billion in sales in 2008. The romance genre has the single largest share of the fiction market. More people buy romances than detective novels, thrillers, science fiction, or science *non*fiction. At least 74.8 million people read a romance novel in 2008 . . . and more than 90 percent of these readers are women.

To put these numbers in perspective, about 100 million men in the United States and Canada accessed online porn in 2008—just slightly more than the number of romance readers. However, though women don't pay for porn, they happily pay for romance. Accurate sales figures are impossible to come by in the adult industry, but there's little doubt that online pornography generated *less* revenue in 2008 than romance publishing.

Sex is ubiquitous in romance, but it is not absolutely essential to the enjoyment of a novel. Many women skim through the sex scenes or skip them completely. (Sex is not essential in porn, either. As we've seen, a man can enjoy simple images of anatomy or non-nude photos of attractive women.) Nevertheless, the sex scene is a very important part of the romance. "The heroine's sexual inexperience remains intact only until the hero's wang of mighty lovin' introduces her to the wonderment of the fizznuckin'," proclaim Sarah Wendell and Candy Tan, authors of *Beyond Heaving Bosoms: The Smart Bitches' Guide to Romance Novels.* "It's part and parcel of the fantasy: the awakening to love is that much more powerful when it's accompanied by a sexual awakening as well."

Different subgenres and different eras of romance treat the sex scene in different ways. Much like *Pamela* three centuries earlier, *The Flame and the Flower* pushed the envelope in its depictions of sexual interactions, offering more graphic descriptions of lovemaking than had previously been seen. But these sex scenes are still rather tame compared to male-targeted erotic stories. Consider this encounter between pirate hero Captain Brandon and innocent heroine Heather Simmons:

> She felt his hardness searching, probing between her thighs, then finding and entering that first tiny bit. In her panic to escape she surged upward. A half gasp, half shriek escaped her and a burning pain seemed to spread through her loins. Brandon stared back in astonishment and stared down at her. She lay limp against the pillows, rolling her head back and forth upon them. He touched her cheek tenderly and murmured something low and inaudible, but she had her eyes closed and wouldn't look at him. He moved against

her gently, kissing her hair and brow and caressing her body with his hands.

The emphasis is on the characters' emotions and interactions. Compare this to the male-targeted erotic story "Princess and the Pirates" by Hamilton_g, where the emphasis is on visual details:

The Captain ran his hands over her perfect ass-cheeks, and he felt a shudder pass through her body. Gently he pulled the globes apart, opening her up to the stares of the lusting pirate crew. He pulled harder, and the lips of her hairless virgin sex parted to reveal the glistening furrow within. It was soaking wet, filled with the copious flow from her aroused pussy.

"Take a good look, men. Our little beauty may protest, but her pussy tells the truth!"
    When she saw the hungry stares of more than a score of ruthless men she groaned in shame and defeat. Her most private secret place was opened to their gazes, and they could see that she was dripping wet. The inner membranes glistened, and they could see the delicate little bump of her sweet clit, sheltered in its pink hood. The entrance to her vagina was spread open, the hole barely protected by the fragile petal of her virgin hymen.

The Flame and the Flower was the first romance novel published solely as a paperback, initiating a transformation of the romance industry from hardcovers into mass-market paperbacks. These days, however, romance is no longer limited to cheap paperbacks with embarrassing covers displaying a muscle-girded Fabio and a windswept vixen locked in a gymnastic embrace—what romance author Nora Roberts called "nursing mother covers—when she's falling out of her dress, and he has his mouth on her tit." Romance has entered the digital age.

"The success of the ebook is being fueled by the romance and erotic romance market," asserts one columnist for the technology news site ITworld. Major romance publishers, such as Harlequin and Avon, were quick to offer their existing titles in digital formats in the mid-2000s. Since then, romance has quickly come to dominate the burgeoning e-publishing industry. Five out of the ten most popular free e-books on Amazon are romance. The actress Felicia Day blogs about her reading tastes on Kindle: "I've read like, 6 books this week and ordered about 10 more. And no ordinary books: Pure unadulterated TRASHY-ROMANCE books! Check out my Goodreads shelf *vaginal-urban-fantasy*, it's bloating to an alarming degree. It's stuff I never would have checked out at the Barnes and Noble, because the gleaming and oily man chests would have made me blush too much."

Many romance publishers and imprints, such as Ellora's Cave, Quill, and Carina Press, now publish many of their titles *only* in e-book format. Women can inconspicuously download their books instead of being seen with a "nursing mother" cover on the subway. This new privacy afforded readers of e-romances has allowed e-romance publishers to take risks, especially by publishing books with spicier sex.

Though there has been a general movement toward more explicit and more frequent descriptions of sex in mainstream romance through the '90s and 2000s, a distinct genre eventually formed in which sex was the primary component: *erotic romance*. Erotic romance is also known as EroRom, while e-publisher Ellora's Cave has trademarked the name *Romantica* to characterize its own books. Other e-EroRom publishers include Loose Id and Total-E-Bound. Authors of EroRom stories still maintain the essential elements of romance, but include more sex scenes with more detail and more kink. But even though EroRom pushes the boundaries of female erotic literature, the books' sensitivity to the emotional experiences of the heroine and her lover would never be mistaken for the emotionless graphic raunch of male-targeted erotica.

Here is an example from Annabel Joseph's e-romance *Comfort Object*.

I grunted as he pulled out of me and pressed his cock against my ass. He entered me all the time this way now, with only the lube from my pussy. He slapped me lightly.

"Open. I want to fuck your ass."

"Yes, Jeremy."

He eased the head of his cock in, then waited for me to relax before thrusting the rest of the way inside. I moaned. I couldn't help it.

"Jeremy." I gasped to the rhythm of his fucking. "If you're tired of the lying, why don't you just stop?"

"Hush. Let me fuck you. And don't you come, you little fuck slut."

Jesus, I'd really ticked him off. "Yes, Jeremy." Yes yes yes, whatever you say.

The main difference between the sex scene in modern romance novels and EroRom is the frequency and kinkiness of sex scenes, rather than the explicitness of the description. E-publishers of Ero-Rom have taken the boldest steps of any commercial publishers, exploring bondage, group sex, and gay sex, though these previously marginalized kinks are becoming common in print romances as well.

But the Internet has delivered a groundbreaking contribution to romance, one that commercial publishers are still scrambling to understand. The democracy of the Web has fueled an explosion of stories written solely by amateurs: *fan fiction*. Here's how one fan named Scartyhlus describes it:

Wake up people! Girlies like porn too, you just have to know where to look. Hello, Fan fiction! There are zillions of pages of boy/girl, boy/boy and even girl/girl stories written online by women, for women. Their ages range from astoundingly young teens to older women in their fifties & sixties & probably older though you'd never guess because no one that old is likely to give their age. Is fan fiction porn? Some fan fiction is porn and is meant to be so. There are communities with names that include fqfest (for F*ck fest(ival). The term used for some such porn heavy fic is "PWP" which stands for "Plot? What plot?"

Fan fiction is a very large and loose-knit community consisting almost entirely of women. These fans are enthusiasts of pop culture "fandoms," such as Harry Potter, Buffy the Vampire Slayer, or Star Trek. Fandoms can be built around books, television shows, movies—even boy bands. The single biggest fan fiction site is FanFiction.net, which boasts more than 2 million different stories and more than 600,000 visitors a day, mostly 18- to 24-year-old women. However, fan fiction sites dedicated to individual fandoms are scattered across the Web, such as Muggle Net (Harry Potter), Wraith Bait (Stargate), and LOTR Fan Fiction (Lord of the Rings). Social networking sites, such as LiveJournal and Dream Journal, are also home to hundreds of thousands of female fans who tend to write more adult stories than the younger women who inhabit FanFiction.net. They are also more social. These women are mostly in their thirties and forties, white, and educated, though as Scartyhlus points out, many women start reading and writing fan fiction as young as eleven or as old as their sixties.

"Continuing the stories of favorite characters after a series has ended is important . . . too many series are cancelled before major storylines conclude, or seem to go astray in their final seasons. Picking up the threads and weaving them into a logical conclusion is fun, especially when it concerns the fates of beloved characters," explains veteran fan Sylvia Volk. Thousands of fan fiction Web sites allow fans to share their enthusiasm for the personalities and relationships of the characters in their favorite books and shows.

Fan fiction is not solely a Western phenomenon, with fanfic Web sites proliferating on every continent except Antarctica. In Russia, there are fandoms for fantasy books by Vera Kamsha and the television show *Ne rodis krasivoy* (a Russian version of *Ugly Betty*), though the three most popular Russian fandoms in 2010 were Harry Potter, the American TV show *Supernatural*, and Guy Ritchie's movie *Sherlock Holmes*. The most popular Russian adult fanfic site is probably Slash World (slashyaoi.borda.ru), featuring stories about the X-Men, South Park, and *Nochnoi Dozor* (*Night Watch*).

Men also have their own versions of fan fiction: celebrity "nip slips" consisting of candid photos of accidentally exposed anatomy (such as a panty-less Britney Spears), "celebrity fakes" that consist of digitally generated nudes of well-known actresses (such as the face of Harry Potter actress Emma Watson pasted onto porn star bodies), and cartoon renditions of fictional characters having sex (such as *Avatar*'s Jake and Neytiri copulating on GoGo Celeb). For decades, the "porn parody" has also been popular among men—hard-core versions of popular movies and TV shows such as *Scrubs: A XXX Parody*, *This Isn't Twilight*, and *Edward Penishands*.

Fan fiction does not need to be romantic, let alone erotic. There are fan fiction stories about Luke Skywalker beating Han Solo in a lightsaber duel and about Gollum getting to keep the One Ring. Nevertheless, most fanfic consists of romantic or erotic relationships between the characters. On FanFiction.net, about half of the stories are tagged as "romance."

Some stories, especially by younger writers, feature G-rated nonsexual romance. But fanfic also allows women to explore and express their kinks. AdultFanFiction.net contains hundreds of thousands of stories rated NC-17. There are also more than a thousand Web sites devoted to the adult stories of a single fandom, such as Twilighted (*Twilight*), Granger Enchanted (Harry Potter), and Valjean Fan Fiction (*Dark Angel*). Most of the sex in fan fiction emphasizes the emotional and psychological over the physical, just as in romance novels. Here is a passage from "Four Months Later," a story pairing Hannibal Lecter and Clarice Starling from *Silence of the Lambs*:

> Lecter was waiting for her to say no, for her to slap him
> or do something. So when he touched her breast and she

gasped he was pleased. Her nipples reacted so easily to his touch that he found himself getting more aroused than he already was. When he brought his mouth around a nipple and toyed with it with his tongue and teeth he was pleased that she brought her hands to rest on his shoulders. She was touching him of her own free will, even if it was instinctive. As his mouth focused on her breasts, his hand was busy trying to bring her pleasure. He was surprised at the way she reacted when he slid a finger within her, and he had all he could do not to take her at that very moment. But he wasn't a thoughtless lover, and he wasn't about to start now with Clarice. He was slow and deliberate with his movements, careful to gauge her reactions and make the slightest change if necessary to ensure she was being pleased. His mouth moved to her stomach where he nipped gently but hard enough to leave a mark on her when he felt her release was approaching.

Fan fiction, EroRom, and e-romances represent the state-of-the-art of the romance novel. But they share the same fundamental elements as romance novels from the past two and a half centuries—including the hero.

BILLIONAIRES AND BAD BOYS

Here are the ten most common professions of the hero, derived from the titles of more than 15,000 Harlequin romance novels:

Doctor
Cowboy
Boss
Prince
Rancher

Knight

Surgeon

King

Bodyguard

Sheriff

Conspicuously absent from the list of romance heroes are blue-collar workers (no janitors or welders), bureaucrats (no claims adjusters or associate marketing managers), and traditionally feminine professions (no hairdressers, secretaries, or kindergarten teachers). All of the hero professions are associated with status, confidence, and competence. As Henry Kissinger famously said, "Power is the ultimate aphrodisiac." Power is a reflection of a man's rank in the dominance hierarchy, and women are attracted to the men near the top. The man at the very top is known as the *alpha male*.

"Alphas are natural leaders—that's pretty much the definition of the alpha—with a strong protective streak and a fierce confidence in their own abilities," writes EroRom author Angela Knight in her book *Passionate Ink: A Guide to Writing Erotic Romance*. "They're who women reach for when the bullets start flying." Most romances introduce their hero with a very clear indication of his alpha status, as in this passage from Angelle Trieste's *Devil Falls*:

Victoria looked up and to her relief saw a man trotting toward her. An umbrella dangled from his hand, and casual but expensive clothes wrapped his long, lean frame. He was gloriously golden, with a face that rivaled Lucifer's in the moment of his fall from grace.

Damien Kirk. A cellist celebrated the world over.

The magazine photos didn't do him justice. They had failed to capture the magnetic vividness of his blue eyes and the electrifying vitality of his presence. She could feel it through the gates, even over the ferocity of the dogs, and she had no doubt he had dominated the vast concert halls, driving the crowds wild. Her heartbeat picked up the pace, and it wasn't all from relief.

Study after study has demonstrated the erotic appeal of male dominance. Women prefer the voices of dominant men, the scent of dominant men, the movement and gait of dominant men, and the facial features of dominant men. The social organization of most primates features a very clear dominance hierarchy. Chimpanzees and baboons boast alpha males, who obtain that position through a combination of physical strength and political savvy, while alpha gorillas attain their status through brute size and strength. Scientists believe that the ventrolateral prefrontal cortex may be responsible for processing cues indicating social status or dominance, and it appears that almost all female brains are susceptible to dominance cues. "I met [Bill Clinton] as part of a governmental panel while he was president. I'm a lesbian, but the powerful attraction I felt toward him for an instant made me question whether I really was!"

Biologists have discovered that the ventromedial region of the prefrontal cortex in female chimpanzees is associated with the determination of other chimps' position in a dominance hierarchy. The sexual authority of the alpha is also recognized by the Pickup Artist culture made famous by Neil Strauss in his book *The Game*. This male "seduction community" has developed a set of techniques its practitioners use to seduce women. The techniques are designed to activate women's psychological cues in the same way that Botox, collagen, and implants are designed to artificially trigger men's visual cues. One of the central commandments of pickup artists is to "always be an alpha." As seduction community spokesman Roissy states on his blog, "You don't have to be an asshole, but if you have no choice, being an inconsiderate asshole beats being a polite beta, every time."

Though romances are dominated by Navy SEALs, knights, and rock stars, some romance writers have felt that always writing alpha heroes was limiting. They've experimented with softer, more deferent protagonists, often called *betas*. "What makes the beta hero so great: an unshakable core of pure and stalwart good, so constant and abiding it's damn near alpha in its strength," explain Wendell and Tan. The most famous beta hero in romance (and perhaps the first) was Freddy Standen, from Georgette Heyer's *Cotillion*. Freddy Standen is a slender, "unarresting" man who is oblivious to the events around him. He has a warm and assured place in the hearts of most romance readers. Often, the hero starts out as a beta but then turns into an alpha, such as Avery Thorne in Connie Brockway's *My Dearest Enemy*, about an eighteenth-century nerd turned unexpectedly hunky.

But for the vast majority of romance readers, the hero should be a strong, confident, swaggering alpha. "I think this is one of the problems we're having in romance in general right now: our heroes have gotten a little too PC. We're portraying men the way feminist ideals say they should be—respectful and consensus-building," muses Angela Knight. "Yet women like bad boys. I suspect that's because our inner cavewoman knows Doormat Man would become Sabertooth Tiger Lunch in short order. In fact, this may be one reason why EroRom is gaining popularity so fast—writers feel free to write dominant heroes with more of an edge."

Though women like alpha heroes, in contemporary novels there are some lines that a hero can never cross, such as excessive physical violence against women or extreme psychological abuse. But in romances written in the 1970s and 80s, the hero was often cruel—or worse. In *The Flame and the Flower*, the hero actually rapes the virgin heroine in the opening scene—later excusing his behavior by saying he presumed she was a whore. In Catherine Coulter's 1982 novel *Devil's Embrace*, the thirty-four-year-old Earl of Clare kidnaps the eighteen-year-old Cassie Brougham just before her wedding to a nice young man, ties her down, and painfully rapes her; later she falls in love with him.

Can a man be *too* dominant for the Detective Agency's alpha cue? What about bona fide bad boys—serial killers, violent offenders, and rapists? It turns out that killing people is an effective way to elicit the attention of many women: virtually every serial killer, including Ted Bundy, Charles Manson, and David Berkowitz, have received love letters from large numbers of female fans. A woman named Lysosome was one of them. "I used to write to Richard Ramirez [the "Night Stalker"] when I was 16–20, he was nice, told me to get an education and that I'm sweet and should sort my life out and not end up in prison lol. I really liked him. I told him I wanted to chop his wifes feet off and he was cool about it. he's a nice guy :-)." Another fan describes her attitude toward Andrei Chikatilo, a Soviet serial killer nicknamed the Butcher of Rostov who killed fifty-three women and children: "My personal favorite is Chikatilo, though. If I could have died by his hands, *sigh*." One woman even managed to have sex with the serial killer Ed Abrams in prison, after marrying him and acquiring conjugal visits.

Among the Yanomamo people of the Amazon, men who have killed the most other men have the most wives and the most offspring. Indeed, killers (known as *chuchu*) are generally regarded by the Yanomamo women as the most desirable. Men from the Ilongots of the Philippines were required to present the shrunken head of a man they had killed to a woman during courtship.

But readers of romance are quick to point out that they *certainly* don't want their heroes to be rapists or murderers. They're willing to tolerate a little misogyny and jerkdom in their heroes at the beginning of a story, as long as they don't stay that way after they meet the heroine. In fact, being an alpha is only half the full hero package. To truly pass Miss Marple's scrutiny, the hero must find his inner goo.

THE TAMING OF THE WILD COCONUT

In psychologist David Buss's classic cross-cultural survey of mate preferences across thirty-seven different cultures, women's number one preference in men was "kindness and understanding." If that's the case, what happened to cartoonist Robert Crumb?

"There was this guy named Skutch . . . he was like this mean bully, but he was also very charming and all the girls liked him. He was the *dreamboat*, but he was also a bully," laments the cartoonist in the biographical film *Crumb*. Robert Crumb is a scrawny, hunched artist with Coke-bottle glasses. The kind of guy teased in high school for being a nerd. "I couldn't understand why girls liked these cruel, aggressive guys and not me, 'cause I was more kind and sensitive. . . . I was not very attractive physically, but I didn't think those things really mattered, it was what's inside that was important."

Crumb clearly never read romances or he would have known that when it comes to women's preferences, they don't just want a nice guy—they want an alpha who learns to be nice to *her*. In other words, women want their romance heroes to be like coconuts: hard and tough on the outside, but soft and sweet on the inside. But the hero's sweet interior can't be available to just anyone. Only the heroine gets to crack him open. The hero is granted free reign to be a badass with everyone else, as long as he's tender and attentive with the heroine.

The heroine's Detective Agency is designed to look for clues indicating that there is a sweet interior worth getting at. Once Miss Marple gathers enough evidence, the female brain then sets out on a mission to tame, heal, or soften the alpha hero's wild heart. The process of the hero getting in touch with his tender side is one of the greatest pleasures of the romance. Scenes where an alpha male expresses his feelings are always described in rich detail. In the same way that women often find the breathless gasping and moaning of female porn stars to be absurdly inauthentic, male readers of romances might find the emotional confessions of romance heroes to be strangely unfamiliar. Consider this scene from Elizabeth Hoyt's *The Serpent Prince*:

He stumbled forward and dropped to his knees before her.

"I'm sorry," she started, and then realised she was speaking over his words.

"Stay." He grasped her shoulders with both hands, squeezing as if he couldn't believe she was solid. "Stay with me. I love you. God, I love you. Lucy. I can't . . ."

Her heart seemed to expand with his words. "I'm sorry. I . . ."

"I can't live without you," he was saying, his lips skimming her face. "I tried. There isn't any light without you."

"I won't leave again."

"I become a creature with a blackened soul . . ."

"I love you Simon . . ."

"Without hope or redemption . . ."

"I love you."

"You are my salvation."

"I love you."

The coconut template of romance heroes has been central to romances for a long time. In the novel *Madame Bovary* by Gustave Flaubert, the narrator describes Emma Bovary's nineteenth-century reading material as full of "gentlemen brave as lions, tender as lambs . . . always well-dressed, and weeping pints." Such men are difficult to find in real life, though one female psychologist suggests that a man who seems to epitomize the male ideal is Denzel Washington: "He is strong, confident, and can be very aggressive. At the same time, you just feel that he is a good man."

Much of the Detective Agency is designed to ferret out a man's true feelings and determine if he is truly "kind and understanding" or whether his emotional expressions are insincere. "Ultimately, I just want to know that this big, strong guy is safe—that he's not going to hurt me, that he really listens to me and cares about me," explains one woman on a romance discussion forum. But sometimes the Detective Agency relies on more direct methods. One young woman describes the things a guy must do to get back together with her: "I needed him to 1. introduce me to his parents. 2. change his facebook relationship status. 3. Give me all his email, Facebook, and phone passwords."

Miss Marple's desire to elicit the latent tenderness of a man is as powerful as Elmer Fudd's desire to make a woman tremble with sexual pleasure. Men frequently attribute sexual pleasure to a woman based upon shaky evidence. Many porn fans express with certitude that adult actresses Sasha Grey, Jenna Jameson, and Cytherea are having *real orgasms* in their movies. There is a similar kind of certainty in many women's conviction that their hyper-masculine lover hides a secret tenderness. "My best friend has written to a couple of high-profile inmates, one sadly now executed," explains JJS811 on the Prison Talk message boards. "She received nice letters in return . . . Even though their names are synonymous with evil, the letters she received showed a human side too."

Though "kindness and understanding" are attractive to women by themselves, they are usually most effective at activating the Detective Agency when a man's sweet interior is packaged together with the tough coconut shell of alpha-hood. This was the final lesson Robert Crumb learned. "When I was a teenager, girls were just utterly out of my reach. They wouldn't even let me draw them." Crumb leans back in his chair and laughs. "Yeah. All that changed after I got famous."

MATERIAL GIRL

Though a man can be an alpha without attaining financial success—a sheriff, for example, or a soldier—the possession of enormous amounts of cash is a sure way to seal one's social dominance. The titles of romance novels demonstrate the high value the Detective Agency places on material wealth. In the romance titles on Amazon, there are 415 millionaires, 286 billionaires, and 263 sheiks, including *The Millionaire's Secretary*, *The Billionaire's Virgin Bride*, and *The Sheik's Secret Harem Girl*.

Material resources are arousing to females all across the animal kingdom. Female chimpanzees prefer males with the largest quantity of meat. Female pelicans prefer males who give them the most fish. The female wolf spider prefers males who bring them the largest insect. The female bower bird famously prefers the male with the most sumptuous and elaborate bower.

Until quite recently, a wealthy husband was the only possible way to ensure a woman's long-term prosperity. In Jane Austen's novels, such as *Pride and Prejudice* and *Emma*, the heroines end up with well-heeled aristocrats as the result of true love—but also to ensure their survival in a world where men control all the purse strings. Things are different in the twenty-first century. In modern romances, the heroine often has a high-powered, high-paying job of her own. Romances feature women who are corporate executives, politicians, and financiers. Since such heroines no longer require a man to provide for their needs, has this cultural transformation led to more romance heroes with limited means?

Not at all. If a heroine is rich, then the hero is even *more* rich. In Judith McNaught's *Paradise* the heroine is from a wealthy family and meets the hero when she is young. He is poor, but ambitious. Her father doesn't approve of their relationship and breaks them up. When they meet again years later, he's made a fortune and is richer than her family. But if the heroine is rich and the hero is poor, a different romantic possibility is to make him an exceptionally macho badass who has to save the heroine from herself, such as this dust jacket description in Lisa Marie Rice's *Midnight Run*:

> Undercover police officer Lieutenant Tyler "Bud" Morrison can't believe his eyes. What's a "princess" doing in a dance club known for its rough trade? She needs rescuing, and rescuing women is what Bud does best.

THE LURE OF THE HUNTER

In the romance, the hero is always *competent*. Usually, he's the best at what he does—a corporate CEO, Hollywood movie star, NFL quarterback, army colonel, or a spy with a license to kill.

Men who don't know what to do with their life, who are midlevel bureaucrats, or who sit around the house watching TV are *never* heroes. The female cue of male competence contrasts with the complete absence of such a cue in men. In pornography and life, men are quite happy pursuing attractive women who are drifting and aimless, who are stuck in minimum-wage jobs, or who seem to botch any task they're assigned. To the OkCupid survey question "Would you date someone who didn't know how to drive a car?" most men answered yes. Most women answered no.

"The hero has to know what he's doing, and be confident in his ability," explains Angela Knight. "In fact, it's often desirable for the hero to be so confident in his talent that he can't even conceive that the heroine has something to offer." In many preliterate cultures, including the Hadza, Yanomamo, Ache, and Hopi, women say that hunting or fighting prowess is an essential quality in a man.

Intelligence is a special kind of competence that is also essential in a romance hero. "Stupidity is never heroic," assert Wendell and Tan. In a peculiar evolutionary tradeoff, men may owe their intelligence in part to women's relative chastity. The brain and the testicles both require large amounts of energy. In species where females are promiscuous, males tend to develop large testicles but smaller brains. The silver-tipped myotis bat has gargantuan testicles that make up 8.4 percent of his body mass, compared to 1 percent in men.

The psychologist Geoffrey Miller believes that a particular kind of evolution known as sexual selection may be responsible for women's valuation of male creativity and intelligence. Whereas natural selection can be described as "survival of the fittest," sexual selection is "survival of the hottest." Sexual selection for male intelligence or creativity may have worked like this: a woman who was attracted to an artist would have children with a good chance of possessing the creative skills of the father—as well as the mother's attraction to creative men. This would produce a genetic feedback cycle, the same evolutionary process that made the peacock's tail so extravagant.

The appeal of competence and dominance could explain why women are far more interested in older partners than men are. Romance heroes are usually older than the heroines, and age gaps of more than ten years are not rare. In *The Flame and the Flower*, there's an age gap of twelve years between the Flower and the older Flame. In historical romances, teenage heroines and thirty-something heroes are quite common, such as Eloisa James's *Pleasure for Pleasure*, where Josie Essex is an eighteen-year old who falls in love with the thirty-five-year old Earl of Mayne. In Suzanne Brockmann's *The Admiral's Bride*, Jake and Zoe are twenty-four years apart. However, many modern romance novels reverse the gap. For example, in *Family Blessings* by LaVyrle Spencer, the heroine is fifteen years older than the hero. But most women prefer their heroes to have greater experience. "I want a mature strong man and I feel I cannot find that with a guy my age or in his 20s," bemoans one woman. "I like older men but I want one who has his shit together and is compassionate. I just feel like I can communicate with older guys better. I've had enough of the boys."

A KNIGHT IN SHINING KEVLAR

The characters populating male fantasies have little in common with those inhabiting female fantasies. In porn, the mind of a woman is usually empty of all thought and feeling—except for an overwhelming urge to have sex with plumbers, pizza boys, and her BFF. Women's hopes and fears are irrelevant. Their skills are inconsequential, except for the admirable ability to satisfy multiple lovers simultaneously and an impressive capacity for moaning. Their bodies, on the other hand, are depicted in lavish, graphic detail.

The heroes of romance novels often seem like members of a more evolved species. They are natural leaders, rich, powerful, and well-connected. Their minds are intelligent and savvy, though they are reticent about their abilities and hide their inner demons. Despite the fact that they are a five-star general or lord of southern England, they hide a troubled and tempestuous soul that can only be healed by the magical balm of a woman's love. While visuals do matter—heroes are handsome, tall, strong, with beautiful gray eyes and a crooked grin—little attention is paid to the details of male genitalia. While almost every male-written erotic story details the precise length of a man's penis to the nearest half inch, in romance, length is seldom given. Instead, and quite curiously, there is far greater emphasis on the activity of the blood within a hero's penis than what his manhood actually looks like.

"Blood surged to his cock, heated, unexpected, inappropriate," writes Christine Feehan in her novel *Burning Wild*. Then, when the heroine kisses the hero, it "makes the blood pound in his shaft." In Shiloh Walker's *Touch of Gypsy Fire*, "His cock throbbed, blood pounding heavily within it" and later "Aryn's blood pounded heavily in his cock." In Ellen Sable's *Days of Flame*, she writes how "blood coursed through his cock" until eventually "it pulsed and throbbed with hot blood." Apparently, female vampires would be well advised to ignore a man's neck in favor of a more nutritious part of his anatomy.

This strange clash of busty, giggling airheads and tall, brooding dukes produces mutual dismay. Where men see sexy, women often see misogyny. Where women see sexy, men often see arrogant jerks with split personalities. Catherine Salmon and Donald Symons imagine what a movie might look like that simultaneously appeals to Miss Marple and Elmer Fudd: "A film genre that combined a number of the ingredients of romantopia, pornotopia, and mainstream commercial cinema, such as romantic comedies and romantic adventures with compelling plots, intelligent and witty dialogue, fully developed characters, first-rate acting, physically attractive stars, happily-ever-after endings, and hard-core sex scenes."

They observe that even if such a movie were produced, it would be a commercial failure, because some of the essential ingredients of romance and porn are incompatible. Impersonal, anonymous sex is a core feature of pornography, but is anathema to romance, in which the careful elaboration of the hidden and special character of both hero and heroine is essential.

In the world of male fantasy—and male desire—the goal is orgasm. The story ends with a man's climax, what masseuses call a "happy ending." In romance, the happy ending (known as an HEA or *Happily-Ever-After*) is always a long-term monogamous relationship, usually marriage. ("In erotic romance, the reader is satisfied with a Happy For Now ending," explains erotic romance author Susanna Carr.) Orgasm is important in modern romances, but it's never the final scene. The moments in bed *after* the orgasm are just as important as the feelings experienced during the orgasm itself. When marriage is depicted in porn, the bride has sex with the best man as often as with the groom, and the wedding ceremony may be followed by an orgy between all the bridesmaids and groomsmen. What are the two most common searches on Dogpile that end in "-ing"? "Wedding" and "fucking."

Romance novels rarely have a sequel—once the hero and heroine are joined in love or matrimony, they get their Happily-Ever-After, presumably with a bevy of children and domestic bliss. Further adventures would violate the female fantasy of true, committed, eternal love. Though there are many series of modern romance novels, once a couple gets their Happily-Ever-After in one book, they only resurface as beloved supporting characters in future books, with each subsequent book's focus on a new hero and heroine. In contrast, porn has more sequels than James Bond, such as *Cotton Panties 11*, *Gang Bang Girl 32*, and *Barely Legal 107*. Even male-targeted adventure stories, such as Patrick O'Brian's Aubrey/Maturin Master and Commander twenty-book series or Warren Murphy's 145-books-and-still-counting The Destroyer, go on and on after marriage, since there's always another macho adventure just over the horizon.

It's also revealing to reverse the roles and consider the men in porn and women in romance. In porn, the male is reduced to a single object: an erect penis. The face of a male porn star is shown far less frequently than close-ups of his sweaty rear end as he pounds away. His personality consists exclusively of the desire to elicit female pleasure through the paradoxical process of attaining his own orgasm.

And the romance heroine?

CHAPTER 6
The Sisterhood of the Magic Hoo Hoo
Female Psychological Cues II: The Heroine

I'm just a girl, standing in front of a boy, asking him to love her.

—Julia Roberts, *Notting Hill*

Skin whitening creams are a big deal in India. They generate hundreds of millions of dollars in sales each year in a country where the average monthly income is $250. In one TV ad for Fair and Lovely (India's best-selling cream) a father and daughter in traditional Hindu garb are looking for the temple. They accidentally walk through a modeling agency's high-glass doors into a vaulted lobby. The duo asks the Western-suited, pale-skinned receptionist for directions to the place of prayer. The receptionist rolls her eyes and informs them they are actually in the hallowed portals of a modern beauty company. She smirks and cattily adds that this wasn't the place for women of *her sort* who belonged in the time of the Vedas. What exactly was her sort? *Dark-skinned.*

The incensed father and his chagrined daughter head back home. He whips out an old parchment and recites an angry Vedic incantation. Through his ancient Ayurvedic sorcery, he concocts a jar of Fair and Lovely. His daughter rubs it on her skin, which quickly lightens to resemble the pale tone of the receptionist.

Obviously, if this advertisement ever aired in the United

States, the NAACP would quite reasonably accuse Fair and Lovely of over-the-top racism. But the ad uses a very revealing incentive to motivate women to buy the cream, one that activates a powerful sexual cue in women.

In the ad, the newly whitened daughter reenters the modeling agency. This time, her appearance produces awestruck reactions from all the men, including the young and handsome director. The curtain drops, revealing that she has become the new face of the agency. She exits an airplane to a crowd of flashing cameras and clamoring men. The message is clear: the enchanted cream has made her *irresistible*.

"The desire of the man is for the woman," Swiss author Madame de Staël famously penned; "The desire of the woman is for the desire of the man." One of the most fundamental and influential psychological cues for women is *irresistibility*: the feeling that you are sexually desirable. "Being desired is very arousing to women," agrees Marta Meana.

The Fair and Lovely ad could have promised women that lighter skin would lead to greater economic achievement, better health, or greater popularity with other women. In fact, the identical product for men, Fair and Handsome, is sometimes marketed with the promise that it will help its male customers rise the corporate ladder. Perhaps these gender-specific incentives are ultimately the result of Indian culture. But the female desire to be irresistible is also a staple of romance novels, where it's often represented as a hero's overwhelming sexual desire for the heroine. In fact, it's so common that Sarah Wendell and Candy Tan have given it a name: the *Magic Hoo Hoo*.

"The Magic Hoo Hoo does it all: it heals all ills, psychic and sexual. It provides unparalleled pleasure to the hero, despite the heroine's reluctance, inexperience, and awkwardness. It's capable of experiencing (and inducing) earth-shattering multiple orgasms on its first outing. It also creates an instant emotional bond that's even more irrational and persistent than a newly hatched chick imprinting on the first living thing it sees. One taste of the Magic

Hoo Hoo is all it takes; the hero won't be satisfied with anything else, physically or emotionally."

The gaze of male desire is focused outward, narrowly, and entirely on the woman. Men do not have sexual cues relating to their self. This unidirectional desire is reflected in the typical porn scene, where the woman is the focus. Male performers are optional, and when they are present, their main contribution is their upright organ. The male viewer of porn doesn't waste any cognitive energy considering how the actor might feel—and he certainly doesn't consider his own emotions as he absorbs the visual cues on display. The wabbit hunter only has eyes for his quarry.

Women have a more panoramic range of considerations. Clues about the character and qualities of the romantic hero are important, of course, as are the hero's looks. But unlike men, Miss Marple also looks inward when deciding whether to release sexual desire. "An increasing body of data is indicating that the way women feel about themselves may be very important to their experience of sexual desire and subjective arousal," observes Marta Meana. "Possibly even outweighing the impact of their partners' view of them."

This gender difference in psychological cues pertaining to self is reflected in a common linguistic distinction. When referring to the self-confidence of a woman, we usually describe it as *female self-esteem*. When referring to the self-confidence of a man, we say *male ego*. "Self-esteem" has a connotation of being something subject to fluctuation, something that must be nurtured and supported. "Ego" has the slightly negative connotation of aggression and conceit, a sense that the ego might get angry or attack. In romance novels, the hero almost always has a strong ego—even to the point of rakish overconfidence and smugness. A lack of confidence, especially at the start of a romance, is a frequent characteristic of the heroine. But after the hero discovers her Magic Hoo Hoo, the heroine's self-esteem is sure to soar.

In Lisa Kleypas's *Only with Your Love*, Celia Vallerand is

"rescued" from a gang of pirates by another pirate named Griffin. But her rescue turns dangerous when Griffin is overwhelmed with lust for her Magic Hoo Hoo.

Never in his life had he wanted anything as much as he wanted her. "But you owe me something."

There was no mistaking his meaning. "When we r-reach New Orleans," Celia stammered, "Monsieur Valle-rand will give you a reward for saving my life."

"I want it now." The bristle of his beard scratched the back of her neck, the velvet heat of his mouth rubbed over the top of her spine. "Please," she said wildly, "don't do this—"

She whimpered in fear, but nothing would stop the ravenous mouth that wandered over her. It didn't matter if his desire was reciprocated or not—he had to bury himself inside her and satisfy his hunger.

"I am not yours and you have no right—"

"You are mine. Until I give you to the Vallerands." He bent over her unwilling mouth once more, thinking that he'd never had to seduce a woman before, not when every corner of the world was filled with willing ones. For him, the act of mating had always been quick and intense. But now he wanted something different, wanted it enough to wait with unnatural patience.

"Don't be afraid. I won't hurt you." Dimly she sensed the terrible guilt that awaited her if she allowed him to take her. If she put up enough of a struggle, there was a slim chance he might let her go. But to her everlasting shame, she found she had no more will to fight . . . her body was welcoming the drugging caresses that eased away all pain, all awareness of everything but rapture.

Donald Symons and Bruce Ellis found that more than half of women's fantasies reflect the desire to be sexually irresistible.

Women frequently fantasize about being a stripper, harem girl, or Las Vegas showgirl and "delighting many men." Sometimes a woman just imagines a stranger being so smitten with her looks that he abandons his friends—or wife—and crosses the room to meet her. In Elizabeth Boyle's *His Mistress by Morning*, Charlotte Wilmont is in love with Sebastien, Viscount Trent, from afar. A magic ring grants her wish to capture his heart. But when she wakes, she finds she has become his mistress—the most notorious and popular mistress in all of London.

The psychological cue of irresistibility explains young women's willingness to enter wet T-shirt contests and flash themselves at Mardi Gras. Whereas male exhibitionism is usually considered a psychiatric disorder and a crime, female exhibitionism is rarely considered a social problem. Indeed, it's frequently exploited commercially. A journalist asked a girl at Spring Break in Miami why she had just stripped naked for the cameras of soft-core pornographers in exchange for a hat. "If a woman's got a pretty body and she likes her body, let her show it off!" was her enthusiastic response. "The only way I could see someone not doing this is if they were planning a career in politics."

The desire to be desired may also explain why many adolescent women participate in *sexting*—exchanging naked photos of themselves taken on a smart phone or webcam. Numerous Web sites, such as JayBee (short for Jailbait), My Ex Girlfriend, and See My Girlfriend, consist of galleries of nude photos that young women have taken of themselves in the mirror or by holding the camera at arm's length.

Sexual irresistibility is often expressed in women's magazines and self-help books as "empowerment." In *Real Sex for Real Women*, Laura Berman suggests that her book will help women "feel empowered" by making their "partners cherish our bodies, crave our touch, and desire passionate, no-holds-barred sex." In other words, to empower women to be the subject of unapologetic male lust.

In women, the urge to feel irresistible may not be part of the conscious, cognitive software of the Detective Agency. It appears to be a primal component of female sexuality, as basic as a man's urge to chase and seduce. Marta Meana believes that there may even be a parallel between female irresistibility and a sexual cue in the female rat. When female rats are in the "proceptive phase"—a period of fertility when they're seeking males for sex—they are in control of the sexual interactions, darting and hopping around the interested male in a process called *pacing*. The female rat wants the male to pursue her. If the male shows sufficient interest and chases her at the pace she sets, then she permits him to mount her and copulate. It's clear that female rats find pacing to be rewarding. Both pacing and the reward for pacing are controlled by software in the rat subcortex.

But the powerful subcortical cue of irresistibility can also cause trouble for the female brain. Women of all ages report dissatisfaction with their body far more often than men do. Anorexia and bulimia are about seven times more likely to occur in women than in men. Women express much greater body image self-consciousness during physical intimacy than men and frequently cite body dissatisfaction as one of the primary impediments to satisfying sex. On the other hand, when a woman does feel empowered by her appearance, she is much more likely to report sexual satisfaction.

The irresistibility cue is so potent and fundamental that it fuels a female fantasy that is very common—and very controversial.

THE CONCUPISCENCE OF COERCION

I blame my recurring rape fantasy on the fact that I'm a feminist. I've never made any bones about getting boned in exactly the fashion that I want. But as a girl, my equipment can be trickier to manage, therefore I need to be a boss in the bedroom to ensure I get worked the right way. It gets really tiresome always being the one in charge, and don't shrinks say that people usually fantasize about the opposite of their reality? I guess that's why I find myself wishing that my typically sugary-sweet sexual encounters were sometimes peppered with assault.

So opens the essay entitled *"One Rape, Please (to go)"* authored by Ms. Tracie Egan Morrissey in the online magazine *Vice*. Egan describes her botched attempt at indulging her coercion fantasy. She hires a male escort: a young, handsome gigolo in New York City. She wants him to wear a ski mask because "it would also be extra scary and thrilling and hot." Unfortunately for Egan, the fantasy peters out prematurely as the hired ruffian ends up falling for her. Instead of violating her resisting body, he begs to see her again.

For both ordinary women and female scientists, the widespread prevalence of female coercive fantasies is an understandable source of discomfort and hand-wringing. The subject frequently leads to defensiveness: getting excited by a fantasy is not the same thing as wanting it in real life. "Arousal is not consent," asserts psychologist Meredith Chivers. In fact, many women emphasize that rape fantasies involve a meaningful level of consent in that the woman consents to having the fantasy. "Perhaps this is why some women can still enjoy rape scenes in romance novels or e-rom," ponders one woman, "they have consented to participate in the mental experience and thus have control over the situation."

In romance novels from the 1970s and '80s, the heroine was frequently raped. And not a verbal seduction followed by gentle coercion, either. Heroines were sometimes violated by a gang of pirates, sold into sexual slavery, or smacked around until their mouths bled. The hero himself often forced himself on the heroine, such as the pirate Griffin raping Celia Vallerand or Woodiwiss's Flame raping the Flower.

Rape romances reached their pinnacle in the classic 1980s "bodice rippers," with feisty heroines and very-bad-boy heroes set on revenge. Here is a sample from Christine Monson's 1984 *Stormfire*. Irish rebel Sean Culhane has abducted Catherine Enderley, an English countess and daughter to the English aristrocrat who arranged the massacre that killed Sean's mother.

> He climbed atop her, caught her hands and pinned them above her head, then threw a leg over her lower body. When she felt the pressure of his sex against her bare thigh, she suddenly went berserk and fought him in dumb, choking terror. Clamping her wrists with one hand, he methodically ripped the camisole and petticoat from her straining body, then lay full length upon her, forcing her to submit to his nakedness until she lay exhausted, heart thudding against his ribs. Sensing the trigger to her fear, he deliberately smeared her breasts with his blood so that her body was slippery under him. Relentlessly, he pursued her into the void.

The author's description is still rather literary and emotional, especially compared to the graphic detail and physical violence of male-targeted coercion erotica. Scientists point out that the men in many of these female coercion fantasies are handsome, appealing alphas—the kind of partner that appeals to Miss Marple. "What is 'wished for' in real life is surrender to a powerful and attractive selected male and a sense of danger, excitement, and passion in real-life relationships," observed two psychologists in a 2008 review of rape fantasy research.

But Meredith Chivers also points out that there is something primordial about female fantasies of submission. "It's the wish to be beyond will, beyond thought. To be all in the midbrain." Though academic research focuses on the notion that coercion involves desirable male partners, many amateur stories written by women depict rapes by unattractive and brutal men in shuddering detail.

Literotica is the single most popular English-language erotic story site on the Web, with 5 million visitors per month. Run by the husband-and-wife team of Laurel and John since the late

'90s the site contains more than 200,000 erotic stories, including more than 10,000 "non-consent/reluctant" stories. There are female-authored fantasies of truckers raping women at rest stops, depraved criminals raping innocent housewives, and soldiers brutalizing captive women.

But fan fiction features the widest variety of female-authored nonconsensual sex—in some cases downright violent and degrading sex. Stories with such themes are common enough to merit their own identifying tags: *Abuse*, *Violence*, *BDSM*, *Tort*[ure] and *Humil*[iation]. Each of these tags is among the ten most popular sexual act descriptors for Harry Potter stories on AdultFanFiction .net. Here is an excerpt from a fan fiction story by Miss Stephanie, featuring the abduction of a muggle by Draco Malfoy:

> She fought with renewed strength then, but he smiled in a wicked grimace as he forced her hands over her head and straddled her. . . . Draco felt the heat flare as he ripped her shirt away and caught sight of her rather large breasts. They jounced and wiggled as she struggled again, and another slap stilled her. . . . Her head turned and he saw a trickle of blood alongside her mouth, but this only spiked his arousal, causing his penis to jump with eagerness as he pulled it out. She pushed against him, ineffectually, but he slapped her regardless, and forced her hands down, gripping them with his own hands on either side of her head. . . . He knew that he was wrong, but he wanted to make this last. He had never in his life felt such heat conjoin in his loins, and he was sure the explosion that was building within him was going to be momentous.

In such fantasies, it often seems like something is going on other than the mere desire to be irresistible. "I get off on stories with the rough stuff," explains Miranda Helmsley, a forty-two-year-old baker. "I don't know why. I definitely would never want to experience any of the things that turn me on. But I need the girl to be exploited, put in her place with real force from the man. I don't like to think too much about it, and I definitely would never tell my husband."

These violent and degrading coercive fantasies may be female counterparts to men's submission fantasies, such as "forced feminization," "cock and ball torture," and "golden showers"—squicky genres we will consider later. It may be that at the bottom of our subcortex, in our hypothalamus and midbrain, we all share the same ancient circuitry associated with dominance and submission. In Czech author Milan Kundera's "The Hitchiking Game," he describes a sexually inexperienced woman who pretends to be a prostitute as part of a sex game with her boyfriend. She ends up losing herself in the role.

> This was exactly what the girl had most dreaded all her life and had scrupulously avoided until now: lovemaking without emotion or love. She knew that she had crossed the forbidden boundary, but she proceeded across it without objections and as a full participant; only somewhere, far off in a corner of her consciousness, did she feel horror at the thought that she had never known such pleasure, never so much pleasure at this moment—beyond that boundary.

WEB 0.0

There's a scene in *Legally Blonde* where Elle Woods returns home to campus and notices her awkward friend David trying to pick up a pretty girl. "You're a dork," replies the girl. "Girls like me don't go out with guys like you." Elle hurries over to David and slaps him. "Why didn't you call me? We spent a beautiful night together and I haven't heard from you since." David plays along as the pretty girl watches attentively. After Elle stalks off, the pretty girl returns to David. "So, when did you wanna go out?"

The maxim "All the best men are taken" is doubly true. If a man is already taken by a woman, then by definition, he's the best man—or certainly a more *desirable* man. If the exact same man is not taken, then his value is questionable—he's certainly not as desirable as a man who has already received the stamp of approval from another woman's Detective Agency.

The *popularity cue* is prominent in romance novels, though it may find its most classic expression in the Cinderella fairy tale. The Prince is sought after by all the ladies of the kingdom—including the bitchy stepsisters—but the glass slipper only fits one girl, the oppressed maid Cinderella. In the romance novel *Heaven, Texas* by Susan Elizabeth Phillips, the hero is a famous professional football player. The heroine is a rather mousy spinster and virgin who's spent most of her life working in nursing homes. Nobody thought she stood a chance with the popular hometown hero. The hero himself said she wasn't his type and didn't expect to stay with her even after they started sleeping together. But even though he can have any woman in town, the virgin's Magic Hoo Hoo captures his full attention and he ends up falling for her.

Popularity cues are one reason many women find married men so attractive. The fact that another woman's Detective Agency has already completed her assiduous detective work and endorsed a man is valuable information. If the man had something to hide, surely the wife's Miss Marple would have ferreted it out. But for the men who are the subject of the popularity cue, it's a case of the rich getting richer. Former Playboy playmate Kendra Wilkinson chronicles her first sexual encounter with Hugh Hefner in the Playboy Mansion:

> One of the girls asked me if I wanted to go upstairs to Hef's room. . . . It seemed like every other girl was going, and if I didn't it would be weird. One by one, each girl hopped on Hef and had sex with him . . . for about a minute. I studied their every move. Then it was my turn . . . it was very weird. I wasn't thinking about how much older Hef was—all the body parts worked the same. I wanted to be there.

Men who are awkward loners or social rejects have a major strike against them in the view of the Detective Agency, unless they offer compensating cues. "Omega" heroes—comedians, art thieves, and nerdy geniuses—rarely show up in romances though, as with Beta heroes, they have their own devoted following. Xander from *Buffy the Vampire Slayer* is an omega, as is the thief Gawain Lammergeier in Claire Delacroix's *The Scoundrel*. Alpha heroes who are dominant in the society of men and desired by the society of women are far more common, and far more appreciated by Miss Marple.

The solitary hunter Elmer Fudd is not receptive to the popularity cue. Other men's opinion about the attractiveness of a woman plays no role in the level of man's desire; indeed, men often prefer that other men had less interest in a potential partner in order to leave her more accessible. The fewer competing wabbit-hunters, the better.

When women are not competing for mates, they frequently solicit one another's opinions on men, relationships, sexuality, health, dieting, fashion, and especially one another's feelings— what we might call *informational cues*. The Detective Agency always craves information to make good long-term investment decisions—and the more information, the better. We saw how women dominate social networking sites like Facebook, MySpace, Twitter, and Bebo. But informational cues are most prominent within the highly networked fan fiction community.

One reason that fanfic has exploded online is because the Internet makes it very easy for female fans to communicate with one another. Most fan fiction stories are posted in forums and blogs that allow readers to comment on the stories. Readers pay particular attention to the emotional qualities of the story and the authenticity of the characters. Remarking on a Harry Potter story, one fan observes, "Oh, and, on a side note, would Ron really use the expression, 'hooking up'? It sounded very Muggle, very American, and very post-early 90s to me." Another fan commends the author, saying, "I liked his surges of anger every now and again, made for a more compelling and realistic Harry. I also thought his spat with Ginny was done very appropriately."

Many fan fiction stories elicit hundreds of comments. A story's author usually responds to comments on her story. Fanfic authors frequently share what they were feeling when they wrote their story, eliciting further discussion. Many women enjoy talking about the process of talking about fan fiction, a type of discussion known as "meta."

One 55,000-word story set in the *Stargate: Atlantis* universe and titled "Written by the Victors" was posted on LiveJournal in 2007 by the author Speranza. It has received more than one thousand enthusiastic comments and still receives comments today. "I will point out that the thing that unequivocally sucked me in was that after seven chapters of theorizing about John's character and motivations we finally get to the emotional truth of the matter," writes one commenter. Miss Marple's joy in analyzing and evaluating informational cues is quite apparent in most comments. "I particularly loved the different truths of the competing historical narratives, their different weightiness in publication type ranging from what I thought were excerpts from more popular and light-weight memoirs/biographies to the more supposedly stringent peer-reviewed articles—how they in literary style cycled through the spectrum of factual history-legend-myth-poetic fantasy and finally degenerated (for us readers—into Latin/Greek and finally glyphs/ideograms)—lost forever perhaps."

In fan fiction, the discussion is as important as the story.

When it comes to desiring a man, women have a love/hate relationship with other women. This is quite different from men's attitude toward other men where women are involved, which is more of an ignore/kill relationship. Why this difference? Miss Marple simply cannot gather enough evidence about a potential partner by working on her own. She always benefits from making a few calls—or a few dozen—to the Detectives at other Agencies.

But at the end of the day, what matters most is the opinion of one man.

SO DAMN EASY TO LOVE

The pop singer Beyoncé croons, "Why don't you love me? Tell me, baby, why don't you love me? When I make me so damn easy to love?" The psychological cue of *adorability*—a woman's desire to feel loved for her unique and special qualities—is as fundamental as irresistibility, and a quality that the Detective Agency is keen to detect.

"For women, being lovable was the key to attracting the best mate. For men, however, it was more a matter of beating out lots of other men even to have a chance for a mate," suggests Roy Baumeister. "Perhaps nature designed women to be lovable, whereas men were designed to strive, mostly unsuccessfully, for greatness."

While a woman's desire to be sexually irresistible may be rooted in the unconscious subcortex, the desire to be loved may involve the conscious cortex, along with conscious emotional mechanisms designed to evaluate a man's love. In romance novels, the hero must show signs of loving the heroine for her unique personal qualities. Some romance fans refer to this as "Twu Wuv." Whereas the Magic Hoo Hoo is about a woman's sexual desirability, Twu Wuv is about a woman's specialness as a human being. The hero must demonstrate that his love is steady, irrational, and everlasting.

The main narrative arc of any romance consists of the hero gradually coming to terms with the powerful and inexplicable love he feels toward the heroine. It is the authenticity and depth of a man's Twu Wuv that the Detective Agency is ultimately designed to plumb. Though a hero may feel the whirling vertigo of love early on, it's not enough for him to simply profess it to the heroine. He must demonstrate its reality through sacrifice and commitment. Often, the hero fights the feeling, sometimes even treating the heroine badly in the hope that by getting rid of her, he will get rid of the throbbing passion in his heart. But love eventually burns through.

The climax of every romance novel occurs when the hero finally confesses his heartfelt Twu Wuv to the heroine in a sudden gush, often accompanied by a marriage proposal, as in this scene from Theresa Michaels's *Once an Outlaw*:

> Logan had eyes for no one but Jessie. Her tears soaked his chin, but her whispers were less frantic now. Wiping the tears with his finger tips, he brought them to his lips.
>
> "I never want to see you cry again," he whispered. She tried to stem the flow, truly tried, but the tears kept coming as she gazed at his battered face. "Ah, Jess, what am I gonna do with a woman who won't obey me?"
>
> "I don't know."
>
> He angled his throbbing head and brushed his swollen mouth against hers.
>
> "Guess that's all you're getting in the way of a kiss for now. But I've the rest of the answer to your question, Jessie. Remember last night? You asked who I am. Logan Kincaid of the Rocking K ranch and the man who wants to marry you. Come home with me, Jess."

There's a fascinating parallel between what may be the greatest sexual self-delusion in men, and the greatest sexual self-delusion in women. Men are quite prone to believing they are inducing feelings of erotic ecstasy in their partner through their own sexual prowess. Women, on the other hand, are more easily manipulated by expressions of love.

This distinction reflects the different jealousies in men and women. The male brain is designed for sexual jealousy. Men are suspicious about whom a woman has slept with and frequently press their partner on how many times she's previously had sex;

most women are savvy enough to round this number down. Likewise, the female brain is designed for emotional jealousy. Women usually push their partner to reveal how many times he's previously been in love; men are often foolish enough to provide a figure other than zero.

Ultimately, a woman wants to feel that a man loves her, and her alone, unconditionally and forever—and that none of a man's previous women ever rose to anywhere near the same level. This is reflected in romances. As Candy Tan writes, "For the vast majority of heroes, falling in love with the heroine represents an emotional deflowering akin to a heroine's loss of virginity. We therefore recommend that heroes protect this tender bud of emotional vulnerability with a series of emotionally unfulfilling—even psychically damaging—relationships. Just remember: physical whoring is not a problem; it is, in fact, recommended for certain hero archetypes. Emotional whoring, on the other hand, is deeply frowned upon; just as the heroine is a whore if she has enjoyed sexual relations with anybody other than you, you, as a hero, are an emotional whore if you fall in love with anybody else other than the heroine."

THE POWER OF AND VS. THE POWER OF OR

Let's review what we've learned so far about the differences between Elmer Fudd and the Detective Agency. We've seen how Elmer Fudd is a trigger-happy hunter who readies, aims, and fires at the slightest hint of any wabbit. Any sexual cue will do. We call this single-cue arousability the *Power of Or*. Nice breasts *or* a round butt *or* a hot MILF *or* a shapely pair of pumps—just one of these is all it takes to goad Elmer into squeezing the trigger. The brain software controlling male desire functions like what computer engineers call an "OR gate"—any sexual cue is sufficient to activate arousal.

But Miss Marple is more demanding. Before the Detective

Agency authorizes psychological arousal, it requires a much longer list of cues to be satisfied. A prospective lover must be financially secure *and* nice to children *and* self-confident. The woman herself must feel safe *and* irresistible *and* physically healthy. We call this multi-cue threshold the *Power of And*. The brain software controlling female desire functions like an "AND gate"—no single cue is sufficient to activate arousal. Instead, a number of cues must be satisfied simultaneously. The exact threshold of the female AND gate depends on many variable factors: the cues themselves, a woman's age, her alternate prospects, her culture, her health, and many other factors.

"It could be that sex is judged not to be worth the risk, effort, or other investment," explains Marta Meana. "That is, there may not be sufficiently high incentive to act out the desire."

For many men, one particular cue can be absolutely essential for arousal, which is one reason why fetishes are so much more common in men than in women. But for most women, no single cue is essential to activate arousal. If a guy is not great-looking, but he's a wealthy, sweet heart surgeon, she can still become aroused. If he's a hot, brilliant alpha who exhibits overwhelming lust for a particular woman, despite his reputation as an impoverished gigolo, perhaps that may be enough to cross the threshold.

Though the Power of Or means that men have little trouble getting aroused, it also means that men are not very flexible in their sexuality. In contrast, the Power of And means that female sexuality is far more plastic. Psychologist Roy Baumeister was one of the first scientists to focus attention on female sexual plasticity, emphasizing "the female sex drive is more malleable than the male in response to sociocultural and situational factors." But the Power of And also means that women have a harder time getting aroused. They simply have more cues to satisfy. This is likely one of the main reasons that clinical psychologists see far more women with desire and orgasm disorders than men. On the other hand, since women are not tied to any particular cue, they have much greater flexibility in getting aroused—including greater flexibility in the gender of their partners.

This is one reason why many more women than men experiment with dating same-sex partners, such as Anne Heche, who was married to a man, then dated Ellen Degeneres, then married another man. Studies have found that high sex drive in women is associated with increased sexual attraction to both women and men, while high sex drive in men only enhances attraction to one or the other, depending on the man's sexual orientation. Many female-targeted porn sites, such as NoFauxxx, East Van Porn Collective, and Crash Pad Series proudly claim to offer a wide variety of models, situations, and sexual orientations. Male-targeted paysites, on the other hand, almost always focus on a single, specific cue.

The Power of Or is designed to help men exploit any sudden opportunity for sex. Since a man pays no physical cost for impregnating a woman, evolution made it easy for him to get aroused. After all, any opportunity is precious. For a woman, however, a man is bound to show up eventually, but pregnancy entails a substantial investment. She doesn't need to chase—she needs to choose.

The Power of And is designed to prevent impulsive sex that could have disastrous consequences. But the Power of And is also designed to help a woman flexibly adapt to the particular cultural and physical environment in which she finds herself. Though round, firm breasts and shapely curves are strong indicators of a woman's health and fertility in any human society, the cues that indicate the most desirable man shift from culture to culture, and generation to generation.

Because of the Power of Or, a sixty-second PornHub clip of a woman unbuttoning her shirt can compel a man to masturbate to ejaculation. But the single most popular artifact used by women to generate arousal takes the form of a 250-page book that requires hours to digest. Even the shorter fan fiction stories invite many hours of analysis and discussion. For the past decade, FanFiction .net has consistently maintained one of the highest stickiness ratings of *any* Web site on the Internet, meaning its users spend more time on the site than users on almost any other site in the world. The only sites that have been stickier were America Online (in the early 2000s) and, more recently, poker sites.

The female brain splits conscious psychological arousal apart from unconscious physical arousal, while the male brain unites them. But the male brain splits apart two neural systems that are united in the female brain: sex and romance. In women, sex and romance are intimately intertwined within the Detective Agency. Sex scenes are integrated into the romance novel as stepping stones leading toward a Happily-Ever-After where sex and love are united in matrimonial bliss. Anonymous, casual sex is anathema in the romance novel.

Men, however, are eminently capable of mentally partitioning sex and romance. This is one reason why men can so easily view porn at work or on a transatlantic flight. Sex is the end of the journey, rather than the journey itself. PornHub is a collection of sexual moments, devoid of romance. On the other hand, men can fall head-over-heels in swooning, romantic love, like Tom Cruise's frenetic display of passion on Oprah's couch. The rock music subgenre called emo (for "emotional hard-core") consists of all-male bands singing about broken hearts and unrequited love. It's just that men are able to separate the tender feelings they feel toward a girlfriend from the more carnal urges they feel toward a hot babe at a nightclub or the MILF next door.

Elmer Fudd and Miss Marple present myriad differences—different cues, different ways of processing cues, and different behaviors in response to cues. But Marta Meana warns of oversimplifying the sexual psychology of men and women. "We could find ourselves caricaturizing both male and female sexual desire with the former portrayed as an unshakable, appetitive drive with a near exclusive penchant for novelty and anonymity, and the latter as a fragile intrapsychic and interpersonal phenomenon requiring a delicate calibration of love, intimacy, and multiple other prerequisites."

Nature is sure to throw a monkey wrench into our tidy distinctions. After all, since our desire software involves so many dynamic components, there's bound to be tremendous individual variation in the way we each experience sexual desire. Indeed, there is one fascinating group of people whose brains mix together desire software from both Marple and Fudd.

Gay men.

CHAPTER 7

Boys Will Be Boys

Gay Cues

I'm a survivor first, a capitalist second, and a
whole bunch of other shit after that.
— Lafayette, gay character on *True Blood*

Here's a tricky question: how does the desire software in gay brains differ from the software in straight brains? If you believe that homosexuality is a choice, then you might assert that all men are born with the same brains. After all, men are all born with the same bodies, right? It turns out that's not entirely true. Gay bodies are different. All men are *not* created equal. Mother Nature has conspired to help gay men exceed straight men in one important respect: penis length.

The average length of the gay penis is 6.32 inches. The average length of the straight penis is 5.99 inches. A common negative stereotype of gay men holds that they are overly effeminate. But when it comes to the prime organ of masculinity, they have been endowed with nearly an extra half inch. If there is such a noteworthy difference in their physical hardware, might there also be a difference in their mental software? Could the gay brain come preloaded with its own special version of desire? And if so, what is the relationship between gay desire and longer penis length?

To answer these questions, let's take a look at a video from a popular Web site.

An attractive-looking guy is walking down the sidewalk. Suddenly, a black van pulls up. The door opens, and two hot girls smile out.

"Hey, you need a ride?" they chirp.

Seeing two luscious babes, the guy grins and nods and hops onto the backseat. The girls sit on either side of him and immediately comment on his manly physique.

"Ooh, you work out, don't you?"

The driver, a bald-headed young man in sunglasses, asks where he's going.

"Across town," replies the guest, eyeing the girls. "But I'm in no hurry."

In the passenger seat is another young man whom the girls introduce as "a friend" before starting to massage the lucky guy's arms and thighs. After a couple minutes of giggling, they remove their shirts and urge him to follow suit. He does so eagerly. They kiss and stroke him, observing that he's rising to the occasion. They get his pants off and lock eyes with him.

"Do you want us to use our mouth?"

The guy nods yes, yes, yes.

"Well, okayyy . . . but we're going to blindfold you, because we don't want you to watch!"

The guy nods yes, yes, yes. Giggling and teasing, the two girls tie a black silk blindfold over his eyes. He feels someone kneel between his legs. A moment later, the lucky guy is moaning with pleasure.

Suddenly, the blindfold is torn off. The guy looks down.

"What the hell!?"

Kneeling between his legs is "the friend" from the passenger seat.

"Welcome to Bait Bus!"

All the videos on the paysite Bait Bus follow the same structure.

Two gay men drive around looking for attractive straight guys to coax into the van, using pretty young women as "the bait." Then, after the women trick the guy out of his clothes, the producer offers him hundreds of dollars if he'll let a gay man continue to perform fellatio on him. Bait Bus is modeled after the heterosexual porn site Bang Bus, which features pornographers who drive around Southern California picking up girls and offering them money to have sex in the van. But what's so interesting about Bait Bus isn't that the target is a guy—it's the fact that he's *straight*.

Straight men are the fifth most popular category of gay sites on the Alexa Adult List. On Broke Straight Boys, young men who are "very hot and very straight" show their naked bodies to the camera in return for a few hundred dollars. In First Auditions, straight guys are told they're auditioning for a heterosexual porn movie, but instead end up spreading their legs for a gay audience. In a video series on Treasure Island Media, straight men sit on a sofa watching heterosexual porn while a gay man licks their nether regions. The Web site Gay Hazing depicts fictional fraternities that haze their straight freshmen pledges by duping them into receiving fellatio from a man or inserting sex toys in their backsides. Straight Hell goes even further, portraying the fictional blackmail of straight men into having abusive sex with other men; for example, one straight man who borrows money to pay for his wedding ends up having to repay his gay lenders by getting gagged, bound, whipped, and penetrated by several men. Many sites simply offer candid shots of straight men collected from Facebook, MySpace, and other social media sites, such as Guys with iPhones, Straight Boy Galleries, and College Dudes 24/7.

In terms of stimulating gay arousal, it really *matters* if a guy is gay or straight. On gay forums, there are frequent and lengthy discussions of whether a purportedly straight actor who appears on a gay site like Broke Straight Boys is truly gay-for-pay or just plain gay. These discussions often manifest the same heated analysis as straight men's discussion of whether a particular porn actress has authentic orgasms. "Peter North isn't really straight, dude, he did gay porn in the 90s." "Hey, does anybody know if the yummy redhead on the latest Dirty Tony is really gay-for-pay?"

So why are straight guys so appealing to gay men? Because gay men are attracted to *masculinity*. Though this may seem somewhat obvious—doesn't being gay mean you like men?—there is a common misconception that gay men are attracted to partners who are feminine and flamboyant. The briefest glance at gay porn sites would quickly dispel this notion. The vast majority of gay men prefer to masturbate while thinking about cowboys, firemen, or David Beckham instead of drag queens, ballet dancers, or Elton John. On the television show *Glee*, the football player Finn and mohawked bad boy Puck are bigger turn-ons for gay men than the effeminate gay character Kurt. On *Ugly Betty*, gay men would much prefer to invite Betty's straight boss Daniel Meade into their bedroom than fashion reporter Suzuki St. Pierre.

Masculine professions dominate gay porn. There are military-oriented gay sites, such as AWOL Marines, Military Shorties, and Hooyah Fags. The slogan of MilitaryJerkoff.com is "Don't ask, don't tell . . . just suck my dick, bro" and features straight American soldiers masturbating for the camera. Firemen and policemen are popular roles in gay porn, as are thugs, construction workers, and jocks.

On Thor and Rocco, the blog of a fortysomething married gay couple, Thor narrates his fantasy about the plumber who replaced the tiles in his shower. "This kid that is here now is so fucking hot. Yeah, he is definitely straight, but what I would give to blow him while his boss is out."

In order to dispel any possible ambiguities about the true sexual orientation of an actor, many gay men prefer to watch straight porn—a man having sex with a woman—since this offers indisputable proof of heterosexuality. "I only watch straight videos," explains one thirty-six-year-old gay man who has sex with multiple men every week. "I prefer gangbang porn, especially European porn, where there's a greater comfort with men being near other men's bodies. Just guys helping a buddy out. Of course, I never really look at the woman at the center of it . . ."

Recently, some Web sites have adapted to the gay interest in straight porn by offering heterosexual content specifically tailored to gay cues. Straight Guys for Gay Eyes and Next Door Hookups present heterosexual couples having sex. There's no doubting the actors are straight: there they are, making love to the ladies and loving it. For a straight man, watching the attentively crafted videos on Straight Guys for Gay Eyes is educational: these videos reveal the central importance of point of view in pornography, something that often goes unnoticed.

In porn targeted at heterosexual men, the woman is always the focus of the camera. We see her expressions, her emotions, the graphic details of her anatomy. We hear her moaning and watch her reaction when the disembodied man ejaculates on her. Other than the penis, the man's body and especially his face are rarely highlighted in contemporary porn. This "man's eye" point of view is a big reason why many women do not like pornography: it's usually shot in a manner designed to maximize activation of male visual cues and completely ignores the visual and psychological cues that appeal to women. In effect, a female viewer is compelled to "have sex" with the woman in the porn—and have sex with her as a man would.

On Straight Guys for Gay Eyes, the situation is completely reversed. Now the camera favors the man. The woman is an afterthought. Sometimes she doesn't even take off her shirt, while the man's shirt gets removed in the first few seconds. The woman herself is often silent, while the man moans or simply tells the girl how much he's enjoying himself. The emphasis is on *male* pleasure. The camera lovingly attends to the man's reactions and feelings, lingering on his brawny chest and arms, moving to a close-up of his butt and thighs as he pumps in and out of the woman. The male body is the center of attention. Perhaps as a result, many straight women report finding Straight Guys for Gay Eyes more arousing than other kinds of porn.

If you think about it, it's a little odd that a man's heterosexuality should be a cue that activates gay desire. If a guy has a hot body, shouldn't that be enough? "Sometimes you're watching a porn and the guy looks straight, like a real macho bad-ass, smoking hot," explains Rocco. "But then suddenly he lisps, 'Oooh, give me a good *th*ucking!' and just ruins the whole thing."

This suggests that gay desire does not solely target anatomical cues. If gay men are merely attracted to male bodies, they shouldn't care whether those bodies are inhabited by a straight mind or a gay mind or an androgynous mind. If anything, one would intuitively expect that gay men would be more aroused by a gay mind, since that would suggest that any attraction could be reciprocated. Instead, the gay sexual brain also hunts for the *psychological* cues associated with masculinity.

There are certainly many gay men who have a strong sexual preference for gay men over straight men. Gay men also fall head-over-heels in love and pursue long-term monogamous relationships with their partners. Gay desire is as varied as straight desire. But numerous studies have demonstrated that the gay interest in masculinity appears to be as fixed and inflexible as David/Brenda Reimer's unchangeable interest in women. Several decades of medical attempts at converting homosexual desire into heterosexual desire through conditioning, electroshock—or, in one case, directly stimulating a gay man's brain while he had sex with a female prostitute—have been notorious failures. The American Psychiatric Association officially opposes such ill-advised and ultimately unethical attempts at reprogramming gays' brain software because of their ineffectiveness and terrible side effects, which resemble the "psychological warfare" experienced by David Reimer.

It might be that by the time males are born, a binary "gender cue" in their brain software gets set to target either masculinity or femininity. There is some evidence that a neural network consisting of core regions in the human reward system may contain receptors for the gender cue. This fundamental, relatively inflexible gender cue then influences and organizes the other male cues—including the visual cues.

THE MALE GAZE

Women often complain that male porn objectifies women, reducing them to a crude collection of anatomical parts. The movie *Angel Eyes* is a useful example to consider.

Angel stands in front of two brutish guys. One ogles Angel's body and purrs, "Nice ass, mind if I squeeze it?" Angel shyly nods, and soon the two guys are probing and poking Angel's body as if it's a slab of meat on a butcher's block. "Great chest!" says the second guy, stroking his rough hands across Angel's nipples. A few minutes later, the two guys have Angel bent over a sofa, one in front, one in back, both pounding away. It's the kind of scene frequently used to demonstrate the misogyny of porn except for one thing.

Angel is a man.

If you're a straight guy, gay porn might be too squicky for you to watch. But if you did take a look (in the interests of science), you'd stand a very good chance of experiencing what many women experience when they watch porn: a feeling that it's *too graphic* with *way too many close-ups*. But if you managed to get past the squickiness, you might experience another feeling: déjà vu. Except for the fact that the male body is the star, gay porn looks and feels *exactly* like straight porn.

Gay porn features similar numbers of explicit anatomical close-ups. We looked at the one hundred top-rated video clips on Gaytube and found:

- 83 featured a graphic shot of a penis.
- 48 featured graphic shots of male butts.
- 46 featured graphic shots of a man's chest.

Like straight porn, gay porn typically jumps right into sex with little or no narrative preamble. Actors on gay tube sites are rarely identified by name; instead, sex is presented as a fast, anonymous, orgasm-focused tangle of bodies.

So what else do gay men want to see online? Below is a list of the seven most popular categories of gay sexual searches on the Dogpile search engine:

% of All Gay Sexual Searches	Popularity Ranking	Category	Example Search
6.2	1	*Youth*	"free twinks"
5.2	2	*Straight*	"straight guys paid to have gay sex"
2.2	3	*Mature*	"well-hung daddies"
2.0	4	*Black*	"hot black gay sex"
2.0	5	*Penises*	"gay college dicks"
.8	6	*Animation*	"gay hentai"
.7	7	*Domination/ Submission*	"gay bondage"

Except for *straight* (#2), every one of these gay interests is also a popular straight interest. In fact, virtually all of the genres of gay porn have a precise parallel in straight porn. *Youth* tops both lists by a large margin. Indeed, fully one-third of the hundred most popular gay sites on the Alexa Adult List feature young men. Within *youth*, gay porn has *twinks*, analogous to *teens* in straight porn. Twinks are young guys, typically college age, most often lean, athletic, with an all-American look and feel. Almost one-half of the hundred most popular gay porn sites feature young men, including Twink's Orgasms, King Twinks, and Cute Young Twinks. Every gay tube site features a twinks section.

Donald Symons explained that men have a preference for younger women, an assertion confirmed by Internet porn. Young women offer the best long-term opportunity for healthy children. But this evolutionary reasoning does not apply to gay desire: a sexual interest in young men will not lead to increased numbers of children. Thus, it seems very likely that gay men inherit the same brain software targeting youth cues as straight men. This male desire for youth contrasts with the sexual desires of women, who generally prefer that their partners be older and more experienced.

But gay men aren't exclusively interested in youth. Like straight men, a large minority of gay men can also be aroused by age and experience. Some gays seek out older men called *daddies*, paralleling the MILFs of straight porn. Also analogous to the tastes of straight men, gays prefer daddies who are confident and authoritative, who unapologetically seduce younger men. Like MILFs, daddies must be fit and physically attractive. And of course, a large penis is always welcome.

While straight men have a deep-rooted fascination with large penises, gay men are positively obsessed with them. There are hundreds of gay sites celebrating the penis, such as We Love Cock, Addicted to Cock, and Cock-n-Dick. The men in gay anime porn always have jumbo-sized members, drawn in a rainbow of bright colors. The famous gay erotic artist Tom of Finland drew men with thick, oversized organs. Many amateur gay sites simply feature collections of close-ups of penises, with no face or body visible, such as Cocks n' Balls ("No bull, just cocks"). There's even a common term for gay men obsessed with large members: "size queens."

Like straight men, gay men also search for heavy actors and models far more than skinny ones. Large gay men are typically referred to as *bears*, paralleling the BBW of straight porn. Bears are usually big, hairy, and older, with a warm and friendly personality. Sites like Lusty Bears, Gay Bear World, and Bear Forest feature explicit imagery of oversized men just like BBW sites feature oversized women. Scrawny boys are relatively more popular among gays than scrawny girls are among straight men, but still remain far less popular than bears.

Gay sites like Asian Boy Feet, Jock Foot Fantasy, and Barefoot Frat celebrate men's feet. Gay men, like straight men, can also become sexually aroused by other body parts or by cued interests in clothing, such as armpits (Armpits.com), saggy jeans (Saggers GoneWild.com), and socks (GaySocks.com). And, unlike women, gay men are also willing to pay money just to *look* at body parts.

Feet, butts, and chests are highly popular in both gay and straight porn, as are domination, submission, group sex, amateurs, and numerous types of squickier interests. With so many parallel interests, Internet porn suggests that gay men share the same visual cues as straight men. This fact overturns many common misconceptions about gay desire. Gay men are not looking for flamboyant, effeminate actors who are preening and emoting. Gay porn is not full of chatty conversation, Cher impersonators, or the elaborate analysis of feelings. Political messages are entirely absent. Instead, gay guys like the same things as straight guys: youth, aggressive and seductive maturity, graphic details of the body, large penises, ejaculation shots, and anonymous, emotionless, nonmonogamous sex.

But what about *psychological* cues? Do gay men share the same preferences expressed in the romance and fan fiction so appreciated by women? What can we learn about gay desire from erotic stories?

Below are two lists. The left column is a list of two-word phrases that appear most frequently in the stories on the all-gay site Nifty Erotic Stories Archive. The right column contains phrases that appear most frequently in the stories on Adult Fan Fiction. Each phrase includes a male pronoun, in order to offer a more accurate comparison of the way each genre handles men.

Most Common Words in Gay Male Erotica	Most Common Words in Women's Erotica
his hole	his gaze
his shorts	his lover
his butt	his teeth
his dad	his heart
his dick	he sighed
his big	his mind
his ass	his skin
his balls	he watched
his cock	he heard
his hard	his neck

There's no overlap in the lists. In gay erotica, there's a graphic emphasis on anatomy, especially penises and butts. In women's erotic fan fiction, there's an emphasis on feelings and softer qualities—*his gaze, his heart, he sighed, his lover.* Gay erotic stories feature little foreplay before jumping into sex: on average, sex appears about a quarter of the way into a gay story; in Harry Potter fan fiction, on the other hand, sex appears about halfway in. It's also worth observing that gay men are no more interested in romance novels than straight men are.

Gay brains appear to possess a gay Elmer Fudd: hunt, aim, fire, repeat. Psychologist Richard Lippa and the BBC conducted a massive international survey with more than 250,000 participants in forty-one nations. Everywhere, they found that both gay and straight men prefer appearance and visual attractiveness over all other qualities when selecting a partner. Another study put gay and straight men in a brain scanner and showed them pornographic videos. Their brain activity was strikingly similar, with comparable activation in the frontal cortex, visual cortex, and subcortex. But, strikingly, both gay and straight brains exhibited different patterns of activation from women's brains.

But gay men don't just *like* the same kind of porn as straight men. They *use* it the same way. In fact, you could even say that gays guys act more like men than straight guys do. Gay men watch more porn, have larger porn stashes, search for more porn online, subscribe to porn sites more often, maintain more subscriptions at the same time, and renew their subscriptions more often. They're more comfortable talking about porn than straight men—and are more tolerant of their partners watching porn than women are. "When you're in a gay relationship, you're both guys, so you understand exactly what's up with the porn," explains a thirty-two-year-old gay man. "It's no big deal. In fact, it's really hot to find your partner watching something good."

Not all gay men like porn and some disapprove of their partners watching it, of course. Generally, however, gay men are free to seek out visual content that satisfies their erotic interests without facing the obstacles sometimes imposed by the female partners of straight men. The adult industry recognizes the financial power of their gay audience. "Gay men are much clearer about what they want, and much more loyal to Web sites that give them what they want," explains the vice president of one company that runs a dozen gay paysites. "You get a smaller audience with a gay site than with many of the vanilla straight sites, but you'll also get more conversions and renewals. It's also easier to generate word of mouth, since gay men are more likely to talk about their favorite sites than straight men."

What percentage of all AOL users search for gay content? About one and a half percent.

After comparing gay porn to straight porn (and considering the tragedy of David/Brenda Reimer), it appears that a preference for masculinity or femininity is preloaded into the male brain as a gender cue. This preference is *not* limited to the physical aspects of a body, since many gay men are especially aroused by straight men. In addition, the gay brain seems to be loaded with the same visual desire software as the straight brain—except that the gay visual cues target *male* bodies instead of *female* bodies.

Thus, it seems likely that the gender cue organizes and influences the visual cues during a critical period in puberty and adolescence. But how does the gender cue control the visual cues? What causes straight guys to become obsessed with large breasts and round butts, while gay men become obsessed with brawny chests and rock-hard butts?

How does the male visual desire software actually work?

THE BODY MAP

The anatomical parts that are searched for the most by gay men, referenced most frequently in gay porn, and referenced most often in gay erotica are: chests, butts, feet, and penises. What's so intriguing about this list is that it parallels the anatomical parts most favored by straight men: breasts, butts, feet, and penises. (The vagina is also exceedingly popular.)

But how might the male brain tell its owner which body parts to look at? You might guess that the male brain is born with a visual template for what an ideal breast looks like, the way you might find an image attached to an e-mail. According to this view, a young man simply consults this mental image to determine what he should look for. But the fact that gay men seek out firm, fit chests instead of soft, round breasts poses a problem for this view. Though it's theoretically possible for evolution to have endowed the male brain with an innate portrait of the ideal breast, it's theoretically impossible for evolution to have designed a gay-brain-only template for a man's ideal chest.

Furthermore, though most men have an interest in breasts, the ideal breast varies dramatically across cultures. Indeed, the physical color, size, areola, and shape of breasts varies with ethnicities, too. It's difficult to imagine how the human brain would come wired with a standard template for breasts that applies across all ethnicities and cultures. We saw how the male brain appears to have a critical period during which the physical details of an ideal breast get set. But how does the male brain know to seek out breasts to begin with?

Scientists have not yet come up with any good answer to this question. No neuroscientist has conducted research intended to identify the neural wiring responsible for men's sexual fascination with particular body parts. But there's enough interesting clues that we can speculate how it *might* work.

One possibility is that men's desire software comes loaded with a sensitivity to "regions of interest"—namely, breasts, feet, butts, and genitals. The brain knows *where* to look, rather than *what* to look for. But doesn't this "regions of interest" proposal suffer from the same problem as the idea of a breast template? Namely, how does the brain know *where* to look? One possibility is that male receptivity to female anatomical the body cues are linked to the male brain's *body map*.

Our brain has several different neural networks that contain mental representations of the body. For example, our somatosensory cortex contains a map of our body based upon our sense of touch. Another part of our brain that processes visual images of bodies is known as the extrastriate body area or EBA. The EBA is activated when looking at the bodies of other people—including individual body parts—but not when looking at faces or objects. Intriguingly, when scientists activated this brain region using a technique called transcranial magnetic stimulation (blasting a brain region with a magnetic field that causes its neurons to fire), subjects altered their aesthetic judgment of body parts.

There is very strong evidence that these body maps are innate. One dramatic example is a strange condition in people who are born without arms or legs, yet can still "feel" the missing arm or leg. This experience of an absent body part is known as a *phantom limb*. Various psychological tests demonstrate that these congenital phantom limbs are anatomically accurate (for example, the owners cannot imagine them doing impossible movements) and are not just the result of "wishful thinking" from watching other people. It appears our mind has its own body map that forms independently of our physical body.

If the male desire software wanted to know what parts of a potential mate's body to target, it could use the brain's body map as a reference point. Perhaps the chest, buttocks, and foot regions of the body map are prewired to subcortical sexual reward centers. Though this is speculative, there are some intriguing clues that support this possibility. First, there is another body map disorder known as body integrity image disorder (BIID) that causes some people to want to amputate their limbs. BIID is the opposite of a phantom limb—these people have a real limb, but it doesn't seem to match their mental representation of the limb, so they want to get rid of it. The first recorded case involved an Englishman who forced a French surgeon at gunpoint to cut off the Englishman's healthy leg. What's so intriguing is that many men who suffer from BIID feel a strong sexual component to their desire for amputation. (Though women also suffer from BIID, they experience sexual feelings must less frequently than men.)

Another piece of evidence is that blind men are aroused by female anatomy, and even seem to prefer the same low waist-to-hip ratio that sighted people do. They also report being aroused by touching breasts and buttocks.

But one of the most intriguing sources of support for the notion that male visual cues activate regions of interest in the brain's body map comes from Syracuse psychologist Stephanie Ortigue. In 2007, Ortigue examined the brain of a thirty-four-year-old man with a very unusual sexual interest. Ortigue dubbed it the "Sleeping Beauty" fetish.

"He was aroused by sleeping women. For a while, his wife voluntarily took sleeping pills to satisfy his desire, but eventually she refused," explains Ortigue. "So he began secretly giving her benzodiazepines, Bromazepam. When she found out, she was furious. But since the man's compulsion was so strong, he put on a latex mask and waited for her to leave work, then sprayed her with pepper spray, apparently intending to put her to sleep. She fought him off, called the police, and that's how he ended up in the emergency psychiatric unit."

But as fascinating as the man's sleeping fetish was, there was more. The man was fixated on hands and feet. The reason he wanted his wife to sleep was so that he could paint and manicure her toenails and fingernails, then masturbate.

Ortigue's team scanned the man's brain using MRI. They discovered lesions in a part of the brain associated with body image. The man also suffered from "personal representational hemineglect": he had an incomplete mental image of his hands. When asked to draw a picture of himself, his arms trailed off into nothingness. The fact that he preferred the hands and feet of sleeping women suggests that he was sexually attracted to disembodied (but living) limbs—an almost exact complement to the sexual desire to amputate one's own limb.

If men's visual cues originate as erotic regions of interest linked to a neural body map, this could explain why gay men are interested in brawny chests and straight men are interested in busty chests. All men instinctively know they should pay attention to chests. But what *kind* of chest should they pay attention to? Perhaps the gender cue plays an important role in this process. If a man is born with the gender cue set to femininity, this cue instructs the regions of interest cues to look for the relevant anatomy on women. If a man's gender cue is set to masculinity, this cue instructs the brain to look at the relevant anatomy on men.

This flexibility in setting the visual cues would also explain why men are interested in such a variety of breasts and chests. Men aren't born liking double-Ds. Instead, the region of interest cue guides a man to examine the chests in the particular environment in which a man finds himself. A feminine gender cue targets female chests. But other fundamental cues might also influence the region of interest cues. For example, the youth cue may guide the chest cue to target *young* female chests. The brain then surveys the available young female chests in the environment to generate its template for an ideal chest.

In this view, culture does play an essential role in determining the exact form of a man's visual cues. This may be one reason that the butt preferences of Latinos and Africans are notably different from the butt preferences of the Japanese and Irish. All men have an innate interest in butts, but the precise kind of butt varies from culture to culture, depending on women's (and men's) bodies in the particular culture, as well as the culture-specific way they are presented.

So far we've only focused on the visual cues that arouse gay men and straight men. But what about psychological cues? Might gay men prefer the same *psychological* cues favored by women?

TOPS AND BOTTOMS

For the past fifteen years, the psychologist Paul Vasey has been studying Japanese macaques, two-and-a-half-foot-tall, pink-faced monkeys. Vasey has been trying to solve a rather intriguing puzzle. Why do some female macaques mount other females during the mating season, the same way males do? At first, Vasey believed that perhaps parts of these females' brains had somehow been masculinized. He thought that their "female software" had somehow been converted into "male software." But when he took a look at their brains, he found that they looked completely female. So he came to a different conclusion about females mounting females.

"It isn't functional. The behavior has no discernible purpose, adaptationally speaking," explains Vasey. "Instead, it's a byproduct of other behavioral mechanisms." The "other behavioral mechanisms" include the brain software for mounting, a typically male behavior. But if the female macaques' brains were typically female, then where did the male behavior come from? In other words, how was "male software" running in a female brain? One possible answer can be found in the brains of another mammal, the rat.

Male and female rats express very different behaviors during sex. The males are dominant, the females are submissive. The male rat is an aggressive stalker, a rodent Elmer Fudd hunting wats instead of wabbits. He looks around for a suitable female, and once he spots one, he takes control. He grabs her around her hips and vigorously thrusts away—a mechanical process of mounting called *intromission*.

The female is more coy. She paces: she runs away from the pursuing male in a series of short dashes. If the male can match her pacing, she will eventually halt and assume a submissive position, thrusting her hips into the air and waiting. This mechanical process is called *lordosis*. Software in the subcortex of the male brain controls intromission. Different software in the subcortex of the female brain controls lordosis. But researchers have discovered something very interesting about this complementary software.

It's possible to make a dominant male behave like a submissive female. How? By stimulating the same part of the subcortex that controls lordosis in females. Using drugs or an electrode, you can elicit lordosis in male rats by activating the ventromedial hypo-thalamus. In other words, *male rat brains naturally contain female sexual software.*

Similarly, if you stimulate a specific part of the female rat brain, you can elicit mounting and hip-thrusting behavior. *The female rat brain naturally contains male sexual software.* Perhaps this is also what's going on with Vasey's female-mounting female macaques: these females are simply accessing the naturally occurring male sexual software.

This choice is very salient in gay men. When gay men have sex, there are two complementary roles: the "top" and the "bottom." Usually the bottom is penetrated by the top, though often the bottom simply performs fellatio on the top. Most gay men eventually come to favor one role over the other. Since most heterosexual men prefer the dominant role in their sexual relations with women, we might speculate that most gay men would also prefer to be tops. After all, we've seen how gay men share the same visual cues as straight men; perhaps they share the same psychological cues, such as the desire to be dominant. At the very least, we might expect that gay men would balance their top and bottom roles, "pitching" and "catching" in relatively equal proportions over their lifetime. However, both of these assumptions are wrong. Most gay men prefer to be bottoms.

"Tops have it so easy," muses one thirty-seven-year-old bottom. "All you need to do is walk into a bar and flex your pecs and a dozen bottoms will throw themselves at you." Online data supports the widespread belief in the gay community that there are more bottoms than tops.

We analyzed 1.9 million men-seeking-men ads on Craigslist that were posted in every major city in the United States in the spring of 2010. These are classified ads that gay men typically use to seek casual sex. Sixty-five percent of the ads were from bottoms seeking tops, and 35 percent of the ads were from tops seeking bottoms. In other words, about two-thirds of American gay men who seek casual sex prefer the more submissive role.

Gay porn is heavily dominated by bottoms. However, though tops are rare, they are the biggest stars with the biggest fan bases and the biggest paychecks. The most successful gay porn stars, such as Jeff Stryker, Wilson Vasquez, Rex Chandler (straight), and Michael Lucas, are all tops. One reason that tops are so valued in gay porn is because they are more straight-acting than bottoms, by virtue of the fact that they are playing the dominant role. In porn, tops are usually taller, more fit, and more dominant than bottoms. In the movie *Thug Home Invasion*, the thug played by Kamrun is a confident, masculine top who penetrates two uncertain, more effeminate men after he breaks into their house. If a straight guy appears in gay porn, he's always the top unless it's a genre that's specifically devoted to forcing straight guys to have penetrative gay sex, such as *Straight Hell*.

Tops rarely get aroused by being sexually submissive, and they identify with the dominant role when they watch domination/submission porn. One forty-five-year-old gay man, who frequently meets men through Craigslist, gives one perspective on what it's like to be a top. "I'm not going to suck any dick, I'm nobody's bitch," he explains. "One of my favorite things is when married straight guys I work with say they want to see what it's like to be with a guy, but don't want anybody to find out. They figure I'm a safe way to try it out. They usually get drunk first, then I fuck them. Sometimes they start crying like a girl. They say, 'oh this was a huge mistake.' But it's always been fun for me."

Most gay porn stories are written from the point of view of the bottom. This is apparent from looking at the possessive pronouns in the three most common five-word phrases in the gay stories on Literotica.

a cock in my mouth

his cock back into my

out of my ass and

So does being a bottom mean a person *enjoys* being sexually submissive? The answer is complicated. "The bottom is really in control," explains one twenty-four-year-old middle school teacher. "He sets the pace, he's the gatekeeper. Think of a woman—she's the one that ultimately chooses what's going to happen and what's not going to happen." Rocco adds, "The bottom willingly puts himself into the position to be dominated." This desire for "submissive control" is reflected in Craigslist ads, such as this ad from a bottom: "Looking for top. Must enjoy and appreciate the cocksucking I will give." Though most gay men agree that the bottom is actually the one who dictates the terms of sex, much as the female rat controls sex through pacing and lordosis, they also agree on something else: "Nobody likes a bossy bottom."

"This one guy kept throwing up demands: stand like this, move like this, do this. It was like I was his personal dildo," explains one very tall thirty-eight-year-old top. "I just wanted him to take it like a man, that's why I told him to come over. So I threw him out." Though the top is typically more dominant, sometimes he simply sits back and passively lets the bottom service him. "Looking for bottom to suck my dick and eat my cum while I watch TV," runs one top's ad on Craigslist.

In other words, getting aroused by being sexually submissive does not seem to be identical with being a bottom, though they're clearly related. "I hook up with a lot of guys off Craigslist," continues the tall top. "Once in a while you get a guy that says, 'Beat me, hit me, piss on me, call me a little slut.' Most bottoms aren't like that, but there's a few that really get off on being degraded."

Out of more than a million Craigslist men-seeking-men ads, only about 2 percent of them specifically requested men willing to dominate another man sexually, above and beyond the usual call of a top. Most bottoms simply want to perform fellatio or receive anal sex—and they want to control what happens. "I'm a bottom and I can tell you I would never want to feel like I'm being humiliated or sexually degraded," explains a twenty-six-year-old Latino man.

"I get off on the pleasure I'm giving to the top. I mean, if a top wanted to call me a little slut, I'd probably enjoy it just because it's sexy talk, but if he tried to tie me up or pee on me or something, I'd throw his ass out."

Most of the time, straight men are aroused by cues of domination, while women are aroused by cues of submission—as seen by the irresistibility cue and the prevalence of female coercion fantasies. But the majority of gay men also seem to favor cues of submissiveness (though most don't appear to respond to irresistibility cues).

If human brains are like rat and macaque brains and contain both male sexual dominance software and female submission software, perhaps the same factors that cause a gay man's gender cue to get set to masculinity also tends to activate a gay man's female submission software.

BORN WITH GAY SOFTWARE

In many ways, gay men seem to live a sexual life that straight men can only fantasize about. If you're heterosexual and male, imagine that at any moment, day or night, you could press a button on your iPhone to see an array of attractive women you've never met before. Then, you could pick the one that struck your fancy and, within five minutes, get together with her. Two out of three times, she will just want to perform fellatio on you, then leave. She's delighted to do it, and it doesn't cost you a penny. This may sound like an impossible fantasy, but this experience is actually available to gay men right now, through Grindr.

Grindr is an iPhone application that displays photos and profile information of all other men using Grindr who are within about three thousand feet, making it easy to get in touch with potential sex partners. "I've met up with a guy in the backseat of his Lexus during my lunch hour," says one thirty-one-year-old Grindr user who works in the Boston Financial District. Grindr is a technological innovation that facilitates the casual, anonymous sex that has long been the fantasy of straight men, but is commonplace among gay men.

Of course, gay men—like straight men—also pursue a "mixed mating strategy." Gay men look for romance and long-term monogamous relationships. Gay men get their hearts broken, get married, and raise children. Like straight men, gay men cheat on their partners and get enraged when their partners cheat on them. In Richard Lippa's BBC survey, he found that the preferred traits in a partner clustered together based upon the *gender* of the subject—not by nationality, and not by sexual orientation. In almost every way, the brain software of gay men appears to be identical to that of straight men.

But as we've seen, there are at least two crucial differences: gay men prefer masculinity, and many (but not all) gay men prefer the submissive role in sex. Both of these preferences are standard in the female brain. Something apparently causes two specific parts of the male desire software to "flip" to female settings, while keeping all of the other male settings. There's also a physical difference between gay and straight men: gay men have longer penises. Is there anything that could possibly cause all three of these differences? It turns out there is: *fetal hormones*.

In the adult brain, androgens ("male hormones") and estrogens (the "female hormones") each control the activity of the brain software involved in several different tasks, including male competition, female ovulation, and sexual arousal in both men and women. But they also play a very important role in *constructing* the brain—and the body.

In the second trimester, the presence or absence of the sex hormones instructs the cells of a fetus to build certain physical structures, such as a penis or ovaries. They influence the growth of fingers and can establish the physiological foundation for male pattern baldness. But they also trigger a cascade of complicated events in the growing brain, influencing the growth and connectivity of neurons.

Though scientists initially suspected that a reduction of testosterone in the third trimester might be responsible for the "feminization" of the gay brain, scientists now understand that things aren't so simple. In fact, an excess of testosterone may ultimately be responsible. Since testosterone can get converted into estrogren, and since there are some parts of the fetal brain that testosterone cannot enter, it seems more likely that some parts of the gay brain are "hypermasculinized" and some parts are "feminized."

It may be that excessive androgens cause gay men to have longer penises and become attracted to masculinity. It might also be the case that even higher amounts of androgens are correlated with changes in the desire software that cause gay men to prefer the bottom role. Intriguingly, in our limited survey of gay men, we noticed an interesting pattern that supports this notion.

Tops were the most straight-acting and did not present any behaviors associated with the Detective Agency—and they anecdotally reported to us that, in their opinion, bottoms had the largest penises. Bottoms generally exhibited behaviors associated with the Detective Agency (such as heightened emotional sensitivity, extended social networking, and a focus on determining how other men "really felt"), yet in most bottoms this Detective Agency did not appear to govern their sexual desire as it does in women—these bottoms sought out anonymous, emotionless sexual encounters. In other words, this gay Detective Agency was not hooked up to his sexual circuits.

However, a minority of bottoms were extremely female-acting, and these men seemed to possess a Detective Agency that governed sexual desire as it does in women. They needed to get to know the personality of a man before hooking up with him, they were not especially attracted to straight men, they believed that whether someone was a bottom or top was entirely socially determined, and they questioned the very existence of the top/

bottom binary—even though they themselves were quite clearly power bottoms. Perhaps future research might determine whether this group of gay men possesses the largest penises of all.

But despite these dramatic alterations, it appears that excessive androgens leave most of the male brain unchanged. Boys will be boys. Even when they like other boys.

CHAPTER 8

A Tall Man with a Nice Tush
Female Visual Cues

I think I might like that.
—Mrs. Alfred Kinsey, upon being asked if she would
like to have sex with her husband's graduate student
in the film *Kinsey*

In the early 1970s, nightclub owner Douglas Lambert had a pioneering idea. He observed that even though there was a flood of men's magazines featuring nude models, like *Penthouse*, *Hustler*, and *Playboy*, there wasn't a single nude magazine for women. Moreover, *Cosmopolitan* magazine was flying off the shelves. He saw an opportunity to combine *Cosmo* and *Playboy* into a single package. So he founded *Playgirl*.

Sounding somewhat like a gender activist instead of the owner of three strip clubs, he proclaimed: "Women have been suppressed sexually for too long. It's healthy for people to view a male body." Lambert hired Marin Scott Milam, a self-described "moderate feminist," to serve as editor in chief. Milam believed that the absence of nude magazines for women reflected the false assumption that only men enjoyed visual stimulation. "Women want to see more male nudes. They love it," she reported enthusiastically, though adding, "I think it's true that women do not accept male nudity in magazines with alacrity. It's a learning process and women are reacting against years of conditioning."

Playgirl was the mirror image of *Playboy*, complete with graphic, high-quality pictures of naked men (though there were no penises in the very first issue, and no erect penises for several years) and a centerfold—the 1973 preview issue featured the Hager twins, Jim and John, from the country variety show *Hee Haw*. Since all the models were selected by women for women, one might have confidently predicted that the magazine would have appealed to female sexual tastes. But things turned out a little differently.

At first, the number of subscriptions to *Playgirl* was a small fraction of subscriptions to *Playboy*, despite the fact that *Playboy* occupied a crowded field of competitors whereas *Playgirl* had a near-monopoly. In fact, the "Magazine for Women" might have gone out of business in its first year, if not for an unexpected set of customers. Here's the AOL search history of one such customer, user #4416126:

gay frat stories

gay drunk college

gay college

nude photos of men

heath ledger nude—playgirl

playgirl magazine

teen male twinks

shower room guys

straight guys

justin timberlake

signs of homosexuality

Though gay men had their own pornographic magazines, like *Mandate* and *David*, *Playgirl* was easier to buy and featured the kind of models gay men prefer—straight guys. In 1999, former *Playgirl* editor in chief Claire Harth admitted the truth:

> Ever since *Playgirl*'s launch in the early '70s, its full-frontal male nudes and steamy copy have attracted an avid gay following. During my time at the magazine, I was constantly aware of the dual nature of *Playgirl*'s sex appeal and the delicate balancing act involved in maintaining its reputation as "Entertainment for Women." The *Playgirl* staff was well aware that we owed much of our 400,000 circulation to gay men. And while we tailored the magazine to a supposedly heterosexual sensibility, we made certain to keep an eye on our loyal male readers.

Though Playgirl.com doesn't feature homosexual acts, its advertising consists primarily of gay sites and penis pumps. Few enterprises have attempted to duplicate *Playgirl*'s business model of nude men for women's pleasure. Titmowse, an adult industry veteran who runs her own resource site for adult webmasters known as Cozy Frog, asserts, "In my 11 years in this business I could count on one hand the number of successful porn for women paysites and after counting I would have three fingers left."

Men often wonder if women prefer soft-core or hard-core porn, or if they prefer girl-on-girl scenes to girl-on-guy scenes. Men ask other men for tips on which porn sites will get their girlfriends hot and bothered. The psychology-focused Detective Agency and *Playgirl*'s failed tryst with women seem to suggest that these questions may be fundamentally misguided.

"Porn is incredibly DULL DULL DULL," laments Isabel, a middle-age woman commenting on Salon.com. "I watched porn made by women, and it was still DULL DULL DULL." Many women find porn unarousing. Others, however, find it downright offensive. "Pornography is the theory, rape the practice," the feminist Robin Morgan famously wrote in 1974, the same year as *Playgirl*'s first full year in print. More than three decades later, sentiments have softened only slightly. In 2010, porn star Ron Jeremy debated antiporn feminist activist Susan Cole at the University of Nebraska. Cole argued that pornography is "not only bad for the people who make it but damaging to society as a whole" and "corrupting of individual sexuality." Also in 2010, Apple banned porn applications from its iPhone. Apple explained, "It came to the point where we were getting customer complaints from women who found the content getting too degrading and objectionable."

So can one safely say that women do not become aroused by graphic sex? Not necessarily. The magazine *Today's Christian Woman* conducted a survey of its readers, and found that a third of them seek out Internet porn. Chief technology officer for Porn-Hub, Perry Stathopoulos, estimates that about a third of its visitors are women. In order to cater to its female audience, PornHub has recently changed its tagline from "It Makes Your Dick Bigger" to the more equal-opportunity "It Makes Your Dick Bigger and Your Pussy Wet." PornHub also initiated the new category, *female friendly*, for videos designed to appeal to women. The selection process for inclusion in this category isn't very scientific, however. A group of women who work in the Montreal office sit together and democratically decide which content merits the pink Venus symbol. The fact is, the tastes of the minority of women who enjoy porn are very hard to pin down.

Here is the abbreviated three-month AOL search history for a female fan of porn, Ms. Juicy:

porn for women

drunk galleries

explicit erotica pictures

juicy gals

explicit movie sex scenes

fucking pictures

erotica for women

drunk springbreak sex

erotic fine art photography

explicit movie stills

x-rated fine art

erotic photography

explicit movie sex scene pictures

pictures of lust

springbreak fuck adventures

washing machine ratings

This searcher avoids using the word "porn" except when qualified by "for women," but clearly does not shy away from seeking out explicit material. Nevertheless, her sexual searches contain the word "erotic" far more often than the sexual searches of a typical male, and she also focuses on erotic "fine art" and "photography." Intriguingly, she even looks for images of desire—"pictures of lust." But these soft-core searches are interspersed with more edgy desires—"drunk galleries" and "springbreak fuck adventures."

Why do some women enjoy visual porn, while most do not, even though most women respond to visual cues? To answer this question, we'll start by exploring a unique component of women's desire software that is even more basic than the Miss Marple Detective Agency.

LADY JEKYLL AND MS. HYDE

Women can only conceive during five days of their ovulatory cycle. Yet women are unique among female mammals in their willingness to have sex every day of their cycle, including *all* nonfertile days. Biologists call a willingness to have sex during nonfertile periods *extended sexuality*.

Among many species, extended sexuality is favored by natural selection because it allows females to trade sex for resources from men. For example, female chimpanzees exhibit a red sexual swelling on their rump for about twelve days during each ovulatory cycle. However, they can only conceive during three days. During the nine days when they have no chance of getting pregnant, female chimps actively solicit sex from males. In fact, though males solicit sex during the entire time a female has a sexual swelling, the female chimps actually initiate *more* sex and are *less* resistant to male solicitations on days of low fertility. They're more sexually active when they *can't* get pregnant, in other words. What do the females get in return for this promiscuity? Food, protection, and perhaps most important, a reduction in the males' aggression toward the females' offspring.

For many years, it was believed that the sexual swellings and bright red butts of female primates signaled fertility (ovulation) to males. But contemporary scientists realized that males need no special prompting to initiate sex. As comedian Mitch Fatel put it, "When it comes to sex, men have the secret ingredient. But unlike any other secret ingredient, we'll give it to anyone who asks." Instead, female ornamentation—such as chimps' bright butts and women's round breasts—evolved to benefit females. Female ornamentation garners attention and resources from males.

Extended sexuality generates a fascinating pattern of behavior in females. Women and their cross-species sisters have two distinct "modes" of sexual interests during their ovulatory cycle. Each mode favors a different set of erotic cues: *short-term interests* during ovulation and *long-term interests* when not ovulating. Most of the time, Miss Marple behaves like a long-term portfolio manager, looking for clues indicating the probable return on investment for investing in a man. When a woman is not ovulating, she prefers men who are willing and able to provide nongenetic benefits, such as food, protection, and child support.

But during ovulation, Miss Marple can become a day trader. Now she gives special preference to males with superior genes, in the form of good looks and social dominance. In women, the sexual cues emphasized during each mode reflect this dual sexuality: visual and physical cues during ovulation, and the Detective Agency's psychological cues when not ovulating.

Female marmosets, Tasmanian devils, and kangaroos all prefer males with superior genes when fertile, but mate less selectively during infertile phases. Though female chimps are highly promiscuous and mate with relatively subordinate males when they can't conceive, they mate much more selectively and strongly favor socially dominant males when they can conceive. Macaques also repeat this pattern: female rhesus macaques who are ovulating prefer males whose faces have been experimentally manipulated to reveal exaggerated red coloration, a testosterone-facilitated male sexual ornament that signals social dominance.

Ovulating women demonstrate a stronger preference for men with masculine faces, masculine voices, and masculine scents, and who display conspicuous signals of social dominance. They also tend to flirt more, dress more provocatively, and express greater interest in going out to bars, clubs, and socializing. One study even found that ovulating women tend to move around more, as if maximizing exposure to new opportunities. Ovulating women express a greater awareness of personal safety and are more likely to avoid risky places. They also exhibit a greater aversion to squicky sex, such as bestiality and incest. Put simply, ovulating women seek out conventional sex with alpha males.

One intriguing study examined the effects of ovulation on the tips that professional lap dancers received while working in gentlemen's clubs. Women with normal ovulatory cycles earned about $185 when they were menstruating, $260 when they were not menstruating nor ovulating, and $335 when they were ovulating. Perhaps the increase in tips was because the dancers unconsciously behaved differently.

When women are not ovulating, they prefer men with more feminized faces. Female steroid hormones such as progesterone appear to drive this shift in attraction: women who are pregnant or using hormonal contraception share the same sexual interests as nonovulating women. It's important to note that nonovulating women do not *ignore* indicators of good genes, but rather the Detective Agency balances physical attraction with many other psychological cues relevant to long-term prospects. Women are always attracted to a physically sexy man, in other words, but they're more likely to actually have sex with him when they might get pregnant. The rest of the time, the Detective Agency decides whether it's worth it to hold out for a hot guy who's *also* sweet.

Women's dual sexuality is indirectly captured in the comments of one woman on Salon.com, who offered, "George Clooney and Sean Connery are sex symbols, but Bill Gates (younger, richer, and more powerful than either of them) is not. Our chances are abysmal for marrying any of the above men. That being the case, of course we're going to fantasize about the good-looking ones, because all we're thinking about is sex. If we were contemplating who to marry and had a choice from among them, that would change things considerably."

Research has found that when ovulating, women in long-term relationships are also more likely to express an interest in an affair. It's not that a woman's attraction to her primary partner goes up and down across the cycle; it appears to be fairly steady. Instead, when a woman is ovulating, her attraction to *other* men goes *up*. One British study asked women to keep diaries of their sexual activity. Married women were significantly more likely to have sex with an outside partner during ovulation. When cheating on a primary partner, women expressed the desire that their lover possess sexiness, sensuality, physical attractiveness, and that he be highly desired by other women. In addition, women focused on sexual gratification—especially orgasms.

If women are more likely to seek affairs when ovulating, have men developed an evolutionary countermeasure? Yes. Studies have shown that men are more protective and guard their mates more during ovulation. But women have evolved counter-countermeasures to combat men's heightened surveillance. When ovulating, women more frequently resist men's efforts to track their activities. All of these ovulation-related behaviors—such as dressing more provocatively and resisting men's surveillance—may occur without a woman's conscious awareness. The unconscious shifts in desire may be designed to prevent her from accidentally betraying her intentions to her long-term partner. Similarly, most women lack conscious awareness of their ovulations, another countermeasure designed to prevent men from discerning when a woman is truly fertile.

The Detective Agency operates most of the time in the female brain to evaluate prospective long-term mates using both psychological and visual cues, giving preference to psychological cues. During ovulation, the Detective Agency still functions, but it appears to increase its valuation of visual cues. In fact, studies have shown that women show a greater interest in visual sexual material if they were first exposed to the material when they were ovulating.

So what visual cues arouse the female brain?

SSSH!

Sssh.com (pronounced "shoosh" to rhyme with "push") is one of only two commercial porn sites that have been able to turn a profit while targeting heterosexual women. One could even argue it's the only successful porn Web site to *exclusively* target heterosexual women, since its main competitor, For the Girls, does attract some gay men, though in much smaller numbers than *Playgirl*.

Sssh was founded by Angie Rowntree in 1995, when 9600 baud modems were the norm and America Online charged an hourly fee for Internet access. Angie, who could pass for a lively, lovable aunt from an Enid Blyton novel, was initially motivated by the same impulse as *Playgirl*'s Marin Scott Milam. "Why do the guys get all the fun? Women like sex, too. I knew there had to be a market for an erotic site for women." But though she shared the same vision as Milam, Angie took Sssh in a different direction. "I used mainstream women's magazines like *Cosmopolitan*, *Redbook*, and *Elle* as my model, rather than *Playboy* or anything else. I wanted to create *Cosmo* with balls."

Unlike *Playgirl* magazine, Sssh is filled with articles on health, diet, and sexual how-to's. It includes a very active forum where women can chat with one another. There is a stable of men, ranging in age from their twenties to their fifties, who answer subscribers' questions about male sexuality. Sssh contains horoscopes, beauty tips, video tutorials on topics such as how to do a striptease, and erotic stories. It also features pornographic videos.

"We've listened to what women wanted to see, and over time we've gotten pretty good at it," says Angie proudly, commenting on her fifteen years of experience. "Women want to see foreplay, a lot of kissing, a lot of talking before the action gets going. They like to see women with a little more weight on them, a little older, not skinny young girls. The guys have to be clean, well-dressed, and well-kept. They hate men that are sloppily dressed."

According to a member survey, the most popular type of sexual content was couples having intercourse. The least popular was facials—a man ejaculating on a woman's face. Sssh costs $19.95 per month. So who subscribes? Most subscribers are age thirty-five to forty-nine, though they range from eighteen to sixty-four. Most are married, though more than 70 percent of members say they view the site alone, without their partner. The average length of a subscription is three months—longer than the average subscription length to male sites—and Angie points out that Sssh has active users who have subscribed for more than a decade.

Though Sssh and For the Girls are the most popular paysites targeting heterosexual women, there are a handful of similar sites for women, such as Candida Royalle and Seska 4 Lovers. There are also sites that sell videos targeted at women (though they often claim to target "couples"), such as Comstock Films and Viv

Thomas. But the greatest growth is in new, smaller Web sites that target lesbian, bisexual, and "alternative" female audiences, such as Feck and I Feel Myself.

So what kinds of men do women like to look at?

WHY WOMEN SHOULD WORK AS NFL SCOUTS

Many of the sensory cues that arouse women are not visual. A sexy voice, a masculine scent, and a sensuous touch all ignite greater arousal in women than feminine versions of these qualities ignite in men. This might be another reason for women's general lack of interest in Internet porn: they can't *feel* it in a physical way that activates their sensory cues. Or perhaps there simply aren't enough cues to meet the threshold of the Power of And.

Though romance novels offer an even more disembodied experience than videos, they contain a greater density of psychological cues, especially in the form of emotional details. And female-targeted stories still contain visual details. "I have consumed vast quantities of female-created (written) porn created for female audiences, written by (mostly) straight women," shared AlaraJRogers on Salon. "And almost no one ever talks about the size of the penis. But the color and intensity of the eyes, the hair color, the general shape of the body, a brief description of the face—those are de rigueur. And occasionally discussion of the butt. Women like butts."

We analyzed the text of more than ten thousand romance novels published from 1983 to 2008 to determine the most common descriptions of the hero's physical appearance. Here are the seven most frequent words describing his masculine features:

cheekbones

jaw

brows

shoulders

forehead

waist

hips

And the seven most common *adjectives* used to describe masculine features?

lean

handsome

blond

tanned

muscular

masculine

chiseled

AlaraJRogers was correct—no synonym for penis appears in the hundred most common physical descriptors used to describe the romance hero. If we wished to describe the ideal-looking hero, we could use the most common two-word physical descriptions: the perfect hero boasts "blue eyes," a "straight nose," "high forehead," and "square jaw" together making a "handsome face." His head is framed by "dark hair," which accents the "white teeth" in his "sensual mouth" curved into a "crooked smile." He stands tall with "broad shoulders," a "broad chest," "narrow waist," "flat stomach," "strong arms," "big hands," "big feet," and "long legs"—though the heroine's eye might ultimately be drawn to his "powerful thighs."

Brain imaging studies show that the female brain processes a man's visual features with the same speed that the male brain processes female features. Attractive visual features trigger similar subcortical circuits responsible for sexual arousal in both men and women, but in women this automatic, unconscious reaction gets intercepted by the Detective Agency before it gets converted into conscious, sex-seeking desire. Because of the Power of And, the Detective Agency weighs other factors—especially contextual cues—before reaching the threshold for generating subjective arousal. This is one reason why almost no women masturbate while looking at a single image. It takes other psychological cues, such as a story about why this rakish man in a tuxedo is lifting up the skirt of the innocent Latina maid, before a woman's sexual imagination takes off.

We saw how men are aroused by the physical features of women associated with estrogen. Similarly, women are attracted to the physical features of men associated with testosterone. This attraction is especially strong during ovulation and when seeking an extramarital affair. But estrogen and testosterone signal very different qualities. Estrogen indicates a woman's health, energy, and future reproductive potential. In contrast, some studies suggest that high levels of testosterone are associated with poorer long-term health. Moreover, testosterone levels do not indicate a man's future reproductive potential: men produce steady levels of sperm during their entire lives regardless of whether they're sick or starving. Even a ninety-year-old man can have kids. Though testosterone does not indicate a man's health or fertility, the hormone is correlated with another quality of great importance to the Detective Agency: *dominance.*

Many scientists view testosterone as the "male competition" hormone, since elevated levels of testosterone cause a man to become more prone to fight with other men to preserve or enhance status. Fans of a losing sports team suffer a drop in testosterone after the game, while the fans of the winners experience a testosterone rush. "My husband has a suit that, when he puts it on, turns him into a real jerk," offered one woman upon hearing that an increase in status will cause a rise in the male hormone. "He swaggers about the room and I just try to stay away from him. I call it his 'testosterone suit.'" Testosterone diverts bodily resources to physiology required for male-male competition, such as musculature and fast energy burning. It also increases sex drive.

Deep, masculine voices and masculine scents are correlated

with testosterone levels; both are attractive to women. Studies have shown that they are more attracted to the odor of sweat from dominant men than subordinate men. Faces that are rated as more masculine—chiseled jaws and well-defined cheekbones—are also correlated with high testosterone levels. Women prefer bodies that are muscular, particularly through the chest, arms, and back, without being clumsily overbuilt; these features also indicate testosterone levels.

One of the most potent visual cues for women is unrelated to testosterone: height. Perhaps height simply serves the same role as it does in the NFL and NBA: it indicates a greater ability to outcompete other men in physical competition. "I do love tall men, especially the ones that are over 6 feet tall who look real strong and masculine," confesses one woman on the Experience Project Web site. "For me, tall men make me feel more secure than guys who are under 6 feet. They look more dominant." Numerous studies find that the vast majority of women prefer to date men who are taller than they are, and virtually no women express a preference for shorter men. Most women cite a desire to feel safe as a reason for their preference for tall men. "It makes me feel small and secure; which is a lovely feeling," says one woman.

Women also express a preference for men in uniform and well-dressed men. A marine in dress blues with white gloves and peak cap, a police officer with boots and a badge, or a well-heeled businessman in an Issey Miyake suit and Testoni loafers all stimulate female arousal. Fashion blogger Teresa McGurk speculates on why women like a man in uniform: "A dress uniform is flattering to the male figure (Ooh-YAH!). The whole demeanor of a man in dress blues, or whites, or whatever is confident and dependable. Very sexy. Since a man in uniform knows all about responsibility and duty, he could well be counted on to take out the garbage. Theoretically, at least." McGurk's analysis also illustrates the influence of the Detective Agency—analyzing visual details and converting them into psychological speculation about a man's character.

Women are far less likely to focus on anatomical details than men are, and generally show little interest in viewing a guy's penis—especially compared to men's special phallic interest. One eye-tracking study found that women spend no more time looking at the penis in images of nude males than any other part of the body. You'll find no "top 10 penises" lists by women on the Internet, though you'll find plenty of "top 10 boobs" lists by men. Whereas most male-targeted porn sites categorize videos according to anatomical features, female-targeted porn sites often lack any anatomical categories at all. For example, the male-targeted HotMovies.com contains video categories for Big Tits, Small Tits, Natural Tits, Tit Fucking, Mouth and Tongue, Shaving, Legs and Nylons, Big Butts, Big Cocks, Big Clits, Camel Toe, and several others. But the female-targeted HotMoviesForHer.com does not contain a single anatomical category.

However, there is one part of a man's body that does appear to interest many women's brains: the butt. The gluteus maximus is a "universal cue": it's the one piece of anatomy that straight men, gay men, and straight women all find exciting. "[John F. Kennedy Jr.] tried to hold the ATM door for me and I wouldn't let him," confesses one woman on Jezebel, "because I wanted to stand behind him and check out his ass." Women generally prefer tight, athletic butts. Interestingly, NFL scouts believe that a football player's butt is the single best indicator of his physical strength and athletic ability. Sportswriter Michael Silver reported on what he saw at the 2010 NFL Scouting Combine: "You'll hear scouts and coaches throwing out compliments like, 'That guy's ass is pretty, now.' You'll see write-ups lauding a prospect's 'big, bubble ass' or 'great explosion in his hips.'"

Nevertheless, the appeal of butts is still modulated by the Detective Agency. Whereas plenty of men will state that breasts or butts are the most important thing, women generally take a more moderate view. On Yahoo! Answers, when someone posed the question "Do women like guys' butts?" more than half the women responded with a variation of one woman's response: "It's not a major priority for a guy to have a nice butt, it's just a nice advantage!"

Even though most women are not as focused on sexual visuals as men, there are still plenty of women who do enjoy hard-core pornography, even if they are much less likely to pay for it than men are. What kind of women watch a lot of visual porn? Consider the AOL search history of Ms. Intuition:

skin massage for stretch marks
look ten years younger fit tv show
fake nude jane seymour
tap your intuition
chakras
pampered chef recipes
sexy vanna white
family nude beach
older men younger women
french country decor
i am in love with him
italian framed art
jealousy between friends
friends jealous after weight loss
anna nicole smith nude
linens & things
labioplasty
celebs pics
free rape movies
what does sex mean to a man
how do men feel about sex
elizabeth montgomery naked

why are single women attracted to married men

when will i see results of pilates

sexy erica hill

anal sex benefits

june carter and johnny cash honeymoon pics

johnny carter cash pics

honeymoon sex

playgirl pics

george clooney nude

brad pitt nude

men in shower pics

porn for women

nude construction workers

making love

erotic nude couples

There has been no research exploring the question of what makes a minority of women become interested in porn, but Ms. Intuition's search history suggests one very intriguing possibility, especially when combined with female responses to OkCupid questions. One particular group of women reported higher amounts of porn viewing, larger porn stashes, greater comfort with their partner watching porn, greater enjoyment of bondage, and more interest in using the Internet for porn. Who were these women? Self-identified bisexuals.

Ms. Intuition seeks out Brad Pitt, George Clooney, nude construction workers, and naked men in the shower. But she also seeks out naked pictures of Vanna White, Jane Seymour, and Elizabeth Montgomery. She also searches for more pornographic material overall than most searchers who search for female-targeted pornography. On OkCupid, the pattern of bisexual women's responses to questions was distinct from straight women and lesbians—but quite similar to the responses of heterosexual men, as shown in the figure below.

Each column represents a single question from the survey. Note how the bisexual women's response patterns are more similar to straight men's than straight women's.

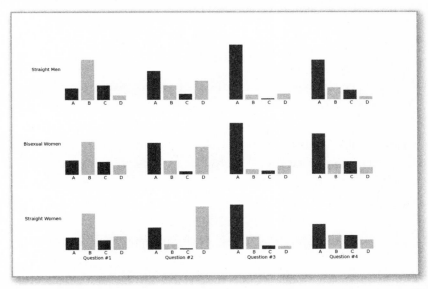

In addition, the responses of bisexual women were similar to heterosexual men on a variety of nonsexual topics, such as aggression, domination, and work habits. Among registered users on the visual porn site Fantasti.cc, 38 percent of the women self-identify as bisexual. In Richard Lippa's BBC survey, he found that bisexual women have a higher sex drive than either heterosexual women or lesbians. A smaller study at the University of Georgia found that bisexual women showed different patterns of arousal from watching pornography from lesbians and heterosexual women. In particular, bisexual women were more aroused than lesbians and heterosexual women by lesbian porn and male-female oral sex.

Though bisexuality in women is poorly understood, one

possibility advanced by scientists is that bisexual women have greater circulating levels of testosterone. This could contribute to bisexual women's higher sex drive and perhaps influences their interest in visual porn. "I can jill off to just about anything," explains a self-proclaimed bisexual woman on reddit.com. "Sometimes I think I watch more porn than my boyfriend. I don't understand why so many girls hate porn—I kinda think they probably are just too embarrassed to try it."

MISOGYNISTIC, IMMORAL, AND SQUICKY AS HELL

So far, we've reviewed the sexual cues in porn that trigger arousal in the vast majority of men and a sizable minority of women. But there's no escaping another obvious fact about porn: it can trigger a variety of negative reactions as well, including anger, jealousy, or moral condemnation. It's almost as if porn has "anti-cues" mixed in with the cues. Just as the sexual cues in the male brain are different from the cues in the female brain, anti-cues manifest differently in men and women. In general, male anti-cues trigger aggressive hostility, while female anti-cues trigger a greater variety of emotions.

"I caught my husband watching porn one night when I came home early," reports one distraught woman on reddit. "I felt completely betrayed, like he was cheating on me." Many women, upon catching their male partner indulging in online erotica, instinctively feel a sense of betrayal. Such emotions likely reflect innate "mate guarding" software in the female brain. Whereas the male brain is designed to become jealous over physical infidelity, the female brain is designed to become jealous over emotional infidelity. Women are instinctively concerned with a man's investment of resources in other women, and instinctively look for signs that a man is losing emotional interest. Even though porn does not represent an actual threat to a woman's relationship, the sense that a man's emotions are getting diverted somewhere else can trigger instinctive feelings of disloyalty.

Perhaps the hardest situation for a woman is discovering that her partner is looking at a qualitatively different kind of female from herself. "I found these links on Jake's browser—they were all to Asian porn sites," writes one twenty-two-year-old woman. "I clicked on one, and it was all these slender, flat-chested Asian girls. I'm blond, somewhat big-boned, with size D cups. I was like—why in the world are you with me???"

This is quite different from the reaction of men. "One night I caught my wife secretly looking at Web Virgins," confesses one twenty-seven-year-old programmer. "It really turned me on. She turned beet red, which just turned me on even more." Most men, including gay men, are aroused by the idea of discovering their partner watching porn. It doesn't appear to activate the male mate guarding software, since there's no cue of physical cheating.

Though many women feel betrayed when their partners watch porn, they rarely feel that they are betraying their husbands by reading romance. In fact, in Janice Radway's *Reading the Romance*, the women in a romance book discussion group insisted that reading romance improved their sex lives with their husbands. Even though the male brain can understand that a woman may be lost in an intimate fantasy world where she is emotionally and erotically connecting with a fictional male, as long as there are no real penises involved, men don't tend to get jealous of a woman's reading habits. However, men can get annoyed. "I think every girlfriend I've had has turned to me after watching a romantic movie and asked 'Why can't you be more like him?'" laments one young man. "I've never put on a Jenna Jameson movie and asked 'Why can't you be more like her?'"

Many women feel threatened by some of the sexual acts depicted in porn, fearing that men will expect them to perform those acts. As one twenty-two-year old woman lamented, "Some of these things, it just makes you ask—do guys *really* want girls that do that?" Women also feel concerned that men will only be satisfied by women who have bodies like porn stars—what some term the "centerfold syndrome." Other women fear that exposure to pornography will induce men to perform violence against women.

Women's brains simply process porn differently than men's brains. Many of women's concerns are the result of the Detective Agency's focus on the psychological and the cultural messages it perceives in porn. In Chapter 1, we compared men and women's divergent sexual cues to a female brain that could only taste sweet and bitter and a male brain that could only taste salty and sour. Porn and romance novels are specifically tailored to appeal to the cues of each sex—porn consists of visual cues appealing to men, romance consists of psychological cues appealing to women. When we each encounter the other's erotica, we can only understand it in terms of our own cues.

Women react to the perceived social messages in porn—that women are sex objects, that women should be promiscuous, that violence against women is acceptable (violence is actually extremely rare in online porn, though it doesn't feel that way to female viewers). Men, however, don't perceive any of these messages. Their brains are focused on the close-ups of the breasts, the seductive manner of the MILF, or the very large penis.

Though women have a broad range of reactions to porn, men are generally more tolerant—up to a point. Then things can get violent. Some straight men have an explosive reaction to gay porn or other porn they find very squicky. Men are also prone to condemning squicky content as immoral. Over the past century, the male-dominated medical profession at various points considered masturbation, fellatio, cunnilingus, anal sex, homosexuality, bisexuality, premarital sex, extramarital sex, and adolescent necking as not just physically unhealthy but morally wrong. Even today, various sexual behaviors can elicit a furious reaction from men.

Why does sex cause some men to react with a righteous rage? One indirect cause may be the very strength of the male sex drive. We've seen that men desire sexual release so intensely that they're willing to risk their jobs by masturbating at work. Any desire that powerful presents grave risks. If a man ends up developing a sexual interest in something nonreproductive—crawling ants, for example, or a doctor's office—then he may be doomed to go childless. Elmer Fudd is designed to easily aim, shoot, and repeat, but he must first be taught what a rabbit looks like, and then be prohibited from shooting at anything else. After a man finishes his sexual imprinting during adolescence, it appears that the male brain labels everything else as deviant, dangerous, or disgusting. This is probably intended to keep the powerful male sex drive focused exclusively on a man's cued interests.

For a woman, the flexible and cautious Power of And prevents women from making sexual mistakes, harnessing feelings of guilt, anger, shame, and insecurity. For a man, disgust and outrage serve a similar purpose—to keep his sexual interests focused on the prize: sexual reproduction.

CHAPTER 9

Cheating Wives and Girls Gone Wild

Male Psychological Cues

> There's a reason they call it Girls Gone Wild and
> not Women Gone Wild. When girls go wild, they
> show their breasts. When women go wild, they
> kill men.
>
> —Comedian Louis C.K.

A man who we will call Mr. Closet is financially successful and married with three children. He also hides a secret. A couple times a week while driving home from work, he takes a wrong exit. And then it starts.

> I go into "autopilot." I start driving aimlessly until I am lost in a neighborhood I have never been to and to which I would never go. I drive until I see a house with a light on or some sign that someone is home, smoke coming from the chimney, the sight of someone through the blinds, but never with a car in the driveway. I am sweating by this time because I know what is coming. I always park right in front of the house and sit there for a minute. I get out of the car and walk to the front door. I try the door knob. I go in without knocking or making any noise. I get into the front coat closet.

Put yourself in his shoes. You're committing a crime, one risking public humiliation and even physical harm. Imagine the danger—and the feeling of *transgression*.

Now the clock is ticking. I strip naked. I am totally sexually excited. I masturbate while I imagine the "lady of the house" walking around. I have some thoughts about what she looks like, but what excites me is knowing that the "man of the house" could be home any minute. He will come home and open the door and then the closet door and then . . . I climax. It is the most exciting sex I have ever had in my life.

Forbidden acts have a very special power to arouse. Unlike breasts and butts, transgression is a *psychological* stimulus. It's an *interpretation* of a situation or person, rather than a piece of anatomy or the sound of a voice. Though previous chapters explored the wide variety of psychological cues used by the Detective Agency, in this chapter we're going to examine a few psychological cues that have the unique power to activate male desire. But first, we're going to consider *transgression*—a psychological stimulus that arouses women and men both.

"I first discovered porn-stories when I was 15-years-old," writes Shannon, a twenty-three-year-old woman on her online journal. "The strange thing, though, was that I was almost immediately attracted to the 'taboo' subjects rather than the 'normal' ones. Stories about humiliation, incest, and other 'disturbing' topics got me off a lot better than stories of romance ever did."

Both sexes can get wildly turned on by situations that are immoral or dangerous, *because* of their immorality or dangerousness. In the 1967 French film *Belle de Jour*, Catherine Deneuve plays a doctor's demure housewife. Surprisingly, she is not turned on by her young, handsome, devoted husband. Instead, she is plagued with dark fantasies that drive her to secretly begin working in a brothel.

By day, she is a prostitute appropriately named Belle de Jour. One of her first clients is an ugly, violent gangster. To her surprise, he incites a wild, lustful passion within her. Though the gangster's alpha male status is surely part of his appeal, the movie makes clear that Deneuve's character is most excited by the danger and wrongness of her behavior; when the gangster eventually tries to romance her, she feels cold. She only wants him for degrading, taboo sex.

Why do Mr. Closet, Shannon, and Belle de Jour all desire the forbidden? Do they all share a psychological cue for transgression? Perhaps not. As Donald Symons points out, cues are evolutionary adaptations, designed with a particular purpose. The male cue for youth guides a man to find a partner who will maximize the number of healthy children he will have. The female cue for social dominance guides a woman to find a man who will maximize the chance of success for her children. A transgression cue that drives people to masturbate in strangers' closets or seek out degrading sex would be a very dangerous guide, indeed.

You might guess that the function of a transgression cue is simply to motivate men and women to engage in ordinary sexual intercourse. After all, sex is often treated as a prohibited act in many societies. Or maybe men need to overcome a natural aversion to penetrating someone else's body. We all instinctively feel it's wrong to jab a stick up someone's nose; perhaps, a transgression cue renders physical penetration exciting instead of horrifying.

But men need little prompting to engage in sex, no matter what the cultural constraints. In addition, it appears that the male psychological cue of dominance and the female psychological cue of submission provide the necessary incentive for a man to physically penetrate a woman and a woman to accept penetration. So if evolution did not design a transgression cue, and if transgression is by definition not a product of socialization, then why is the forbidden so thrilling? Surprisingly, it might be a strange quirk of our brain wiring.

Our *visceral nervous system*, also called the autonomic system, manages many unconscious processes in our body, such as digestion, salivation, and respiration. The visceral nervous system is like a team of air traffic controllers: you never see them doing their job, but without their constant effort everything would come crashing down. One part of our visceral nervous system known as the *sympathetic nervous system* is responsible for our fight-or-flight response. When confronted with a scary or risky situation, the sympathetic nervous system readies our body for action. It speeds up our heart rate, increases blood flow to our muscles, and makes us take deeper breaths. We get ready to battle or bolt. But the sympathetic nervous system also controls another critical bodily process: orgasm.

Could the sympathetic nervous system influence our capacity to become sexually aroused from transgression? Two Canadian psychologists decided to test this hypothesis with an ingenious experiment. In North Vancouver, British Columbia, the Capilano River winds through a deep canyon. The experiment used two bridges. The Capilano Canyon Suspension Bridge is a footbridge constructed of wooden boards attached to wire cables. The bridge is 450 feet long but only five feet wide, with low handrails of wire cable. The bridge tilts, sways, and wobbles, creating the impression that you are about to fall over the side and plunge 230 feet to the rocks and shallows below.

The other bridge is farther upriver. It is wider, firmer, and constructed of heavy cedar with high handrails. Below is just a ten-foot drop to a small rivulet. An attractive female interviewer approached men as they were crossing each bridge and asked them to fill out a questionnaire while they remained on the bridge. They were also asked to write a brief dramatic story based upon a picture of a young woman. The interviewer also offered her phone number to each man "in case he wanted to talk further." Presumably, the only difference between the two groups of interviewed men was the level of activation of their sympathetic nervous system. So what did the psychologists find?

The men on the rickety, anxiety-provoking bridge wrote stories with significantly more sexual content than the men on the safe bridge. Nine out of eighteen men on the rickety bridge eventually called the female interviewer. Only two out of sixteen men on the safe bridge ended up calling her. The increased sense of danger appeared to enhance sexual arousal in men. But what about women?

In women, things are a little more complicated. As we've learned, the software controlling sexual arousal in women is split into two components—conscious psychological arousal and unconscious physical arousal. The separation of the two types of arousal is governed by the Detective Agency. When it comes to the activation of the unconscious sympathetic nervous system, the Detective Agency appears to get involved, as can be seen in an experiment by two other Canadian psychologists.

The experiment presented female subjects with two different conditions. In one, subjects watched a neutral movie about traveling, followed by an erotic movie containing heterosexual foreplay and sex. In the other condition, subjects watched an anxiety-provoking movie about threatened amputation, followed by an erotic movie. Women's physical arousal was measured using a vaginal plethysmograph. Psychological arousal was measured using a questionnaire.

After watching the amputation movie (and then the erotic movie), women showed significantly increased *physical* sexual arousal. Their bodies were turned on. But they reported significantly decreased *psychological* arousal. Miss Marple was still reacting to the amputation, even if her body was getting excited. But perhaps amputation is not really the right stimulus to test anxiety—after all, some people might react to a threatened amputation with revulsion rather than nervousness or fear. Perhaps we should look at a more frightening stimulus.

In his book *Who's Been Sleeping in Your Head?*, psychologist Brett Kahr recounts a sexual fantasy shared with him by an elderly Jewish woman. Her parents died in the Nazi Holocaust. One imagines that her attitude toward the Nazi regime must be one of anger and terror. This makes her fantasy seem quite surprising. "She imagines a group of S.S. officers in jackboots and other Nazi regalia forcing her to strip naked before strapping her to Josef Mengele's medical examination table, where she must submit to probing of the most deadly surgical nature." The same men who murdered her parents have become the subject of her most intimate, secret fantasies, producing "the most explosive of orgasms."

This Nazi fantasy, Mr. Closet's masturbatory behavior, and the bridge experiment provide convergent hints at one reason we may find transgression so exciting: the part of our nervous system that reacts to threats can also generate a sexual response. If so, that would make transgression a unique source of desire in both women and men. Transgression may not be an evolutionary cue like small feet or tall men. Instead, it could be a counterintuitive enhancement of erotic feeling due to our quirky brain wiring—an evolutionary by-product, rather than an adaptation. Anything perceived as dangerous or taboo—including sociocultural risks and violations—may simultaneously activate a fight-or-flight response and enhance sexual arousal.

We now turn to a psychological cue exclusive to the male brain that seems just as counterintuitive as transgression.

LOVING WIVES AND INDECENT PROPOSALS

Jealousy is the green-ey'd monster. When Shakespeare penned this line in *Othello*, he certainly had *sexual* jealousy in mind. Evolution has endowed men with a paranoid vigilance for sexual betrayal. Unlike women, a man can never be certain of his paternity. In an analysis of about twenty-four thousand children across nine mostly Anglo-Saxon countries, about 3 percent were found to have been fathered by a man other than the presumed father. That means that about one out of thirty men was unknowingly raising someone else's child—a seemingly small number, unless you happen to be one of the duped fathers. In 2007–2008, about 3,500 paternity claims were brought to the British Child Support Agency. These were cases in which a man suspected that he wasn't the real father. Nineteen percent of the children in these cases had not been fathered by the presumed dad.

Men have always faced a non-negligible risk that they might

devote time, emotion, and resources to another man's child. Sexual jealousy motivates a man to conduct his own detective work looking for clues of a partner's promiscuity. Jealousy is a dark, consuming emotion that can instantly explode into a violent rage when confronted with evidence of a wife's infidelity. This fury can even drive a man to murder, as shown by Othello and possibly O. J. Simpson.

So then, what are we to make of the enormous popularity of *cuckold porn*?

A cuckold is a man whose wife has sex with another man. Paradoxically, many men are intensely aroused by the thought of their wife cheating on them. Here's the account of one such man, writing on a cuckold message board:

> She wore her very best lingerie, an expensive and very hot silky set from Victoria's Secret. She never wore that for me. I didn't even know she had bought it. She spent hours on her hair and makeup. As soon as I got to see her, fully decked out in her erotic best, there was a knock at the door. He had arrived. She sashayed to the door and opened it, completely ignoring me. He walked in. He was a foot taller than me, with huge biceps. He looked my wife over from head to toe and smiled. He was very happy. I could tell how happy by the huge bulge in his pants. But I already had a bulge in my pants, too.

Cuckold porn is the second most popular heterosexual interest on English-language search engines. Only *youth* is more popular. On PornHub, men who search for "cheating wife" view the greatest number of videos. There are 343 Web sites on the Alexa Adult List that portray female partners having sex with strangers, including Please Bang My Wife, Cream My Girlfriend, and Cheater Sex Spy.

One of the most common scenarios in cuckold porn is wives getting *paid* to have sex with another man. Usually, these Internet videos are nothing like the 1993 movie *Indecent Proposal*, where Demi Moore's character receives a million dollars for an evening of adulterous lovemaking in an expensive penthouse with the handsome Robert Redford. Instead, the videos on Sell Your Girlfriend are more typical. The girls are paid a few hundred bucks to have sex with a tattooed biker on a ratty sofa.

In cuckold porn, the boyfriend or husband almost always watches from the sidelines, usually with a look of frustration and dismay. Frequently, the wife calls out to her husband as she's being serviced, touting the superior skills or better equipment of the *bull*—a common term for the cuckolder. (The woman is known as a *hotwife* or *cuckoldrix*.) On a small minority of cuckold sites, like Forced BiCuckolds, after the hotwife has been satisfied she compels the husband to perform fellatio on the bull.

One of the most popular categories of stories on Literotica is *Loving Wives*. Apparently, what these wives love most is having sex with men other than their husband. The sex is usually voluntary, though some of the narratives involve coercion or blackmail. Wives have sex with loan officers to acquire a mortgage, with their husband's boss to help him get a promotion, or with a dozen of her husband's friends to celebrate a Super Bowl victory.

But there is another intriguing element to cuckold erotica. Look over this list. It shows the most common two-word phrases in cuckold stories on Literotica.

Most Common Phrases in Cuckold Stories
black cock
black man
your wife
another man
your husband
big black
other men
my wife
her lover

Much of cuckold porn consists of a well-built, well-hung black man having sex with a man's white wife while he watches. Many cuckold porn sites exclusively feature black cuckolders, such as Interracial Hotwife, My Wife Went Black, and Black Mother-Fuckers. In Craigslist ads posted by couples seeking a man, nearly one-third specify they want a black guy. On Fantasti.cc, fifteen of the top twenty-five videos tagged "cuckold" feature black men and white wives. Of particular interest in cuckold porn is the black penis. It's inevitably large, and always elicits high praise from the wife when compared to the husband's smaller organ. Why is there such a strong interest in watching black men have sex with cheating wives? There's a clue in a genre of porn without any wives—or even any women. Gay porn.

"Black guys are hot," explains Rocco. "They're the ultimate in 'you're going to suck me off,' the ultimate in 'I'm going to throw you down and mandhandle you.' They're the ultimate tops. Big, strong, dominant, with a huge dick." In Chapter 7, we saw that the fourth most popular category of gay sexual searches is *blacks*. Gay men search for *blacks* even more than they search for *penises* or *anal*. Why? One clue can be found in gay porn. On It's All Gay, in videos containing a white man and a black man, black men are tops about seven out of eight times.

As revealed by online videos and stories, the black man possesses one very special quality in the imagination of both gay and straight men: *dominance*. But why would a straight man get *more* turned on by watching a dominant, masculine man have sex with his wife? What makes a man's sexual desire overcome his sexual jealousy? The science of biology offers one intriguing answer to this question.

Sperm competition.

Sperm competition refers to a variety of physiological and behavioral adaptations that enable a male's sperm to compete head-to-head with other males' sperm in the battle to impregnate a female's egg. These adaptations are found in a dazzling variety of species. The giant testicles of the chimpanzee, which can blast out an enormous volume of sperm, is one such *physiological* adaptation. Female chimpanzees have sex with multiple males while ovulating, so a male that can produce more sperm has a better chance of dislodging other males' sperm and a better chance of his own sperm surviving future matings. Many biologists hypothesize that the bulbous head and extended length of the human penis is another physiological adaptation. Its shape is very effective at shoveling out the sperm of any rivals. Perhaps the inevitable flaccidity men experience after ejaculation is intended to prevent men from shoveling out their own sperm.

Dogs, deer, and kangaroos exhibit *behavioral* adaptations for sperm competition. If males from these species sense that a female might be exposed to sex with other males, they will exhibit premature ejaculation, more vigorous thrusting, and multiple ejaculations. Mice, owls, and beetles adjust the number of sperm they release in response to sperm competition cues. The motility of their sperm and the force of their ejaculation also depend on the perceived risk of male competition for a female. Male stickleback fish will release more sperm if they see a *video* of another male.

A man getting aroused by the psychological cue of cuckoldry is another *behavioral* adaptation. If a man believes that his sexual partner may have been with a rival, this adaptation drives him to have sex with her as quickly and as vigorously as possible. One hotwife describes her cuckolded partner's physical response: "My steady boyfriend, nicknamed IFuckAmy, is mentally strong and physically weak. He is definitely monogamous and he picks my boyfriends—they are always physically well built and fit. He watched me fuck the same guy a few times. I can tell that IFuckAmy is jealous but when he fucks me afterwards, I also noticed that his load is strong and heavy and he cums fast."

In many species, the more dominant the potential rival, the stronger the sperm competition cue and the more intense the arousal, perhaps because dominant males tend to ejaculate more vigorously than submissive males. Since black men are frequently perceived as more dominant, they may activate the sperm competition cue more effectively. British psychologist Nicholas Pound even speculates that the erect penis and the "money shot" are both visual cues of sperm competition that trigger arousal. If Pound is right, this would also explain why large penises play such a prominent role in cuckold porn, especially large black penises. (It would also underscore the penis's special role as a visual cue in the male brain.)

Sperm competition cues may also help explain another popular genre of male-targeted online porn: *group sex*. On the Web, group sex porn has exploded into a variety of subgenres. There are the straightforward "gang bang" sites featuring one woman and multiple men, such as Gang Bang Squad, Gang Bang Arena, and Her First Gangbang. There are "orgy" sites such as Teenage Group Sex, Orgy World Girls, and Anal Party Orgies, which feature staged group sex scenes with professional stars. There's a surging genre of "party" porn such as Frat House Fuck Fest, Party Hard Core, and In the VIP—sites that portray real college parties or nightclubs where girls have raucous sex in front of large crowds, often with multiple partners. A similar "reality" group sex genre features amateurs having group sex without any audience, such as Dare Dorm, Russian Orgy, and Frat House Hazing.

Nicholas Pound conducted a series of studies using videos portraying "polyandrous sexual activity" (in other words, gang bangs and group sex). He discovered that men are consistently more aroused by multiple men than by multiple women or by a man and a woman. Another piece of online evidence for sperm competition cues in group sex porn is the marked asymmetry in the *gender* of group sex participants. Many Web sites feature large numbers of men but only one woman, such as 6 Buck Orgy, 10 Man Cum Slam, and 15 on 1. But the site with the highest female to male ratio is Fuck Team Five. This site's videos feature between three and five professional actresses who often please one lucky guy. But, tellingly, the videos just as often show the Fuck Team actresses with groups of guys.

Though *threesome* Web sites featuring two ladies and one man are certainly popular, Fuck Team Five is the only multi-female, one-male gang bang site on the Alexa Adult List. In contrast, there are 381 multi-male, one-female gang bang sites on the list. (There are a number of multi-female, one-male sites within a genre known as CFMN: Clothed Female Naked Man. However, this genre specifically portrays a man getting teased, dominated, or humiliated by a group of clothed women, and thus appeals to a different psychological cue: submission.)

On PornHub, in the three hundred most-viewed group sex videos, there are forty-four videos with three or more guys and one girl; there are twenty-five videos with three or more girls and one guy. The extremes of the group sex genre are also revealing. There are dozens of "mega–gang bang" videos featuring more than one hundred guys having sex with a single woman. In contrast, there are no videos featuring a guy having sex with more than a dozen women, not even if we include CFNM porn. (Of course, this might also say something about how much easier it is to round up one hundred guys to be in porn than it is to find one hundred willing girls, especially considering that the guys would be willing to do it for free. But if you're a straight male, ask yourself—would you pay to see one guy have sex with a hundred women?) There's also a gender difference in sexual fantasies about group sex. Men fantasize about group sex more often than women do—and imagine larger numbers of *males* in group sex fantasies than women do.

One final piece of evidence from the Internet supports the existence of a sperm competition cue in the male brain. In gay porn, gang bangs are also extremely popular. Gay men even appear to exhibit the cuckold cue. "Sometimes I fantasize about walking in on Thor with another guy. It really gets me hot thinking about it and we've role-played it before," explains Rocco. "Of course, if it really happened, I'd cut his balls off."

SHE'S GOTTA HAVE IT

Long before the Internet, male-targeted pornography featured shrieking, shivering female orgasms. Howling moans and vocal encouragement culminate in a moment of egregious ecstasy that often seems as artificial as the one famously faked by Meg Ryan in *When Harry Met Sally.*

Why does porn contain such conspicuous signals of female pleasure? It's certainly not for the female viewers. "I just don't get how these women are supposed to be having orgasms because some guy shoots a big load on her face?" complains one woman. Another woman put it even more succinctly: "Yeah, right."

The women are moaning and swooning for the men. Female sexual pleasure is one of the most potent psychological cues for male arousal. Indeed, this may be the most common cue across all varieties of online porn. "Seeing and hearing a woman who is truly turned on like crazy has to be the biggest aphrodisiac I can think of for me," lauds one man on reddit. "If this happens in porn, and it rarely does, I find it to be fucking amazing."

But true pleasure might be hard to find, according to Stephen Yagielowicz. "While I suspect that most fans believe that the girls are actually having orgasms (just as most guys believe they always give their lover an orgasm), I also suspect that many performers are thinking about the new shoes they will buy. It's like big-time wrestling: some believe it's all real, from the hits to the back story. Same with porn."

Because of men's desire to believe, women who lack typical male visual cues can still excite men through the energetic expression of sexual pleasure. One example is porn superstar Sasha Grey, who crossed over into mainstream filmmaking in Steven Soderbergh's *The Girlfriend Experience.* Sasha Grey is skinny, flat, and lacking in feminine curves, yet she has a large and devoted male following. This enthusiasm is apparent in the comments section on the porn star review site FreeOnes:

"No tits, too damn skinny but god damn i will watch her vids all day."

"I totally am into fake Blondes with huge fake tits, but this girl knows how to suck and take a facial. Don't know what it is, maybe she likes it that much, and it is showing . . . that might be why I am turned on by her actions . . ."

"Sasha actually puts enthusiasm into her work. No one works it harder than she does on the set. I'd kill to be with a girl with that much energy."

Indeed, the surest way for a female porn star to increase her popularity is to be known for having authentic orgasms. Any casual discussion of porn actresses on forums or comments inevitably finds intricate discussions of whether favored stars have orgasms or not—and those that attain consensus that their orgasms are real, such as Sasha Grey, Nina Hartley, Chloe, Cytherea, and Jenna Jameson, tend to have the most devoted fans. Gay men are also aroused by conspicuous signs of sexual pleasure from their partner. Gay porn contains as much moaning and groaning and dirty talk as straight porn.

On Fantasti.cc, we analyzed ten thousand comments on one hundred top-rated videos. The third most common type of comment is acknowledgment of the woman's pleasure. For example, "She loves it!", "Look at how excited she is," "Would more cocks make her even happier?" (The most common type of comment is praise for a woman's attractiveness. The second most common type of comment is variations of "What a delightful piece of anatomy.")

Why are men so interested in determining the authenticity of a woman's sexual pleasure—even when the objective odds of her experiencing bona fide pleasure are low, such as when a man ejaculates on her chest? And conversely, why do men get so upset when they believe a woman is faking pleasure? Perhaps for the same reason that the male brain is designed for sexual jealousy: to ensure a woman's fidelity.

In order to figure out if a woman was faithful, men's brains developed their own detective skills. But unlike Miss Marple's chatty agency filled with a variety of sleuths, the male detective is more like an obsessive and irascible private investigator, permanently hired for a single task: determining whether a woman is cheating on him. Men are wired to pay attention to whether his partner is engaged and responsive during sex. If a woman seems apathetic or distant, that triggers suspicions. The private investigator starts asking questions. If I'm not turning her on, then who is?

A woman's sexual pleasure isn't just important for long-term relationships, but also matters in a short-term partner. The more pleasure a man provides a woman, the more likely she'll want to have sex with him again instead of someone else, even if she's someone else's wife and "fidelity" per se isn't at issue. But another reason why it would behoove a man to pay close attention to satisfying a short-term lover: female gossip. "For most of human history, if Ann rejected Andy for being a bad lover, it's a good bet that everybody in the community would find out about it. That would lower Andy's mate value among other women. So Andy better make sure that Ann is feeling good!"

Another genre of porn that appears to be based upon the female pleasure cue is *squirting*. Through a process that is still poorly understood, when some women orgasm they squirt out a jet of clear liquid, similar to male ejaculation. Since this is taken as an unfakable sign of female pleasure, squirting is quite popular with male viewers, ranking as the thirty-sixth most popular category of sexual search on Dogpile and the third most popular search on PornHub.

It's clear that the male psychological cue of female pleasure is so potent that men are easily convinced of a woman's pleasure, even when objectively there's reason to be skeptical—especially considering that more than 65 percent of women say they've faked orgasms. For a woman, it appears there's no better way to elicit a man's devotion than to make him believe he's taken her to the heights of sexual ecstasy. Men want to believe in their own sexual prowess and that sex is a source of boundless pleasure for their partner. The male cue for female sexual pleasure is entirely analogous to the female cue for a man's emotional commitment.

Consider how often you might expect to hear the heroine in a romance novel say: "Oh, you sure like cunnilingus, don't you? I can see how much you love cunnilingus! You're just a big, dominant cunnilingus lover, aren't you!"

Or, conversely, how often might you expect to hear a naked guy in porn sob, "Oh, you had me at hello!"

GIRLS GONE WILD

Most of the men and women who produce the adult content on the Internet live from paycheck to paycheck. The rest are middle class, making somewhere between the salaries of a rookie policeman and a senior computer programmer. "Despite the new sports cars gracing the splash pages of affiliate marketing Web sites, many more folks drive Pontiac Sunfires than Porsche Carreras," admits Stephen Yagielowicz. There's precious few millionaires in the business, not since the glory days of the 1990s, when there was little competition and even less free porn, though even then there were very few people who struck it rich.

But there's one man who's earned at least $100 million from his adult movie empire and who continues to rake in the dollars today. Amazingly, he's achieved this success without filming any intercourse or fellatio, without hiring any actresses, and without building any sets. His movies aren't available in stores and until recently weren't even available for sale over the Internet. The man's name is Joe Francis. His company is called Girls Gone Wild.

Francis's videos feature college-age women voluntarily disrobing for his ultra-low-budget camera crews at Spring Break spots and university parties. He built his empire hawking his soft-core porn on late-night cable infomercials. How does he get the girls to take off their clothes? He offers them a free Girls Gone Wild T-Shirt and a chance to be ogled by millions of men. Why are men willing to shell out $19.99 just to see a collection of five-second clips of intercourse-free nudity? Joe Francis's Gulfstream jet and silver Ferrari owe their existence to the male psychological cue of *authenticity*.

Authenticity is important to both men and women, but in different ways. Women focus on *emotional* authenticity. This is one of the primary tasks of the Detective Agency: looking for clues indicating whether a man is being honest about his level of ambition and commitment. Is he really an alpha, or is did he just learn the strategies of the Pickup Artist community? Did he really mean it when he said he loves me, or is he just trying to get me into bed?

Men, in contrast, focus on *physical* authenticity. Are those breasts that big or is she wearing a Victoria's Secret push-up? Is she really twenty-five or just dressing young? Is her face expressing genuine sexual pleasure or is she faking it? This desire for physical authenticity manifests itself in the extraordinary popularity of "amateur" or "candid" porn. *Amateurs* is the ninth most popular category of sexual searches on Dogpile and is very popular on search engines around the world. Why is authenticity a psychological cue rather than a visual cue? Because just as most gay men prefer a hot straight guy over a hot gay guy even if they look exactly the same, most straight men prefer a hot amateur to a hot professional even if they're identical twins.

There are a flood of Web sites that feature personal photos or videos taken from ordinary women's MySpace or Facebook accounts, donated by ex-boyfriends, or captured by an iPhone in public without the subject's awareness. For example, Watch My Girlfriend, Busty Candids, JayBee, Girls Next Door, and Real Emo. On reddit, one of the largest social news sites on the Web, there is a very popular Gone Wild forum where users post their own photos. Dare Dorm features videos of actual college students having group sex, purportedly sent in by the students themselves. (There is a gay version of this site called Dick Dorm.) Though many of these sites contain nudity, a very sizable portion of amateur content is non-nude and simply features attractive women going about their lives.

"I pretty much can't watch professional porn anymore. Too many fake tits, fake orgams, fake moaning, almost every single fuck session ends with the guy blowing cum on the girl's face," complains one fan of amateur porn. "It reminds me of that scene from Ace Ventura 2 when he blows a gigantic loogie inside the hut, and then he and three other people come out of the hut with snot all over their faces . . . everything's fake and retarded, especially the story."

Amateur sites often seem to offer "proof" of women's authenticity by their very medium, such as low-resolution photos from digital cameras or blurry shots taken at a crowded beach. On Girls Gone Wild videos, the girls are frequently filmed at Mardi Gras or Spring Break, settings with too many people and too much activity to fake. Of course, objectively speaking, there is nothing authentic about a pixelated image of a stranger whom you will never meet and whose name you may never know. Indeed, there is at least the remote possibility that a professional porn star might be contacted and persuaded to engage in sex for money. An unidentified amateur, on the other hand, is far more likely to be unattainable. But this doesn't stop men from preferring the girl next door to *Playboy*'s Girls Next Door.

"All the porn stars are just fake, fake boobs, fake hair, fake orgasms," writes another reddit commentator. "But you get one of those college videos, just some girl fucking her boyfriend, the girl loving it, her natural body, it's like night and day."

There's a related genre known as "reality porn," which *emulates* the authenticity of amateur porn. The Web site Mike's Apartment presents women who trade sexual favors for a free stay in an urban apartment. Another long-lasting and highly popular example is Bang Bus (the original source of the gay Bait Bus), where pornographers ride around California in a van, looking for girls who might need a ride. They find a remarkable number of solitary ladies willing to get into a vehicle with a bunch of strange guys— and have sex with them. Sites like these try to cash in on the male desire for authenticity.

....

But there is another important psychological cue offered by amateur porn, especially genuine amateurs: *novelty*. Males of most species are wired to become aroused by novelty, a process first studied systematically in rats in the 1950s. Researchers observed that after a male rat had copulated with the same female a few times, he would become exhausted. He'd do the rodent equivalent of collapsing on the sofa and reaching for the remote to watch *SportsCenter*. Often, the female rat would be eager for more. She would nudge and lick him, doing her seductive best to arouse him, but he would simply lie in the nest, flaccid and unresponsive.

Then the researchers would place a new, unfamiliar female in the cage. Immediately, the male would jump to his feet and strut around, flexing his masculine haunches and showing off his versatile tail. Gone was the exhausted, drooping rodent of a moment before. Within minutes, he would be feverishly copulating with the new female. The researchers repeated this process with another female, then another. Each time, like a ragged marionette, the male would respond to the brain's command to perform. In one study, a male copulated with a dozen females before finally collapsing in a bleary heap.

In one study of novelty conducted at the State University of New York, Stony Brook, forty male volunteers were exposed to images of heterosexual couples engaged in sexual activity. Arousal was quantified by a penile plethysmograph. One group of young men was shown the same image five times, while another group was shown five different erotic images. In the first group, the plethysmograph slowly deflated. In the second group, the plethysmograph maintained steady arousal.

After orgasming, why do men have such a difficult time getting aroused again by the same woman, but get erect so easily at the sight of a new woman? We think it's to prevent a man from dislodging his own sperm—the same reason we believe men become flaccid after orgasming. Since the penis appears to be physically designed to shovel out competitors' sperm, it can just as easily shovel out a man's own sperm. By becoming flaccid and losing all sexual interest in a woman once he ejaculates inside her, a man increases the chances of impregnating her. But if a new woman appears, it's in his biological interest to get erect and jump back into action. There might even be another man's sperm to shovel out of the way. Of course, once he ejaculates inside the new woman, he will again become flaccid and uninterested for the very same reason: sperm preservation.

As Lord Byron lamented, "How the devil is it that fresh features/Have such a charm for us poor human creatures?" Fresh features certainly charmed Giacomo Casanova, history's most famous rake, who narrated his eighteenth-century erotic adventures with 122 women in his detailed memoirs, *Story of My Life*. Though Casanova's seductive prowess is dwarfed by the notorious conquests of Wilt Chamberlain (who claimed to have had sex with more than twenty thousand women), Casanova's description of the usual course of his love affairs is revealing: "After the most pleasant highs derived from the physical enjoyment of a woman's charms have been absorbed, there is always a notable reduction of ardor upon the repetition. Excitement diminishes, attraction wanes. Soon, and inexorably, boredom sets in. Then I must plead my unworthiness and arrange to pair the woman with some other, more suitable man, as a means to extract myself from the frustrations of apathy."

Porn stars, by virtue of their very prevalence in porn, quickly lose their novelty value. Amateur porn offers new bodies with fresh faces. Women who strip naked and perform on webcams for paying men lament the "New Girl Effect," whereby webcam performers make the most money they'll ever make in their very first week. One reason that Girls Gone Wild is so very popular is that it offers an endless stream of authentic young women, each appearing just long enough to maximally activate the novelty cue before being replaced by another fresh face, igniting the male brain yet again.

But in one of the many ironies of the adult industry, the women who stand to make the most money from selling nude photos of themselves—namely, young amateurs who have never appeared in porn before—are also the ones most willing to give it away for free. In fact, many young women enjoy snapping self-portraits of themselves in their underwear or completely naked and posting them online. JayBee, Sexbook, and My Ex Girlfriend contain thousands of provocative photos of young women taken by their own hands.

These true amateur sites manage to cross the abyss separating the divergent desires of men and women. Women are satisfying their own psychological cue of irresistibility, the exhibitionist desire to be desired. Men, on the other hand, are very willing to pay to see such authentic, novel expressions of female sexual pleasure. Everybody's happy.

Especially Joe Francis.

CHAPTER 10

Lords and Lordosis

Human Psychological Cues

You must submit to supreme suffering in order to discover the completion of joy.

—John Calvin

Geladas are a peculiar and little-known species of monkey that science has largely overlooked. They live in large troops in the towering Simien Mountains of northern Ethiopia. They have golden manes that are the stuff of shampoo commercials, and burning red eyes. They graze on grass, but have vampiric canines. But what's particularly interesting is a very special patch of skin on their chest shaped like an hourglass.

On males, this hourglass indicates its owner's social status. The color ranges from a meek eraser pink to a fiery red for alphas. Gelada society is broken into harems. Each harem is composed of an alpha male, between two and twelve females, and their young. Even though the male is in charge, the females expect to be well taken care of. Otherwise, they may turn on their leader.

There are always bachelors with bright hourglasses—though not as bright as alphas'—who skulk around the edges of harems, testing for weakness. Often the alpha will scream and kick up dust, demonstrating his dominance. But sometimes his display is unconvincing. Then a bachelor may attack.

Biological anthropologist Jacinta Beehner remembers one fight that lasted three days. It appeared to be a stalemate until a treacherous female edged away from the harem. As her champion looked on, she sidled up to the bachelor. The former alpha "didn't even try to prevent it," Beehner recalls. "He just quit."

A deposed leader may be allowed to stay with a harem, where he cares for the young. Of course, he loses mating rights and must take on a sort of avuncular role. Within a few months of being dethroned, the flaming redness of his chest patch subsides to an anemic pink.

We conclude our survey of sexual cues with a Siamese twin pair of psychological cues that is found in both men and women: *sexual domination* and *sexual submission*. In the male brain, only the gender cue (whether you're attracted to men or women) is more basic and influential. The sexual submission cue is also fundamental to the female brain.

But first, we need to make a distinction between *social* dominance and *sexual* dominance. Though not much studied by science, social dominance and sexual dominance appear to involve different parts of the brain. Social dominance specifically involves social status and is almost exclusively a male trait. Social dominance in the geladas is indicated by the redness of the male hourglass. (Female geladas also have an hourglass, but its redness indicates the status of her ovulatory cycle.) Sexual dominance has to do with one's physical role in sex. In rats, intromission is the sexually dominant role, and lordosis is the sexually submissive role. Similarly, tops and bottoms among gays correspond to the sexually dominant and sexually submissive roles. Social dominance and sexual dominance are related but distinguishable.

We're going to start with a discussion of social dominance. We saw in Chapter 5 how male dominance is a potent cue for the Detective Agency, with Miss Marple valuing alpha males, dominant voices, dominant scents, dominant gaits—if it suggests dominance, women like it. In fact, social dominance in most mammals is exclusively a male domain. As we saw in Chapter 7, male social dominance is mediated by testosterone. This "male competition hormone" provides the redness for the male gelada hourglass.

Testosterone levels are associated with aggression. Superior fighting ability and a will to fight typically increase a male's social status. When the rage center of a monkey's brain is artificially stimulated, the monkey will rise swiftly up the dominance hierarchy, by virtue of frequently fighting other monkeys. Testosterone levels are associated with many physical qualities in males, including greater musculature, deeper vocalizations, and various skin coloration.

There's a very important fact to understand about male social dominance. No man is born dominant. He must strive for it—and he may fail. The male brain is designed to go through life shifting between dominant and submissive states. Though a man might be born with physical and personality traits that facilitate an easy rise to dominance—height, vigorous upper-body strength, a deep voice, an aggressive temperament, an indomitable will—dominance must still be attained through social interactions with other males. In other words, social dominance is fluid and flexible, not hard-wired into the male brain.

The Sandra Bullock movie *The Blind Side* (based on the book by Michael Lewis) tells the true story of Michael Oher, one of the best offensive tackles in the NFL. He is a mountain of a man at six feet four inches and 304 pounds. But despite his size, he started out as a "gentle giant"—timid and submissive. It took time and experience to build up his confidence until he became a dominant All-Star left tackle for the Baltimore Ravens.

Social dominance influences a man's financial success. It also influences his attractiveness to women. But male dominance also has another consequence: it directly influences his sexuality. The link between social dominance and male sexuality is most apparent in one of the oddest mammals on Earth, the naked mole rat.

The naked mole rat is what biologists call a *eusocial* creature. Like the ant or the termite, naked mole rats have separate behavioral castes, including a sterile caste. There is a naked mole rat queen that has unlimited reproductive privileges. There are "worker" naked mole rats, called subordinates. What's interesting is that the subordinates are asexual. The male and female workers are almost indistinguishable, in both body and brain. They do not breed, just like worker ants or worker termites. Their life mission is to serve the greater good of the colony, digging and finding food and caring for young. They obey and serve the queen without question. In contrast, a small set of naked mole rats are "breeders." They get to have sex.

But naked mole rats are not genetically predetermined to become a breeder or a subordinate. The naked role rat brain is designed to become either one. There are specific hormones responsible for the change: androgens, a class of hormone that includes testosterone. If the androgen levels rise in a subordinate, some remarkable changes occur. Suddenly, the rat develops prominent sexual characteristics. But just as dramatic are the changes in the brain. New neurons form, the receptors on existing neurons change, and the brain's wiring changes. No longer is the subordinate deferent and asexual. Now it claims its role as a dominant member of society—and its main reward is sex.

Though the relationship between social dominance and sexuality in humans is not quite as dramatic as in naked mole rats, socially dominant humans do share one essential quality with socially dominant members of all mammal societies: an increased sex drive. The more dominant a human male becomes, the more testosterone he produces, which in turn increases his sex drive. Men with high levels of testosterone lose their virginity earliest, have the most sexual partners, and convince women to have sex the fastest. Alpha males have the greatest sex drive of all.

In the television series *Breaking Bad*, the high school chemistry teacher Walter White learns that he has lung cancer. The doctor tells him he only has a few months to live. He decides to "break bad" and become a crystal meth dealer. He ends up killing another drug dealer. Later, he blows up the headquarters of a vicious gang leader, a true alpha male. After each of these incidents of unexpected male dominance, he returns home and has fervent sex with his wife, who is overwhelmed by his unprecedented levels of lust.

In the beautiful documentary *Man on Wire*, tightrope walker Phillipe Petit accomplishes an extraordinary feat: he illegally strings a cable between the twin towers of the World Trade Center and performs 120 floors above the ground without any kind of safety equipment. He is arrested, but is quickly released because of the outcry of the public, who claims him a hero. He triumphantly walks out of the police station to an adoring crowd. A woman rushes up to him, clearly enamored of his newly attained alpha status. Though Petit's team is waiting for him—as well as the media—Petit immediately ignores them to return to the unknown woman's apartment and has hours of passionate sex with her.

HEADS OR TAILS

In primates, social dominance is a complex cognitive process that appears to be partially managed by regions in the frontal cortex. This conscious part of the brain is responsible for evaluating the social ranking of others and whether there is enough social support to make a move to increase one's own status.

In contrast, sexual dominance and sexual submission appear to be entirely managed by subcortical processes, mediated by several nuclei in the hypothalamus. These subcortical circuits control very physical processes, such as hip thrusting or passiveness. As we saw in Chapter 7, both males and females in several mammal species appear to possess both sexual dominance and sexual submission circuitry. Female dogs sometimes mount other males or even mount the legs of humans, an act controlled by sexual dominance circuitry. Both types of circuits are wired to the pleasure centers of the brain. It's rewarding for a female rat to perform lordosis or for a male rat to perform intromission. Since heterosexual female macaques mount other females, and heterosexual male bonobos allow themselves to be mounted by other males, it's reasonable to presume that they also feel pleasure from switching over to the other side.

Domination and submission are usually cast together like the two sides of a coin, which can show heads or tails but never both. Though the vast majority of gay men have a clear preference, they can and do shift flexibly between the top and bottom roles. But this flexible switching isn't the sole domain of gay men. Consider the AOL search history of Mr. Panties:

> any bondage
>
> daddy gets excited so much wearing daughter's pink panties
>
> daddy was forced by his boss to start wearing daughter's panties
>
> kidnap a very pretty girl for fucking her in every tight hole
>
> watching your teenage daughter being fucked
>
> you're all tied up and forced to watch your daughter being fucked
>
> so slip your panties now little girl i've got something for you to suck

Some of Mr. Panties' searches take a dominant point of view, some take a submissive one, demonstrating that a single individual can derive satisfaction from either a sexually dominant or sexually submissive role. One thirty-three-year-old male performer who has appeared in many "fetish shows" and adult movies also switches between dominant and submissive roles. "Sometimes I like to dress up like a blond girl, with high heels, a wig, miniskirt, makeup, the works. It's very empowering. But most of the time I just like to tie girls up and whip them. The feeling of power, that's a real rush."

When combined together, *domination and submission* is the sixth most popular category of sexual search on Dogpile. Since any act of sexual dominance requires an act of sexual submission by the partner, sometimes it was difficult to determine whether a particular search was better categorized as *domination* or *submission*. For example, one forty-two-year-old gay top reports that he enjoys watching sexual submission Web sites like Straight Hell and Frat Hazing because he identifies with the dominant men in the videos. That's why we did not separate *domination* and *submission* into separate search categories.

Nevertheless, despite the ambiguity in determining whether specific searches were better categorized as *domination* or *submission*, when viewing individual search histories on AOL, it was clear that most people prefer one or the other. There were a minority of people like Mr. Panties who appeared to flexibly shift between the two. But most were focused on one or the other, as illustrated by the sexual submission content preferred by Mr. Diapers:

diaper punishment stories

sissy diaper stories

forced to be a girl at school

femdom at school

sissy slut cartoons

prison slut stories

adult babies in wet diapers pictures

On the other side of the coin is Mr. Gardens:

rape stories

forced seduction

forced deepthroat

female oral humiliation

botanical gardens

throatfucking

Heterosexual domination porn involves the male coercion of a female partner. The man is always in the dominant role. One subcategory of domination porn is financial exploitation—where men persuade women to have sex for money. Exploited Teens, Black Girls That Need Cash, or College Teens Book Bang are popular examples—the last one featuring college women (actually actresses) who have sex in exchange for textbooks. (These parallel gay Web sites such as Twinks for Cash, Gay 4 Cash, and Paid to Play Gay.) Another subcategory is psychological exploitation, including sites featuring sex with drunk girls (Drunk Chix, Free Drunk Bitches, and Only Drunk Porn), hypnotized girls (Hypnogirls, Smart in Hypnosis, and HypnoKing), and tricked girls (Chick Tricks, The Nasty Cop, and Teens Porn Casting). There's also physical domination sites: Smack My Bitch, Forced Witness, and Forced Sex Scenes.

Though sexual domination sites are very popular, sexual submission sites are even *more* popular—and still maintain a majority male audience. Sexual submission sites are even more varied than their domination counterparts. There's forced feminization sites: Strapped in Silk, House Boys, and Sissy School. There's CFNM (Clothed Female Naked Male) sites, where a man is stripped and taunted by groups of clothed women, frequently at school or work; this is one of the very few genres of porn frequently featuring small penises. There are also sites featuring water sports (urination), male milking (forcing a man to orgasm), CBT (Cock and Ball Torture), Ballbusting (just what it sounds like), Ball Kicking, FemDom (Female Domination), Foot Femdom, male spanking, facesitting, FemDom Assfucking (women with strap-on dildoes having anal intercourse with men), trampling (women in boots walking on men), and castration (eek!). The vast majority of these submission sites feature role reversal: a dominant woman sexually exploiting a submissive male.

So why would a man, with desire software that is biologically and socially programmed to be dominant, enjoy watching porn that features a submissive, degraded, or humiliated male? Perhaps the simplest neural explanation is that male fans of sexual submission porn are accessing the female submissive circuitry their brain shares with women. After all, the submission circuitry is still wired to the brain's reward centers.

But does this imply that women access their very own male sexual dominance circuitry?

FEMALE DOMINANCE

It's often observed that men strive for control and domination, while women strive for consensus and equality. One likely reason is because women are not motivated by a testosterone-fueled drive for social dominance. Though Miss Marple prefers her partners to be dominant, most women do not feel the burning ambition to outcompete other women on the way to becoming alpha female.

Of course, many women are driven to succeed—political opposites Hillary Clinton and Sarah Palin demonstrate that women of all persuasions have the inner fire to strive for the highest positions of executive authority. But generally speaking, women avoid physical competition and personal clashes in favor of what psychologists call "tending and befriending"—establishing strong interpersonal bonds.

This changes if you give women testosterone. They become more aggressive, perform more rough and tumble play, initiate more fights, and become more prone to risk-taking, just like men. It also increases their sex drive. Female Viagra already exists and it's called testosterone. "There was a time when I had to take testosterone supplements, and it increased my compassion for men four-fold," reported one woman. "Not only did my sex drive go up, but I felt more aggressive and a lot more willing to take risks. It was amazing!" Unfortunately, though testosterone can be prescribed by a doctor, it has a number of negative side effects, including problems with blood fats, liver function, and body hair growth.

But even without testosterone supplements, many women prefer to be the seducer rather than the seduced, such as cougars

Samantha on *Sex and the City* and Gabrielle on *Desperate Housewives*. During the five-year period from 2001 to 2005, about 250 female teachers in America had their teaching credentials revoked because of sexual misconduct—making sexual advances on a student. (Compared to about nine times that number of male teachers.) One of the first female teachers to make headlines for sexual misconduct was Mary Kay Letourneau, who at age thirty-four began an affair with a thirteen-year-old student. When Letourneau's husband discovered the affair, she was arrested for second-degree child rape. Three months later, Letourneau gave birth to a Audrey, a baby girl, the daughter of the thirteen-year-old lover. Seven years later Letourneau married her student and, with her new husband, celebrated with a "Hot for Teacher" night at a Seattle bar.

Rebecca Bogard, a twenty-seven-year-old science teacher in Mississippi, allegedly seduced a fifteen-year-old in her Jaguar with plates that read "GRRRR." She later texted the boy, "I love you, yeah it was the best, which night was the best 4 you, I'm sensitive but not sore, you were good." One Alabama teacher was even arrested for allegedly having sex with eight members of the high school baseball team.

These examples aren't necessarily indicative of female arousal from dominance; they may reflect arousal from irresistibility (consider the intensity of desire from most adolescent boys). Still, they all demonstrate a willingness to violate social norms (and criminal laws) in the pursuit of sexual fulfillment with the woman assuming a dominant role. Nevertheless, it's safe to say that most women have a very complex relationship with their desire to be dominant or submissive, one that is much more problematic than that experienced by men. One woman writes about this knotty attitude:

> I can read and am very fond of [dominant and submissive roles] between two male characters, whereas a male-dom-female-sub heterosexual pairing has to be very specifically written for it not to be upsetting for me. The most

seemingly-innocuous things, stuff that's normal enough in such fiction not to merit a warning, will turn it in my head from consensual to rape and/or abuse of power, and the male character from a desirable lover into a threatening tormentor.

There was a large gender difference in the responses to the OkCupid survey question "How does the idea of being slapped hard in the face during sex make you feel?" Two-thirds of women answered "horrified," compared to only one-third of men. But despite this clear preference for no abuse, many women—just like men—are aroused by degradation and humiliation. Web sites like Hogtied, Public Disgrace, and Wasteland feature many actresses who participate because they enjoy it. "I like being choked," admits one performer and bondage enthusiast. "Especially from behind. I need to be slapped around a bit. I like to be put in my place."

Several popular categories of fan fiction involve salient cues of submission, such as *rape*, *submission*, and *hurt/comfort*. Hurt/comfort stories typically involve a character who is harmed or suffering in some fashion. He may be physically injured, have cancer or AIDs, or simply face discrimination for publicly admitting he is gay. There's often a very erotic overtone to the comforting. Here's a scene from "Breakfast in Bed," a hurt/comfort story set in the Harry Potter universe:

Remus opened his mouth to speak, but his voice cracked. He winced, and Sirius leapt up to get him a glass of water. "What happened?" Remus asked, not minding the absent teasing of his bangs.

"Dumbledore looked at your dinner plate. Someone mixed silver shavings into your potatoes." Sirius' face paled even further. "It's my fault. Please, eat some fruit."

"I don't feel well enough. What if I throw it up?"

"Just take it slow," he whispered. He reached out and picked up a piece of melon. He touched it to his lips and smiled. Remus' heart hammered in his chest. Sirius turned the piece and held the kissed end for Remus. Remus grinned and opened his mouth. The melon was sweet on his tongue, wet with juice and Sirius' kiss.

However, many women are aroused by more intense submission cues. "[In my fantasies] my 'hero' is shorter than everyone else, darker, and therefore highly desirable, but as he is totally vulnerable and powerless he is sexually abused," explains fan fiction scholar Brita Hansen of the University of Melbourne. "My identical twin sister also has a paracosm fantasy, but she won't tell me what hers is." As an example of her fantasy, she points to the story "Cleansing" based on the (nonpornographic) family television show *21 Jump Street*. The story is about the police officer named Tom Hanson, played by Johnny Depp on the show. Tom has been captured by criminals, who send a videotape to Tom's partner Doug:

> Doug could feel his face growing hotter and hotter by the minute as he watched the abuse of his partner.
> "Who wants him?" Andrew asked. "Or am I first?" He traced his finger down Tom's cheek, making the young cop recoil from the contact. The four other captors sniggered and hooted at this. "I'll just take him."
> He pushed Tom to the bed and shoved him to lay on it. Eric covered the officer's mouth with duct tape that stretched from Hanson's right ear to his left. It was evident that Hanson was already thoroughly exhausted, and he could not bring himself to waste his strength on trying to force Andrew off of him.
> The camcorder focused on Tom's battered face, catching every flinch of pain and the utter shame present in his usually lively brown eyes. They were soon shut tightly as he arched upward and practically screamed from Andrew thrusting into him.

It appears that just as men are flexible but generally prefer sexual domination, women are also flexible but generally prefer sexual submission. But things are simpler for Elmer Fudd, who can divorce sexual gratification from his other thoughts and feelings. Miss Marple has a more difficult time separating the intellectual discomfort with sexual submission from her physical and sexual response. Perhaps this is another reason so many women enjoy fan fiction: it provides them with an opportunity to explore their complex feelings about sexuality.

So what exactly is the relationship between social dominance and sexual dominance? One special genre of sex may shed some light on this question.

IVY LEAGUE DEANS AND LOST GIRLS

BDSM is an acronym for the very intimidating phrase "Bondage, Discipline, and Sadomasochism," a sexual subculture that has long befuddled mainstream society—and mainstream science. Until recently, scientists erroneously believed that BDSM participants were concerned with the infliction and experience of pain. This is also how BDSM is often portrayed in movies and daytime talk shows. Certainly the accoutrements of BDSM, such as whips, gags, and nipple clamps, seem like they would *hurt*. But fans of BDSM—and the precious few scientists who study them—now agree it's about something else entirely.

"It's about the voluntary exchange of power," explains Tiiu, a female BDSM enthusiast who performs in fetish shows and stars in online videos on the BDSM Web site Wasteland. "The submissive gives the dominant power out of respect and trust. This is called The Gift." This centrality of power in BDSM is reflected in the names of many private bondage clubs, like Arizona Power Exchange (APEX), People Exchanging Power (PEP), headquartered in New Mexico, and the Memphis Power Exchange in Tennessee.

Those who participate in BDSM are *doms* (short for dominant), *subs* (short for submissive), or *switches* (able to play either role). It's frequently said that even though the sub gives power to the dom, the sub is still ultimately in control. (This parallels the conviction in the gay community that the bottom is really in charge.) The sub often has a safe word that will put an instant end to a play session, in the event that things start to progress beyond the sub's limits. A good dom pays very close attention to the sub's experience and determines when a sub may be approaching his or her limits. It takes training and experience to become a good dom—usually by serving as a sub for an established dom.

But what kind of person would derive sexual satisfaction from relinquishing control of his or her body to another? Are subs all young, mentally unbalanced slackers, perhaps enamored of the goth lifestyle? Not at all, says Gloria Brame, a clinical sexologist who works with BDSM participants. "[They] are as romantic, loving, and committed to relationships as anyone else. But instead of finding a kiss romantic, they may find wearing someone's collar to be romantic."

More insight into the BDSM community can be obtained by considering the Web site Wasteland.com. Wasteland is the oldest continuously operating Web site devoted to BDSM themes. It was formed in 1994 after owner Colin Rowntree (husband to Angie Rowntree, owner of Sssh.com) put a catalog of goth fashion on the nascent Internet. At the time, Colin himself had no connection to either goth or BDSM. In fact, the warm, witty Rowntree, who works out of a rambling colonial home tucked between New Hampshire apple orchards and pumpkins patches, resembles an enthusiastic and slightly rakish humanities professor. His catalog site quickly obtained a lot of traffic, but nobody was buying anything. Visitors just wanted to look at the pictures of attractive models wearing black leather clothes. As an experiment, Colin charged people $10 a month just to look at the pictures. Hundreds of people signed up. Soon people were requesting models in specific poses and situations. Wasteland was born.

Today, Wasteland contains hard-core videos of people acting out various BDSM scenarios, such as getting locked in cages, getting suspended from the ceiling, getting mummified, and getting tied up with ropes that look like they could be used to anchor an ocean liner. So who pays money to join the site? "We've got bankers, stockbrokers, Ivy League deans, CEOs," explains Rowntree with a smile. "People who have a lot of responsibility in real life, and who want to get away from the burden of being in charge. People for whom this is a lifestyle, a chance to play." The average age of Wasteland members is forty-five. The average income is upper-middle class.

Many of the fans of BDSM are socially dominant, yet prefer to be sexually submissive. Social dominance does not imply sexual dominance—only an increased sex drive. How that sex drive is satisfied varies from individual to individual. Certainly, most alpha males prefer the sexually dominant role. But perhaps a minority feel a kind of psychological relief when taking the submissive role. Or another possibility is simply that the motivation required to become socially dominant is unrelated to one's preference for sexual dominance. For example, many gay alpha males are power bottoms.

BDSM play is usually not aimed at generating an orgasm, though its practitioners usually consider it erotic. "A sub might orgasm, if the dom allows it, but it's not typical," explains Tiiu. "It's more about getting something you need, and that need isn't always an orgasm." The domination and submission cues provided by BDSM seem to have a direct line to our reward centers. Wasteland has one of the highest retention rates (the rate at which people maintain their sign-ups) in the industry, with an average subscription rate (before the 2008 recession) of seven months. Colin also notes that "a goodly number of the members who cancel return to join again after an average 3 month 'rest period,' presumably where they spent scarce money on other things in life."

The very structured and ritualistic culture of BDSM poses a very interesting question. Do its practitioners satisfy the same cues of sexual domination and sexual submission experienced by viewers of Exploited Teens videos or by readers of coercion scenes in fan fiction?

One possible way to answer this question is by looking at erotic stories. In the following table, the left column lists the ten most common phrases in BDSM stories on Literotica; the right side lists the ten most common phrases in coercion stories.

Most Common Phrases in BDSM Stories	Most Common Phrases in Coercion Stories
my master	the guy
her master	the guys
the crop	the fuck
Master, I	please don't
yes mistress	the knife
yes master	two men
the plug	his dick
the whip	her bra
your fingers	couldn't believe
your hand	was happening
the leather	her husband
Sir, I	the man
the chain	the young
feel your	grabbed her

There's a clear difference in the content between the two types of stories. At the top of the BDSM list is *her master* and *my master.* At the top of the coercion stories is *the guy.* BDSM uses *the crop,* while coercion stories use *the knife.* BDSM emphasizes the relationship, the coercion stories emphasize the threat. Another intriguing difference is the fact that there aren't any overt sexual words on the BDSM list. On the coercion list, there's *the fuck* and *his dick.*

Reading BDSM stories and coercion stories, one is struck by the feeling that BDSM tends to emphasize the formal relationships of control and dominance without delving too deeply into explicitly sexual territory. In contrast, coercion stories tend to emphasize sexual humiliation and helplessness, and always have graphic sexual descriptions. This emphasis on the raw experience of power is also suggested by the fact that many people in positions of authority and power are drawn to BDSM, often as subs. BDSM might simply be a very sophisticated means of accessing the reward mechanisms associated with the psychological mechanisms of social dominance that guide all primates.

THE NATURE OF DESIRE

We've completed our survey of sexual cues, ending with a set of cues that are perhaps responsible for more erotic creativity on the Internet than any other. There is greater diversity and inventiveness in sexual submission and sexual domination Web sites than within Web sites associated with any other sexual subgenre. This fertile sexual imagination extends to both male visual sites and female story sites.

But the two sexes differ on most other cues. Men are visual. They respond to a gender cue that is fundamental and fixed. They respond to visual cues that are flexible during adolescence, then very fixed. They respond to a cuckold cue from sperm competition, an authenticity cue, a novelty cue, and a partner pleasure cue. Transgression can intensify arousal.

The brains of both gay and straight men are like Elmer Fudd: any cue triggers an immediate, powerful reaction directed toward seduction and orgasm. Men hunt for the perfect single cue, the ever elusive Bugs Bunny, though any wabbit will do.

Several key factors have shaped male desire. First, the need to evaluate potential female partners. The best woman was one who could provide and raise the most and healthiest children. Second, the need to be instantly ready for sex should the opportunity arise. Third, the need to physiologically compete with other men who might have had sex with the same woman. Fourth, the need to compete with other men socially for access to women.

In a very real sense, there is something tragic about male sexuality. It is never satisfied. Tomorrow is another day for the hunt—whether a single guy cruising for a one-night stand, or a married guy searching a tube site for something new. The novelty cue ensures that whatever is delicious today is bland tomorrow—and male desire is frequently a solitary affair.

But male desire is also powerful, intense, urgent. It can take a man to strange, new places and open up new doorways of experience. It's never tied down, never sedated, and can incite a man to wander great distances in search of fortune and adventure. It drives dazzling visual creativity, such as Japanese anime.

Women are more focused on emotional and psychological cues, which generate erotic stories suited for satisfying female appetites. Women respond to a truly astonishing range of cues across many domains. The physical appearance of a man, his social status, personality, commitment, the authenticity of his emotions, his confidence, family, attitude toward children, kindness, height, and smell are all important to Miss Marple's Detective Agency. Unlike men, who become aroused after being exposed to a single cue, women need to experience enough simultaneous cues to cross an ever-varying threshold. Sometimes, just a few overwhelming cues can take a woman there. Other times, it takes a very large number of moderate cues. For a man, a single cue is often sufficient, and sometimes necessary. For women, no single cue is either necessary or sufficient.

Women have unique psychological cues. Irresistibility and adorability are feelings a woman has about herself that influence her self-esteem. Women are also sensitive to environmental cues, like food, shelter, and security. Unlike the solitary Elmer Fudd, Miss Marple is garrulous, frequently chatting with other detectives. Writing and reading erotica is far more of a social enterprise for women than for men. Women's desires also change across the monthly cycle and sometimes droop, whereas men's desires are constant all year long.

These portraits appear so different as to describe two different species separated by an abyss. And yet, our race has always found harmony within this chasm. Our very lives are a testament to the millions of times our ancestors have bridged this gap and found the cues we craved staring back at us from the other side.

CHAPTER 11

Erotical Illusions

The Creative Power of Cues

Illusion is the first of all pleasures.

—Oscar Wilde

For more than five centuries, the enigmatic smile of Lisa del Giocondo has enchanted millions of visitors to the Louvre. Completed by Leonardo da Vinci in 1507, the painting more commonly known as the *Mona Lisa* portrays an Italian woman with a famously mysterious expression. The *Mona Lisa* smile appears to simultaneously convey mischievousness and a staid worldliness. Why does it have such a bewitching, dynamic effect? Because Leonardo da Vinci painted an optical illusion.

If you peer very closely at Mona Lisa's mouth, it appears to be rather neutral, almost a horizontal line. However, if you look into her eyes, her expression changes. Now she seems to be smiling merrily, almost like she's teasing you. How does this work? Margaret Livingstone, a professor of neurobiology at Harvard who studies human vision, discovered da Vinci's visual trick.

Our brain perceives high-resolution details in the center of our vision and coarse, low-resolution shapes in the periphery. When you look directly at the high-resolution details of Mona Lisa's mouth, you see her relatively flat lips. But if you step back and look at her eyes, nose, or forehead—anywhere but her mouth—your peripheral vision picks up only the coarse details of her mouth: now her lips seem to follow the strong curving lines of her cheekbones and semi-dimpled cheeks into a smile, almost like the Joker's makeup-extended grin in *Batman*.

This juxtaposition of two different visual cues—a high-frequency cue and a low-frequency cue—is the basis of the most famous optical illusion in art.

Neurally, the *Mona Lisa* shares something in common with Chicken McNuggets and the luscious desserts at the Cheesecake Factory. The mouthwatering tastes of these foods are also perceptual illusions that have been specifically crafted to exploit our brain's gustatory cues. Professional "food engineers" at restaurant corporations like McDonald's, the Cheesecake Factory, and T.G.I. Friday's combine sweet, salty, and savory tastes to produce entrees that maximize *cravability*. This is the food industry's term for dishes that dupe the mind's gustatory system in order to make diners want more and more and more. "Cravable foods stick in customers' imagination and bring them back," explains Bennigan's chef David Sonzogni.

The manufactured cravability of Cold Stone Creamery's Hunka Chunka Burnin' Fudge or Chili's Texas Cheese Fries brings together combinations of tastes that never existed before in nature. When they hit our tongue, our brain swoons with a pleasure more intense and thrilling than when we bite into a mere bar of chocolate or fried potato. The unique juxtaposition of tastes, textures, and temperatures in manufactured cravable foods trick the brain in the same way the *Mona Lisa* smile manipulates the perception of two different visual cues. But if visual and gustatory cues can be combined to produce surprising new perceptual effects, what about sexual cues? Is it possible to create the erotic equivalent of the Mona Lisa smile?

The answer is a resounding yes.

Certain kinds of sexual stimuli merge together multiple sexual cues in a kind of perceptual trickery we call *erotical illusions*. With modern technology and some very human creativity, ancient sexual cues are now spliced together in novel combinations that can dupe or hyperstimulate our sexual perception, giving rise to curious new erotic cravings in both men and women. But there is one crucial difference between optical and erotical illusions. In his book *Stumbling on Happiness*, psychologist Daniel Gilbert asserts that "optical illusions are the same for everyone." Men and women both perceive the same shifty Mona Lisa smile. But things are quite different with erotical illusions. Since they rely on sexual cues, male erotical illusions have no effect whatsoever on the female brain and female erotical illusions have no effect on the male brain.

In this chapter, we're going to review some of these erotical illusions and demonstrate how our brain's desire software is one of the most potent and overlooked sources of creative inspiration in the human mind.

FUTANARIA

Sage Agastya, a renowned Vedic scholar and the author of many couplets in the Rig Veda, occupies a special orbit in the constellation of Indian mythology. According to legend, Agastya came across many ancestors hanging upside down in a cave. When asked why they hadn't proceeded to their well-earned place in the heavens, the inverted ancestors bemoaned the lack of an heir to continue their line and perform the proper rites to send them on their way. So Agastya decided to create a wife for himself. Using Vedic wizardry, he selected the most desirable parts of various domesticated animals to fashion a beautiful and perfect wife named *Lopamudra*, which means "assembled from the most beautiful parts."

Based on traditional depictions of Lopamudra, we can presume that Agastya selected those body parts that best satisfied his male visual cues: firm breasts, round butt, wide hips, small feet. Similarly, when men search for porn on the Internet, they also seek out the perfect combination of cues. They hope to find a body that maximizes their desire by activating as many cues as possible. Many Web sites make it easy. Thumbnail Web sites like Dan's Movies, Cliphunter, and Bravo Vids display rows of photographs laid out like a catalog. The images feature attractive female bodies in a wide variety of shapes and sizes. But once in a while, a different kind of body pops out.

"I call it the 'Trannie Peek,'" explains one industry veteran. "Adult webmasters figured out that straight guys will click on shemales out of curiosity and take a look. It grabs about 5% of the clicks on straight TGPs [thumbnail galleries]."

The terms "trannie" and "shemale" are frequently used as slang within the adult industry and in adult content for a transsexual woman who has been treated with hormones so that she possesses breasts and a female figure but still possesses a penis. (Some in the transsexual community consider both "trannie" and "shemale" to be derogatory terms.) They are also known as "T-girls" and "ladyboys." PornHub and many other tube sites also features the occasional T-girl porn on their front page, but they only present gay porn if you actively search for it. This is because the main audience for T-girl porn is heterosexual men.

"Transsexual Porn is classified as Straight Specialty," blogs Wendy Williams, a bulky transsexual performer who has starred in eleven movies. "So obviously the adult industry had to market our porn to those who buy it, guess what that is STRAIGHT men. There is no market for a gay company to produce this content so most are all big straight companies like Evil Angel and Devils Film." Housekeeper, who runs several transsexual porn sites, including Transsexual Brazil and Stroking Queens, agrees. "My main audience, and the audience for most shemale porn, are straight dudes. That's how it's always been. I will say that all of the visitors to transsexual sites are straight. Many of them are married men, men in relationships with real women, and single men."

T-girl porn has exploded in popularity over the past decade, with a dazzling variety of sites on the Alexa Adult List: She Gods, Shemale Fly, Evil Shemales, TranSex Domination, and Submissive SheMale. In fact, if you categorize the sites on the Alexa Adult List by the names of the sites, then T-girl sites are the fourth most popular category of adult Web site. "Transsexual porn is one of the largest-selling niches in all of straight porn. It's a huge money-maker," asserts Wendy Williams. T-girl porn is popular in every country on the Internet, but especially in Brazil and Southeast Asia. "Shemales" is the sixteenth most popular sexual search on Dogpile, more popular than "butts," "threesomes," and "interracial sex."

Here is the search history for one T-girl fan, Mr. Miami Latino.

transexuales calientes

chat de transexuales latinos

transexual cum

transexuals fucking women

lesbian transexuals

miami hot latin girls

semen transexual

Most men who search for T-girl porn either search exclusively for T-girl content or a mix of T-girl porn and straight porn. But there is a minority of men who search for both gay and T-girl content. For example, Mr. Squirt.

absolute shemale

squirt

gay male porn galleries

squirt

absolute shemale

squirt

gaybeef

squirt

Does this suggest that perhaps some gay men really do like T-girls? Not necessarily. Two sociologists visited a Chicago bar frequented by transsexual women and their male admirers. Scientists refer to these T-girl fans by the rather intimidating term *gynandromorphophiliacs*. The sociologists approached various men at the bar and interviewed them about their sexual orientation and tastes. So how many T-girl fans were straight? About 60 percent. And the others? The remaining 40 percent were bisexual men. There were no gay men at the bar.

So what drives straight men's interest in T-girls? The fact that as represented in online porn, the T-girl is an erotical illusion.

The T-girl consists of the novel juxtaposition of two kinds of male visual cues. First is a set of cues for *femininity*: breasts, butts, curvy figures, and feminine facial features and mannerisms. All of these cues trigger the male brain's usual arousal from an attractive female body. But there is another vivid cue: the penis. As we've learned, the penis has a special power to activate the male sexual brain. When you superimpose these two cues, the result is an erotic version of the *Mona Lisa* smile.

"I like her soft looks, sexy body. Very nice long legs," muses one T-girl fan on Fantasti.cc. "And then there's that added bonus . . . I can't really explain why it affects me."

A sense of inexplicable enigma often colors men's response to shemale porn, similar to most people's reactions to optical illusions. "I'm enchanted by her figure. It's svelte, and the long hair is really nice and feminine. Plus a sex toy that just kind of pops out in my brain," explains another shemale fan. Wendy Williams is used to it. "They like the feminine qualities that make us a transsexual and the dick is sort of a fetish." The femininity cues are the reason gay men aren't interested.

Like Agastya's hand-crafted Lopamudra, the T-girl porn is an erotical illusion comprised of a conjunction of different anatomical cues. Many men who search for T-girl porn also search for specific female body parts, such as Mr. Sexy:

shemale galleries

sexy butt babes

sexy boob babes

sexy bikini babes

sexy boobed babes

Searches for T-girl porn are also highly correlated with searches for strap-on dildos. The nature of the erotical illusion of T-girl porn is made even more vivid in artistic erotica freed from physical constraints. In Japanese anime, transsexual characters are known as *futanari*. Futanari porn reveals exactly what appeals to straight men about T-girls. Futanari characters are drawn with hyperfeminine bodies, typically very young, with large round breasts and hourglass figures, large eyes with long eyelashes, and beautiful faces. They also possess giant horse-sized penises. Typical futanari features schoolgirls with giant protrusions beneath their plaid skirts, teenage girls with pink hair and a bulge in their jeans, slender ballerinas in tutus sporting erections as long as their slender legs.

Recently, contemporary adult webmasters have begun to understand the precise appeal of T-girl porn. They've found ways to manufacture "artificial shemales" that do not involve the use of actual transsexual actresses. One site, Futanaria.com, uses real women. The women are voluptuous and curvy, with enormous strap-on dildos that look like authentic if colossally oversized penises. The site is full of scenes of attractive, busty women stroking their giant artificial manhood until geysers of fake semen spray across the room. The site makes the erotical illusion very clear: visual cues of femininity juxtaposed with the visual cue of a penis.

What about the opposite? What about someone with strong muscular arms, tattooed biceps, a bald head, a beard—and a vagina? The most famous (and perhaps only) transsexual male porn star is the cigar-puffing Buck Angel. Buck Angel combines a number of visual cues of masculinity with the single feminine cue of a vagina. Straight men express no interest in Buck Angel, and some find him disquieting. Many gay men, however, find Buck Angel extremely intriguing. "I would definitely love to try out Buck," explains one thirty-two-year-old gay man. "He's hot, and there's just something very dizzying about him that whirls around in my brain."

Women have created their own parallel world of protagonists accessorized with unnatural add-ons. But in keeping with the kind of female cues preferred by Miss Marple, these extra appendages are of the emotional and psychological variety.

VAMPIRE ANGST

Beth's neck jacked back up as she met the man's steady, feral gaze. She couldn't see the color of his eyes through the glasses, but his stare burned.

As he stopped in front of her, she felt a blast of pure, unadulterated lust. For the first time in her life her body got wickedly hot. Hot and wet.

Pure, raw, animal chemistry. Whatever he had, she wanted.

On impulse her hands went to the lapels of his jacket, and she tried to pull him down to her mouth. He captured both her wrists in one of his hands. "Easy."

She struggled against his hold, and when she couldn't get free she arched her back. Her breasts strained against her T-shirt, and she rubbed her thighs together, anticipating what it would feel like to have him between them. "Sweet Jesus," he muttered. She smiled up at him, relishing the sudden hunger in his face.

Wrath was dumbfounded. And he wasn't a vampire who got struck stupid very often.

This half-human was the hottest thing he'd ever gotten anywhere near. And he'd cozied up to a lightning strike once or twice before.

This abridged passage, from J. R. Ward's *Dark Lover*, is representative of a female erotical illusion that has rocketed to the top of best-seller lists and the heights of box office sales: *paranormal romance*. Over the past decade, sexy vampires, lusty werewolves, and a wide variety of supernatural beasties have replaced mere mortals as the most popular romance heroes and heroines. Stephenie Meyer leads the pack of paranormal authors with her Twilight series of novels about a pretty high school senior named Bella Swan who must choose between angsty vampire hottie Edward Cullen and loyal werewolf hottie Jacob Black. Twilight is so popular that U.S. senator Amy Klobuchar asked Supreme Court nominee Elena Kagan if she belonged to Team Edward or Team Jacob. At times Meyer's Web site has received more than a million visitors a day. The vast majority of her fans are women.

The rapid rise of the paranormal in romance is largely due to an extraordinary variety of erotical illusions. The paranormal takes the psychological cues inherent to the genre and twists them into marvelous new variations that satisfy Miss Marple in deliciously fresh new ways. Paranormals are the cream cheese sushi of the female sexual brain.

Consider paranormal heroes: wizards, necromancers, werewolves, and—most common of all—vampires. These supernatural males are alphas among alphas. Vampires are exceptionally strong and powerful. They're often immortal. They know how to fight and are willing to annihilate the competition. They are fully capable of protecting the ones they love from a range of mundane and otherworldly dangers. In most tellings, such as Laurell K. Hamilton's Anita Blake series and Anne Rice's Lestat series, vampires are fabulously wealthy, having acquired land and treasure across centuries. They're prone to owning mansions and castles, and inevitably have far-flung networks of "old money" and behind-the-scenes power. The Validus vampires in F. E. Heaton's *Winter's Kiss*, for example, are a one-thousand-year-old vampire bloodline that influences European politics.

"Edward Cullen has, for millions of passion-starved better halves worldwide, become the undead embodiment of everything the contemporary schlub seems to have shed: danger, poetry, strength, speed, eternal devotion, and an insatiable hunger for the jugular," complains Jeff Gordinier, the editor at large at *Details* magazine. "Meanwhile, the defanged mortal males of Earth, their rumps firmly planted in front of the flat-screen and their breath faintly fragrant of Pirate's Booty, have become, thanks to Edward, one big collective cuckold."

Werewolves are also alphas—even when they're not. In most paranormals, including the works of Stephenie Meyer, Charlaine Harris, and Keri Arthur, werewolves operate in packs. Every pack has a true designated alpha wolf. However, any werewolf has monstrous strength and ferocity and refuses to back down from a challenge. They are intensely loyal to protecting anyone who is part of the pack, including human girlfriends.

Most supernatural heroes, whether storm-calling wizards, fire-breathing demons, or mind-reading psychics, have the kind of strength, competence, confidence, and willingness to defend women that sends Miss Marple into happy fits of fast-track approval. Particularly considering that paranormal heroes offer especially sweet emotional centers inside their tough supernatural shells.

In J. R. Ward's Black Dagger Brotherhood series of erotic paranormals, the vampires are led by the blind vampire prince Wrath, a super-alpha who is introduced as follows:

Wrath was six feet, six inches of pure terror dressed in leather. His hair was long and black, falling straight from a widow's peak. Wraparound sunglasses hid eyes that no one had ever seen revealed. Shoulders were twice the size of most males'. With a face that was both aristocratic and brutal, he looked like the king he was by birthright and the soldier he'd become by destiny.

Wrath is an erotical illusion. The description of Wrath comes close to the exaggerated caricature of an impossibly broad-shouldered, improbably thin-waisted hero on the Cartoon Network, but since Wrath is a mythic being it makes this impossible blend of cues possible—and highly exciting to his female audience. The Amazon Kindle allows readers to highlight passages in their e-books and displays the passages that are most frequently high-lighted by *all* readers of the same book. The above description of Wrath is one of the five most popular passages in *Dark Lover.*

Wrath has other cues that enrapture the Detective Agency. He is a thousand years old, immortal, the leader of an elite, inter-nationally influential brotherhood of vampires, controls a kingly amount of investments in banks across the globe, and has killed hundreds of human men who pissed him off for various reasons. He's an erotic concoction that hyperstimulates female psychologi-cal cues of experience, wealth, competence, and Miss Marple–swooning dominance.

Though vampires turbocharge cues of masculinity, the eroti-cal illusions are only complete when these invincible heroes are brought to their knees by the irresistibility of an ordinary woman and her ability to unlock his secret heart. In the *Dark Lover* excerpt that opens this section, the half-human Beth has a Magic Hoo Hoo that dumbfounds Wrath, even though his palate has been jaded by "cozying up to lightning." Another J. R. Ward vampire, named Rhage, has been cursed so that he possesses an unchecked lust for blood and women. When roused, his beast within is only satisfied by merciless, mindless sex with women he can hardly remember. And yet this formidable vampire ends up being vanquished by his deep and instant love for an average-looking cancer survivor named Mary who volunteers at a suicide hotline.

Mary's very first utterance enraptures Rhage:

> Rhage shivered, a balmy rush blooming out all over his skin. The musical lilt of her voice, the rhythm of her speech, the sound of her words, it all spread through him, calming him, comforting him. Chaining him sweetly.

The paranormal allows for the irresistibility cue to take even more fervent forms. In *Twilight*, the vampire Edward Cullen doesn't just lust after Bella's body . . . he lusts after her blood. Because of his vampire nature, his heart pounds and his mind gets dizzy whenever he's close enough to smell the sweet red platelets pulsing through her carotid artery. He has a voracious hunger for her—but can't let himself give in, producing one of the most famously angsty alphas in all of paranormal romance. As a result, Bella gets to be desired forever with a supernatural longing, by a boyfriend who continuously proves how much he loves her by controlling himself. Bella has the ultimate Magic Hoo Hoo.

Edward Cullen exerts such influence over the brains of his female fans that he is the frequent subject of sexual searches on the Internet. In fact, one woman professed her love—and lust—for Edward Cullen in a series of dozens of Dogpile sentence-length searches in 2009:

> i'm a single woman in her 44 years old and i love edward cullen's like a sex object.

> ok edward cullen i'll go down on you if you can give into me and my clit is going out of control for you

> you fucking people edward cullen is not gay he totally love's bella to death and i love him cause i'm not gay either

> edward cullen please let me do naughty and dirty things to you all night long you wouldn't let bella do

The art of erotical illusions also allows paranormal romance authors to write rape scenes that aren't quite rape. In Laurell K.

Hamilton's series of books about a female necromancer/vampire hunter named Anita Blake, an evil wizard forcefully infects Blake against her will with a metaphysical hunger called the *ardeur*. It is a forced violation not of her body, but of her very psyche. Its erotic nature is emphasized by the fact that the *ardeur* compels her to have sex with all manner of supernatural beasties.

In vampire romances from Stephenie Meyer to Charlaine Harris, savage male vampires sink their fangs into the bodies of human women, changing them against their will into bloodsucking creatures of the night. Often, these paranormal coercion scenes are written in a way that leaves little doubt of their status as erotical illusions, such as this scene from J. R. Ward's *Dark Lover*:

> As the last shudder left his body and went into hers, at that moment when he was finally spent, the balance of his desires was thrown. His bloodlust surged forward in a wicked, consuming rush, as powerful as the lust had been.
>
> He bared his teeth and went for her neck, for the vein deliciously close to the surface of her pale skin.
>
> His fangs were about to sink deep, his throat dry with thirst for her, his gut spasming with a starvation that cut to his soul, when he pulled himself up short, horrified by what he was about to do.

If Japanese anime offers the greatest creative freedom for erotical illusions that titillate the male brain, then the paranormal romance is its match for the female brain.

RIDING THE EXPRESS CUE TRAIN

Back when men had to trek all the way out to a gritty downtown movie theater in order to watch a 16mm skin flick, the money shot landed on a variety of places, including—once in a while—a woman's face. In Internet porn, however, facials are the most common money shot by a wide margin. On Fantasti.cc, out of the one hundred top rated videos that show ejaculation, fifty-four of them are facials.

The facial is an erotical illusion that merges the visual with the psychological. Specifically, facials juxtapose three sexual cues within a single stimulus: the penis (a visual cue), the ejaculation (which may be a sperm competition cue or possibly a cued interest in some men), and—most important—the woman's emotional reaction, which may be a psychological cue of female pleasure (if she expresses delight) or a psychological cue of sexual submission (if she expresses surprise or dismay).

It's a way of adding an emotional commentary on the ejaculation, a kind of pornographic emoticon that guides and enhances the reaction of the male sexual brain. In contrast, ejaculating on a woman's stomach, chest, or butt does not provide the same psychological cue, even if a woman is moaning with pleasure.

This juxtaposition of psychological cues with visual cues has been developed into a cinematic technique adopted by more sophisticated pornographers, such as the French director Hervé Bodilis. He frequently uses split screens to simultaneously show close-ups of female anatomy or male ejaculation on one side and a close-up of a woman's facial expressions on the other. In his Russian Institute series, there is a scene where the left screen shows a close-up of two women's hands masturbating a large penis, while the right screen shows the two women's faces pressed together, smiling with delight at the unseen man—a *Mona Lisa*–like erotical illusion that induces a perceptual shift depending on exactly where you look.

One type of porn intensifies the effect of the facial erotical illusion: *bukkake*. Bukkake consists of multiple men simultaneously ejaculating on one woman's face. Bukkake offers the same sexual cues as a one-man facial—namely, the penis, the ejaculation, and the emotional reaction of the woman—but adds two more. First, bukkake repeats the same set of cues each time a new man ejaculates on the woman, repeatedly activating the novelty cue in quick succession. Second, the multiple men likely trigger sperm competition cues, and perhaps the copious semen does as well.

A similar effect is achieved through video editing. The seventh most common search on PornHub is for "compilations." A compilation is an edited collection of brief clips around some theme, such as facials, large breasts, or anal sex. "Cumshots" are the most common theme for a compilation; the most popular cumshot compilation on PornHub consists of thirty separate ejaculations edited into a three-minute video. A compilation is basically a staccato succession of similar cues. It's like getting the Uno's appetizer sampler. You get a collection of highly cravable bite-sized morsels you can pop into your mouth, one after another: potato skins, nachos, chicken fingers, onion rings, chicken wings.

The idea of enhancing erotic pleasure by duplicating cues is also found in a surprising kind of female erotica.

DOUBLE THE PLEASURE, TRIPLE THE FUN

"For me, gay porn has always been arousing because of its masculinity," writes *Wired* columnist Regina Lynn. "The strength and power, plus the double dose of raw male drive and sexuality, add up to more than the sum of their parts."

Lesbian sex has been a mainstay of male-targeted porn since the nineteenth century. The sight of two girls making out in mainstream movies like *Wild Things* and *Mulholland Drive* (not to mention the Girls Gone Wild videos) is well known to stoke men's libidos. But it's not widely known that many women are just as turned on by watching two guys sexually satisfy each other.

In the breakout indie movie, *The Kids Are All Right*, the lesbian couple played by Julianne Moore and Annette Bening watch a gay porn video while having sex. Though the raunchy physicality of gay porn is too overwhelming for many women, this is exactly what appeals to its female fans. "What do you like to see in porn? More than anything, I like to see the people enjoying themselves and really getting into it," writes one woman. "I have to admit, I'm a straight female, but my preference is for gay male porn—twice the dicks to enjoy looking at! And when the guys are really into it, and making all kinds of sexy noises, that's my favorite stuff."

Over the past five years, gay porn has surged in popularity among heterosexual women and doesn't show any sign of having peaked. But despite the growing numbers of female fans of gay sex, gay romance stories are even more popular. But these female-targeted stories are quite different from gay stories aimed at homosexual men. Below are two literary snippets: the first from erotic fanfic, the second from gay erotica.

Draco took a quill from Harry's case and, watching Harry with a sly, mischievous smile on his face, dropped it on the floor right under their desk. Draco slid down to reach it, and found himself between Harry's unconsciously parted legs.

He slowly unzipped Harry's fly and stroked his stomach, asking him to relax and give into the provided pleasure. Harry obeyed and breathed in, shivering from the sudden sensation of soft fingers on his bare flesh.

Glorious, Harry thought before closing his eyes and entering another row of Nirvana, unable to bear the slowlyness of erotic movements. "Draco, please," he whispered under his breath, as low as he could so the teacher wouldn't hear him . . . if professor Binns ever heard anything other than historical facts.

"I bet my weapon's bigger than yours," the cop joked as he raised his nightstick for the boy to see. It was a thick baton, easily over a foot long. The cop gobbed on the end of the stick. "This is gonna go right up into your guts boy."

The boy moaned in fear as he stared at the stick. "Please, no sir. No . . ." The lad shook his head weakly.

The cop tugged at the flimsy cotton briefs causing the lad's heavy cock and balls to fall out. "Nice thick cock you have there; full loaded balls," the cop moaned as he feasted his eyes on the lad's equipment.

The fastest expanding subgenre of EroRom is *male-male romances.* These stories didn't even exist a decade ago—at least, not as a commercial genre. But now every major romance publisher has published or is planning gay love stories. Authors such as Erastes, Chris Owen, Claire Thompson, and Ruth Sims write about two male heroes and no heroines—but their books are most definitely targeted at women. The largest audience for the groundbreaking film *Brokeback Mountain* was not the gay community, but straight women eager to hear two alpha male cowboys say to each other, "I wish I knew how to quit you." The movie was based on a short story written by a woman.

As the two passages quoted earlier demonstrated, there is no mistaking gay erotica written by a woman for gay erotica written by a man. Stories by men are designed to activate male cues. They feature hard-core sex (including anilingus and fisting), lots of obscenities, graphic descriptions of anatomies, physical roughness, and very few expressions of emotion or tenderness. They often delight in humiliating a character and are rife with gang bangs, anal rape, and enormous penises.

Gay stories written by women have quite a different feel and tone. The emotional journeys of the characters are almost always the main thing, and a scene is rarely depicted without identifying the vivid feelings of the participants. Anatomy is not described in detail, the physical violence is markedly toned down, and even though there's plenty of domination and submission, the stories almost always end with some kind of lasting emotional bond.

Gay porn may also appeal to women by eliminating any interference from Detective Agency concerns about whether a scene involving a woman depicts misogynistic, dangerous, or degrading activities. Men are doing things to other men—there's nobody to potentially feel bad for.

Gay EroRoms are even starting to make their way into mainstream publishing lines like Harlequin and Avon. But the Internet is the real engine driving the surging popularity of gay romance, in the form of a subgenre of fan fiction known as *slash*. Slash takes its name not from any kind of violence, but rather from a punctuation mark. The content of slash stories is indicated by a particular pairing of two heterosexual men, such as Kirk/Spock, Harry Potter/Severus Snape, or Frodo/Legolas. Over the course of a slash story, the two "slashed" heroes will end up emotionally and sexually involved.

There are more than a half million slash stories on the Web, across more than a hundred different fandoms, virtually all written by female amateurs in the privacy of their homes. *Harry Potter*, *Twilight*, and *Buffy the Vampire Slayer* boast the greatest number of slash stories. Though sex is often a key element of slash, the main focus is always how the two strong males share their tender side with each other. Though none of us can truly compare what it's like to experience both a male erotical illusion and a female erotical illusion, it seems reasonable to assume that slash offers women an even more intense illusion than lesbian porn offers men. As Regina Lynn noted, gay romance is "more than the sum of its parts" because it's the emotional interactions that activate female arousal, and having two alphas work out their inner coconut together builds more complex and engaging stimulation than watching two busty blondes gyrate together.

Though sex is often a key element of a slash story, the main focus is always how the two strong males share their tender side with each other. Here's a scene from "Happy Birthday," a Frodo/Sam slash story set in the *Lord of the Rings* universe:

> Sam smiled, love and joy and sheer bliss swelling so big inside his heart that he felt he would surely burst. He could easily recall the very first time he and Frodo had become intimate, finding love and comfort in each other's arms while surrounded by the purest form of evil each had ever known.

A love so deep and pure that it went far beyond mere friendship. Sam remembered gazing into those soul-weary eyes after that first time and seeing the blazing emotion lying just beneath the surface.

"I love you, Mister Frodo," Sam whispered.

"And I love you, Sam Gamgee."

In slash, one of the men is usually portrayed as slightly more feminine than the other: smaller, physically weaker, lighter in coloring, more seductive, more in touch with his emotions, and quicker to perceive the development of mutual love. "One of the guys is almost always written as shorter, even if they were the same height in the fandom," explains slash scholar Brita Hansen. "He usually ends up being the bottom."

Though many American fans of slash are somewhat reluctant to publicly disclose their interest, it is widely understood in Japanese society that women enjoy gay romances, which are often called *yaoi* (or "boy-love"), such as *Fujimi Orchestra* and *Constellation in My Palm*. The most popular comic books (known as manga) among Japanese girls feature handsome, slightly feminine heterosexual boys who have sex with one another. During the 1992 Tokyo Gay and Lesbian Film Festival, an estimated 80 percent of the audience were straight women who wanted to watch men have sex. As journalist Richard McGregor writes, "In Japan, almost anything homosexual can attract an all-female audience." In a cultural variation of slash, whenever a Japanese animated television series or male-targeted manga series becomes extremely popular, the producers almost always issue a boy-love version, where the male characters have sex with each other. "It's widely understood that the audience for these boy-love stories is women."

Slash, gay EroRom, and paranormal romance all demonstrate that literary erotical illusions are predominantly the province of women. But the male brain can also experience erotic mental trickery in the form of text. In fact, there's one literary erotical illusion that is the exclusive domain of the male mind.

THE RELUCTANT CHEERLEADER

In his seventeenth-century autobiography, the Abbé de Choisy describes the pleasure of being mistaken for a woman: "I wore embroidered corsets and gold and black robes de chambre, with sleeves lined with white satin, a girdle with a bust and a large knot of ribbons behind to mark the waist."

On the Internet it's possible for a man to experience de Choisy's unique thrills vicariously, through a genre of erotica known as *transformation fiction*. Web sites featuring transformation stories and graphics include Six Pack Site, TG Comics, and the largest and oldest site, Fictionmania. In transformation stories, a man is changed into a woman through a dazzling variety of methods: magic, chemicals, alien technology, genetic manipulation, or surgery. This change almost always occurs unwillingly. Sometimes a man is tricked, sometimes he suffers an accident, often he is punished for some crime of masculine hubris. Eventually, however, the victim adjusts to his change and comes to happily accept his new life, and all the perks that womanhood brings.

We opened our book with the tragic story of David Reimer, who was raised as a girl for fourteen years before rebelling against his fate and returning to manhood. We end with an erotical illusion that enables men to derive erotic pleasure from imagining themselves as a woman. What can we learn from this strange contrast? In Chapter 7, we examined the cues that arouse gay men in order to gain a better understanding of the differences in the desire software of men and women. Transformation fiction offers the same opportunity, by revealing which cues men believe they would get to experience if only they had the body of a woman.

Even though transformation stories contain ample psychological details about what it's like to be a woman, nobody would mistake these desires or experiences for those of a genuine lady. The stories usually contain copious amounts of promiscuous sex, as the newly minted tart is inevitably compelled to provide sexual gratification for a variety of well-endowed men. In transformation fiction, there's a remarkable number of policemen with a penchant for blackmailing newly created women into performing fellatio on them. Men who visit strip clubs are inevitably turned into strippers who must service all the patrons. In the story "Team Spirit," the misogynistic football quarterback Josh is transformed into a sexy cheerleader named Honey who meets a suitable fate.

> Honey looked at Anthony, her face stricken. It'd already been over a day since he fucked her and she was feeling her pussy getting more and more aroused. She didn't know if she could stand waiting until tomorrow for his semen.
>
> "Well Honey! Looks like now's your chance to show a little team spirit," Amy said with a spiteful grin.
>
> Billy took her hand and led her into a room filled with an entire football team flushed with victory, celebrating the biggest win of the year.
>
> "Anthony said to tell you the entertainment committee promised him $100 a pop! He said there's a special treat if you manage to fuck every single member of the team!"

One of the key moments in these stories is when a new woman interacts with others for the very first time. Inevitably, there is a positive reaction to her physical appearance. Men drool with lust, women confess their envy, bouncers unhook the velvet rope. Often the man wins a beauty contest, is voted homecoming queen, or wins a lap dance competition at a strip club. This is because he has inevitably been endowed with a female body stitched together with every male visual cue. In "Slow Justice," a boy named Russ who date-raped a girl is transformed into Rose. Each morning, he becomes more and more feminine, until the transformation is complete in this scene:

> She could hardly believe what she saw in the mirror. Her hair was a mass of chestnut curls that framed her now heart shaped face and hung down almost to her waist. Her eyebrows were shaped to narrow lines, and her eyelashes seemed much longer. Her complexion was peaches and cream perfect. Her lips seemed fuller, and her expression fell into a natural, but very sexy pout.
>
> She stepped back to get a look at her figure. Her hips seemed wider, too, and her waist narrower. The nightie was cut low and barely contained her larger breasts. She posed this way and that in front of the mirror, marveling at her new figure. She felt feminine and sexy, and a growing part of her loved the feeling.

There is an obsessive interest with breast size in much of transformation fiction. It's rare for a newly transformed woman to have breasts smaller than a D, while double-D, double-E, and even double-G breasts are not uncommon. Feet are always small and dainty, and usually clad in four-inch heels. In fact, careful attention is paid to another component of the male fantasy of womanhood: fashion. Most transformation stories include elaborate, almost baroque descriptions of female clothing and the methodical process of putting it on: silky stockings, thong underwear, lacy bras—the stories sometimes read like an advertisement for Frederick's of Hollywood. Shopping is often the first step of the newly transformed, followed by a trip to the salon for a makeover, complete with a sultry new coiffure, a manicure, and professional cosmetics. In the transformation comic *How Annie and Toni Became Best Friends Forever Part 2*, more than three-fourths of the 125 panels feature shopping. There's even a sequence of twenty consecutive panels that simply show the new girl in different dresses.

Here is a list of some of the most common two-word phrases in stories on Fictionmania:

a boy

a dress

his mother

a girl

my new

the doctor

the mall

to wear

little girl

my mother

high heels

the old

her new

to change

the boys

the mirror

"The mall" is a common place to shop for something "to wear," such as "a dress" or "high heels." "The doctor" usually confirms that "a girl" is no longer "a boy." Sometimes the "little girl" simply confirms "the change" in "the mirror." Interestingly, "the mother" usually plays an affirming role in transformation fiction; the father features less prominently.

Contrasting the male conception of the female mind with the real thing is as amusing as it is illuminating. Men, imagining women to share their psychology, envision becoming promiscuous women with an overriding interest in anonymous sex. Transformation stories obsess over penises, with far more time spent on the details of other men's penises than the loss of the main character's own penis, which is usually small to begin with. Intriguingly, when men become women, they often become bimbos as well. Boys who are straight-A students as males become C students as girls. Men who run international financial firms are barely able to survive as secretaries. Though fan fiction plumbs the emotions of its heroines in great detail, in transformation fiction the transformed heroines seem to desire only shopping, dressing up, and sex.

The audience for transformation fiction is mainly heterosexual males, though actual transsexuals appear to form a significant portion of the audience. In fact, a recent study found that enjoyment of transformation stories was the single factor that best predicted whether a transsexual would eventually seek sex change surgery. Nevertheless, judging from online comments, most fans of transformation stories don't appear to seek sex reassignment, though many may dress up in women's clothes. A significant number of fans are married, heterosexual men.

So why do straight men get turned on by the thought of themselves as a woman—a desire that psychologists call *autogynephilia*? It may ultimately be a kind of erotical illusion that combines the sexual submission cue with the male visual cues of female anatomy, as well as psychological cues such as female pleasure (since the transformed woman usually experiences sexual ecstasy), and sperm competition (since she frequently experiences group or serial sex). Since searches for transformation fiction are moderately correlated with searches for other kinds of submission porn, perhaps reading transformation fiction activates the subcortical sexual circuitry associated with female sexual submission.

It may be that some men are born with a stronger connection between the hypothalamic submission circuitry and the subcortical reward system than in other men, and this connection manifests itself as an inexplicable, unconscious urge to assume the submissive role. Psychologists draw attention to the fact that in transformation stories, the man is always forced to change against his will. Some external force compels the transformation, which is initially resisted by the man. This may reflect an unconscious (i.e., subcortical) urge that imposes itself on the conscious (i.e., cortical) mind. This urge *feels* like an external compulsion. But once this subcortical compulsion is accepted by the conscious mind, a powerful psychological satisfaction can result. Perhaps this is why most stories end up with a happy ending, the new girl living as an internationally famous teen pop star or leading the dance as the high school prom queen—or even serving as a brainwashed but satisfied high-end prostitute for wealthy businessmen.

A man gets to feel the pleasure of his submissive circuitry by living as a woman who is meek, ditzy, and ravished by dominant men. He gets to experience the visual pleasures of youth cues (a very popular category of transformation stories is "age regression") and female anatomy cues. Most transformees spend considerable time ogling their female anatomy in the mirror, describing their new breasts and hips and derriere with the same level of assiduous detail that we find in male porn. The fondness for group sex and penis-focused promiscuity also reflects typical male cues. However, even within this experience of sexual submission, the male is still focused on the sexual pleasure of the partner. There is far more emphasis on the pleasure the "real" male characters receive from the transformee then there is on the transformee's own pleasure—though the new woman does usually experience thunderous orgasms that far outclass anything she experienced as a man.

It's possible that transformation fiction also involves a disruption or deception of the brain's erotic body map we speculated on in Chapter 7. The extrastriate body area in the cortex shows different activation when looking at others' body parts than when looking at one's own body parts. Perhaps by imagining that one's own body is other, one can create a neural feedback loop that tricks the male desire software into believing it is perceiving external cues of female anatomy.

But for some fans of transformation fiction, it may simply be a desire to be the center of sexual attention. To have everyone lust after you. If women get to have a Magic Hoo Hoo, then why can't I?

....

Erotical illusions—including T-girl porn, paranormal romance, slash fiction, and transformation fiction—are unrecognized pinnacles of human imagination, as inventive and creative as the sushi in the Ginza district of Japan or the harmonizing melodies of the Beatles. These illusions reveal a hidden fact about all erotic experiences: that what ultimately binds sexual cues together into a single experience is our *imagination*.

Many believe that by reducing our desires into a set of narrow biological cues, we eliminate all the magic of sex. Instead, by identifying those cues, we can liberate ourselves and appreciate the magic more clearly. A penis and a female body can be combined within the sorcery of the male sexual imagination to produce an entirely new creation. Dominant men and irresistible women can be magnified by the erotic artistry of the female sexual imagination to produce thrilling tales of vampires and demons.

By investigating the software of our sexual brain, we can finally appreciate the true nature of human desire. There is no such thing as an absolute, unitary "male sexuality" or "female sexuality," but instead a number of gender-specific software components, subject to the vagaries of biology and experience. We each respond to our own unique pattern of sexual cues—some male, some female, some fixed, some flexible. Cues can flip, change, or transform, resulting in endless variations of sexual identity that defy easy labeling. But it is our sexual cues, our finite, identifiable, biological cues, that grant us all the pleasures of sex.

Our cues release us, even as they bind us.

CONCLUSION
Happy Ending or Happily-Ever-After?

Different but equal.
—Roy Baumeister, social psychologist

Now that we've finally seen what's on the end of a billion forks, we can draw some conclusions. One of the most encouraging is this: if you are a woman, then no matter what your attributes—big or skinny, A-cup or double-E, mother or grandmother—you are the sexual ideal and greatest erotic fantasy for an abundance of men. Similarly, if you are a man, no matter what your character—aggressive or pacifist, witty or stoic, rich or penniless, scarred or delicate—there are plenty of women who can fall in love with you, and if their love is reciprocated, feel intense desire for you.

Some of us may have a harder time finding a sexual match than others, and perhaps the one we find the most attractive may not reciprocate our sentiments. Sexual attraction may not always lead to long-term compatibility. Fortunately, the Internet—in addition to being the genie of a million squicks—offers myriad new ways of finding someone whose desires complement our own.

Why is human sexuality so diverse, with homosexuality, bisexuality, and transsexuality appearing so often alongside heterosexuality? Over the past few hundred thousand years, the design of women's brains have diverged more and more from men's brains in order to manage the different challenges confronted by each sex: the primary challenge of long-term investment planning for women, the primary challenge of attaining status for men. But as the software of the male brain has become ever more different from the software of the female brain, this has increased the number of opportunities for disruptions during neural development. Sometimes female software ends up with male components, sometimes male software gets female components. The very gulf that separates a woman's brain from a man's brain is responsible for all the wondrous diversity of human sexuality.

As our world becomes more technologically sophisticated and socially complex, this has introduced even more variations in the way our sexual cues get set and triggered. Our sexual software, originally designed to play the odds, now allows us to play the field, searching for partners who match our unique sexual tastes with unprecedented precision.

The greatest hurdle to sexual harmony is ignorance of the fact that members of the other sex (and other sexual orientations) are fundamentally different from ourselves. We all instinctively feel that other people must be *just like us*. "It just seems so natural to like men," insisted one thirty-year-old gay man when asked why he liked gay porn that featured straight men. "To be completely honest, I guess I believe that all guys must feel the same attraction to men that I do, but straight guys just repress these feelings. So when I see a straight guy having sex with other men, it feels like validation. It's like—*see, he's just like me after all*."

Similarly, many straight men believe that, deep down, all women secretly yearn for casual, no-strings-attached sex with strangers. Many straight women believe men have been socialized to be aggressive and promiscuous—but hide a secret emotional life that, with the proper attention, will blossom into tenderness and monogamy. It's hard for us to accept that other people's most intimate desires are different from our own—and when confronted with this fact, we often dismiss their desires as deviant or dangerous or just plain hurtful. When literary scholar Janice Radway asked the women in a romance discussion group about male sexuality, the women reported that they did not want to adopt male standards; they wished that men would learn to adhere to theirs. Doubtless, most men feel the same way. By identifying and understanding one another's sexual cues, we can develop greater comfort, confidence, and compassion; only then will we have an authentic opportunity to truly connect.

Some might argue that not all of our sexual cues should be indulged—that some should be ignored or repressed. Science can't offer any moral prescription about which cues should be judged acceptable and which unacceptable; but science does tell us that it's difficult or impossible to modify men's rigid cues, and even though women's tastes are more plastic, it's simply not possible to shut off the sleuthing of Miss Marple or her detectives. It's also worth remembering that at various points in the twentieth century, the medical profession and mainstream society were in perfect agreement that certain sexual activities were *unacceptable*, including masturbation, oral sex, anal sex, adolescent make-out sessions, homosexuality, and interracial sex.

Our brain has a conscious, thinking cortex that is fully capable of pondering human sexuality and forming its own judgment. That's part of the joy of being human—figuring out what to do about the unique pattern of cues that nature and experience have endowed us with. We can accept our fantasies without becoming slaves to them. Maybe you'll explore your own cues in solitude; perhaps you'll seek those places where your cues intersect someone else's.

But a lucid consideration of our unique suite of cues holds tremendous potential for deep personal fulfillment—a fulfillment we may not be able to experience from anything else. As American author Edward Abbey writes, "Modern men and women are obsessed with the sexual; it is the only realm of primordial adventure still left to most of us. Like apes in a zoo, we spend our energies on the one field of play remaining; human lives otherwise are pretty well caged in by the walls, bars, chains, and locked gates of our industrial culture."

ACKNOWLEDGMENTS

Accumulating and interpreting a billion wicked thoughts required the support, guidance, and kindness of a great many folks.

We're grateful for the excellent research assistance provided by Jess Kamen, Jessie Sementelli, Kyra Smith, Lyndsey LaRiviere, Matt Feltz, Lingqiang Kong, Thao Nguyen, and Brian Wilder. Lauren Clark and Dan Schneider deserve special notice for their talent and effort.

We'd like to thank anonymous individuals who shared ideas with us: Axay, Irlemochrie, countryadameve, xannate, pbjane, contractor72. We'd also like to thank the anonymous workers of Amazon Turk.

We'd like to thank the following individuals for advice and ideas: Erik Larsen, Jeannie Larsen, Denise Leclair of the International Foundation for Gender Education, Anna Schwind, Gennady Livitz, Tom Standage, Alex Davis, Joe Rogan, Andrea Cendrowski, Chris Betke, and Eddie Ramsey.

We'd also like to thank the scientists and professionals who answered our questions or sent us material: Debra Lieberman, David Buss, Roy Baumeister, Richard Wrangham, Leda Cosmides, Elaine Hatfield, Meredith Chivers, Nicholas Pound, Albert-László Barabási, Robert Boyd, Joseph Plaud, Anne Lawrence, Peter Brugger, Serge Stoleru, William Reiner, Joshua Greene, Elizabeth Hines of Project HAL, Peter Gray, Matthew McIntyre, Larry Cahill, Dominique de Quervain, Ernst Fehr, Daniel Kruger, J. Michael Bailey, Simon Lajeunesse, Sherif Karama, Irv

ACKNOWLEDGMENTS

Binik, James Roney, Margaret McCarthy, Diane Halpern, Gilbert Herdt, Ed Hagen, Carla Harenski, Jonathan Haidt, Tom Standage, Jim Jansen, Eujern Lim, Alan Said, Sam Gosling, Leonard Koziol, Dan Ariely, Melita Giummarra, Isabelle Henault, Benjamin Edelman, Yonie Harris, Alice Dreger, Elise Seip, Julie Albright, Peter Skomoroch, Lisa Ruble, George M. Realmuto, Daniel Kruger, William Tooke, Lindsay Weekes, Tyler Cowen, Andrey Anokhin, Joe Henrich, Henry Jenkins, Adam Wilson of Mira Books, and Raelene Gorlinsky of Ellora's Cave.

We'd also like to thank Jasun Mark of Straight Guys for Gay Eyes, Laurel of Literotica, Paul Morrisson, Randy McAnus, Collin Ireland, Xvideos, Mack Mack, Max the Cat, Twilight Wars Author, Sam Lawrence of Blackbox Republic, Doug of Rabbit Reviews, Kellie Barker and Chris Baker of Adult Entertainment Broadcast Network (AEBN), Wetlook model and producer TracieZ, Erik Elsas of eewetlook.com, Joan Irvine of ASACP, Bob Smart of Booble, Lewis at Viv Thomas, Steve Lightspeed, Mark Greenspan of CCBill, Monica of Monica's Reviews, and Scott Rabinowitz.

We'd also like to thank Dan Bullock and Barbara Shinn-Cunningham for their support at Boston University. We'd especially like to thank Ron Tanner for his literary guidance.

We'd like to thank those who helped us with women's literature, including Erastes, Bo Balder, Susanna Carr, Alla Kalinina, Brita Hansen, Sylvia Volk, and Caroline Seawright.

We'd like to thank the publishing professionals who made this book possible, including attorney Gary Mailman, copy editors Rachael Hicks and Richard Willett, Jennifer Manguera, the magnificent Anna Sproul, editorial assistant Lily Kosner, Brian Tart, Christine Ball, and Gail Ross. Ogi would also like to thank Chris Castellani and Chip Cheek of Grub Street.

We'd like to thank the following individuals for reviewing drafts of our manuscript: Heather Ames, Greg Amis, Arash Fazl, Meredith Wright, Nico Foley, Arup Sen, Sara Trowbridge, Chris Yeomans, Karen Ferreira, Rena Xu, David Mou, Nicole Sarofeen, Peter Crossley, Antje Ihlefeld, Arash Fazl, Arun Ravindran,

ACKNOWLEDGMENTS

Darja Djordjevic, Elizabeth Ricker, Max Versace, Rohit Nambisan, Sameer Vaidya, Bo Balder, Sylvia Volk, Jess Kamen, Peter Kouroubacalis, John LaVerde, Kevin Jiggetts, Jessie Sementelli, Diwakar Chada, Aishwarya Mantha, Paulo Figueiredo, John Ogas, Ajish Potty, Shubhakoti Srikanth, Sameer Vaidya, Seema Rao, Jayaram Iyer, Murthy Bhavaraju, Santiago Olivera, Robert Kozma, Harsha Vellanki, Thomas Heiman, Sara Al-Tukhaim, Robin Sherk, Diksha Kuhar, Mrinmoyee Das, and Polina Ogas.

Special thanks to Eric X and Tiiu for sharing so much about their relationship and a mysterious world previously unknown to us.

Special thanks to Chris Coyne of OkCupid, who generously supplied us with terrific data.

Special thanks to C. Curtis Sassaman, who gave us invaluable information about running a porn site affiliate. His new Web site is poundedink.com.

We'd like to thank the extraordinarily generous and supportive Alec Helmy, who shared so many contacts and granted us the opportunity to attend the Xbiz conference.

Extra special thanks to Angie Rowntree and Colin Rowntree, who invited us into their home and shared so much precious data with us.

Thanks to Paul Vasey, whose help was so meaningful. We'd also like to thank the brilliant and always-diligent Stephanie Ortigue. Very special thanks to Frank Guenther.

We feel deep gratitude toward Steven Pinker, whose books, ideas, and research influenced us so profoundly.

Titmowse is one-of-a-kind and we hope we get to meet her in person one day. We'd also like to give very special thanks to Perry Stathopoulos of PornHub, who provided us with so much useful data and gave us an illuminating tour of the Manwin Canada offices.

We'd like to give outrageous thanks to Peter Kouroubacalis and John LaVerde, who showed us movies we never knew existed.

The remarkable Stephen Yaglieowicz was unfailingly helpful and interesting. He's a bright light in a murky industry.

ACKNOWLEDGMENTS

We'd like to give great thanks to Snake and Naif of Fantasti.cc, who invited us in and gave us the run of the place.

We'd really like to single out Marta Meana, whose feedback was unparalleled. She is a role model for all female scientists.

Of course, this book wouldn't exist without the creative energy of Peter Morley-Souter and Rosa Morley-Souter—two Internet legends who may not be quite so anonymous after this book.

We'd like to offer our heartfelt thanks to Stephen Morrow, who believed in this book from the start, and gave us the freedom and support to pursue it the way we wanted.

We'd also like to thank the very best literary agent in America, Howard Yoon. You're the grandmaster. Your support and talent mean everything to us.

But one man deserves our greatest praise. His intelligence, erudition, and unstinting generosity affected every atom of this book: Donald Symons. We walk in his shadow and follow his light. He opened up a universe to us, larger than our imagination, that never stops growing. Though we believe he has found the true path, any flaws, errors, misinterpretations, or outright howlers are our full responsibility. If we've strayed from the path, it's on us and us alone.

NOTES

PREFACE

xii **almost all of these people are still "WEIRD"** Henrich, et al. (2010). The WEIRD paper was coauthored with Ara Norenzayan and Steven Heine.

CHAPTER 1

1 **The study of desire** Personal communication, August 12, 2010, based upon original in Meana (2010).
"That researchers can distill sexual desire and separate it from its historical, cultural, and interpersonal context may be an illusion, but striving to be conscious of this complexity is a requirement. The study of sexuality, and desire in particular, has never been for the faint of heart."

1 **Heinrich Hertz built the very first radio antenna** Hertz stated, "I do not think that the wireless waves I have discovered will have any practical application." Photos of Hertz's original setup can be found at http://www.sparkmuseum.com/BOOK_HERTZ.HTM. Also see Buchwald (1994).

2 *Psychopathia Sexualis* The original is Krafft-Ebing (1887). We used Krafft-Ebing & Rebman (1906). available at http://www.archive.org/details/psychopathiasexu00krafuoft.

2 **"see what's on the end of everyone's fork"** Burroughs et al. (2003).

3 **Many social institutions don't want sex to be studied** Phoenix (1961). "Research on the relationships between the hormones and sexual behavior has not been pursued with the vigor justified by the biological, medical, and sociological importance of the subject. Explanation may lie in the stigma any activity associated with sexual behavior has long borne. In our experience, restraint has been requested in the use of the word sex in institutional records and in the title of research proposals. We vividly recollect that the propriety of presenting certain data at scientific meetings and seminars was questioned."
Locating Strategic Research Funds for Sexuality Science: An Exploratory Guide

(http://www.thefreelibrary.com/Locating+strategic+research+
funds+for+sexuality+science:+an . . . -a0154757389, retrieved on August
30, 2010.) "Investigators should ideally start with the question: 'what
is the sensitivity level of my particular research area?' If a researcher
wishes to investigate, for example, 'health risks of engaging in BDSM',
searching federal, or state and even local health sources is probably not
going to be successful. Such agencies normally do not fund such relatively
sensitive inquiry. Conversely, a wide variety of private organizations
and foundations may be quite interested in such research if it advances
knowledge and safer practices among the population who practice such
unique sexual activities."

Pfaus et al. (2003). "All too often our questions are obscured by scientific
blinders and constrained by research review committees. with certain
moral limitations imposed by ethics review boards and government
agencies pressured to enforce 'community standards.'"

Farmer and Binik (2005). "There are far more graduate training
opportunities in psychology departments for the study of depression
than for the study of sexual disorders. This is surprising considering the
high prevalence of sexual dysfunction compared to that of depression."
"Mainstream psychologists have not pursued sexology with the
enthusiasm aimed at other areas of psychological research. Ambivalence
is evident in the ideological marginalization of sexology by mainstream
psychology."

http://entertainment.timesonline.co.uk/tol/arts_and_entertainment/
books/book_extracts/article7060908.ece. "I always take it for granted
that sexual moralising by public figures is a sign of hypocrisy or worse,
and most usually a desire to perform the very act that is most being
condemned. This is why, whenever I hear some bigmouth in Washington
or the Christian heartland banging on about the evils of sodomy or
whatever, I mentally enter his name in my notebook and contentedly
set my watch. Sooner rather than later he will be discovered down on
his knees in some dreary motel or latrine, with an expired Visa card,
having tried to pay well over the odds to be peed upon by some Apache
transvestite."

3 **"But if you're studying sex"** Personal e-mail communication,
August 12, 2010.

3 **only one scientist has managed to survey a large number of
people on a broad range of sexual interests** http://sexademic
.wordpress.com/2010/03/19/before-there-was-kinsey-mosher-
davis-and-dickinson-surveyed-victorian-sex/, retrieved on August 30,
2010. Dr. Katharine Davis worked in New York as a corrections officer
and social reformer during the early 1900s. Sexual studies were not
the focus of her career, but in 1929 she published the results of 2,200
sexual questionnaires filled out by educated women. Dr. Robert Latou
Dickinson was an East Coast gynecologist and researcher during the
early twentieth century. He studied sexuality in marriage, personal
sexual histories of his female patients, and was one of the first doctors to

use vibrators on female patients. In his survey of one thousand married women he found that they most frequently complained about failure to reach orgasm and that obstacles to sexual pleasure were primarily inorganic, i.e., not physiological in nature. http://www.stanfordalumni.org/news/magazine/2010/marapr/features/ mosher.html, retrieved on August 30, 2010. Dr. Clelia Duel Mosher conducted possibly the first known female sexual attitudes survey in 1892 in the Midwest. Her study was meant to fill her own knowledge gaps for a married life presentation for the Mothers Club of the University of Wisconsin. She created forty-five sexual profiles that offer a peek into Victorian female sexuality, affirming that the public record of values often disappears in private conduct. The majority of women in the forty-five profiles reported enjoying sex and experiencing sexual desire.

3–4 **Alfred Kinsey** Jones (1997).

4 **"Too darn hot"** Lyrics taken from http://www.stlyrics.com/songs/e/ ellafitzgerald1351/toodarnhot862082.html, retrieved on August 28, 2010.

4 **Kinsey was denounced** Jones (1997). http://www.kinseyinstitute .org/about/Movie-facts.html, retrieved on August 30, 2010.

4 **The eighteen thousand men and women** The eighteen thousand figure is from the Kinsey Institute: http://www.iub.edu/~kinsey/about/ photo-tour.html, retrieved on August 30, 2010.

5 **many intellectual heirs of Richard von Krafft-Ebing have been pilloried** Some examples: the reaction to J. Michael Bailey's *The Man Who Would Be Queen*, Susan Clancy's *The Trauma Myth*, Randy Thornhill and Craig Palmer's *A Natural History of Rape*, and E. O. Wilson's *Sociobiology*. Also, the University of Illinois firing Leo Koch.

5 **The 1971 Stanford prison experiment** Zimbardo (2007).

5 **The 1960s Milgram obedience experiments** Miller (1986).

5 **"What do people do under conditions of extreme anonymity?"** Gergen et al. (1973), http://articles.sun-sentinel. com/1995-11-12/features/9511100325_1_james-latona-computer-network-anonymous-internet/4, retrieved on August 30, 2010.

6 **a much, much, much larger version of the Gergen experiment** Cooper (1998).
Anonymity is one of the A's in Al Cooper's "Triple A engine" (accessibility, affordability, anonymity) often cited as driving Internet porn use.

7 ***Rule #34*** Peter's story was communicated through e-mail during 2009–2010. The original comic is visible at http://rule34.blogspot .com/2007/06/first-post.html.

7 **"Rule 34 Challenge"** The competition is described at http:// boingboing.net/2008/04/18/irc-game-rule-34-cha.html.

7 **"'Specify type of goat'"** From Richard Jeni's *A Big Steaming Pile of Me*.

8 **ninety different adult magazines** Based on lists of pornographic magazines provided on http://en.wikipedia.org/wiki/List_of_ pornographic_magazines and http://www.absoluteastronomy.com/topics/ List_of_pornographic_magazines, both retrieved on August 30, 2010.

8 **nine hundred pornography sites** Stack et al. (2004).

8 **2.5** *million* **adult Web sites** http://www.cybersitter.com/, retrieved on August 30, 2010.

8 **sex-related online activities have become routine** Doring (2009).

8 **you can see more naked bodies in a single minute** "I can download 3 million vaginas in one minute." Louis C.K, *Chewed Up*.

8 **We no longer have to interact with** *anyone* **to obtain erotica** http://gizmodo.com/5316206/the-desperate-times-before-internet-porn/ gallery/#pager, retrieved on August 30, 2010. Also worth considering: http://getahead.rediff.com/report/2009/aug/12/videos-sex-porn-top-kids -internet-searches.htm, retrieved on August 30, 2010.

9 **an actual search someone entered on the Dogpile search engine** Dogpile searches were collected by scraping displayed searches on http://www.dogpile.com/dogpile/ws/searchspy. Also worth considering is the following list of the most common Dogpile searches that start with "how to":

Search	Frequency
how to offset your carbon footprint	5228
how to have sex	2730
how to get a dog to mount you	2536
how to give head	1957
how to finger a girl	1829
how to train your dragon	1772
how to last longer in bed	1538
how to eat a girl out	1417
how to masturbate	1415
how to eat pussy	1332
how to make a girl wet	1330
how to write a resume	1316
how to tie a tie	1302
how to masterbate	1256
how to give great head	1187
how to kiss	1143
how to make a girl squirt	1116
how to cook a turkey	1010

9 **a popular term for unusual sexual interests:** *kinks* See http:// www.urbandictionary.com.

10 **David Reimer** Colapinto (2001). http://www.slate.com/id/2101678, retrieved on August 30, 2010. http://reason.com/archives/2004/05/24/ the-death-of-david-reimer, retrieved on August 30, 2010.

11 **Dr. John Money of Johns Hopkins University** Ogi Ogas
previously interviewed John Money, though not about David Reimer, in
Ogas (1994).

12 **a report on fourteen genetic males who underwent neonatal
sex reassignment** Reiner & Gearhart (2004). Also personal
communication with William Reiner, April 2010.

13 **the Sambia** Herdt (1982). Herdt (2006), Bancroft (2000).

13 **semen is the essence of manhood** The idea of semen as male mojo
was also expressed by Robert Baden-Powell, founder of the Boy Scouts:
"Masturbation prevents you from becoming the strong manly man
you would otherwise be. You are throwing away the seed that has been
handed down to you as a trust instead of keeping it and ripening it for
bringing a son to you later on."

13 **a Sambian woman** The feminine mojo of Sambian women is believed
to reside in their menstrual blood.

13 **"natural experiments"** Diamond (1983). "Natural experiments permit
one to examine conditions that cannot be created experimentally and
reveal the end results of ecological and evolutionary processes."

13 **some things we *instinctively* find arousing** A biological male
preference for men or women is also supported by Lippa (2007).

13 **express precisely what they would like to pop up** It's important
to remember that online porn itself may represent the practical aspects
of pornography production, such as perceived financial returns, actor
availability, ease of production, and other business factors unrelated to
the ability to sexually arouse consumers.

14 **start by looking for patterns in these wishes** "I will focus on
the determinants of female sexual attractiveness, not on actual matings,
because the former more clearly illuminate the design of the
psychological machinery underpinning male sexual attraction. Who men
actually mate with depends on many things (such as opportunity and
risk) in addition to sexual attraction." Donald Symons in Abramson and
Pinkerton (1995), p88.

14 **400 million different searches that were entered into the
Dogpile** We collected 398,944,925 searches. We classified 55,170,457
of the searches as "sexual." We scraped from July 10, 2009, to July 28,
2010. We missed some days in September, for a total of 352 days of
scraping.

14 **some users are from India, Nigeria, Canada, and the United
Kingdom** Dogpile traffic from different countries is taken from
Quantcast (www.quantcast.com).

15 **AOL released a data set** You can view the AOL data set here:
http://www.aolstalker.com/
The scandal surrounding the release of the data is described in: http://
techcrunch.com/2006/08/06/aol-proudly-releases-massive-amounts-of
-user-search-data/, retrieved on August 29, 2010, and http://news.cnet.com/
AOL-apologizes-for-release-of-user-search-data/2100-1030_3-6102793
.html, retrieved on August 29, 2010.

NOTES

15 **"101 Dumbest Moments in Business"** http://money.cnn.com/ magazines/business2/101dumbest/2007/full_list/index.html, retrieved on August 29, 2010.

15 **the search phrase "college cheerleaders"** The expected number of overlapping searchers for "cheerleaders" and "porn" in the AOL data set: 50.3. Obtained: 382. The expected number of overlapping searchers for "college cheerleaders" and "porn," assuming independence: 0.6. Obtained: 8.

16 **we counted the search in the appropriate category** Obviously, this means there is a near-certainty of overcounting the frequency of certain sexual search categories. Some people searching for cheerleaders are no doubt searching for nonerotic reasons.

16 **most popular sexual interests on Dogpile** Here is a more complete list of sexual search categories from the Dogpile data set:

	%	Sexual Search Category
1	13.54	Youth
2	4.70	Gay
3	4.27	MILFs
4	3.95	Breasts
5	3.37	Cheating wives
6	2.82	Vaginas
7	2.41	Penises
8	2.36	Amateurs
9	2.11	Mature
10	2.11	Animation
11	2.1	Domination and Submission
12	1.02	Incest
13	1.86	Lesbian
14	1.76	Black
15	1.66	Bestiality
16	1.62	Fat
17	1.29	Transsexuals
18	1.24	Anal sex
19	1.23	Nudism
20	1.02	Grannies
21	0.93	Buttocks

NOTES

	%	Sexual Search Category
22	0.88	Voyeurs
23	0.88	Celebrities
24	0.86	Group sex
25	0.73	Hairy
26	0.72	Tattoo
27	0.69	Games
28	0.66	Fellatio
29	0.61	Asian
30	0.58	Skinny
31	0.55	Girlfriends
32	0.52	Spanking
33	0.49	Prostitutes
34	0.48	Webcam
35	0.48	Watersports
36	0.48	Rape
37	0.47	Squirting
38	0.46	Creampie
39	0.42	Swingers
40	0.41	Panties
41	0.35	College
42	0.33	Interracial
43	0.32	Pantyhose
44	0.31	Lingerie
45	0.31	Handjob
46	0.31	Upskirt
47	0.27	Nipples
48	0.27	Skirt
49	0.27	Sleep
50	0.27	Drunk
51	0.26	Massage
52	0.25	Fan fiction
53	0.25	Public

continued

	%	Sexual Search Category
54	0.24	Feet
55	0.24	Vintage
56	0.23	Vomit
57	0.17	Cfnm
58	0.16	Tickling
59	0.16	Injection
60	0.16	Daddies
61	0.16	Virgin
62	0.15	Cameltoe
63	0.15	Pregnant
64	0.15	Crossdress
65	0.13	Nipslip
66	0.13	Vaginal fisting
67	0.13	Enema
68	0.13	Gloryhole
69	0.11	Uniforms
70	0.11	Furry
71	0.10	Milking
72	0.10	Bisexual
73	0.09	Midget
74	0.09	Romance
75	0.09	Babysitter
76	0.09	Showers
77	0.08	Lactating
78	0.07	Grandpa
79	0.07	Cheerleader
80	0.07	Gym
81	0.07	Small breasts
82	0.07	Sybian
83	0.07	Facesitting
84	0.06	Dogging
85	0.06	Vore

NOTES

	%	Sexual Search Category
86	0.06	Clown
87	0.05	Emoporn
88	0.05	Groping
89	0.05	Areolas
90	0.05	Female masturbation
91	0.05	Testicles
92	0.05	Shaved
93	0.04	Transgender
94	0.04	Leather
95	0.04	Amputee
96	0.04	Bareback
97	0.03	Wet shirt
98	0.03	Cunnilingus
99	0.03	Lactation
100	0.03	Gagging

18 **The following tables list the most popular "erotic" Web sites**
Visitor information from Quantcast: www.quantcast.com. Rankings from
Alexa: www.alexa.com.

19 **men prefer images. Women prefer stories.** Women also enjoy
reading erotica more than men do. It's no surprise that the eleventh
century *Tale of Genji*, the world's first erotic novel, was written by a
woman. But erotic stories on the Web were initially targeted toward men,
who were far more prevalent on the Web than women in the
early years. See http://www.asstr.org/~JournalofDesire/v3n2/
JekyllSexStories.html
Pre-Internet studies of erotic fantasy include Leitenberg & Henning
(1995). "75% of boys and only 39% of girls responded yes to sexual
fantasy items, whereas 36% of boys and 50% of girls responded yes to
romantic fantasy items. In addition . . . explicit sexual scenes, as opposed
to romantic scenes, produced the greatest physiological (genital) arousal,
women did not rate these scenes as most arousing." "Female participants
were more likely to say that their first fantasies were stimulated by a
relationship (31% of women vs. 6% of men), whereas male participants
were more likely to have their first sexual fantasies in response to a visual
stimulus."
Hamann et al. (2004). "Men are generally more interested in and
responsive to visual sexually arousing stimuli than are women."

NOTES

GENDER DIFFERENCES ON SELF-REPORTED PREFERRED ONLINE SEXUAL ACTIVITIES

Activity	% Male	% Female
Looking for love contacts	4	2
Flirt	11	10
Looking for a partner	10	8
Staying in contact with a love/sex partner	8	21
Reading erotica (text)	6	9
Viewing erotica (pictures/ movies)	37	6
Visiting contact sites	8	8
Replying to sex ads	1	0
Chat with people with same interest	10	17
Educating myself about sex/ getting professional help	2	9
Buying sex products	1	3
Contacting prostitutes	0	-
Other things	4	7
	n=1090	*n=895*

Table from Cooper et al. (2002).

PRIMARY REASON FOR ONLINE SEXUAL ACTIVITIES, USA

	% of Men	% of Women
Distraction	60	37
Education	9	30

19 **Preferred Online Sexual Activity** Table from Cooper et al. (2003).

19 **different modes of stimulation** Leitenberg & Henning (1995). "Females are more likely to say that their first sexual fantasies were triggered by a relationship, whereas males report having theirs triggered by a visual stimulus."

19 **"In the male fantasy realm of pornotopia"** From personal

communications with Donald Symons and Catherine Salmon, August 2010. Based upon original text in Salmon & Symons (2003).

19 **Biological anthropologist Donald Symons** Kinsey's work parallels Galileo, who pointed a telescope at the heavens and was the first to document Saturn's rings and Jupiter's moons. Kinsey pointed his survey at men and women and was the first to systematically document their true sexual interests. Symons is more akin to Charles Darwin. Darwin patiently synthesized biological data from a broad variety of sources in order to forge a unifying theory of natural selection which explained the design of all life on Earth. Similarly, Symons synthesized a diverse range of findings to offer something that was missing from previous inquiries into human desire: an explanation. Masters and Johnson also contributed to sex science by reporting on what they observed, with very little theoretical contribution.

20 **Harvard psychologist Steven Pinker** Personal e-mail communication, August 26, 2010.

21 **our brains contain innate mechanisms designed to detect specific sexual cues** Toates (2009). "Incentives and cues associated with them (conditional stimuli) impinge on the nervous system, which triggers sexual motivation." Also worth considering: McCall & Meston (2006).

21 **"It is clear that human beings evolved psychological mechanisms"** From personal communications with Donald Symons and Catherine Salmon, August 2010. Based on original text in Salmon and Symons (2003).

22 **men and women are wired to detect the same taste cues** In fact, there is evidence that men and women do differ in their relative sensitivity to different taste cues. cf. http://carlacompanion.hoppress .com/2010/07/12/women-make-better-beer-tasters/, retrieved on August 30, 2010.

22 **how an apparent infinitude of appealing stimuli can be reduced to a finite set of cues** Also worth considering: language, which is infinitely expressive, despite a finite set of grammatical rules and a limited vocabulary.

CHAPTER 2

23 **Researchers led by neurobiologist Michael Platt** Deaner et al. (2005). Also personal e-mail communications with Michael Platt, March 2010.

23 **The most popular paysites featuring adult videos** Personal communications with Perry Stathopoulos, chief technology officer for Manwin Canada, parent company for Brazzers; Steven Yagielowicz, senior editor for Xbiz; Colin Rowntree, owner of Wasteland.com; and Titmowse, webmaster for Cozy Campus.

24 **only 2 percent of all subscriptions to pornography sites**

Personal communications with Mark Greenspan, vice president of CCBill.

24 **The National Science Foundation (NSF) is** http://www.nsf.gov/nsb/.

24 **a certain activity was stealing so many hours** See http://www.washingtontimes.com/news/2009/sep/29/workers-porn-surfing-rampant-at-federal-agency/
http://www.washingtontimes.com/news/2009/sep/29/workers-porn-surfing-rampant-at-federal-agency/
http://trueslant.com/level/2010/05/03/bored-florida-state-senator-caught-viewing-porn-on-senate-floor/
http://www.washingtontimes.com/news/2009/sep/29/workers-porn-surfing-rampant-at-federal-agency/?page=1.
In the NSF/OIG Semiannual Report to Congress, September 2008, that reports on the investigations, all investigated employees are referred to using the male pronoun. Example: "An NSF employee continued to store sexually explicit image files on his NSF computer, despite being previously reprimanded for downloading inappropriate files and peer-to-peer software on his NSF computer. The employee also sent emails from his NSF account that contained numerous sexually explicit image and video files to users outside NSF. Based on our findings and his recidivism, NSF issued a formal Proposal to Remove followed by a Decision terminating the employee. After being terminated, the employee invoked his right to grieve under NSF's CBA, and that process is pending."
http://www.nsf.gov/pubs/2009/oig0901/oig0901_3.pdf.

25 **the Securities and Exchange Commission (SEC)** http://www.cnn.com/2010/POLITICS/04/23/sec.porn/index.html.
http://ac360.blogs.cnn.com/2010/04/23/evening-buzz-viewing-porn-on-the-job/.

25 **Department of Defense at the Pentagon** http://www.dodig.mil/fo/Foia/PDFs/OperationFlickerReportsJuly2010pdf.pdf.
http://www.boston.com/news/nation/washington/articles/2010/07/23/pentagon_workers_tied_to_child_porn/.
http://www.heraldnet.com/article/20100724/NEWS02/707249949.

25 **Minerals Management Service** http://www.politico.com/static/PPM156_100524_mms_report.html.

25 **Men are so highly motivated to look at graphic sex** "Is There Anything Good About Men?" Roy Baumeister, American Psychological Association, Invited Address, 2007.
http://www.psy.fsu.edu/~baumeistertice/goodaboutmen.htm, retrieved on August 30, 2010.
"men recorded approximately 7.2 sexual fantasies per day as compared with 4.5 for women" and "men estimated they had approximately one sexual fantasy per day, whereas the women estimated they had only one sexual fantasy per week."
Leitenbergand Henning (1995).
"Male university students were found to masturbate to ejaculation about

every 72 hours, and on the majority of occasions, their last masturbation is within 48 hours of their next in-pair copulation." If they're not having intercourse every day, that is to say, men tend to pleasure themselves to completion no more than two days prior to having actual sex." http://www.scientificamerican.com/blog/post.cfm?id=one-reason-why -humans-are-special-a-2010-06-22, retrieved on August 20, 2010. Incidentally, male dolphins also have a very strong sex drive, and can mate dozens of times a day. They often try to have sex with inanimate objects and other animals, like sea turtles, using a penis as prehensile as an elephant's trunk. When a pack of male dolphins happen upon a female, they frequently attempt to force her to mate.

25 **one out of every six** 16.8 percent of all sexual searches.

25 **frequency of sexual searches on Dogpile that contain** *specific* **ages** We collected 398,944,925 searches. We classified 55,170,457 searches as "sexual" searches. We scraped from July 10, 2009, to July 28, 2010. We missed some days in September, for a total of 352 days of scraping. The figure shows age-specific sexual searches. The mode (not shown) is age thirteen. When including searches for ages 16 and under, the median age is 15 and the mean age is 20.

26 **cluster of searches** In the United States, all women in porn must be over eighteen. If you are looking at a porn site and don't see "18 USC 2257 Compliant," Chris Hansen of *To Catch a Predator* will be asking you to take a seat faster than you can say "statutory rape."

26 **"MILF falls into the 35–50-year-old category"** Personal communication from Stephen Yagielowicz, August, 2010.

27 **single most popular search term users enter** Perry Stathopoulos, the CTO of PornHub, supplied us with a variety of data about users' activities on their Web site. One data set was a list of search terms that were most frequently entered into the PornHub search engine in February 2010.

27 **frequency of specific age-related** *adjectives* We generated the age-related adjectives by reviewing the most common age-related terms in our sexual search age categories.

28 **became a profitable online niche in the early 2000s** Personal e-mail communication with Stephen Yagielowicz, senior editor for Xbiz, August 10, 2010; personal e-mail communication with Colin Rowntree, owner of Wasteland.com, August 2010.

28 **An erotic online comic titled** *Savita Bhabhi* The comic continues to be published on a different Web site and now requires a paid subscription. In homage to *Savita Bhabhi*, an online talk show, Jay Hind features an advice segment titled "Savita Bhabhi ke Sexy Lessons." It contains racy innuendo-filled suggestions from an attractive female host who copies the cartoon avatar's titillating look.

29 **searches for content they don't immediately see** Perry Stathopoulos, CTO of PornHub, supplied us with a variety of data about users' activities on their Web site. One data set was a collection of all search terms entered into the PornHub search engine in February 2010.

NOTES

29 **More than a quarter of all men** Leitenberg & Henning (1995).

29 **a greater willingness to have casual sex** Easton et al. (2010).

29 **know exactly what they want** Personal communication, August 2010. The names of all individuals who shared personal information about their sexual interests have been changed to pseudonyms. Ages and professions are accurate.

29 **The "MILF-lovers" Facebook group** http://www.facebook.com/ group.php?gid=2254123384, retrieved March, 2010.

30 **one out of four people who searched for MILFs** Number of *MILF* searchers: 3,405. Number of *teen* searchers: 22,103. Expected overlap for *MILF* and *teen* searchers, assuming independence: 114. Obtained: 812. Percent of *MILF* searchers who also searched for *teen*: 23.9. Percent of *teen* searchers who also searched for *MILF*: 3.67.

30 **one out of four GILF searchers** Number of *granny* searchers: 942. Number of *teen* searchers: 22,103.
    Expected overlap for *granny* and *teen* searchers, assuming independence: 31.7. Obtained: 202. Percent of *granny* searchers who also searched for *teen*: 21.44. Percent of *teen* searchers who also searched for *granny*: 0.91.

30 **one granny fan, Mr. Playstation** User #1183669.

31 **the Alexa Adult List** We used the Alexa list of the million most popular Web sites from March 27, 2010. Of the sites in the top million, 953,702 were successfully crawled. We classified 42,337 as porn sites based on textual pattern matches. We classified Alexa Web sites by analyzing titles and keywords from the textual content of the Web sites. In ambiguous cases, we used independent raters' evaluations. Here is a list of the top categories of Web sites on the Alexa Adult List:

# of Sites	% of All Sites on Alexa Adult List	Adult Web Site Category
2462	5.81	Youth
1725	4.07	Amateur
1672	3.95	Breasts
1625	3.83	Mature
1577	3.72	Animation
1465	3.46	Penis
1237	2.92	MILF
1052	2.48	BDSM
984	2.32	Transsexual
788	1.86	Interracial
760	1.79	Asian
741	1.75	Celebrities
692	1.63	Black

NOTES

# of Sites	% of All Sites on Alexa Adult List	Adult Web Site Category
688	1.62	Webcam
677	1.60	Vagina
643	1.51	Anal
525	1.24	Lesbian
504	1.19	Fat
433	1.02	Bestiality
381	0.90	Group Sex
373	0.88	Incest

31 **men prefer smooth skin to wrinkles** . Symons (1979), Buss (2005).

31 **the grandmother is often the confidante** Brockman (1997). Also see http://kisii.com/profile-and-coverage.

31 **might have been their first intimate contact** Personal communication, February 2010.

31 **where he goes to pick up GILFs** http://www.grannysexforum .com/forums/showthread.php?t=65655, retrieved on August 29, 2010.

32 *Youth* **is the number one sexual interest** Russian data scraped by us from the Russian search engine Yandex in spring 2010, from http://www.yandex.ru/last20.html. India, Japan, and Europe data were calculated using Google trends and refers to searches entered into Google USA from those territories.

32 **"Legal teen content has been a consistent earner"** Personal communication, February 2010.

32 **"fashion world sees toothpicks toppling"** http://thefbomb .org/2010/08/its-not-all-skinny-love/, retrieved on August 29, 2010. "Essentially the fashion world sees toothpicks toppling under the weight of their false lashes as attractive. Arms must be willowy, stomachs trim and God forbid your thighs touch; but appropriate facial features must be amplified. We are trained as consumers, convinced we require powders to contour our features into submission. We as women are coached into painting ourselves like dolls—doe-eyed creatures with pillowy lips, meek in demeanour—and all for the convenience and pleasure of the male population."
Though it's sometimes suggested that medieval Europe preferred a large, "Reubenesque" female body size, others argue that a broader analysis of art from the time reveals an average body size similar to that preferred today. See http://www.femininebeauty.info/ medieval-body-size-preferences.

32 **pressured by the fashion and media industries to be skinny** http://www.huffingtonpost.com/2010/02/02/9-in-10-teen-girls-feel -p_n_445630.html, retrieved on August 29, 2010.

33 **For every search for a "skinny" girl** Number of sexual searches

containing the word "fat": 137, 324. Number of sexual searches containing the word "skinny": 47,669.

33 **There are also more than 150 nonerotic BBW dating networks** Counted and checked by hand from BBW links and Google results for "BBW dating." We estimate there were between 150 and 200 English-language BBW Web sites on the Internet in the summer of 2010.

33 **BMI and weight of 202 popular American porn actresses** We scraped biographies of all porn actresses listed on *Wikipedia* (See here: http://en.wikipedia.org/wiki/List_of_pornographic_actresses_by_decade; retrieved July 2010). We further extracted biographies that listed weight and height information. A cutoff birth date for inclusion, January 1, 1980, was then used to create the final list of actresses.
The porn actresses with the highest BMI include: Chelsea Charms (30), Lisa Sparxxx (25), Sunny Lane (23), SaRenna Lee (23), Vanessa Lane (22). Porn actresses with the lowest BMI include: Jenna Haze (16), Lela Star (16), Nikky Blond (15), Dominica Leoni (15), Meggan Mallone (14).

33 **bodies of mainstream European porn actresses** Voracek & Fisher (2006).

33 **weights of these porn stars with other women** Celebrity BMIs taken from http://diet.health.com/2009/01/08/surprising-celebrity -bmis/2/, retrieved on August 1, 2010. The healthy and average numbers are taken from the Centers for Disease Control and Prevention at http://www.cdc.gov/nchs/data/ad/ad347.pdf.

34 **waist-to-hip ratio (.7) to be most arousing** Singh (1993), Singh (2002), Furnham et al. (2006), Karremans et al. (2010). But also consider Donohoe et al. (2009). The average WHR of the top fifty high-fashion models as of March 30, 2007, was reported as 0.7. http://www .femininebeauty.info/i/top.models.txt. "It should be noted, however, that this finding is based in part on studies that included 0.70 as the lowest WHR in their stimulus materials, e.g., Singh, 1993; when participants are able to choose from lower WHRs, it is sometimes found that WHRs lower than 0.70 are considered more attractive, e.g., Gray et al., 2003.

34 **activated when a man views an ideal waist-to-hip ratio** Platek & Singh (2010).

34 **no hip fetishes reported in the clinical literature** A PubMed search for paraphilias and fetishes failed to turn up any hip-related obsessions. Major contemporary lists of paraphilias do not include hip paraphilias, including very extended lists, such as in Levine et al. (2010). Incidentally, many of the paraphilias presented in these oft-reproduced lists do not find expression in online porn. We wonder how accurately these lists reflect actual clinical paraphilias, considering how different they are from the actual sexual interests people seek out online.

35 **biggest growth area in bra sales** http://www.news.com.au/ entertainment/fashion/dd-cup-runneth-over-for-aussie-women/story -e6frfn7i-1225699623920. http://www.guardian.co.uk/lifeandstyle/2010/ may/16/womens-breasts-are-getting-bigger.

35 **the most popular body part in sexual searches** Russian data

scraped by us from the Russian search engine Yandex in spring 2010, from http://www.yandex.ru/last20.html. Germany, India, and Saudia Arabia data calculated using Google trends, and refers to searches entered into Google USA from those territories.

35 **the number of times she was approached by men** Gueguen (2007).

36 **4,287 large breast Web sites in the Alexa Adult List** See our description of our Alexa Adult List data.

36 **synonyms for "large" appear in sexual searches** From our Dogpile data.

36 **"I like small breasts"** Fatel, *Miniskirts and Muffins* (2004).

36 **"Delicious Flat Chest" or DFC** See http://www.facebook.com/pages/Delicious-Flat-Chest/91503929877.

37 **a twenty-two-year-old's breasts often resemble a Western forty-year-old's** Personal e-mail communications, Donald Symons, 2010. Also see Dixson et al. (2010).

Out of the 55 million Dogpile sexual searches, there were 2,868 searches for "dark areola," 423 for "brown areola," and 305 for "pink areola." The color of a woman's nipples is an even less influential visual cue. There are no adult sites on the Alexa Adult List dedicated to dark nipples or light nipples. Overall, men seem to place much greater emphasis on the size of nipples and areolas (the bigger the better), rather than their color. Below is a list of the most frequently occurring adjectives with sexual searches for "nipple" on Dogpile:

Most Frequent "Nipple" Adjective	Frequency
puffy	12532
big	11212
long	9270
hard	5546
large	4362
erect	3811
huge	3508
teen	1666
young	1367
pierced	1291
small	1118
mature	1007
asian	938

continued

Most Frequent "Nipple" Adjective	Frequency
perky	809
black	798
suck	787
dark	749
nice	653
hairy	600
tiny	593
little	590
pointy	589
pink	585
giant	561
lactating	544

37 **"I do have a bit of a foot fetish"** http://www.playboy.co.uk/the -articles/interview/78872/3/Dirty-Dozen-Jack-Black/commentsPage/1/ contentPage/1, retrieved on August 29, 2010.

37 **explaining the widespread male interest in feet** Krafft-Ebing & Rebman (1906). In pornography, it's quite common for actresses to keep their high heels on during sex. Many men find this arousing. However, men typically do not keep their footwear on during sex, and when they do, women frequently urge men to take them off, including their socks.

38 **rate small female feet as more attractive** Fessler et al. (2005). Another study found similar results in Austria and Canada: Voracek et al. (2007).

38 **additional clues supporting an innate male interest in foot cues** Personal e-mail communications, June 2010.

39 **searches for foot erotica are highly correlated with searches for bondage and submission porn** The expected number of overlapping searchers for *feet* and *domination/submission* searchers in the AOL data set: 1.40. Obtained: 34.

39 **stockings are also highly correlated with sexual searches for feet** The expected number of overlapping searchers for *feet* and *pantyhose/ stocking* searchers in the AOL data set: 0.17. Obtained: 13. "Ludacris: I have. I try not to judge. I let God judge. But I definitely love girls with beautiful feet. I have a foot fetish. Messed up feet man, sometimes she can trick me and just wear boots and not even show her feet.

But when I see the feet, it's a wrap. And I don't like girls with hairy legs. I kind of like it to be nice and smooth. A little hair never hurt anybody. But when it gets a little too much, that's when it's not good anymore."

39 **"I told him we're all gay, buddy"** http://www.imdb.com/title/tt0811045/. Quotes retrieved on August, 30, 2010

40 **45 percent of men wanted a larger penis** Lever et al. (2006).

40 **men consistently direct their gaze to the male crotch** Nielsen & Pernice (2009). Also worth considering: Ponseti et al. (2006): The temporal-occipital junction is hypothesized to respond to sexual stimuli. In homosexual men, it responds strongly to penises, but not to vaginas. In heterosexual men, however, it responds to both vaginas and penises. (In heterosexual women, it responds to penises, but not vaginas.)

40 **twenty-one feature close-up shots of a penis** We downloaded the one hundred highest-rated images on Fantasti.cc on May 10, 2009. We submitted these images to workers on Amazon Turk. There were three taggers for each image, and we counted any tag that was shared by two or more raters (e.g., "close-up of penis").

40 **.2 percent of men wish they had a smaller penis** Lever et al. (2006).

40 **9 percent of women who wish they had smaller breasts** http://www.mynippon.com/women/bsize.htm, retrieved on August 29, 2010. There were 144,000 breast reductions in 2004, according to: http://www.imageps.com/pdf/Liposuction%20Breast%20Recuction.pdf.

40 **more than six times the number of searches for "big dick"** "Big dick" searches: 47,476. "Small dick" searches: 7,861.

40 **1,072 Web sites in the Alexa Adult List** Another 313 gay Web sites are devoted to large penises.

40 **Mr. Amish** User #2567521.

41 **One possible explanation may lie with our primate cousins** "Anyways, if that isn't enough bad behavior for you, think about this: macaque males will attack their enemy when he is at his weakest: during orgasm. Attackers often use considerable cunning to get near their victim without arousing any suspicion. They may feign indifference by barely glancing at him, digging casually in the sand or pretending to collect handfuls of pebbles. But the moment their victim ejaculates, they jump him, hitting, biting and tugging at his fur." http://www.newscientist.com/article/mg13618502.900-science-macaque-attacks-succeed-best-during-sex-.html

41 **erect penis can provoke hostility and attacks** Edwards (1997).

41 **a visual cue that motivates males to copulate** Pound (2002).

41 **visible sign of a male's general health** Dawkins (2006) [1978], endnote, p. 158. "It is not implausible that, with natural selection refining their diagnostic skills, females could glean all sorts of clues about a male's health, and robustness of his ability to cope with stress, from the tone and bearing of his penis."

41 **"the fondling of the penis and scrotum"** Bagemihl (1999).

41 **among the Australian Walbiri and Aranda people** Bagemihl (1999).

42 **men have inherited our primate cousins' attentiveness to the penis** Some pictures and a description are contained here: http://rbg-web2.rbge.org.uk/ethnobotany/Yali2.pdf, retrieved August 29, 2010.

42 **what he saw on 1,276 consecutive Chat Roulette sessions** http://www.cpeterson.org/2010/02/12/dispatches-from-the-front-12-hours-on-chatroulette/, retrieved on August 29, 2010.
"1276 cams viewed:
Conversations: 34
Avg. Conversation Duration: 23.7 sec
Long: 5 min 56 sec
298 naked masturbating men
678 non masturbating males
152 fake cams
148 females or mixed m/f boobs shown you ask? 0.0
EDIT: Cum shots: 2
man having sex with raccoon viewed 23 times.
Not counted: repeats, no cam, empty rooms, people with dolls and signs."
One person even developed software to track penis sightings on Chat Roulette: http://chatroulettecockmap.com/.
A video of people counting penises during five minutes on Chat Roulette can be found here: http://mprodgers.posterous.com/chatroulette-challenge-how-many-penises-can-y. The total count of Chat Roulette sessions that contained nudity or actions of a sexual nature: 14 penises and a masturbating girl.

42 **an image of their penis as their avatar** We collected 5,626 male avatars and 958 female avatars from Fantasti.cc in May 2010 and had three workers on Amazon Turk tag each image according to its visual category (e.g., "penis"). We then categorized and counted those avatars where two or more workers applied the same tag.

42 **On reddit's heterosexual Gone Wild forum** We downloaded 768 images from http://www.reddit.com/r/gonewild in May 2010 and submitted them to three Amazon Turk raters. We used ratings where two or more workers used the same tag to annotate the image.

42 **clinical psychiatrists do not consider them dangerous** Levine et al. (2010).

42 **the urge to exhibit oneself** Leitenberg and Henning (1995). "Freund, Scher, and Hucker (1984) did not find any difference in arousal to consenting scenes between exhibitionists and a control group of nonoffenders. Both groups showed greatest arousal to consenting intercourse imagery. A subsequent study conducted by Marshall, Payne, Barbaree, and Eccles (1991) found that only 13.6% of exhibitionists had greater arousal to cues of exposure than to cues of consenting sexual activity. However, 34% of the exhibitionists but none of the controls had a response to the exposure stimuli that was at least 70% of the response to normal consenting stimuli. In addition, as a whole, the exhibitionists

showed greater arousal than the control participants to the exposure scenes. Even so, Marshall, Payne, et al. (1991) concluded that the importance of deviant sexual arousal in exhibitionism is exaggerated." Contrary to what one might expect, voyeurs rarely go to strip shows, look at pornography, or attend nudist camps. Yalom (1960), Sagarin (1973).

42 **"The act was more magical than sexual"** Rentzel (1973).

43 **released the floodgates on Japanese animated erotica** http://www.hawaii.edu/PCSS/biblio/articles/1961to1999/1999 -pornography-rape-sex-crimes-japan.html, retrieved on August 30, 2010. http://www.nationmultimedia.com/2008/02/15/entertainment/ entertainment_30065550.php, retrieved on August 29, 2010.

44 **Her voice is extremely high-pitched** Bryant & Haselton (2009). Also see http://www.futurepundit.com/archives/cat_brain_sexuality .html, retrieved on August 30, 2010.

44 **sometimes longer than a girl's arm** cf. http://www.sayhentai.com/.

CHAPTER 3

45 **"given enough time, I'm going to have sex with it"** Joe Rogan's *Shiny Happy Jihad* (2007). "We have reason to believe that man first walked upright to free his hands for masturbation." —Lily Tomlin.

45 **What does a hen need to turn a rooster on?** From a paper with one of the most unintentionally amusing titles in biology: Carbaugh, B. T., M. W. Schein, et al. "Effects of Morphological Variations of Chicken Models on Sexual Responses of Cocks." *Animal Behaviour* 10(3–4): 235–238.

45 **a red comb.** Cornwallis & Birkhead. (2007).

45 **Turkeys are even less discriminating** Schein & Hale (1957), Schein & Hale (1958).

46 **bigger and brighter the fake butt** Girolami & Bielert (1987).

46 **far more men than women obsessed with body parts** See http://www.psychiatrictimes.com/display/article/10168/54866, retrieved on August 30, 2010. "Paraphilias are predominantly male sexuality disorders with an estimated sex differences ratio of 20:1 in sexual masochism. *(The other paraphilias are almost never diagnosed in females, although some cases have been reported.)*"

46 **Male arousal itself relies on two structures located in the subcortex** Pfaus (2009).

46 **the amygdala and the hypothalamus** Karama et al. (2002), Hamann et al. (2004), Ferretti et al. (2005), Walter et al. (2008), Schiffer et al. (2008).

46 **men remember more visual details from sexual encounters** "Men report more sexual fantasies than women; however, women may not report sexual fantasies as frequently because they do not realize that they are sexually aroused by certain romantic images or because they

simply do not consider romantic fantasies without explicit sexual acts to be sexual fantasies even if they are sexually arousing." Leitenberg and Henning (1995).

46 **use more visual descriptions than stories written by women** See discussions and analysis in Chapters 5,6, 7, and 11.

46 **"Martha Stewart" searchers were four times more likely** The expected overlap of "Martha Stewart" and "porn" searchers in the AOL data set, assuming independence: 90.40. Obtained: 75 (not different from random). The expected overlap of "Martha Stewart" and "stories" searchers in the AOL data set, assuming independence: 24.70. Obtained: 85. Worth considering: AOL user #10193632, who searches for Martha Stewart recipes and food sex fetishes.

46 **swiftly experiences physical and psychological arousal** Toates (2009).

46 **Male arousal itself relies on two structures** Pfaus (2009). "Brain dopamine systems (incertohypothalamic and mesolimbic) that link the hypothalamus and limbic system appear to form the core of the excitatory system. This system also includes melanocortins, oxytocin, and norepinephrine. Brain opioid, endocannabinoid, and serotonin systems are activated during periods of sexual inhibition, and blunt the ability of excitatory systems to be activated."

47 **their sexual motivation pathways have more connections** Becker. (2009), Joyal et al. (2007), Baird et al. (2004), Stark (2005), Pfaus (2009), Toates (2009), Walter et al. (2008). Greater male sex drive and sociosexuality were found across many diverse cultures in Lippa (2009).

47 **men's brains are designed to objectify females** "The notion that *Playboy* turns women into sex objects is ridiculous. Women are sex objects." —Hugh Hefner

47 **The famous 26,000-year-old Venus of Willendorf statuette** A photo and description can be found here: http://witcombe.sbc.edu/willendorf/willendorfdiscovery.html.

47 **The 40,000-year-old Venus of Hohle Fels** A photo and description can be found here: http://www.livescience.com/history/090513-first-figure.html.

47 **twenty-three feature close-ups of female anatomy** We downloaded the one hundred highest-rated images on Fantasti.cc on May 10, 2009. We submitted these images to workers on Amazon Turk. There were three taggers for each image, and we counted any tag that was shared by two or more raters (e.g., "close-up of penis").

47 *zettai ryouiki*, **translated as "the absolute territory"** http://whatjapanthinks.com/2009/09/06/favourite-fetishes-of-japanese-men/, http://burogublog.wordpress.com/2008/06/08/the-art-and-science-of-zettai-ryouiki/, http://www.facebook.com/ZettaiRyouiki?v=photos, http://zettairyouikicafe.wordpress.com/category/zettai-ryouiki, http://whatjapanthinks.com/image10/zettai-ryoiku.jpg.

48 **"socks and skirt are usually darker shades"** http://animedesho.animeblogger.net/?p=2585, retrieved on August 30, 2010.

48 **categorize the bewitching strip of skin into six different types**
See http://burogublog.wordpress.com/2008/06/08/the-art-and-science
-of-zettai-ryouiki/.

48 **in order to derive a "golden mean** "A Mathematical Analysis and
Alternative of the Zettai Ryouiki Ratio," on http://kevo.dasaku
.net/?p=92, retrieved August 30, 2010.

48 **"memorizing this formula"** Quote from DarkMirage on http://
burogublog.wordpress.com/2008/06/08/the-art-and-science-of-zettai
-ryouiki/, retrieved August 30, 2010.

48 **belly is a common male obsession** Aki Sinkkonen of the University
of Helsinki has suggested that navels are used to attract potential mates.
His hypothesis "makes a lot of biological sense," according to Gerald
Weissmann of the New York University School of Medicine. We have
doubts.

48 **claimed to be aroused by a woman's earlobe** Dalí (2004).

49 **experiment run by psychologists Joseph Plaud and James
Martini** Plaud & Martini (1999).

50 **or a box of Kleenex** "Few people are turned on by doorknobs,
bedroom dressers, or bathroom fixtures, even though these cues are often
in the environment when sexual arousal and orgasm take place. Instead,
there is probably a biological preparedness as well as a socialization
process." Leitenberg & Henning (1995).

50 **sexual interests in men first form during adolescence** Woodson
(2002).

50 **what neuroscientists call a** *critical period* "The most plausible
suggestion, in my view, is that males actually do have a brief period
of plasticity during childhood, after which the sexual patterns are
reasonably rigid." Baumeister (2000).

51 **same pattern of irreversible male sexual imprinting** Kendrick
et al. (1998). For sexual imprinting in other animals see Woodson (2002).

52 **"I don't know why I like breasts"** Mitch Fatel, *Miniskirts and Muffins*.

53 **Chaminda was a young Buddhist** Dewaraja & Money (1986). The
subject's name is not provided.

54 **a name for the oversized parts of female anatomy** Thornhill &
Gangestad (2008). "If mammary glands were no longer directly or
indirectly selected in descendants, they would likely degrade through
mutation and drift if neutral."
Gottschall (2007). Also consider: Hooper & Miller (2008).

54 **indicate how many years of healthy childbearing remain**
Thornhill & Gangestad (2008) refer to future fertility as "residual
reproductive value" or RRV.

54 **men should find visual cues associated with** *youth* Symons (1979).

55 **"would have had more living relatives to invest in"** Abramson &
Pinkerton (1995).

55 **age of first menstruation is happening earlier** Clavel-Chapelon &
Grp (2002). "There was thus a steady increase in the interval between age
at menarche and at onset of regular cycling, mainly due to an increase in

NOTES

the percentage of women in whom regular cycling started at least 5 years after menarche (from 9.0% among women born in 1925–1929 to 20.8% in those born in 1945–1950). The increase in the interval between menarche and onset of regular cycling was even greater among women with a late menarche."

55 **Male chimps do not find adolescents sexually attractive** Thornhill & Gangestad (2008).

55 *mixed mating strategies* Buss (2003).

56 **the most attractive ones received jewelry** Personal telephone communications with Steve Lightspeed, founder and owner of Lightspeed, August 2009.

56 **influenced by the same molecule:** *estrogen* The discussion of estrogen-based female ornamentation is taken mainly from Thornhill & Gangestad (2008).

57 **estrogen limits the growth of foot bones** Thornhill & Gangestad (2008).

57 **prefer women who weigh a pound more** Personal e-mail communication, March 2010.

57 **Breast size is not correlated with milk production** Thornhill & Gangestad (2008).

58 **went from 36B in 1997 to 34D today** Mackay (2000).

58 **the baby geese will imprint upon the scientist** Lorenz (1935).

59 **"Smaller breasted women just look better to me!!!"** http://www.answerbag.com/q_view/863803#ixzz0y6vp8qIS, retrieved on August 30, 2010.

60 **Male desire is instantly activated by visual cues** Ponseti et al. (2006). "We reasoned that the observation of sexually arousing stimuli may cause automatic activation of motor representations in the PMv because exposure to visual sexual stimuli is frequently followed by sexual behavior."

60 **"my mother's decapitated head"** Louis C.K. *Chewed Up* (2008).

CHAPTER 4

62 **Women were not allowed to dine at the Faculty Club** Hatfield's story is from *Commentary*, HBES E-Newsletter (Human Behavior and Evolution Society), Summer 2007, pp. 1–10. Also personal e-mail communication with Elaine Hatfield, August 12, 2010.

64 **Hatfield and fellow psychologist Russell Clark** Clark & Hatfield (1989).

65 **Hatfield and Clark couldn't get these dramatic results published** Clark & Hatfield (2003).

65 **study was replicated in Belgium, Denmark, and Germany** Molzer (2003), Voracek et al. (2005), Voracek et al. (2006). According to Elaine Hatfield (personal e-mail communication, September 29, 2010), the study was also replicated by Charlotte De Backer, Ghent University, Department of Philosophy and Moral Sciences.

NOTES

65 **on the online dating site OkCupid** OkCupid is one of the largest social networking and dating Web sites. One primary feature of OkCupid is the creation and answering of member-created quizzes containing questions on all manner of topics. Users are free to answer any number of such quizzes or questions posed by other users. This, paired with the user demographics, provide an unparalleled wealth of data on user preferences. Some questions elicit answers for a few hundreds of thousands of users, allowing for a fine-grained analysis of preferences based on age, sexual preference, gender etc. OkCupid has been showcasing some remarkable results from the analysis of its data on its excellent blog, OkTrends. OkCupid also offered access to anonymized data consisting of 369 million answers to 3,989 questions by 6.4 million users. This data consists of the randomized IDs of OkCupid users and the coded answers to questions. Only the gender, stated sexual orientation, year of birth, and stated location were provided. The response dataset was generated in July 2009. Information for OkCupid question #1597 Would you consider sleeping with someone on a first date?
Straight Males: # of respondents: 300,402; 72.1% YES; 20.4% NO.
Bisexual Females: # of respondents: 33,592; 61.0% YES; 30.0% NO.
Straight Females: # of respondents: 195,689; 10.4%; 40.7% YES; 48.9% NO.

66 **test compound known as 5 cyclic GMP-specific phosphodiesterase inhibitor** Ghofrani et al. (2006), Terrett et al. (1996), http://inventors.about.com/od/uvstartinventions/a/ Viagra.htm, retrieved on August 30, 2010.

67 **its share price doubled** http://www.guardian.co.uk/business/2009/ nov/16/viagra-pfizer-drug-pill-profit, retrieved on October 1, 2010.

67 **multinationals turned their attention to developing "pink Viagra"** An academic review of the search for female Viagra can be found in Brown et al. (2007).

67 **twice as many women as men suffering** First & Tasman (2010).

67 **Vivus vasodilator failed to boost female desire** Rosemary et al. (2002). http://medicaldevicelicensing.com/public/companies/view/1382/ vivus.

68 **stimulating female desire through "peripherally acting agents"** Brown et al. (2007).

68 **to find out what turns women on** Chivers et al. (2004). http:// www.stanfordalumni.org/news/magazine/2010/marapr/features/mosher .html. Of the forty-five women in Mosher's survey, thirty-five said they desired sex; thirty-four said they had experienced orgasms; twenty-four felt that pleasure for both sexes was a reason for intercourse; and about three-quarters of them engaged in it at least once a week.

68 **plethysmograph** "The first invention came in the 1950s. Soldiers could get out of the Czech army by claiming they were gay, and researcher Kurt Freund needed to find a way to confirm their orientation. He invented a kind of barometer that measures changes in air pressure around the penis when a man has an erection. A more modern device—nicknamed a

'peter meter'—uses mercury and an electrical current to measure changes in the size of a band placed around the penis. In women, scientists use a tampon-like gizmo that shines light into the vagina and tracks blood flow by measuring the diffusion of light in the surrounding tissues." http://www.wired.com/medtech/health/news/2004/04/63115, retrieved on August 30, 2010.

69 **"all this conflicting stuff flying around my brain and body"** http://letters.mobile.salon.com/mwt/broadsheet/2006/11/27/porn/view/index13.html, retrieved on August 30, 2010.

69 **"being aroused by something that *disgusts* you"** http://letters.mobile.salon.com/mwt/broadsheet/2006/11/27/porn/view/index11.html, retrieved on August 30, 2010.

69 **Chivers reviewed 132 different laboratory studies** Chivers et al. (2010).

69–70 **vaginal lubrication is a poor predictor of what she is actually feeling** Meana (2010): "The best predictors of sexual distress were general emotional well-being and emotional well-being with partner during sex. Arousal, lubrication, and orgasm were poor predictors of sexual distress."

70 **women report lubrication and even orgasm during unwanted and coercive sex** Meana (2010).

70 **if a man is erect** There are exceptions; men can have spontaneous erections (*morning wood*) after sleep.

70 **rare sex survey in the 1920s** http://sexademic.wordpress.com/2010/03/19/before-there-was-kinsey-mosher-davis-and-dickinson-surveyed-victorian-sex/. "In his survey of one thousand married women he found that they most frequently complained about failure to reach orgasm and that obstacles to sexual pleasure were primarily inorganic, i.e., not physiological in nature."

70 **likely involve conscious mechanisms** Brown et al. (2007). "The failure of the peripherally acting PDE5 inhibitors, coupled with the clinical findings that subjective and objective arousal in women may be different, suggested that centrally acting agents may be more appropriate for the treatment of FSD. Indeed many animal studies have shown the importance of the brain, especially a number of hypothalamic nuclei, in mediating female sexual response in rodents. Thus, attention has turned to centrally acting agents in the search for an effective treatment of FSD."

71 **why are they separated in women?** Meana (2010). "The model of sexual response propagated by Masters and Johnson (1966), by Kaplan (1974), and by the third and fourth editions of the *Diagnostic and Statistical Manual of Mental Disorders* (*DSM*; American Psychiatric Association [APA], (1987; 2000) has problematized women's sexual experience through the damaging application of a male analog." "The accumulation of data [supports] the existence of quantitative and qualitative gender differences in desire."
"Although there have been suggestions that this gender difference may be

NOTES

a function of measurement artifacts or socially desirable responding on the part of women, the bulk of the data generally does not support these possibilities. More pointedly, they suggested that, in contrast to men, women's genital arousal had a weaker relation to their sexual preferences."

71 **dramatic differences in how these** Meana (2010). "The accumulation of data supporting the existence of quantitative and qualitative gender differences in desire." "It appears that physical sexual arousal is the same in men and women—what differs is the way the conscious mind processes and reacts to it."
Walter, Bermpohl, et al. (2008). "men recorded approximately 7.2 sexual fantasies per day as compared with 4.5 for women" and "men estimated they had approximately one sexual fantasy per day, whereas the women estimated they had only one sexual fantasy per week."
Leitenberg & Henning (1995). "Male university students were found to masturbate to ejaculation about every 72 hours, and "on the majority of occasions, their last masturbation is within 48 hours of their next in-pair copulation."
http://www.scientificamerican.com/blog/post.cfm?id=one-reason-why -humans-are-special-a-2010-06-22, retrieved on August 20, 2010. "If they're not having intercourse every day, men tend to pleasure themselves to completion no more than two days prior to having actual sex."

71 **low sexual desire much more often than men** "The most common presenting sexual complaint in women attending clinics is low desire. In contrast, men most often present with erectile difficulties. Bachman surveyed 1,946 health professionals attending four major specialty conferences (the American College of Obstetricians and Gynecologists, the Endocrine Society, the North American Menopause Society, and the American Society for Reproductive Medicine) and found that 67% of respondents reported that low sexual desire was the most common type of sexual dysfunction among their female patients. Of note is the fact that 85% of these health professionals believed HSDD to be a medical disorder."

71 **"theory of women's desire as being substantially different"** Meana (2010).

71 **separation of the physical from the psychological** Becker (2009). "Sex differences in motivation are apparent for the motivation to engage in sexual behavior, the motivation to take drugs of abuse, and the motivation to engage in parental behavior. In both males and females there is an increase in NAcc DA associated with motivated behaviors. Here it proposed that sex differences in the regulation of DA activity in the ascending mesolimbic projections may underlie sex differences in motivation. In particular, sex differences in the neuroendocrine regulation of this brain system play a role in the expression of sex differences in motivated behaviors. Here it is proposed that sexual differentiation of motivation is mediated, at least in part, by a novel mechanism in which ovarian hormones secreted at puberty in the female actively feminize the DA system."
Also see Lippa (2009).

NOTES

73 **a section called Missed Connections** Craigslist is the largest
free online classifieds Web site in the United States. See http://www
.craigslist.org/about/sites. We scraped posts/classifieds from listings
in the following 52 American cities and regions: Akron, Anchorage,
Albany, Atlanta, Austin, Baltimore, Boise, Boston, Buffalo, Charlotte,
Chicago, Cincinnati, Columbia, Dallas, Denver, Detroit, Fresno,
Hartford, Honolulu, Houston, Indianapolis, Kansas City, Las Vegas,
Los Angeles, Memphis, Miami, Milwaukee, Minneapolis, Nashville,
New Orleans, New York City, Norfolk, Oklahoma City, Omaha,
Orange County, Orlando, Philadelphia, Phoenix, Pittsburgh,
Portland, Providence, Raleigh, Richmond, Sacramento, Salt Lake
City, San Antonio, San Diego, Seattle, St. Louis, Tampa, Tucson,
and Washington, D.C.
Classifieds on Craigslist are categorized into several specific
subcategories. Our scraping included six subcategories in the personals
section: m4m (Men Seeking Men), m4w (Men Seeking Women), w4m
(Women Seeking Men), w4w (Women Seeking Women), mis (Missed
Connections), msr (Miscellaneous Romance). Missed Connections is
a section where men and women post messages for people they desire
to reconnect with. These messages can be for long lost friends and
acquaintances, or strangers encountered in everyday life. We scraped
565,597 listings in this category. Listings by men for women and vice
versa are denoted by using m4w and w4m respectively. Men post roughly
twice as often as women. Analysis of the most frequent two-word phrases
in post titles by men (for women) and women (for women) reveals that
"looking for" and "miss you" are among the ten most common phrases
used by both sexes. Relative frequency of usage shows that women are
more likely to use the phrase "miss you" and men use "looking for."
Expanding the relative frequency of phrase usage analysis to top fifty
phrases reveals that men are looking for women they met "at Walmart"
or at the "gas station." Women on the other hand confess they "love you"
and are thinking "about you."
74 **A physical detective** Ellison & Gray (2009), Jasienska & Ellison
(2004).
74 *He's Just Not That Into You* Behrendt & Tuccillo (2004).
75 **women ruminate over emotional situations more than men**
Bjorklund & Kipp (1996), Arrais et al. (2010), Thornhill & Gangestad
(2008).
76 **women's sexual fantasies have higher romantic and emotional
content** Meana (2010). "The research on sexual fantasy has repeatedly
shown that women's fantasies have higher romantic–emotional content
than those of men."
76 **"sex differences in the human brain may be the norm"**
Gillies & McArthur (2010).
76 **men are more likely to suffer from Parkinson's** Gillies &
McArthur (2010), Blakemore (2008), Burnett et al. (2009).
76 **twice as likely to suffer from mood disorders** Becker (2008).

76 **susceptibility to mood disorders is one of the costs** Paus et al. (2008), Perrin et al. (2008).

76 **The insular cortex and the hippocampus are both involved** During the luteal phase, women show more activation in the emotion-related areas. Superior activation for luteal women in anterior cingulate, left insula, left orbitofrontal cortex. Gizewski et al. (2006), Bartels & Zeki (2004), Bush et al. (2000), Van Overwalle (2009), Arnow et al. (2009), Bianchi-Demicheli & Ortigue (2007), Arrais et al. (2010), Rupp et al. (2009).

78 **women performed better than men on verbal tasks** Kansaku et al. (2000), Burman et al. (2008).

78 **More women than men use social networking sites** http://www.briansolis.com/2010/08/influence-is-bliss-the-gender-divide-of-influence-on-twitter, retrieved on August 30, 2010.

78 **greater connectivity between the two cortical hemispheres** Van Overwalle (2009), Insel and Fernald (2004).

79 **or a celebrity's views on mental health** http://newsinfo.iu.edu/tips/page/normal/10912.html, Baumeister (2000), Baumeister et al. (2000).

79 **likely to attribute sexual anxiety to social pressures** Meana (2010).

80 **behaviors are appropriate and inappropriate in a given situation** Rupp et al. (2009), Harenski et al. (2008), Fumagalli et al. (2010), Baron-Cohen et al. (2005), Kaasinen et al. (2001).

80 **"Most men who ever lived did not have descendants who are alive today"** Georgiadis et al. (2006), Arnow et al. (2009), http://www.psy.fsu.edu/~baumeistertice/goodaboutmen.htm.

82 **"The Case for Settling for Mr. Good Enough"** Gottlieb (2010).

83 *objectum sexualis* http://www.ejhs.org/volume13/ObjSexuals.htm.

84 **Erika Naisho, married the Eiffel Tower** http://www.independent.co.uk/extras/sunday-review/living/i-married-the-eiffel-tower-832519.html.

CHAPTER 5

86 **"romance for men"** Here's one guy that likes romance: "Hi! I'm that odd guy out who reads romance novels, and lots of them :) The reason that I read romance novels is that my Mother read, amongst many other things, romance novels, and therefore a lot of the books in the house when I went through my 'read everything I can lay my hands on' stage were of that genre. And quite a few of them I enjoyed. So I picked up the habit at an impressionable age and never stopped." http://pandagon.net/index.php/site/comments/why_dont_men_read_more_romance_novels/, retrieved on August 30, 2010.

86 **Catherine Salmon and Donald Symons in their book,** *Warrior Lovers* Salmon & Symons (2003).

86 *Pamela* **was one of the earliest bestsellers** Doody (1995).

86 **1972 novel** *The Flame and the Flower* Woodiwiss (1972).

87 **90 percent of these readers are women** http://www.laweekly
.com/2009-12-17/art-books/man-on-man-the-new-gay-romance/,
retrieved on October 15, 2010. http://www.rwanational.org/cs/the_
romance_genre/romance_literature_statistics, retrieved on August 30,
2010.

87 **about 100 million men in the United States and Canada**
Albright (2008). Also see Edelman (2009).

89 **erotic story "Princess and the Pirates" by Hamilton_g**
Abridged from http://www.literotica.com/stories/showstory
.php?id=100201, retrieved on August 30, 2010.

89 **what romance author Nora Roberts called "nursing mother
covers"** http://www.newyorker.com/reporting/2009/06/22/090622fa_
fact_collins, retrieved on August 30, 2010.

90 **"success of the ebook is being fueled"** http://www.bookpatrol
.net/2009/08/romance-and-erotic-novels-drive-ebook.html.

90 **offer their existing titles in digital formats** http://
eromancewriters.com/publishers.cfm.

90 **actress Felicia Day blogs about her reading tastes** http://
feliciaday.com/blog/kindle-oh-kindle, retrieved on August 30, 2010.

90 **Other e-EroRom publishers** Loose Id, LLC—Loose Id (www
.loose-id.com), Total-E-Bound Publishing—Total-E-Bound (www
.total-e-bound.com), Jasmine Jade Enterprises, LLC—Ellora's Cave
(www.jasminejade.com/default.aspx).

91 **"Girlies like porn too"** http://letters.salon.com/mwt/broadsheet/
2006/11/27/porn/view/index9.html, retrieved on August 30, 2010.

92 **2 million different stories and more than 600,000 visitors**
Traffic from Quantcast.com. Also http://www.oprah.com/relationships/
Online-Pornography-Why-Men-Are-Visual-and-Women-Are-Textual/
print/1, retrieved on August 30, 2010. "The leading site in this category is
AdultFanFiction.net, with visitors that are predominately 18- to 24-year-
old women."

92 **"Continuing the stories of favorite characters"** Personal e-mail
communication with Sylvia Volk, September 2010.

93 **about half of the stories are tagged as "romance"** Based on
scraping of tags on fanfiction.net in March 2010.

93 **"Four Months Later," a story pairing Hannibal Lecter and
Clarice Starling** Abridged from http://community.livejournal.com/
apckrfansfic/113090.html, retrieved on August 30, 2010.

94 **derived from the titles of more than 15,000 Harlequin
romance novels** Cox & Fisher (2009).

95 **absent from the list of romance heroes are blue-collar
workers** Some other romance heroes: Josef Serafin aka Killian from
Anne Stuart's *Ice Storm*: For the majority of the book, the reader is led
to believe that the hero is "the most dangerous man in the world." He
is portrayed as a well-known warlord and arms dealer who's caused the
deaths of hundreds if not thousands of people. It turns out that he was
just deep undercover for the CIA portraying the mercenary Serafin.

NOTES

Simon Cross from Linda Howard's *Death Angel*: he's an assassin hired to kill the heroine. Viktor Drakovich from Lisa Marie Rice's *Dangerous Passion*: the hero is an arms dealer.

95 **"Alphas are natural leaders"** Knight (2007).

96 **processing cues indicating social status** Waismann et al. (2003), Allison et al. (2000).

96 **"I'm a lesbian, but the powerful attraction"** http://www.thegreatstory.org/stories-awaken.html.

96 **"an inconsiderate asshole beats being a polite beta"** http://roissy.wordpress.com/the-sixteen-commandments-of-poon/, retrieved on August 30, 2010.

97 **"women like bad boys"** Knight (2007).

98 **"I used to write to Richard Ramirez"** http://www.experienceproject.com/groups/Find-Serial-Killers-Fascinating/forum/Serial-Killer-Penpals/3533, retrieved on August 30, 2010. http://www.sfgate.com/cgi-bin/article.cgi?f=/c/a/2009/09/28/BA8M19PDAN.DTL. "Oh my favorite is Kendall Francois he is such a wonderful guy and so friendly and caring." Also: http://groups.yahoo.com/group/killer_groupies/message/507. "I write to Richard Ramirez. He is realy nice, sweet & funny. And I'm happy over every day he has." http://www.experienceproject.com/stories/Find-Serial-Killers-Fascinating/839889. "Poptart: In the words of Steven Tyler 'Groupies are fantastic man, they make an old man young, & keep a young man hard-kkkkkkow'! No man i know ever gets tired of hearing a young hot girl say 'omg i wanna suck your cock'. Well, no hetero man anyway! RichardsGirl: hahaha poptart maybe so but i'd never say it at least, not to richard anyway. okay, maybe not in my FIRST letter, anyway . . . HAHAHA. Poptart: haha now your gettin' it darlin'—you are a babe—he is gonna luv ya! Good girls corrupted & turned bad are a fave!" http://skcentral.com/forum/viewthread.php?thread_id=816&rowstart=100. "I am obessed with them. I have a friend who asks me when I'm going to write one. I say the ones in prison are the safest. Then they can't cheat on you" —LostLittleGirl http://www.unexplained-mysteries.com/forum/index.php?s=0c41a4ec25d11c09ad6ed34a02e03861&showtopic=64212&st=15

98 **"If I could have died by his hands"** http://www.experienceproject.com/stories/Find-Serial-Killers-Fascinating/839889, retrieved on August 1, 2010.

98 **regarded by the Yanomamo women as the most desirable** Personal e-mail communication with Donald Symons, June 2010.

98 **required to present the shrunken head of a man** http://www.bukisa.com/articles/26013_bizarre-culture-of-primitive-tribes-from-around-the-world.

98 **tolerate a little misogyny and jerkdom** Knight (2007).

98 **mate preferences across thirty-seven different cultures** Stone

et al. (2007). Lippa (2007): "Women ranked honesty, humor, kindness, and dependability more important than men did."

99 **it was what's inside that was important** From *Crumb*: "In this strip I talk about all my problems with women, starting with high school, where I learned a lot about women because there was this guy named Skutch . . . who was like this mean bully, but he was also very charming, and all the girls liked him. He was, like, the *dreamboat* but he was also a bully. . . . [Points to another part of the comic strip.] Here it shows all these girls talking about how one of their friends got a date with Skutch and how envious they all are. And this is how I felt about it." [Chuckles as he points to a drawing of himself in the comic. He looks distraught and angry, and there is a bubble showing him saying "Arghh!"] "I'm a little bitter about it as you can see here. I show here how I thought that most teenage boys were very cruel and aggressive and everything like that, and if girls could see that I was more kind and sensitive they would like me more, they would be kinda impressed by the fact that I could draw. But I couldn't understand why they liked these cruel, aggressive guys and not me, 'cause I was more kind and sensitive and everything, more like them, I was more like *them*. I didn't realize that they didn't *want* you to be like them, basically. I felt very hurt and cruelly misunderstood because I considered myself talented and intelligent and yet I was not very attractive physically, but I didn't think those things really mattered, it was what's inside that was important. When I was thirteen and fourteen and trying to be a normal teenager I was really a jerk. I tried to act like I thought they were acting and it just came out all wrong and weird. So then I just stopped completely and just became a shadow, and I wasn't even there, people weren't even aware that I was in the same world they were in."

100 **a man who seems to epitomize the male ideal** In an episode of *Sex and the City*, the women all say their fantasy male is Russell Crowe.

100 **things a guy must do to get back together** Abridged from http://www.enotalone.com/forum/showthread.php?t=348168. "I was actually considering getting back together with him (I think I must have forgotten about him sleeping with another girl part) I needed him to 1. introduce me to his parents, 2. change his facebook relationship status 3. Give me all his email, FB and phone passwords, 4. Call his stupid ex and tell her to stop calling him amongst other things. He agreed to it all. . . . to my surprise."

101 **"She received nice letters in return"** http://www.prisontalk.com/forums/showthread.php?t=239749.

101 **415 millionaires, 286 billionaires, and 263 sheiks** Scraped from all book titles in the romance genre on Amazon.com in September 2010.

103 **who sit around the house watching TV are *never* heroes** Knight (2007).

103 **date someone who didn't know how to drive a car** See OkCupid data description.

NOTES

QUESTION #48960 WOULD YOU CONSIDER DATING SOMEONE WHO DOES
NOT KNOW HOW TO DRIVE A CAR?
  Straight Males: # of Respondents: 74410; 79.0% YES; 11.72% NO.
  Bisexual Females: # of Respondents: 9460; 67.73% YES; 20.39% NO.
  Straight Females: # of Respondents: 49039; 48.00% YES; 37.67%
  NO.

  The Hadza people are an ethnic group of hunter-gatherers living
  around the Rift Valley in central Tanzania. For tens of thousands
  of years, they have survived on the berries and nuts gathered by the
  women, and the antelope meat obtained by the men. Anthropologist
  Frank Marlowe asked the Hadza women what characteristic they most
  desired in a husband. Marlowe always received the same answer. "He
  must be a good hunter."

103 **"be confident in his ability"** Knight (2007).
103 **hunting or fighting prowess is an essential quality in a man**
  Escasa et al. (2010), Marlowe (2004).
103 **silver-tipped myotis bat has** http://www.timesonline.co.uk/tol/news/
  uk/article749435.ece
103 **valuation of male creativity and intelligence** Miller (2000).
104 **why women are far more interested in older partners**
  Symons (1979). Lists of romance novels with age gaps (in both
  directions): http://www.likesbooks.com/may-dec.html, http://forums
  .rtbookreviews.com/viewtopic.php?t=8094.
  Generally, in historicals, the heroines are either debutantes (eighteen
  to twenty-two), widows (late twenties to late thirties), or spinsters (late
  twenties to midthirties).
  From Kresley Cole's *A Hunger Like No Other*:

  She frowned as a sudden thought occurred. "You said 'every age that I
  have lived.' So how old are you? Six hundred? Seven hundred years?"
  "Does that matter?"
  She shook his hand free. "How—old?"
  "Roughly twelve hundred years."
  She gasped. "Do you know what 'robbing the cradle' means? I am almost
  seventy-one. This skeeves me out!"

104 **"I've had enough of the boys"** Abridged from http://www.blogher
  .com/dating-older-men-how-old-too-old#comment-119801. "I am stuck
  I guess. I want a mature strong man and I feel I cannot find that with
  a guy my age or in his 20s. I like older men but I want one who has his
  sh!t together and is compassinate and I just feel like I can communicate
  with older guys better. Communication is very important. Being able to
  TALK instead of having to explain EVERYthing to a childish BOY is
  something I have to go for. I've had enough of the boys."

Nineteen-year-old actress and singer Gabriella Climi did an interview with Gossiptiva.com about how she wants to date older men like Robert Downey Jr. and John Travolta. http://gossipvita.com/2010/06/gabriella -cilmi-likes-date-older-man-sex-boyfriend-love/. Lily Allen talks about why she likes to date older men: "They make me feel grown up." http:// www.metro.co.uk/showbiz/830110-lily-allen-i-date-older-men-as-they -make-me-feel-grown-up.

104 **natural leaders, rich, powerful, and well connected** On Support and Advice for Escorts (www.saafe.info), women explicitly look for "sugar daddies" (wealthy men who pay women to be their girlfriend): "The only sugar daddy that I could tolerate would have to be super-mature, handsome, fit, funny, witty and too busy with his amazing life to be whiny or insecure. Because it sounds like the sugar daddy relationship is way too up-close-and-personal, despite the money (which has to be disguised as gifts? WTF? I can't eat shoes!) so if you don't actually like each other, it's a nightmare. I have rather high standards for my male company unless I'm getting an hourly fee." http://www.saafe.info/main/index.php?topic=2755.30

105 **what a movie might look like that simultaneously appeals** Salmon & Symons (2003).

106 **"the reader is satisfied with a Happy For Now ending"** Personal e-mail communication with Susanna Carr, April 22, 2010.

106 **"Wedding" and "fucking"** Number of searches for "wedding": 406,416. For "fucking": 321,198.

106 **each subsequent book's focus on a new hero and heroine** For example: the Desperate Duchess series stretches the story arc of Elijah and Jemma, the duke and duchess of Beaumont, through Books 1 to 5 (*Desperate Duchesses*, *An Affair Before Christmas*, *Duchess by Night*, *When the Duke Returns*, and *This Duchess of Mine*). In *Desperate Duchesses* (Book 1), Elijah has called Jemma home from Paris, where she has been living for many years during their estranged marriage. She left him because she walked in on him with his mistress, but now it's time for him to have an heir, and he'll need his wife to do it. Throughout each novel, they fight and make up, are pulled emotionally apart, and then brought together. *This Duchess of Mine* (Book 5) features Jemma and Elijah as the main couple, and it's in this novel that they finally get their Happily-Ever-After.

CHAPTER 6

108 **In one TV ad for Fair and Lovely** http://www.youtube.com/ watch?v=F-9tcXpW1DE.

109 **"Being desired is very arousing to women"** Meana (2010).

109 **"The Magic Hoo Hoo does it all"** Wendell & Tan (2009).

110 **"the way women feel about themselves may be very important"** Meana (2010). "An increasing body of data is indicating that the way women feel about themselves may be very important to their experience of sexual desire and subjective arousal, possibly even outweighing the impact of their partners' view of them."

111 **half of women's fantasies reflect the desire to be sexually irresistible** Ellis & Symons (1990).

112 **Women frequently fantasize about being a stripper** Strassberg & Lockerd (1998). Forty-seven percent of women reported the fantasy of "seeing themselves as a striptease dancer, harem girl, or other performer," and 50 percent had fantasized about "delighting many men."

112 **"If a woman's got a pretty body"** Levy (2006).

112 *sexting* http://www.thebostonchannel.com/news/18688245/detail .html, retrieved September 12, 2010.

112 *Real Sex for Real Women* Berman (2008).

113 **a parallel between female irresistibility and a sexual cue in the female rat** Meana (2010).

113 **Both pacing and the reward for pacing are controlled by software** Becker (2008). Also Meana (2010): "Bancroft deftly reviewed research suggesting that in the proceptive phase, female rats are in control, darting and hopping around the interested male, thereby pacing the frequency of his mounts. These sexual contacts have been shown to be rewarding (as evidenced by the conditioning of place preference) to the female rat, quite apart from intromission."
The female giraffe also performs a kind of pacing. http://www .bio.davidson.edu/people/vecase/Behavior/Spring2004/breedlove/ matingsystem.html.

113 **Anorexia and bulimia** Becker (2008).

113 **Women express much greater body image self-consciousness** Meana (2010).

114 **"One Rape, Please (to go)"** http://www.viceland.com/int/v14n8/ htdocs/rape.php, retrieved on August 30, 2010.

114 **widespread prevalence of female coercive fantasies** Critelli & Bivona (2008).

114 **an understandable source of discomfort and hand-wringing** Meana (2010), http://www.nytimes.com/2009/01/25/magazine/25desire-t .html?pagewanted=all, retrieved on August 30, 2010.
Leitenberg & Henning (1995): Thirty percent of women had the fantasy "I'm a slave who must obey a man's every wish," and 22 percent had the fantasy "I'm made to suffer before a man will satisfy me sexually."

114 **"Arousal is not consent"** http://www.nytimes.com/2009/01/25/ magazine/25desire-t.html?pagewanted=all, retrieved on August 30, 2010.

114 **Christine Monson's 1984 *Stormfire*** "Because as I've said before, if the hero had a beer gut and one droopy eye with caterpillar eyebrows, the woman would be screaming her head off and running for the sunset. But if the hero is a 'dark Irish devil' with all the beauty of a fallen angel and abs like rock-hard nuggets of goodness, the woman would be screaming her head off and running for the sunset but not upset if she gets caught by him again." http://www.ripmybodice .com/2010/04/05/even-with-1-ball-more-alpha-than-the-rest/.

115 **It's the wish to be beyond will** http://www.nytimes.com/2009/01/25/ magazine/25desire-t.html?pagewanted=all, retrieved on August 30, 2010.

NOTES

115 **Literotica is the single most popular English-language erotic story site** More on the history of erotic stories on the Web: http://www .asstr.org/~JournalofDesire/v3n2/Jekyll-SexStories.html.

116 **Harry Potter stories on AdultFanFiction.net** Top sexual tags for Harry Potter stories on AdultFanFiction.net, scraped in May 2010:

Anal	4143
Oral	3752
BDSM	1228
Lemon	1209
Abuse	1144
SoloM	1081
Violence	960
Rim	861
Bi	857
Humil	839
Toys	746
Inc	712
Tort	697
MPreg	694

116 **a fan fiction story by Miss Stephanie** http://hp.adultfanfiction .net/story.php?no=600025374, retrieved on August 30, 2010.

116 **"the explosion that was building within him"** One reader admiringly comments on Miss Stephanie's story, "He may be a psychopath, but a HOT psychopath. Damn. I like how he pulled his cock out of her and slapped her clit with it. Nice visual."

117 **a scene in *Legally Blonde*** Other movies that feature enhanced male sex appeal due to faked female interest: *She's Out of My League, Love Don't Cost a Thing, Sex Drive, American Pie, Year One, Along Came Polly, The Heartbreak Kid*. Also worth considering: Rachel Uchitel, one of Tiger Woods's mistresses, is still attracted to Tiger despite—or because of?—all his other mistresses. http://www.telegraph.co.uk/sport/golf/tigerwoods/7962948/ Rachel-Uchitel-wants-to-rekindle-Tiger-Woods-romance.html.

118 **the virgin's Magic Hoo Hoo captures his full attention** Similar narratives: *The Golden Touch* by Laura London. The heroine is a vicar's daughter, the hero a famous musician. She also wrote one called *The Lightning That Lingers*, about a librarian and a (male) stripper. Very charming books, and surprisingly un-rapey for the early eighties. *There's Perfect*, by Judith McNaught. The heroine is a librarian, the hero a film

star on the run. *Rock Star* by Roslyn Hardy Holco. The heroine is a librarian, the hero is a rock star. *The Good, the Bad and the Sexy* by Emily Carmichael. He's a movie star, she owns a ranch.

118 **Former Playboy playmate Kendra Wilkinson** Abridged from http://www.huffingtonpost.com/2010/07/12/hugh-hefner-i-have-sex -tw_n_643303.html, retrieved on August 20, 2010.

119 **"Omega" heroes** Knight (2007).

119 **"It sounded very Muggle"** http://hp.adultfanfiction.net/story .php?no=600025374, retrieved on August 30, 2010.

120 **a type of discussion known as "meta"** http://www.angelfire.com/ falcon/moonbeam/terms.html.

120 **"the thing that unequivocally sucked me in"** http://cesperanza .livejournal.com/174095.html, retrieved on August 30, 2010.

121 **pop singer Beyoncé** Beyoncé, "Why Don't You Love Me?"

121 **"nature designed women to be lovable"** Roy Baumeister, "Is There Anything Good About Men?"American Psychological Association, Invited Address, 2007. http://www.psy.fsu.edu/~baumeistertice/ goodaboutmen.htm, retrieved on August 30, 2010.

122 **the greatest sexual self-delusion in men** http://roissy.wordpress .com/2008/12/17/common-shit-tests/.

122 **The male brain is designed for sexual jealousy** Symons (1979).

123 **falling in love with the heroine represents an emotional deflowering** Wendell & Tan (2009).

124 **"sex is judged not to be worth the risk"** Meana (2010).

124 **reason why fetishes are so much more common in men** Laws & O'Donohue (2008).

124 **focus attention on female sexual plasticity** Baumeister (2000). "The greater consensual lesbianism in prison (as compared with consensual homosexuality among imprisoned males) would be interpreted by the selective control explanation as a sign that prison frees women from the compulsive heterosexuality enforced by society, reinforcing greater female erotic plasticity."

125 **Anne Heche** http://en.wikipedia.org/wiki/Anne_Heche, retrieved on August 30, 2010.

125 **found that high sex drive in women** Lippa (2006).

126 **FanFiction.net has consistently maintained one of the highest stickiness rating of *any* Web site** http://www.zdnet .com/blog/itfacts/nielsen-stickiest-brands-in-august-2003/4699, http:// www.internetnews.com/stats/article.php/3096631/Traffic-Patterns-of -September-2003.htm, http://books.google.com/books?id=ZKv43-YsSvQC&pg=PA123&lp g=PA123&dq=fanfiction.net+stickiest&source=bl&ots=K-2GU-YJ6a& sig=eSdMXqUDuQZQBEo2THmjlIDUkwQ&hl=en&ei=sR -NTIbyKoO88ga3t53ICw&sa=X&oi=book_result&ct=result&resnum= 3&ved=0CB4Q6AEwAjgK#v=onepage&q=fanfiction.net%20 stickiest&f=false, http://www.clickz.com/clickz/stats/1713182/

top-us-parent-companies-stickiest-brands-web-december-2008, http://
www.clickz.com/clickz/stats/1703722/top-us-parent-companies-stickiest
-brands-web-february-2009.

126 **Men, however, are eminently capable of mentally partitioning sex and romance** Fisher et al. (2002).

CHAPTER 7

128 **The average length of the gay penis** Bogaert & Hershberger (1999). Gay men are thicker too: straights have a penis circumference of 4.80 inches, while gay men have 4.95 inches.

131 **"This kid that is here now is so fucking hot"** http://thorandrocco .wordpress.com/.

133 **the gay interest in masculinity appears to be as fixed and inflexible** APA (2009), *Report of the American Psychological Association Task Force on Appropriate Therapeutic Responses to Sexual Orientation.*

133 **converting homosexual desire into heterosexual desire through conditioning** Moan & Heath (1972).

133 **opposes such ill-advised and ultimately unethical attempts** APA (2009), *Report of the American Psychological Association Task Force on Appropriate Therapeutic Responses to Sexual Orientation.*

133 **a binary "gender cue"** Ponseti et al. (2006).

134 **the one hundred top-rated video clips on Gaytube** The hundred top-rated videos were retrieved on October 21, 2010.

135 **the seven most popular categories of gay sexual searches** See Dogpile data description for more information. Dogpile gay sexual searches:

Rank	% of All Gay Sexual Searches	Sexual Category
1	6.22	youth
2	5.23	straight
3	2.23	daddies
4	1.99	black
5	1.98	penis
6	0.84	animation
7	0.72	college
8	0.65	domination and submission
9	0.63	mature
10	0.61	anal
11	0.52	college

Rank	% of All Gay Sexual Searches	Sexual Category
12	0.51	amateurs
13	0.50	bestiality
14	0.46	incest
15	0.44	celebrities
16	0.41	group sex
17	0.37	massage
18	0.36	interracial
19	0.33	asian

136 **Tom of Finland** http://www.eroticarts.com/.

137 **Below are two lists** Gay stories consist of all stories in the category *gay* on Nifty, scraped in February 2010. Fanfic stories consist of stories across multiple fandoms on AdultFanFiction.net scraped in March 2010. The genres scraped were: *anime, books, buffy, comics, Barry Potter, movies,* and *television*. These genres contained the most stories.

138 **sex appears about a quarter of the way into** Heterosexual stories consist of all stories in the category *erotic couplings* on Literotica, scraped in April 2010. Gay stories consist of all stories in the category *gay* on Literotica, scraped in February 2010.
Fanfic stories consist of all Harry Potter stories on AdultFanFiction .net scraped in March 2010.
Percentage of length into a story when a sexual encounter takes places in gay and fan fiction stories (the presence of a sexual encounter in a passage is determined using the density of masculine and feminine pronouns, and anatomical descriptors that were found to be a staple of such descriptions): Harry Potter fan fiction: Median: 50.0%, mean: 48.9%
Gay erotica: Median: 20.0%, mean: 26.6%

138 **Psychologist Richard Lippa and the BBC** Lippa (2007).

138 **both gay and straight brains exhibited different patterns** Safron et al. (2007). "Comparisons of activation to preferred sexual stimuli, non-preferred sexual stimuli, and sports stimuli revealed large networks correlated with sexual arousal, spanning multiple cortical and subcortical areas. Both homosexual and heterosexual men exhibited category-specific arousal in brain activity. Within the amygdala, greater preference-related activity was observed in homosexual men, but it is unclear whether this is a cause or a consequence of their sexuality. In a subsequent analysis of regions hypothesized to support arousal, both participant groups demonstrated widespread increases in evoked activity for preferred stimuli."
Schiffer et al. (2008). "The results for the sexual > neutral block contrast in the boys condition, together with the appendant regression analyses

with sexual arousal ratings in homosexual pedophiles, confirmed an activation pattern previously reported in heterosexual males."

138 **Gay men watch more porn** Traeen et al. (2006).

140 **impossible for evolution to have designed a gay-brain-only template** Symons (1979).

140 **the male brain's *body map*** Aleong & Paus (2010). Arzy et al. (2006), Poliakoff. (2010), Chan et al. (2004), David et al. (2007), Peelen & Downing (2007), Urgesi et al. (2004).

142 **blind men are aroused by female anatomy** Karremans et al. (2010).

142 **dubbed it the "Sleeping Beauty" fetish**. Bianchi-Demicheli et al. (2010). Intriguingly, there is an online genre of pornography that features sleeping women, including sites like SleepingLand.com, 3XSleep.com, and SleepingPortal.com. Though most of the interest in this genre is probably due to natural urges rather than brain damage, perhaps *some* of these Sleeping Beauty fetishists have the same brain lesion as Ortigue's fascinating patient.

143 **the psychologist Paul Vasey has been studying Japanese macaques** Vasey & Pfaus (2005).

144 **"a by-product of other behavioral mechanisms"** http://www .nytimes.com/2010/04/04/magazine/04animals-t.html?pagewanted=all, retrieved on August 30, 2010.

144 *intromission* Becker (2008), Pfaus (1996).

144 **pacing** Becker (2008). Pfaus (1996). "At first, rat copulation was studied by putting a female rat in a small cage. It was after placing the female rat in a larger cage was it discovered that she liked to control the pace of copulation."

144 *lordosis* Patchev et al. (2004). Researchers produced mice lacking one of the genes responsible for the animals' sensitivity to estrogen. These mice never exhibited lordosis. "Female sexual receptivity was severely disrupted, as disclosed by abolition of lordosis behavior."

144 **make a dominant male behave like a submissive female** Becker (2009).

145 **you can elicit mounting and hip-thrusting behavior** Becker (2009).

145 **widespread belief in the gay community** Cf. http://answers .yahoo.com/question/index?qid=20100306222159AAicFCT.

145 **We analyzed 1.9 million men-seeking-men ads on Craigslist** Posters are disarmingly direct and top or bottom self-identification is commonly made in the short post titles itself (for example: "Suck your cock and more," "Submissive cocksucker in hotel," "Use my mouth," "Looking for masculine guy who like to be serviced," "Smooth white bottom for hung top"). We took advantage of this feature to categorize posters as tops and bottoms by conservatively matching titles with string patterns. A small random sampling of posts that did not match any of the string patterns showed the distribution to be same as obtained from pattern-matched titles.

Interestingly, we also found that posters lie about their age. The most commonly reported ages are 28, 35, 30, 25, 38, and 29, suggesting a tendency toward rounding off toward milestone numbers when above, and subtracting when close. About 30,000 ads among the 1.9 million were posted by married men. This was also determined by pattern-matching the titles.

146 **in the three most common five-word phrases in the gay stories on Literotica** http://www.literotica.com/stories/stories_by_ category.php?category=6&page=44.
The three hundred most common five-word phrases from *gay male* stories on literotica were compared to the most common five-word phrases from stories in the erotic coupling genre. The resulting list was sorted according to relative frequency.

MOST COMMON PHRASES SORTED ACCORDING TO RELATIVE FREQUENCY

a cock in my mouth
his cock back into my
out of my ass and
out of his mouth and
on his knees in front
the back of his throat
and i felt his cock
on his back on the
cock in his hand and
and i could see his

147 **"Must enjoy and appreciate the cocksucking I will give"** This listing was retrieved in April 2010. Craigslist does not archive old listings. See http://www.craigslist.org/about/help/faq#lifespan.

147 **Looking for bottom to suck my dick** Retrieved from Craigslist in April 2010.

147 **about 2 percent of them specifically requested men willing to dominate another man sexually** At least 1.6% or 31,667 listings out of total 1.95 million m4m craigslist posts seek out sexual domination. This was determined by solicitations in post titles that used the keywords *rough, rape, slut, whore*. These keywords were chosen after verifying that such usage was highly correlated with requests for sexual domination.

148 **"I've met up with a guy in the backseat of his Lexus"** See also: http://articles.sfgate.com/2010-03-19/entertainment/18838701_1_grindr -gay-men-marriage.

149 **casual, anonymous sex that has long been the fantasy** Two classic jokes illustrate the difference between male sexuality and female sexuality: What does a lesbian bring on a second date? A moving van. What does a gay man bring on a second date? What's a second date?

150 **excessive androgens** LeVay (2010), Wilson & Rahman (2005).

NOTES

CHAPTER 8

152 **So he founded *Playgirl*** See http://findarticles.com/p/articles/mi_
g1epc/is_tov/ai_2419100965/

153 **the 1973 preview issue featured the Hager twins** See http://
findarticles.com/p/articles/mi_g1epc/is_tov/ai_2419100965/.

154 **editor in chief Claire Harth admitted the truth** http://books
.google.com/books?id=WWIEAAAAMBAJ&pg=PA52&dq=playgirl+edi
tor&hl=en&ei=X4tuTL6dF8O78gaO9KH1Cw&sa=X&oi=book_result&
ct=result&resnum=4&ved=0CD8Q6AEwAw#v=onepage&q=playgirl%20
editor&f=false.

154 **I could count on one hand the number of successful porn
for women paysites** Personal e-mail communication with Titmowse,
August 2009.

154 **"Porn is incredibly DULL DULL DULL"** http://letters.salon
.com/mwt/broadsheet/2006/11/27/porn/view/index11.html?show=all.

154 **"Pornography is the theory, rape the practice"** Morgan (1980).

155 **"not only bad for the people who make it but damaging to
society as a whole"** http://journalstar.com/news/local/education/
article_fae8d340-107b-11df-a90b-001cc4c03286.html.

155 **"customer complaints from women"** http://gizmodo.com/5477864/
why-apple-banned-sex-apps-we-were-getting-complaints-from-women.

155 **Chief technology officer for PornHub** Personal face-to-face
communication with Perry Stathopoulos, February 2010.

155 **about a third of its visitors are women** Also see Albright (2008).
Based on a survey of 15,246 respondents in the United States 75 percent
of men and 41 percent of women had intentionally viewed or downloaded
porn. Men and gays/lesbians were more likely to access porn or engage
in other sex-seeking behaviors online compared with straight men or
women. Also see Cooper et al. (2003).

155 **Ms. Juicy** User #3194921.

156 **Women can only conceive during five days** Wilcox et al. (1995).

156 ***extended sexuality*** Thornhill & Gangestad (2008).

157 **"men have the secret ingredient"** Mitch Fatel, *Miniskirts and
Muffins.*

157 **two distinct "modes" of sexual interests during their
ovulatory cycle** Thornhill & Gangestad (2008).

157 **different set of erotic cues** Kruger & Fisher (2005). Female college
students read brief sketches of characters from nineteenth-century
novels exemplifying alternative male mating strategies. The proper
hero "dad" advertises high potential for paternal investment by being
compassionate, romantic, and industrious, whereas the dark hero "cad"
advertises high genetic quality by being competitive, dominant, and
brave. Women preferred the "dad" for long-term relationships, but were
more likely to choose the "cad" for brief sexual relationships. These
preferences were expected, as they benefit the women's reproductive
success. Participants also inferred critical attributes and behaviors

from the character descriptions that omitted this information. Also see
Kruger et al. (2003).

157 **she gives special preference to males with superior genes**
Haselton & Miller (2006), Gizewski et al. (2006). Also http://www
.eurekalert.org/pub_releases/2010-08/uocp-mwp082410.php: "Not
unlike the chimps featured on the Discovery Channel, women become
more competitive with other females during the handful of days each
month when they are ovulating. The desire for women at peak fertility
to unconsciously choose products that enhance appearance is driven
by a desire to outdo attractive rival women."

157 **good looks and social dominance** Haselton & Miller (2006).
"Comparing women in mid-luteal phase and during their menses,
superior activation was revealed for women in mid-luteal phase in the
anterior cingulate, left insula, and orbitofrontal cortex. The superior
cerebral activation in the mid-luteal phase is also correlated with the
differing subjective rating of women in the two cycle times. The women
within the mid-luteal phase rated their sexual arousal similar to men
and women within the menstrual phase rated significantly lower than
men or women in mid-luteal phase. The reported results indicate that
the differences in cerebral activation are more prominent in comparison
between men and women than between women in different cycle phases."

158 **and strongly favor socially dominant males** Matsumoto-Oda
(1999).

158 **prefer males whose faces have been experimentally
manipulated** Waitt et al. (2003).

158 **a stronger preference for men with masculine faces** Thornhill
& Gangestad (2008).

158 **tend to flirt more** Haselton et al. (2007), Thornhill & Gangestad
(2008).

158 **likely to avoid risky places** Chavanne & Gallup (1998), Broder &
Hohmann (2003), Petralia & Gallup (2002).

158 **a greater aversion to squicky sex** Fessler & Navarrete (2003).

158 **tips that professional lap dancers received** Miller et al. (2007).
"To see whether estrus was really 'lost' during human evolution (as
researchers often claim), we examined ovulatory cycle effects on tip
earnings by professional lap dancers working in gentlemen's clubs.
Eighteen dancers recorded their menstrual periods, work shifts, and
tip earnings for 60 days on a study Web site. A mixed-model analysis
of 296 work shifts (representing about 5300 lap dances) showed an
interaction between cycle phase and hormonal contraception use.
Normally cycling participants earned about US$335 per 5-h shift during
estrus, US$260 per shift during the luteal phase, and US$185 per shift
during menstruation. By contrast, participants using contraceptive
pills showed no estrus earnings peak. These results constitute the first
direct economic evidence for the existence and importance of estrus in
contemporary human females, in a real-world work setting. These results
have clear implications for human evolution, sexuality, and economics."

NOTES

158 **When women are not ovulating, they prefer men with more feminized faces** Jones et al. (2005).

159 **nonovulating women do not** *ignore* **indicators of good genes** Thornhill & Gangestad (2008).

159 **"George Clooney and Sean Connery are sex symbols"** http://letters.salon.com/mwt/broadsheet/2006/11/27/porn/view/index11.html.

159 **One British study asked women to keep diaries** Thornhill & Gangestad (2008), Bellis & Baker (1990), Jones et al. (2005).

159 **Studies have shown that men are more protective** Thornhill & Gangestad (2008).

159–160 **women more frequently resist men's efforts to track their activities** Gangestad et al. (2004), Garver-Apgar et al. (2007).

160 **most women lack conscious awareness of their ovulations** Thornhill & Gangestad (2008).

160 **women show a greater interest in visual sexual material** Wallen & Rupp (2010).

160 **Sssh was founded by Angie Rowntree** Personal face-to-face and e-mail communication with Angie Rowntree, spring and summer 2010.

162 **A sexy voice, a masculine scent, and a sensuous touch** Thornhill & Gangestad (2008).

162 **"I have consumed vast quantities of female-created (written) porn"** http://letters.salon.com/mwt/broadsheet/2006/11/27/porn/view/index2.html?show=all.

162 **analyzed the text of more than ten thousand romance novels** We extracted the entire text from 10,344 romance novels by a total of 1,878 different authors. The median length of the romance novels was 55,615 words and the mean length was 54,168 words. We extracted probable description passages based on pronoun density. Most often, passages with the highest density of masculine pronouns and located in the first quarter of the text were descriptions of male protagonists. Passages with the highest combined density of masculine and feminine pronouns tend to be sexual or erotic descriptions. We extracted such high-density passages from the novels and used Mechanical Turk for annotation as person or scene description. Anatomical nouns were then extracted from the scene descriptions by sorting according to the frequency of words relative to the baseline frequency of all romance novels (and manual validation). Adjectives used in physical descriptions by limiting the search to two-word phrases containing anatomical nouns.

163 **female brain processes a man's visual features with the same speed** Rupp & Wallen (2008).

164 **associated with poorer long-term health** Ellison & Gray (2009).

164 **men produce steady levels of sperm** Ellison & Gray (2009).

164 **"My husband has a suit"** http://www.thegreatstory.org/stories-awaken.html.

164 **musculature and fast-energy burning** Leitenberg & Henning

(1995). "That serum testosterone level, independent of pubertal development per se, was a significant predictor of sexual fantasy frequency, whereas six other hormones were not."

Blakemore et al. (2010). "Rather, there is emerging evidence from both human and nonhuman primate studies that testosterone increases motivation to attain higher status, but the specific effects on behavior are dependent on the social and developmental context."

164–165 **masculine scents are correlated with testosterone levels** Thornhill & Gangestad (2008).

165 **"tall men make me feel more secure"** http://www .experienceproject.com/stories/Love-Tall-Men/1099298

165 **"It makes me feel small and secure"** http://www.experienceproject .com/stories/Love-Tall-Men/506030.

165 **a preference for men in uniform** See OkCupid data description.

QUESTION #2792: ARE MILITARY UNIFORMS A TURN ON? YES, NO, I WEAR ONE TO WORK.

Straight Males: # of respondents: 17315; 18.45% YES, 58.79% NO, 2.61%.

Bisexual Females: # of respondents: 2685; 35.83% YES, 47.3% NO, 0.34%.

Straight Females: # of respondents: 9201; 43.22% YES, 39.18% NO, 0.37%.

165 **Fashion blogger Teresa McGurk** http://hubpages.com/hub/Why -do-women-find-men-in-uniform-so-attractive_.

166 **One eye-tracking study found that women spend no more time looking at the penis** Rupp & Wallen (2007).

166 **"because I wanted to stand behind him"** http://jezebel.com/ comment/26261416/.

166 **Women generally prefer tight, athletic butts** Abramson & Pinkerton (1995).

166 **Sportswriter Michael Silver** http://sports.yahoo.com/nfl/ news?slug=ms-thegameface022208.

"They talk about 'Winning the Beauty Contest'—that was Brodrick Bunkley . . . When he weighed in, there were murmurs throughout the room. His legs were exploding out of his shorts, and it looked like his skin was swathed in Saran Wrap. You had a bunch of grown men who acted like they were at a strip joint outside of town. I thought they were going to offer him money for a lap dance."

166 **"Do women like guys' butts?"** http://answers.yahoo.com/question/ index?qid=20100330113037AA8qFo6.

167 **Ms. Intuition** User #2976906.

168 **One particular group of women reported higher amounts of porn viewing** See OkCupid data description.

NOTES

QUESTION #25: WOULD YOU WATCH A PORNO MOVIE WITH YOUR IDEAL MATCH? YES, NO.
>Straight Males: # of respondents: 94903; 83.51% YES, 6.13% NO.
>Bisexual Females: # of respondents: 12292; 88.06% YES, 4.0% NO.
>Straight Females: # of respondents: 55679; 74.71% YES, 11.18% NO.

QUESTION #9668: NOT AS IN WHIPS AND CHAINS, BUT IN GENERAL, DO YOU PREFER YOUR PARTNER TO BE . . . DOMINANT, SUBMISSIVE, BALANCED.
>Straight Males: # of Respondents: 77158; 14.1% Dominant, 20.19% Submissive, 42.34% Balanced.
>Bisexual Females: # of Respondents: 9681; 50.05% Dominant, 6.0% Submissive, 27.91% Balanced.
>Straight Females: # of Respondents: 45389; 50.69% Dominant, 3.14% Submissive, 20.39% Balanced.

QUESTION #1134: DO YOU HAVE A DESIRE (EVEN IF IT'S SECRET) TO TAKE PART IN SEXUAL ACTIVITIES INVOLVING BONDAGE? YES, NO ABSOLUTELY NOT.
>Straight Males: # of Respondents: 99053; 51.54% YES, 30.51% NO, 1.56%.
>Bisexual Females: # of Respondents: 13611; 81.63% YES, 8.53% NO, 0.54%.
>Straight Females: # of Respondents: 61933; 55.83% YES, 23.15% NO, 1.49%.

QUESTION #27262: YOU WALK IN ON YOUR PARTNER SURFING A PORNO SITE. HOW DO YOU FEEL? ANGRY/JEALOUS/SHOCKED/CHEATED, INTERESTED, INDIFFERENT.
>Straight Males: # of Respondents: 68397; 8.79% Angry/jealous/shocked/cheated, 61.91% Interested, 10.57% Indifferent.
>Bisexual Females: # of Respondents: 7434; 8.8% Angry/jealous/shocked/cheated, 64.47% Interested, 11.19% Indifferent.
>Straight Females: # of Respondents: 48488; 23.41% Angry/jealous/shocked/cheated, 39.34% Interested, 13.28% Indifferent.

>Also see discussion on authenticity of bisexual self-identification and commentary by bisexuals on differences in online and real-life dating preferences: http://blog.okcupid.com/index.php/the-biggest-lies-in-online-dating/.

168 **Self-identified bisexuals** The expected overlap of *nude men* and

nude women searches in the AOL data set, assuming independence: 8.86, obtained: 130. We can't differentiate between male and female searchers, however.

169 **Each column represents a single question from the survey**
Question #1 (OkCupid Question# 86615): Would you pay for porn? A: Yes. B: No. C. Only if I couldn't get it for free. D. I'm not interested in porn. (Respondents: 826 straight men, 106 bisexual women, 268 straight women.)
Question #2 (OkCupid Question# 13103): How big is your porn collection? A. Small B. Medium C. Large D. Don't have one. (Respondents: 8,147 straight men, 762 bisexual women, 3,394 straight women.)
Question #3 (OkCupid Question# 35624): You discover a huge porn collection on your significant other's computer. You are: A. Unaffected . . . "So what?" B. Embarassed or disgusted . . . "This is filthy!" C. Angry or hurt . . . "This is cheating!" D. Masturbating . . . "This is so hot!" (Respondents: 253,460 straight men, 27,639 bisexual women, 163,804 straight women.)
Question #4 (OkCupid Question# 18966): Do you prefer hardcore or softcore when it comes to your porn? A: Hard! B: Soft! C: I'm not sure. D: I don't like porn. (Respondents: 57,876 straight men, 8,245 bisexual women, 36,799 straight women.)

169 **38 percent of the women self-identify as bisexual** Fantasti.cc users self-identification, based on user information scraped in July 2010:

WOMEN: 958
> bisexual, 368 (38%)
> open-minded, 286 (30%)
> straight, 184 (19%)
> single, 133
> relationship, 115

MEN: 5626
> straight, 3912 (70%)
> open-minded, 980 (17%)
> single, 818
> relationship, 364
> bisexual, 279 (5%)

169 **In Richard Lippa's BBC survey** Lippa (2007).
170 **bisexual women have greater circulating levels of testosterone**
Van Wyk (1995). "Several studies seem to indicate that some bisexuals have a predominantly heterosexual or homosexual orientation, but high erotic responsiveness and more 'masculine' characteristics, leading to versatility in sexual behavior. Early exposure to masculinizing hormones

seems to predispose human females toward bisexuality rather than exclusive homosexuality." Also Vinegas & Conley (2000).

170 **can trigger a variety of negative reactions** Spinella (2007). "The analysis indicated that several brain structures are commonly involved in the processing of disgust-inducing and erotic pictures (occipital cortex, hippocampus, thalamus, and the amygdala). The ventral striatum was specifically activated when subjects saw highly sexually arousing pictures. This indicates the involvement of the human reward system during the processing of visual erotica."
http://www.boston.com/bostonglobe/ideas/articles/2010/08/15/ewwwwwwwww: "The disgust response gets pulled into these higher moral domains having to do with social rules," says Daniel Kelly, a philosopher at Purdue University and author of a forthcoming book on morality and disgust. Paul Rozin. In all those instances, most people refused, even though they knew the cockroach and sweater were clean and that the fudge was in fact fudge. They just felt disgusted. According to Rozin, the power of our disgust reaction leads us to a sort of magical thinking. "The sense of contamination is what's so interesting," Rozin says. "When the cockroach touches something, we feel like something of the cockroach actually enters it."

171 *Reading the Romance* Radway (1984).

172 **"centerfold syndrome"** Albright (2008).

172 **prone to condemning squicky content as immoral** See http://www.obscenitycrimes.org/Senate-Reisman-Layden-Etc.pdf

172 **as not just physically unhealthy but morally wrong** http://www.scientificamerican.com/blog/post.cfm?id=one-reason-why-humans-are-special-a-2010-06-22: "Between 1969–1989, for example, a single institution in the United States performed 656 castrations with the aim to stop the men from masturbating. One clinical study reported some success in eliminating this problem behavior by squirting lemon juice into the mouth of a young patient every time he pulled out his penis in public."

173 **powerful male sex drive focused** There is a neurological condition known as Kluver-Bucy syndrome that results from the destruction of temporal lobe tissue. This condition removes all sexual inhibitions. Men who suffer from Kluver-Bucy will try to have sex with trees, animals, and rocks. They can no longer control their sexual urges. "Male hang-ups" may actually be nature's way of narrowing the focus of the powerful drive of male sexuality.

CHAPTER 9

174 **Mr. Closet** Abridged excerpt is from Levine et al. (2003).

175 **I first discovered porn-stories when I was 15** http://www.asstr.org/~Forbidden_Fantasies/stuff/what.htm.

177 **also controls another critical bodily process: orgasm** Marthol & Hills (2004).

177 **to test this hypothesis with an ingenious experiment** Dutton & Aron (1974).

178 **The experiment presented female subjects with two different conditions** Schacter & Singer (1962), Dutton & Aron (1974), Meston & Heiman (1998), Brotto & Gorzalka (2002), Palace & Gorzalka (1990), Meston (2000), Meston & Gorzalka (1995).

178 **to Josef Mengele's medical examination table** Kahr (2008).

179 **an analysis of about twenty-four thousand children** http://blogs .discovermagazine.com/gnxp/2010/06/the-paternity-myth-the -rarity-of-cuckoldry/

179 **3,500 paternity claims** http://www.telegraph.co.uk/news/ uknews/2483751/Mothers-wrongly-identifying-fathers-in-Child -Support-Agency-claims.html.

180 **"She wore her very best lingerie"** http://www.hotwifeblog .com/2010/06/11/her-first-time-alone/.

180 **men who search for "cheating wife"** Perry Stathopoulos, the CTO of PornHub, supplied us with a variety of data about users' activities on their Web site. One data set was a collection of most frequent search terms entered into the PornHub search engine, and number of videos viewed per search term. The data was collected in February 2010.

181 **the most common two-word phrases in cuckold stories** Stories were scraped from the *Loving Wives* category on Literotica in April 2010.

182 **in videos containing a white man and a black man** 43 out of 50 videos feature black and white men feature the black male as the top. Videos were retrieved and examined in August 2010.

182 **Sperm competition refers to a variety of physiological and behavioral adaptations** Birkhead & Maller (1998).

183 **giant testicles of the chimpanzee** Dixson & Brancroft (1999).

183 **the bulbous head and extended length of the human penis** Gallup et al. (2006). Also see http://www.scientificamerican.com/article .cfm?id=secrets-of-the-phallus.

183 **the inevitable flaccidity men experience after ejaculation** Gallup et al. (2006).

183 **Dogs, deer, and kangaroos** Birkhead & Hosken (2008).

183 **Male stickleback fish** Zbinden et al. (2004).

183 **"My steady boyfriend, nicknamed IFuckAmy"** http:// cuckoldinglifestyle.blogspot.com/2006/02/cuckolding-today .html?zx=a5f050a3291bc87e.

184 **frequently perceived as more dominant** A female Duke undergraduate gained notoriety in October 2010 for her parody of a thesis presentation that detailed her actual sexual liaisons with student athletes at Duke. The PowerPoint presentation listed the sexual perks and quirks of the thirteen men she allegedly slept with. She makes note of how one of her partners—a Caucasian man—implores her to

NOTES

profess love for big black penises while in bed with her. http://www
.huffingtonpost.com/2010/10/07/karen-owen-duke-sex-rati_n_754186
.html.

184 **British psychologist Nicholas Pound** Pound (2002).
184 **videos portraying "polyandrous sexual activity"** Pound (2002).
185 **the three hundred most-viewed group sex videos** The three
hundred most-viewed group sex videos were collected from PornHub on
January 9, 2010, and "compilation" videos were removed.

mean # of males per video: 2
mean # of females per video: 2.6

Then, we removed "threesome" videos, which left a set of videos with
four or more sexual partners:

mean # of males per video: 3.75
mean # of females per video: 3.31

In the set of threesome videos, there were more males in 63 videos and
more females in 91 videos.

185 **Men fantasize about group sex more often than women do**
Ellis & Symons (1990).
186 **shrieking, shivering female orgasms** When asked whether female
orgasms in porn were fake or real, one porn director replied, "More fake
than real. I have some girls who always fake it, they find the pressure of
the cameras and lights, the added self-awareness stop them from getting
to orgasm. Other girls find that as soon as the cameras are on they come
from the smallest of things. One girl in particular will come multiple
times in every scene she does. Everyone is wired different, I don't think
you can say everyone does this or everyone does that." He added, "I
really dislike guys using Viagra or similar drugs. Anything that raises
the blood pressure makes their faces go bright red as soon as they start
fucking, which really shows up on camera. I think it looks terrible."
Personal e-mail communication from Stephen Yagielowicz, August,
2010. In the same communication, Yagielowicz observed, "While some
actresses are better at acting than others, it appears that acting is all
it is—and that even when the guy is 'acting' it does not go unnoticed,
or undesired. While I suspect that most fans believe that the girls are
actually having orgasms (just as most guys believe they always give their
lover an orgasm), I also suspect that many performers are thinking about
the new shoes they will buy or whatever, rather than being immersed in
the scene. It's like big time wrestling: some believe it's all real, from the
hits to the back story. Same with porn. Having said that, girls like Lezley
Zen and Aria (not Giovanni, just Aria), Tory Lane and others have been
thought of as 'giving it their all,' while the 'squirters' tend to carry more
of a 'she's really cumming!' audience, with girls such as Tianna Lynn
and Annie Cruz coming to mind with no pun intended. I also think you

used the right word: 'actresses'—this is after all about fantasy, not reality. Audiences are not there to see their bored wives wearing hair curlers and saying 'hurry up.'

186 **one of the most potent psychological cues** Bogaert (2001). "The results indicated that, when given a choice to view different media materials, the men chose a broad range of media materials, although the 'female insatiability' films were more popular than the other sexual films (e.g., 'erotic' or 'violent')." Also, Brewer & Hendrie (2010).

186 **"Seeing and hearing a woman who is truly turned on"** http://www.reddit.com/r/AskReddit/comments/9pzlt/is_there_a_reason_that_so_much_hetero_porn_is/.

186 **Sasha Grey** http://www.freeones.com/html/s_links/Sasha_Grey/.

187 **Sasha Grey, Nina Hartley, Chloe, Cytherea, and Jenna Jameson** http://www.nina.com/vboard/showthread.php?p=315, http://forum.adultdvdtalk.com/forum/topic.dlt/topic_id=150466/forum_id=1/cat_id=1/150466.htm, http://www.adultdvdtalk.com/chat/chloe.asp.

187 **On Fantasti.cc, we analyzed ten thousand comments** We scraped 10,000 comments posted in response to the hundred highest rated videos on Fantasti.cc in March 2010. These comments were then categorized by workers on Amazon Mechanical Turk. The comments were binned into seven categories. A particular comment was categorized and counted if at least two of three workers applied the same category tag.

> subject is attractive, 6033
> praise of anatomy, 5157
> subject is expressing pleasure, 4806
> comment on sex, 4047
> None of the above, 3443
> subject is "dirty," 2739
> subject is expressing surprise or fear, 1148

188 **are wired to pay attention to whether his partner is engaged** See http://www.nytimes.com/books/first/b/buss-passion.html.

188 **"if Ann rejected Andy for being a bad lover"** Personal e-mail communication with Donald Symons, 2010.

188 **more than 65 percent of women say they've faked orgasms** Muehlenhard & Shippee (2009), Brewer & Hendrie (2010).

189 **the men and women who produce the adult content on the Internet live from paycheck to paycheck** Personal e-mail communication with Stephen Yagielowicz, August 2010. Profitability has been further eroded by tube sites, including illegitimate tubes based in eastern Europe.

189 **Joe Francis** http://www.latimes.com/features/magazine/west/la-tm-gonewild32aug06,0,2664370.story?coll=la-home-headlines.

191 **"I pretty much can't watch professional porn anymore."** http://www.consolecity.com/forum/archive/index.php/t-63740.html.

NOTES

192 **especially genuine amateurs** Symons & Ellis (1990). From http://
www.scientificamerican.com/blog/post.cfm?id=one-reason-why-humans
-are-special-a-2010-06-22: "In a 1990 study published in the *Journal of
Sex Research*, evolutionary psychologists Bruce Ellis and Donald Symons
found that 32 percent of men said that they'd had sexual encounters in
their imagination with more than 1,000 different people, compared
to only 8 percent of women. Men also reported rotating in from their
imaginary rosters one imagined partner for another during the course
of a single fantasy more often than women did."
Toates (2009). "Novelty and increased appetitive behavior is associated
with increased activation of dopamine in the N.acc." Also see Fiorino
et al. (1997), Woodson (2002).

192 **a process first studied systematically in rats in the 1950s**
Wilson et al. (1963).

192 **one study of novelty conducted at the State University of New
York, Stony Brook** Odonohue & Geer (1985).

CHAPTER 10

195 **Geladas are a peculiar and little-known species of monkey**
http://www.smithsonianmag.com/science-nature/Ethiopias-Exotic
-Monkeys.html.

197 **increase a male's social status** Blakemore et al. (2010). "Rather,
there is emerging evidence from both human and nonhuman primate
studies that testosterone increases motivation to attain higher status,
but the specific effects on behavior are dependent on the social and
developmental context."

197 **the monkey will rise swiftly up the dominance hierarchy**
Panksepp (1998).

197 ***The Blind Side*** Lewis (2007). See http://en.wikipedia.org/wiki/
Michael_Oher.

197 **the naked mole rat** Holmes et al. (2007), Holmes et al. (2008).

198 **more dominant a human male becomes** Holmes et al. (2008),
Bernhardt et al. (1998). Boston men may have experienced the most sex in
America during the 2007 sports season, when the Red Sox, Celtics, and
Patriots all made it to the championships in their respective sports.

199 **social dominance is a complex cognitive process** Marsh et al.
(2009), Allison et al (2000), Chiao et al. (2008).

199 **sexual dominance and sexual submission appear to be entirely
managed by subcortical processes** There's precious little research
on the neural underpinnings of sexual dominance and submission in
humans, but sexual behavior in rats has proved to be a good model for
basic sexual behavior and endocrine action in humans. Becker (2008),
Agmo and Ellingsen (2003), Pfaus (2009), Paredes (2003).
Herbert (2008): "The medial preoptic area of the hypothalamus (MPOA)
is known to be involved in masculine patterns of sexual behaviour in

298

rodents and monkeys, and to be sexually dimorphic, though, it should be pointed out, there are suggestions that it promotes sexual performance (the ability to copulate) more than motivation for masculine-type sex. Garcia-Garcia-Falgueras and Swaab find that part of this area, INAH3 in humans, is larger and has a greater number and density of neurons in males than females, and that male-to-female transsexuals (MtF) resemble females."
Evidence from rat studies: Becker et al. (2001), Hoshina et al. (1994), Paredes & Baum (1997).

200 **Mr. Panties** User #13263062.

201 **Mr. Diapers** User# 23251711.

201 **Mr. Gardens** User # 3214991.

203 **women are not motivated by a testosterone-fueled drive** Mazur & Booth (1998). A normal man has about ten nanograms of testosterone per milliliter of blood; women have roughly one-seventh this amount. Female testosterone levels are not responsive to anticipated or successful status competition.

203 **This changes if you give women testosterone** van Honk et al. (2004), Dabbs & Hargrove (1997).

203 **Female Viagra already exists and it's called testosterone** Because people who are deprived of food tend to have more frequent daydreams about food, it might be expected that sexual deprivation would have the same effect on sexual thoughts. The little evidence that exists, however, suggests otherwise. Those with the most active sex lives have the most sexual fantasies. Studies have shown that frequency of fantasy is positively correlated with masturbation frequency, intercourse frequency, number of lifetime sexual partners, and self-rated sex drive.

203 **"increased my compassion for men four-fold"** http://evolutionarytimes.org/files/bd4988b205d403c244617c86dcf34e8c-21.php

203 **number of negative side effects** Basaria & Dobs (2004).

203 **many women prefer to be the seducer** Targosz (2008).

204 **250 female teachers in America** http://www.zimbio.com/The+50+Most+Infamous+Female+Teacher+Sex+Scandals/articles/7hrWhfmeIcL/50+Most+Infamous+Female+Teacher+Sex+Scandals.

204 **Rebecca Bogard** http://sabrinaerdely.com/docs/SexLiesPhysEd.pdf.

204 **allegedly having sex with eight members** http://www.zimbio.com/The+50+Most+Infamous+Female+Teacher+Sex+Scandals/articles/7hrWhfmeIcL/50+Most+Infamous+Female+Teacher+Sex+Scandals.

204 **complex relationship with their desire to be dominant or submissive** Here's one woman's comment on http://pandagon.net/index.php/site/comments/why_dont_men_read_more_romance_novels: "Fanfiction fanfiction fanfiction. Thank you kindly. Though gay sex is still the major content of fanfiction, and while I think that some of that is just the plain old two-hot-dudes-for-the-price-of-one thing, I also think it's because to many women two male bodies read as kind of neutral and equal—one doesn't start off coded as passive/receptive or active/

NOTES

aggressive. And then there's the whole subset that I think is women acting out their issues with sex on 'neutral' male bodies. Pretty much every trope that Amanda has decried as being disturbing in male-oriented porn has a fairly popular fanfiction equivalent."

204 **"I can read and am very fond of [dominant and submissive roles]"** An interesting anecdote from a submissive: "i sleep with a collar on at night. i find it comforting and it gives me a sense that there is more than me, i am not the biggest thing in the world, and that i'm not meant to control everything. i submit to plenty of things in my life and the collar symbolizes that, even though a collar usually symbolizes submission to your Master." http://hislittlepet.blogspot .com/2006_07_01_archive.html.

205 **"How does the idea of being slapped hard in the face during sex make you feel?"**

QUESTION #11: HOW DOES THE IDEA OF BEING SLAPPED HARD IN THE FACE DURING SEX MAKE YOU FEEL? HORRIFIED; AROUSED; NOSTALGIC; INDIFFERENT.

Straight Males: # of Respondents: 104,623; 37.0% Horrified; 16.14% Aroused; 1.97% Nostalgic; 20.59% Indifferent.
Bisexual Females: # of Respondents: 12,786; 42.59% Horrified; 21.63% Aroused; 2.40%; 12.33%.
Straight Females: # of Respondents: 66,646; 62.58% Horrified; 8.44% Aroused; 1.11%; 7.23%.

206 **fan fiction scholar Brita Hansen** Personal e-mail communication with Brita Hansen, June 2010.

206 **"Cleansing"** http://www.fanfiction.net/s/4403887/1/Cleansing.

207 **generally prefer sexual submission** Troisi & Carosi (1998) reported that female Japanese macaques experience orgasm more frequently when mating with dominant males.

207 **scientists erroneously believed that BDSM participants** Wright (2006), Richters et al. (2008).

207 **"It's about the voluntary exchange of power"** Personal face-to-face and e-mail communication, June 2010.

207 **This centrality of power** See http://www.iron-rose.com/IR/support_groups.htm, http://www.bdsm-texas.com/state.htm.

208 **would derive sexual satisfaction from relinquishing control** Lawrence & Love-Crowell (2008). "One therapist suggested, however, that the negotiation skills required in BDSM play tended to weed out persons with significant psychopathology: It takes really good boundaries to negotiate anything in sex and in particular around dealing openly with fantasy and stuff. And mentally ill people really aren't good at that and they don't get very far. (Therapist L). They seem smarter than the

average client, I think. . . They tend to be articulate, imaginative, creative people. (Therapist J)."

Richters et al. (2008). "Our findings support the idea that BDSM is simply a sexual interest or subculture attractive to a minority, and for most participants not a pathological symptom of past abuse or difficulty with 'normal' sex."

Stark et al. (2005). "This interpretation is also supported by an unpublished investigation of our group, in which 110 sadomasochists had shown only minor differences with regard to various personality traits in comparison to a nonSM group. The SM group depicted more activation in the ventral striatum than the nonSM group when they saw the pictures with a sadomasochistic content, which were rated highly erotic by them and disgusting by the nonSM group."

208 **"wearing someone's collar to be romantic"** http://gloria-brame .com/therapy/kinkoverview.html
"Men who had engaged in BDSM scored significantly lower on a scale of psychological distress than other men. Engagement in BDSM was not significantly related to any sexual difficulties."

209 **"A sub might orgasm, if the dom allows it"** Personal communication with Tiiu, June 2010.

209 **"goodly number of the members who cancel"** Personal email communication with Colin Rowntree, August 2010.

210 **the left column lists the ten most common phrases in BDSM** The 1,500 most frequent two-word phrases from stories in the BDSM category on Literotica were compared to the most frequent two-word phrases from stories in the NonConsent/Reluctant category on Literotica. Thus, each column lists the most frequent two-word phrases relative to the two-word phrases in the other genre.

CHAPTER 11

213 **Margaret Livingstone, a professor of neurobiology** Livingstone (2002).

214 *cravability* http://www.americanwaymag.com/david-leong-food-kevin -reilly-amsterdam-joe-horn. Also see Kessler (2009).

214 **"Cravable foods stick in customers' imagination"** http:// findarticles.com/p/articles/mi_m3190/is_4_37/ai_97314567/.

215 *Lopamudra* Parameshwaranand (2001).

216 **"I call it the 'Trannie Peek'"** Personal communication, August 2009.
Shemale porn has even made its way into mainstream television, such as this clip from *Dexter*: http://www.youtube.com/watch?v=JE0N103hkS4. "'Cause I can explain all that shemale stuff."

216 **"Transsexual Porn is classified as Straight Specialty"** http:// blogs.myspace.com/index.cfm?fuseaction=blog.view&friendId= 22387538&blogId=496679913.

216 **"the audience for most shemale porn, are straight dudes"** http://blogs.myspace.com/index.cfm?fuseaction=blog.view&friendId= 22387538&blogId=496679913.

217 **"Transsexual porn is one of the largest-selling niches"** http:// www.amydaly.com/blog/grooby/the-tranny-awards-show.html "We are one of the if not the most profitable genre in porn" says transsexual star Amy Daly.

217 **Mr. Miami Latino** User #5083529.

217 **Mr. Squirt** User #3018011.

218 **Two sociologists visited a Chicago bar frequented by transsexual women** Weinberg & Williams (2010).

218 **"I like her soft looks, sexy body"** http://www.psychologytoday .com/blog/cupids-poisoned-arrow/201006/losing-porn-roulette.

219 **Mr. Sexy** User #4317947.

221 **U.S. senator Amy Klobuchar** http://filmdrunk.uproxx.com/ 2010/06/supreme-court-hearing-includes-question-of-team-edward-or -team-jacob.

221 **Meyer's Web site has received more than a million visitors a day** Traffic information from Quantcast.

222 **"insatiable hunger for the jugular"** http://www.details.com/ celebrities-entertainment/movies-and-tv/200911/new-moon-twilight -edward-cullen-girlfriend-wife?currentPage=2#ixzz13QR6TJJW.

226 **fifty-four of them are facials** Of the hundred top-rated videos on Fantasti.cc in March 2010 that were tagged "hardcore" (which means hetero sex, not lesbian or solo girl), fifty-four featured facials.

227 **"compilations"** PornHub search data for February 2010.

227 **"gay porn has always been arousing"** http://www.villagevoice .com/2008-05-13/columns/girls-love-gay-male-porn/.

227 **just as turned on by watching two guys sexually satisfy each other** "I am a 100% heterosexual 19 year old girl. And there is nothing better than two men having sex with one another. I can't stand hetero porn. Gay male sex is so erotic. Ive been looking at it sense I was 14 or 15 and it only gets better. If I ever get married I think I would encourage my husband to have lots of gay sex that way I can watch in person, and I can join in. It's my dream! I can't wait to see my husband having gay sex. Sometimes I dream about how great it would be to come home and find my man in bed with another man. I bet he would probly think I'm mad but then I would tell him how turned on I get from watching with other men and how I want to see himm have gay sex everyday because it brings out th freak in me." http://www.ukblackout .com/entertainment-mainmenu-76/film-theatre-tv/873-women-who -like-to-watch-gay-porn-.html.

228 **my preference is for gay male porn** http://blog.babeland .com/2007/11/28/new-ideas-for-sex-research/#comments.

228 **"Draco took a quill from Harry's case"** http://www.kvraudio.com/ forum/viewtopic.php?t=270398.

NOTES

228 **"'I bet my weapon's bigger than yours'"** http://www.agaysex.com/ Tortured-by-Cop/index.html.

229 **The fastest expanding subgenre of EroRom is *male-male romances*** http://www.laweekly.com/2009-12-17/art-books/man-on -man-the-new-gay-romance.

229 **The largest audience for the groundbreaking film *Brokeback Mountain*** http://www.newyorker.com/ archive/1997/10/13/1997_10_13_074_TNY_CARDS_000379463.

230 **a subgenre of fan fiction known as *slash*** http://www.laweekly .com/2009-12-17/art-books/man-on-man-the-new-gay-romance.

230 **more than a half million slash stories** Estimated from the number of slash stories tagged on the social bookmarking engine Delicious. Delicious alone lists 536,243 stories tagged "fic" (a commonly used abbreviation for fiction), and 167,028 tagged as "slash" and "fic." Almost all stories tagged using "fic" on Delicious belong to the slash genre. The "slash" tag is less common and character pairing tags are used more often. For instance, stories pairing Harry Potter and Draco Malfoy from the Harry Potter series are tagged as "harry/draco." There are 24,691 stories tagged as "harry/draco," but only 10,622 of these also employ the tag "slash."

230 **"Happy Birthday"** http://libraryofmoria.com/frodosam/ happybirthday.txt.

231 **"One of the guys is almost always written as shorter"** Personal e-mail communication with Brita Hansen, August 2009.

231 ***yaoi*** Macwilliams (2008).

231 **1992 Tokyo Gay and Lesbian Film Festival** McLelland (2006/2007).

232 **"I wore embroidered corsets and gold and black robes"** Choisy (1994).

234 ***How Annie and Toni Became Best Friends Forever Part 2*** http:// tgtony.deviantart.com/art/BFF-Best-Friends-Forever-Pt1-168406985.

236 **enjoyment of transformation stories** Veale et al. (2008).

236 ***autogynephilia*** Bailey (2003).

236 **in transformation stories, the man is always forced** Beigel and Feldman (1963).

241 **Edward Abbey writes** Abbey (1982).

BIBLIOGRAPHY

Abbey, E. (1982), *Down the River.* New York: Dutton.

Abel, G. G., and E. B. Blanchar (1974). "Role of Fantasy in Treatment of Sexual Deviation." *Archives of General Psychiatry* 30(4): 467–475.

Abel, G. G., L. Coffey, et al. (2008). "Sexual Arousal Patterns: Normal and Deviant." *Psychiatric Clinics of North America* 31(4): 643–+.

Abel, G. G., and C. Osborn (1992). "The Paraphilias—The Extent and Nature of Sexually Deviant and Criminal Behavior." *Psychiatric Clinics of North America* 15(3): 675–687.

Abramson, P. R., and S. D. Pinkerton (1995). *Sexual Nature, Sexual Culture.* Chicago: University of Chicago Press.

Abramson, P. R., and S. D. Pinkerton (1995). *With Pleasure: Thoughts on the Nature of Human Sexuality.* New York: Oxford University Press.

Adams, H. E., L. W. Wright, et al. (1996). "Is Homophobia Associated with Homosexual Arousal?" *Journal of Abnormal Psychology* 105(3): 440–445.

Adolphs, R. (2010). "What Does the Amygdala Contribute to Social Cognition?" *Year in Cognitive Neuroscience* 2010. Oxford: Blackwell Publishing. 1191: 42–61.

Agate, R. J., W. Grisham, et al. (2003). "Neural, Not Gonadal, Origin of Brain Sex Differences in a Gynandromorphic Finch." *Proceedings of the National Academy of Sciences of the United States of America* 100(8): 4873–4878.

Agmo, A. (2008). "On the Concept of Sexual Arousal: A Simpler Alternative." *Hormones and Behavior* 53(2): 312–314.

Agmo, A. (2007). *Functional and Dysfunctional Sexual Behavior: A Synthesis of Neuroscience and Comparative Psychology.* Amsterdam; Boston: Elsevier/ Academic Press.

Agmo, A., and E. Ellingsen (2003). "Relevance of Non-Human Animal Studies to the Understanding of Human Sexuality." *Scandinavian Journal of Psychology* 44(3): 293–301.

Agmo, A., A. L. Turi, et al. (2004). "Preclinical Models of Sexual Desire: Conceptual and Behavioral Analyses." *Pharmacology Biochemistry and Behavior* 78(3): 379–404.

Ahmed, E. I., J. L. Zehr, et al. (2008). "Pubertal Hormones Modulate the Addition of New Cells to Sexually Dimorphic Brain Regions." *Nature Neuroscience* 11(9): 995–997.

Ahmed, S. F., A. Cheng, et al. (2000). "Phenotypic Features, Androgen Receptor Binding, and Mutational Analysis in 278 Clinical Cases Reported as Androgen Insensitivity Syndrome." *Journal of Clinical Endocrinology and Metabolism* 85(2): 658–665.

Albright, J. M. (2008). "Sex in America Online: An Exploration of Sex, Marital Status, and Sexual Identity in Internet Sex Seeking and Its Impacts." *Journal of Sex Research* 45(2): 175–186.

Alcaro, A., R. Huber, et al. (2007). "Behavioral Functions of the Mesolimbic Dopaminergic System: An Affective Neuroethological Perspective." *Brain Research Reviews* 56(2): 283–321.

Aleman, A., and M. Swart (2008). "Sex Differences in Neural Activation to Facial Expressions Denoting Contempt and Disgust." *PLoS One* 3(11).

Aleong, R., and T. Paus (2010). "Neural Correlates of Human Body Perception." *Journal of Cognitive Neuroscience* 22(3): 482–495.

Alexander, G. M., and M. Hines (2002). "Sex Differences in Response to Children's Toys in Nonhuman Primates (Cercopithecus Aethiops Sabaeus)." *Evolution and Human Behavior* 23(6): 467–479.

Alexander, G. M., and B. B. Sherwin (1993). "Sex Steroids, Sexual-Behavior, and Selection Attention for Erotic Stimuli in Women Using Oral-Contraceptives." *Psychoneuroendocrinology* 18(2): 91–102.

Allen, L. S., and R. A. Gorski (1991). "Sexual Dimorphism of the Anterior Commissure and Massa Intermedia of the Human Brain." *Journal of Comparative Neurology* 312(1): 97–104.

Allen, L. S., and R. A. Gorski (1992). "Sexual Orientation and the Size of the Anterior Commissure in the Human Brain." *Proceedings of the National Academy of Sciences of the United States of America* 89(15): 7199–7202.

Allen, L. S., M. Hines, et al. (1989). "2 Sexually Dimorphic Cell Groups in the Human-Brain." *Journal of Neuroscience* 9(2): 497–506.

Allen, L. S., M. F. Richey, et al. (1991). "Sex-Differences in the Corpus-Callosum of the Living Human-Being." *Journal of Neuroscience* 11(4): 933–942.

Allen, M., T. M. Emmers-Sommer, et al. (2007). "The Connection Between the Physiological and Psychological Reactions to Sexually Explicit Materials: A Literature Summary Using Meta-Analysis." *Communication Monographs* 74(4): 541–560.

Allison, T., A. Puce, et al. (2000). "Social Perception from Visual Cues: Role of the STS Region." *Trends in Cognitive Sciences* 4(7): 267–278.

Aloni, R., and S. Katz (1999). "A Review of the Effect of Traumatic Brain Injury on the Human Sexual Response." *Brain Injury* 13(4): 269–280.

Andersen, B. L., J. M. Cyranowski, et al. (2000). "Beyond Artificial, Sex-Linked Distinctions to Conceptualize Female Sexuality: Comment on Baumeister (2000)." *Psychological Bulletin* 126(3): 380–384.

Andersen, M. L., D. Poyares, et al. (2007). "Sexsomnia: Abnormal Sexual Behavior During Sleep." *Brain Research Reviews* 56(2): 271–282.

Andersen, S. L., M. Rutstein, et al. (1997). "Sex Differences in Dopamine Receptor Overproduction and Elimination." *Neuroreport* 8(6): 1495–1498.

Anderson, C. A., and B. J. Bushman (2001). "Effects of Violent Video Games on Aggressive Behavior, Aggressive Cognition, Aggressive Affect, Physiological Arousal, and Prosocial Behavior: A Meta-Analytic Review of the Scientific Literature." *Psychological Science* 12(5): 353–359.

Anderson, C. A., A. J. Lindsay, et al. (1999). "Research in the Psychological Laboratory: Truth or Triviality?" *Current Directions in Psychological Science* 8(1): 3–9.

Anderson, J. L., C. B. Crawford, et al. (1992). "Was the Duchess of Windsor Right—A Cross-Cultural Review of the Socioecology of Ideals of Female Body Shape." *Ethology and Sociobiology* 13(3): 197–227.

Anderson, S. W., A. Bechara, et al. (1999). "Impairment of Social and Moral Behavior Related to Early Damage in Human Prefrontal Cortex." *Nature Neuroscience* 2(11): 1032–1037.

Andreano, J. M., and L. Cahill (2009). "Sex Influences on the Neurobiology of Learning and Memory." *Learning & Memory* 16(4): 248–266.

Andreasen, N. C., and R. Pierson (2008). "The Role of the Cerebellum in Schizophrenia." *Biological Psychiatry* 64(2): 81–88.

Andrews, L., G. Kiel, et al. (2007). "Gendered Perceptions of Experiential Value in Using Web-Based Retail Channels." *European Journal of Marketing* 41(5–6): 640–658.

Angier, N. (1994). "Deaf to Estrogen's Call: A Man's Strange Story." (October 25, 1994) *New York Times*.

Angrilli, A., D. Palomba, et al. (1999). "Emotional Impairment After Right Orbitofrontal Lesion in a Patient Without Cognitive Deficits." *Neuroreport* 10(8): 1741–1746.

Anokhin, A. P., and S. Golosheykin (2006). "ERPS Elicited by Affective Pictures: Early Anterior Sensitivity to Erotic Content." *Psychophysiology* 43: S20–S20.

Anokhin, A. P., S. Golosheykin, et al. (2006). "Rapid Discrimination of Visual Scene Content in the Human Brain." *Brain Research* 1093: 167–177.

Anson, J. A., and D. T. Kuhlman (1993). "Post-Ictal Kluver-Bucy Syndrome After Temporal Lobectomy." *Journal of Neurology Neurosurgery and Psychiatry* 56(3): 311–313.

APA (2009). *Report of the American Psychological Association Task Force on Appropriate Therapeutic Responses to Sexual Orientation.*

Aragona, B. J., Y. Liu, et al. (2006). "Nucleus Accumbens Dopamine Differentially Mediates the Formation and Maintenance of Monogamous Pair Bonds." *Nature Neuroscience* 9(1): 133–139.

Arendash, G. W., and R. A. Gorski (1983). "Effects of Discrete Lesions of the Sexually Dimorphic Nucleus of the Preoptic Area or Other Medial Preoptic Regions on the Sexual-Behavior of Male-Rats." *Brain Research Bulletin* 10(1): 147–154.

Ariely, D. (2008). *Predictably Irrational: The Hidden Forces That Shape Our Decisions.* New York: Harper.

Ariely, D., and G. Loewenstein (2006). "The Heat of the Moment: The Effect of Sexual Arousal on Sexual Decision Making." *Journal of Behavioral Decision Making* 19(2): 87–98.

Arndt, W. B., J. C. Foehl, et al. (1985). "Specific Sexual Fantasy Themes—A Multidimensional Study." *Journal of Personality and Social Psychology* 48(2): 472–480.

Arnold, A. (2004). *Sex Chromosomes and Brain Gender.* New York: Wiley-Liss.

Arnow, B. A., J. E. Desmond, et al. (2002). "Brain Activation and Sexual Arousal in Healthy, Heterosexual Males." *Brain* 125: 1014–1023.

Arnow, B. A., L. Millheiser, et al. (2009). "Women with Hypoactive Sexual Desire Disorder Compared to Normal Females: A Functional Magnetic Resonance Imaging Study." *Neuroscience* 158(2): 484–502.

Arrais, K. C., J. P. Machado-de-Sousa, et al. (2010), "Social Anxiety Disorder Women Easily Recognize Fearful, Sad and Happy Faces: The Influence of Gender," *Journal of Psychiatric Research* 44(8): 535–540.

Arzy, S., G. Thut, et al. (2006). "Neural Basis of Embodiment: Distinct Contributions of Temporoparietal Junction and Extrastriate Body Area." *Journal of Neuroscience* 26(31): 8074–8081.

Attwood, F. (2009). "Intimate Adventures Sex Blogs, Sex 'Blooks' and Women's Sexual Narration." *European Journal of Cultural Studies* 12(1): 5–20.

Audet, M. C., and H. Anisman (2010). "Neuroendocrine and Neurochemical Impact of Aggressive Social Interactions in Submissive and Dominant Mice: Implications for Stress-Related Disorders." *International Journal of Neuropsychopharmacology* 13(3): 361–372.

Auger, A. P. (2003). "Sex Differences in the Developing Brain: Crossroads in the Phosphorylation of Camp Response Element Binding Protein." *Journal of Neuroendocrinology* 15(6): 622–627.

Augustine, J. R. (1996). "Circuitry and Functional Aspects of the Insular Lobe in Primates Including Humans." *Brain Research Reviews* 22(3): 229–244.

Awh, E., and E. K. Vogel (2008). "The Bouncer in the Brain." *Nature Neuroscience* 11(1): 5–6.

Aylwin, A. S., J. R. Reddon, et al. (2005). "Sexual Fantasies of Adolescent Male Sex Offenders in Residential Treatment: A Descriptive Study." *Archives of Sexual Behavior* 34(2): 231–239.

Baeken, C., R. De Raedt, et al. (2010). "Right Prefrontal HF-rTMS Attenuates Right Amygdala Processing of Negatively Valenced Emotional Stimuli in Healthy Females." Behavioural Brain Research 214(2): 450–455.

Bagemihl, B. (1999), *Biological Exuberance: Animal Homosexuality and Natural Diversity.* New York: St. Martin's Press.

Bailey, J. M. (2003), *The Man Who Would Be Queen: The Science of Gender-Bending and Transsexualism.* Washington, DC: Joseph Henry Press.

Bailey, J. M. (2009). "What is Sexual Orientation and Do Women Have One?" *Contemporary Perspectives on Lesbian, Gay, and Bisexual Identities* 54: 43–63.

Bailey, J. M., S. Gaulin, et al. (1994). "Effects of Gender and Sexual Orientation on Evolutionarily Relevant Aspects of Human Mating Psychology." *Journal of Personality and Social Psychology* 66(6): 1081–1093.

Baird, A. D., S. J. Wilson, et al. (2002). "Hypersexuality After Temporal Lobe Resection." *Epilepsy & Behavior* 3(2): 173–181.

Baird, A. D., S. J. Wilson, et al. (2004). "The Amygdala and Sexual Drive: Insights from Temporal Lobe Epilepsy Surgery." *Annals of Neurology* 55(1): 87–96.

Baird, A. D., S. J. Wilson, et al. (2007). "Neurological Control of Human Sexual Behaviour: Insights from Lesion Studies." *Journal of Neurology, Neurosurgery and Psychiatry* 78(10): 1042–1049.

Bakker, P. and T. Saara. (2007). "The Irresistable Rise of Porn: The Untold Story of a Global Industry." *Observatorio* 1: 99–118.

Balon, R., and R. T. Segraves (2005). *Handbook of Sexual Dysfunction.* Boca Raton, FL: Taylor & Francis.

Bancroft, J. (1998). "Central Control and Inhibitory Mechanisms in Male Sexual Response." *International Journal of Impotence Research* 10: S40–S43.

Bancroft, J. (1999). "Central Inhibition of Sexual Response in the Male: A Theoretical Perspective." *Neuroscience and Biobehavioral Reviews* 23(6): 763–784.

Bancroft, J. (2000), *The Role of Theory in Sex Research.* Bloomington: Indiana University Press.

Bancroft, J. (2005). "The Endocrinology of Sexual Arousal." *Journal of Endocrinology* 186(3): 411–427.

Bancroft, J., A. L. Beckstead, et al. (2003). "Peer Commentaries on Spitzer (2003)." *Archives of Sexual Behavior* 32(5): 419–468.

Bancroft, J., C. A. Graham, et al. (2009). "The Dual Control Model: Current Status and Future Directions." *Journal of Sex Research* 46(2–3): 121–142.

Bancroft, J., J. Loftus, et al. (2003). "Distress About Sex: A National Survey of Women in Heterosexual Relationships." *Archives of Sexual Behavior* 32(3): 193–208.

Barak, A., W. A. Fisher, et al. (1999). "Sex, Guys, and Cyberspace—Effects of Internet Pornography and Individual Differences on Men's Attitudes Toward Women." *Journal of Psychology & Human Sexuality* 11(1): 63–91.

Barlow, D. H. (1986). "Causes of Sexual Dysfunction—The Role of Anxiety and Cognitive Interference." *Journal of Consulting and Clinical Psychology* 54(2): 140–148.

Baron, N. S. (2004). "See You Online—Gender Issues in College Student Use of Instant Messaging." *Journal of Language and Social Psychology* 23(4): 397–423.

Baron-Cohen, S., R. C. Knickmeyer, et al. (2005). "Sex Differences in the Brain: Implications for Explaining Autism." *Science* 310(5749): 819–823.

Barron, M., and M. Kimmel (2000). "Sexual Violence in Three Pornographic Media: Toward a Sociological Explanation." *Journal of Sex Research* 37(2): 161–168.

BIBLIOGRAPHY

Bartels, A., and S. Zeki (2004). "The Chronoarchitecture of the Human Brain—Natural Viewing Conditions Reveal a Time-Based Anatomy of the Brain." *Neuroimage* 22(1): 419–433.

Bartels, A., and S. Zeki (2004). "The Neural Correlates of Maternal and Romantic Love." *Neuroimage* 21(3): 1155–1166.

Basaria, S., and A. S. Dobs. (2004). "Safety and adverse effects of androgens: How to counsel patients." *Mayo Clinic Proceedings*, 79(Suppl): S25–S32.

Basson, R. (2001). "Human Sex-Response Cycles." *Journal of Sex & Marital Therapy* 27(1): 33–43.

Basson, R. (2008). "Women's Sexual Function and Dysfunction: Current Uncertainties, Future Directions." *International Journal of Impotence Research* 20(5): 466–478.

Basson, R., J. Berman, et al. (2000). "Report of the International Consensus Development Conference on Female Sexual Dysfunction: Definitions and Classifications." *Journal of Urology* 163(3): 888–893.

Basson, R., J. Berman, et al. (2001). "Report of the International Consensus Development Conference on Female Sexual Dysfunction: Definitions and Classifications." *Journal of Sex & Marital Therapy* 27(2): 83–94.

Basson, R., R. McInnes, M. D. Smith, G. Hodgson, and N. Koppiker (2002), "Efficacy and Safety of Sildenafil Citrate in Women with Sexual Dysfunction Associated with Female Sexual Arousal Disorder." *Journal of Women's Health & Gender-Based Medicine* 11(4): 367–377.

Basson, R., and W. W. Schultz (2007). "Sexual Dysfunction 1—Sexual Sequelae of General Medical Disorders." *Lancet* 369(9559): 409–424.

Bateman, A. J. (1948). "Intra-sexual Selection in Drosophila." *Heredity* 2 (Pt. 3): 349–368.

Bauman, M. D., J. E. Toscano, et al. (2006). "The Expression of Social Dominance Following Neonatal Lesions of the Amygdala or Hippocampus in Rhesus Monkeys (Macaca Mulatta)." *Behavioral Neuroscience* 120(4): 749–760.

Baumeister, A. A. (2000). "The Tulane Electrical Brain Stimulation Program: A Historical Case Study in Medical Ethics." *Journal of the History of the Neurosciences* 9(3): 262–278.

Baumeister, R. F. (1999). "The mastery of submission: Inventions of masochism." *Journal of the History of the Behavioral Sciences* 35(1): 87–88.

Baumeister, R. F. (2000). "Gender Differences in Erotic Plasticity: The Female Sex Drive as Socially Flexible and Responsive." *Psychological Bulletin* 126(3): 347–374.

Baumeister, R. F. (2008). "Free Will in Scientific Psychology." *Perspectives on Psychological Science* 3(1): 14–19.

Baumeister, R. F., K. R. Catanese, et al. (2000). "Nature, Culture, and Explanations for Erotic Plasticity: Reply to Andersen, Cyranowski, and Aarestad (2000) and Hyde and Durik (2000)." *Psychological Bulletin* 126(3): 385–389.

Baumeister, R. F., K. R. Catanese, et al. (2001). "Is There a Gender Difference in Strength of Sex Drive? Theoretical Views, Conceptual Distinctions, and a Review of Relevant Evidence." *Personality and Social Psychology Review* 5(3): 242–273.

Baumeister, R. F., C. N. DeWall, et al. (2009). "Social Rejection, Control, Numbness, and Emotion: How Not to Be Fooled by Gerber and Wheeler (2009)." *Perspectives on Psychological Science* 4(5): 489–493.

Baumeister, R. F., E. J. Masicampo, et al. (2009). "Prosocial Benefits of Feeling Free: Disbelief in Free Will Increases Aggression and Reduces Helpfulness." *Personality and Social Psychology Bulletin* 35(2): 260–268.

Baumeister, R. F., K. D. Vohs, et al. (2007). "Psychology as the Science of Self-Reports and Finger Movements: Whatever Happened to Actual Behavior?" *Perspectives on Psychological Science* 2(4): 396–403.

Baumeister, R. F., K. D. Vohs, et al. (2007). "The Strength Model of Self-control." *Current Directions in Psychological Science* 16(6): 351–355.

Bazzett, T. J., and J. B. Becker (1994). "Sex-Differences in the Rapid and Acute Effects of Estrogen on Striatal D-2 Dopamine-Receptor Binding." *Brain Research* 637(1–2): 163–172.

Beach, F. A., and P. Rasquin (1942). "Masculine Copulatory Behavior in Intact and Castrated Female Rats." *Endocrinology* 31(4): 393–409.

Beauregard, M., J. Levesque, et al. (2001). "Neural Correlates of Conscious Self-Regulation of Emotion." *Journal of Neuroscience* 21(18): 6.

Bechara, A. (2004). "Disturbances of Emotion Regulation After Focal Brain Lesions." *International Review of Neurobiology*, Vol. 62. San Diego: Elsevier Academic Press Inc., pp. 159–193.

Bechara, A. (2005). "Decision Making, Impulse Control and Loss of Willpower to Resist Drugs: A Neurocognitive Perspective." *Nature Neuroscience* 8(11): 1458–1463.

Bechara, A., and A. R. Damasio (2005). "The Somatic Marker Hypothesis: A Neural Theory of Economic Decision." *Games and Economic Behavior* 52(2): 336–372.

Bechara, A., and M. Van der Linden (2005). "Decision-making and Impulse Control After Frontal Lobe Injuries." *Current Opinion in Neurology* 18(6): 734–739.

Beck, J. G., D. H. Barlow, et al. (1987). "Shock Threat and Sexual Arousal— The Role of Selective Attention, Thought Content, and Affective States." *Psychophysiology* 24(2): 165–172.

Beck, J. G., A. W. Bozman, et al. (1991). "The Experience of Sexual Desire— Psychological Correlates in a College Sample." *Journal of Sex Research* 28(3): 443–456.

Becker, J. B. (2008). *Sex Differences in the Brain: From Genes to Behavior.* Oxford; New York: Oxford University Press.

Becker, J. B. (2009). "Sexual Differentiation of Motivation: A Novel Mechanism?" *Hormones and Behavior* 55(5): 646–654.

Becker, J. B., C. N. Rudick, et al. (2001). "The Role of Dopamine in the Nucleus Accumbens and Striatum During Sexual Behavior in the Female Rat." *Journal of Neuroscience* 21(9): 3236–3241.

Beckley, J., H. Ashman, et al. (2004). "What Features Drive Rated Burger Craveability at the Concept Level?" *Journal of Sensory Studies* 19(1): 27–47.

Bedard, L. E., and M. G. Gertz (2000). "Differences in Community Standards for the Viewing of Heterosexual and Homosexual Pornography." *International Journal of Public Opinion Research* 12(3): 324–332.

Beer, J. S., M. V. Lombardo, et al. (2010). "Roles of Medial Prefrontal Cortex and Orbitofrontal Cortex in Self-evaluation." *Journal of Cognitive Neuroscience* 22(9): 2108–2119.

Behrendt, G., and L. Tuccillo (2004). *He's Just Not That Into You: The No-Excuses Truth to Understanding Guys.* New York: Simon Spotlight Entertainment.

Beigel, H. G., and R. Feldman (1963). "The Male Transvestite's Motivation in Fiction, Research, and Reality." *Advances in Sex Research* 1: 198–210.

Bejot, Y., N. Juenet, et al. "Sexsomnia: An Uncommon Variety of Parasomnia." *Clinical Neurology and Neurosurgery* 112(1): 72–75.

Bellis, M. A., and R. R. Baker (1990). "Do Females Promote Sperm Competition—Data for Humans." *Animal Behaviour* 40: 997–999.

Bem, D. J. (2000). "Exotic Becomes Erotic: Interpreting the Biological Correlates of Sexual Orientation." *Archives of Sexual Behavior* 29(6): 531–548.

Benbow, C. P., D. Lubinski, et al. (2000). "Sex Differences in Mathematical Reasoning Ability at Age 13: Their Status 20 Years Later." *Psychological Science* 11(6): 474–480.

Benuto, L., and M. Meana (2008). "Acculturation and Sexuality: Investigating Gender Differences in Erotic Plasticity." *Journal of Sex Research* 45(3): 217–224.

Bereczkei, T., P. Gyuris, et al. (2004). "Sexual Imprinting in Human Mate Choice." *Proceedings of the Royal Society of London*, Series B: Biological Sciences 271(1544): 1129–1134.

Berglund, H., P. Lindstrom, et al. (2006). "Brain Response to Putative Pheromones in Lesbian Women." *Proceedings of the National Academy of Sciences of the United States of America* 103(21): 8269–8274.

Berlin, F. S. (2008). "Basic Science and Neurobiological Research: Potential Relevance to Sexual Compulsivity." *Psychiatric Clinics of North America* 31(4): 623–+.

Berlin, F. S., W. Berner, et al. (2002). "Peer Commentaries on Green (2002) and Schmidt (2002)." *Archives of Sexual Behavior* 31(6): 479–503.

Berman, L. (2008), *Real Sex for Real Women: Intimacy, Pleasure & Sexual Well-Being.* New York: DK Pub.

Bernhardt, P. C., J. M. Dabbs, et al. (1998), "Testosterone Changes During Vicarious Experiences of Winning and Losing Among Fans at Sporting Events," *Physiology & Behavior* 65(1): 59–62.

Berridge, K. C. (2003). "Pleasures of the Brain." *Brain and Cognition* 52(1): 106–128.

Berridge, K. C., and J. W. Aldridge (2008). "Decision Utility, the Brain, and Pursuit of Hedonic Goals." *Social Cognition* 26(5): 621–646.

Bevc, I., and I. Silverman (2000). "Early Separation and Sibling Incest: A Test of the Revised Westermarck Theory." *Evolution and Human Behavior* 21(3): 151–161.

Beyer, C., W. Kolbinger, et al. (1992). "Sex-Differences of Hypothalamic Prolactin Cells Develop Independently of the Presence of Sex Steroids." *Brain Research* 593(2): 253–256.

Bezeau, S. C., N. M. Bogod, et al. (2004). "Sexually Intrusive Behaviour Following Brain Injury: Approaches to Assessment and Rehabilitation." *Brain Injury* 18(3): 299–313.

Bhugra, D., Q. Rahman, et al. (2006). "Sexual Fantasy in Gay Men in India: A Comparison with Heterosexual Men." *Sexual & Relationship Therapy* 21: 197–207.

Bianchi-Demicheli, F., and S. Ortigue (2007). "Toward an Understanding of the Cerebral Substrates of Woman's Orgasm." *Neuropsychologia* 45(12): 2645–2659.

Bianchi-Demicheli, F., and S. Ortigue (2008). "Are All Types of Orgasm Mentally Represented Alike in a Woman's Brain? An Event-Related fMRI Study." *Journal of Sexual Medicine* 5: 71–71.

Bianchi-Demicheli, F., and S. Ortigue (2009). "Mental Representation of Subjective Pleasure of Partnered Experiences in Women's Brain Conveyed Through Event-Related fMRI." *Medical Science Monitor* 15(11): CR545–CR550.

Bianchi-Demicheli, F., C. Rollini, et al. (2010). "Sleeping Beauty Paraphilia: Deviant Desire in the Context of Bodily Self-Image Disturbance in a Patient with a Fronto-Parietal Traumatic Brain Injury." *Medical Science Monitor* 16(2): CS15–CS17.

Bickham, P. J., S. L. O'Keefe, et al. (2007). "Correlates of Early Overt and Covert Sexual Behaviors in Heterosexual Women." *Archives of Sexual Behavior* 36(5): 724–740.

Bickham, D. S., E. A. Vandewater, et al. (2003). "Predictors of Children's Electronic Media Use: An Examination of Three Ethnic Groups." *Media Psychology* 5(2): 107–137.

Bimber, B. (2000). "Measuring the Gender Gap on the Internet." *Social Science Quarterly* 81(3): 868–876.

Binik, Y. M., and M. Meana (2009). "The Future of Sex Therapy: Specialization or Marginalization?" *Archives of Sexual Behavior* 38(6): 1016–1027.

Birbaumer, N., and A. hman (1993). *The Structure of Emotion: Psychophysiological, Cognitive, and Clinical Aspects*. Seattle: Hogrefe & Huber.

Birkhead, T. R, and A. P. Maller. (1998). *Sperm Competition and Sexual Selection*. New York: Academic Press.

Birkhead, T. R, and D. J. Hosken. (2008). *Sperm Biology*. New York: Academic Press.

Birnbaum, G. E. (2007). "Beyond the Borders of Reality: Attachment Orientations and Sexual Fantasies." *Personal Relationships* 14(2): 321–342.

Birnbaum, G. E., N. Svitelman, et al. (2008). "The Thin Line Between Reality and Imagination: Attachment Orientations and the Effects of Relationship Threats on Sexual Fantasies." *Personality and Social Psychology Bulletin* 34(9): 1185–1199.

Birnbaum, M. H. (2004). "Human Research and Data Collection Via the Internet." *Annual Review of Psychology* 55: 803–832.

Bischof, H. J. (2003). "Neural Mechanisms of Sexual Imprinting." *Animal Biology* 53(2): 89–112.

Bivona, J., and J. Critelli (2009). "The Nature of Women's Rape Fantasies: An Analysis of Prevalence, Frequency, and Contents." *Journal of Sex Research* 46(1): 33–45.

Bjorklund, D. F., and K. Kipp (1996), "Parental Investment Theory and Gender Differences in the Evolution of Inhibition Mechanisms," *Psychological Bulletin* 120(2): 163–188.

Blair, C. D., and R. I. Lanyon (1981). "Exhibitionism—Etiology and Treatment." *Psychological Bulletin* 89(3): 439–463.

Blakemore, S. J. (2008). "The Social Brain in Adolescence." *Nature Reviews Neuroscience* 9(4): 267–277.

Blakemore, S. J., S. Burnett, et al. (2010). "The Role of Puberty in the Developing Adolescent Brain." *Human Brain Mapping* 31(6): 926–933.

Blanchard, R., and P. I. Collins (1993). "Men with Sexual Interest in Transvestites, Transsexuals, and She-Males." *Journal of Nervous and Mental Disease* 181(9): 570–575.

Blanchard, R., and R. A. Lippa (2007). "Birth Order, Sibling Sex Ratio, Handedness, and Sexual Orientation of Male and Female Participants in a BBC Internet Research Project." *Archives of Sexual Behavior* 36(2): 163–176.

Blanke, O., S. Ionta, et al. (2010). "Mental Imagery for Full and Upper Human Bodies: Common Right Hemisphere Activations and Distinct Extrastriate Activations." *Brain Topography* 23(3): 321–332.

Blanke, O., S. Ionta, et al. (2010). "Mental Imagery for Full and Upper Human Bodies: Common Right Hemisphere Activations and Distinct Extrastriate Activations." *Brain Topography* 23(3): 321–332.

Blankstein, U., J. Y. W. Chen, et al. (2009). "The Complex Minds of Teenagers: Neuroanatomy of Personality Differs Between Sexes." *Neuropsychologia* 47(2): 599–603.

Bleske, A. L., and T. K. Shackleford (2001). "Poaching, Promiscuity, and Deceit: Combatting Mating Rivalry in Same-Sex Friendships." *Personal Relationships* 8(4): 407–424.

Bloemers, J., J. Gerritsen, et al. (2010). "Induction of Sexual Arousal in Women Under Conditions of Institutional and Ambulatory Laboratory Circumstances: A Comparative Study." *Journal of Sexual Medicine* 7(3): 1160–1176.

Bocher, M., R. Chisin, et al. (2001). "Cerebral Activation Associated with Sexual Arousal in Response to a Pornographic Clip: A O-15-H2O, PET Study in Heterosexual Men." *Neuroimage* 14(1): 105–117.

Bogaert, A. F. (2001). "Personality, Individual Differences, and Preferences for the Sexual Medial." *Archives of Sexual Behavior* 30(1): 29–53.

Bogaert, A. F., and S. Hershberger (1999). "The Relation Between Sexual Orientation and Penile Size." *Archives of Sexual Behavior* 28(3): 213–221.

Bolding, G., M. Davis, et al. (2006). "Heterosexual Men and Women Who Seek Sex Through the Internet." *International Journal of STD & AIDS* 17(8): 530–534.

Bolding, G., M. Davis, et al. (2007). "Where Young MSM Meet Their First Sexual Partner: The Role of the Internet." *AIDS and Behavior* 11(4): 522–526.

Boller, F., and E. Frank (1982). *Sexual Dysfunction in Neurological Disorders: Diagnosis, Management, and Rehabilitation.* New York: Raven Press.

Boneva, B., R. Kraut, et al. (2001). "Using E-mail for Personal Relationships the Difference Gender Makes." *American Behavioral Scientist* 45(3): 530–549.

Borg, J. S., D. Lieberman, et al. (2008). "Infection, Incest, and Iniquity: Investigating the Neural Correlates of Disgust and Morality." *Journal of Cognitive Neuroscience* 20(9): 1529–1546.

Both, S., E. Laan, et al. (2008). "Appetitive and Aversive Classical Conditioning of Female Sexual Response." *Journal of Sexual Medicine* 5(6): 1386–1401.

Both, S., M. Spiering, et al. (2004). "Sexual Behavior and Responsiveness to Sexual Stimuli Following Laboratory-Induced Sexual Arousal." *Journal of Sex Research* 41(3): 242–258.

Both, S., M. Spiering, et al. (2008). "Unconscious Classical Conditioning of Sexual Arousal: Evidence for the Conditioning of Female Genital Arousal to Subliminally Presented Sexual Stimuli." *Journal of Sexual Medicine* 5(1): 100–109.

Both, S., G. Van Boxtel, et al. (2005). "Modulation of Spinal Reflexes by Sexual Films of Increasing Intensity." *Psychophysiology* 42(6): 726–731.

Bradford, A., and C. Meston (2007). "Correlates of Placebo Response in the Treatment of Sexual Dysfunction in Women: A Preliminary Report." *Journal of Sexual Medicine* 4(5): 1345–1351.

Bradford, J. M. W. (2000). "The Treatment of Sexual Deviation Using a Pharmacological Approach." *Journal of Sex Research* 37(3): 248–257.

Bradford, J. M. W., J. Boulet, et al. (1992). "The Paraphilias—A Multiplicity of Deviant Behaviors." *Canadian Journal of Psychiatry—Revue Canadienne De Psychiatrie* 37(2): 104–108.

Breedlove, S. M., and A. P. Arnold (1980). "Hormone Accumulation in a Sexually Dimorphic Motor Nucleus of the Rat Spinal-Cord." *Science* 210(4469): 564–566.

Breedlove, S. M., and A. P. Arnold (1983). "Hormonal-Control of a Developing Neuromuscular System .1. Complete Demasculinization of the Male-Rat Spinal Nucleus of the Bulbocavernosus Using the Anti-Androgen Flutamide." *Journal of Neuroscience* 3(2): 417–423.

Brenowitz, E. A. (1991). "Altered Perception of Species-Specific Song by Female Birds After Lesions of a Forebrain Nucleus." *Science* 251(4991): 303–305.

Brewer, G., and C. Hendrie (2010). "Evidence to Suggest That Copulatory Vocalizations in Women Are Not a Reflexive Consequence of Orgasm." *Archives of Sexual Behavior*, in press. Epub ahead of print, retrieved August 30, 2010, from http://www.ncbi.nlm.nih.gov/pubmed/20480220.

Brewis, A., and M. Meyer (2005). "Demographic Evidence That Human Ovulation Is Undetectable (At Least in Pair Bonds)." *Current Anthropology* 46(3): 465–471.

Brewis, A., and M. Meyer (2005). "Marital Coitus Across the Life Course." *Journal of Biosocial Science* 37(4): 499–518.

Briere, J., K. Smiljanich, et al. (1994). "Sexual Fantasies, Gender, and Molestation History." *Child Abuse & Neglect* 18(2): 131–137.

Briggs, K. E., and F. H. Martin (2009). "Affective Picture Processing and Motivational Relevance: Arousal and Valence Effects on ERPS in an Oddball Task." *International Journal of Psychophysiology* 72(3): 299–306.

Briken, P., and M. P. Kafka (2007). "Pharmacological Treatments for Paraphilic Patients and Sexual Offenders." *Current Opinion in Psychiatry* 20(6): 609–613.

Brockman, N. (1997). "Kenya," in R. T. Francoeur (ed.), *The International Encyclopedia of Sexuality*, Vol. 2. New York: Continuum.

Broder, A., and N. Hohmann (2003). "Variations in Risk Taking Behavior Over the Menstrual Cycle: An Improved Replication," *Evolution and Human Behavior* 24 (6): 391–398.

Brody, S. (2004). "Slimness Is Associated with Greater Intercourse and Lesser Masturbation Frequency." *Journal of Sex & Marital Therapy* 30(4): 251–261.

Broos, A. (2005). "Gender and Information and Communication Technologies (ICT) Anxiety: Male Self-Assurance and Female Hesitation." *Cyberpsychology & Behavior* 8(1): 21–31.

Brotto, L. A., and B. B. Gorzalka (2002). "Genital and Subjective Sexual Arousal in Postmenopausal Women: Influence of Laboratory-Induced Hyperventilation," *Journal of Sex and Marital Therapy* 28 (1): 39–53.

Brotto, L. A., C. Klein, et al. (2009). "Laboratory-Induced Hyperventilation Differentiates Female Sexual Arousal Disorder Subtypes." *Archives of Sexual Behavior* 38(4): 463–475.

Brown, A. D., J. Blagg, et al. (2007). "Designing Drugs for the Treatment of Female Sexual Dysfunction." *Drug Discovery Today* 12(17–18): 757–766.

Brown, D. E. (2004). "Human Universals, Human Nature & Human Culture." *Daedalus* 133(4): 47–54.

Brown, J. D., and K. L. L'Engle (2009). "X-Rated Sexual Attitudes and Behaviors Associated with US Early Adolescents' Exposure to Sexually Explicit Media." *Communication Research* 36(1): 129–151.

Brown, J. J., and D. H. Hart (1977). "Correlates of Females Sexual Fantasies." *Perceptual and Motor Skills* 45(3): 819–825.

Brown, J. K. (1970). "A Note on Division of Labor by Sex." *American Anthropologist* 72(5): 1073–+.

BIBLIOGRAPHY

Buchwald, J. Z. (1994). *The Creation of Scientific Effects: Heinrich Hertz and Electric Waves*. Chicago: University of Chicago Press.

Buhler, M., S. Vollstadt-Klein, et al. (2008). "Does Erotic Stimulus Presentation Design Affect Brain Activation Patterns? Event-Related Vs. Blocked fMRI Designs." *Behavioral and Brain Functions* 4: 30.

Buhrich, N., and N. McConaghy (1976). "Transvestite Fiction." *Journal of Nervous and Mental Disease* 163(6): 420–427.

Bullock, T. H. (1984). "Comparative Neuroscience Holds Promise for Quiet Revolutions." *Science* 225(4661): 473–478.

Bullough, V. L. (2003). "Understanding Bestiality & Zoophilia." *Journal of Sex Research* 40(2): 222–223.

Burgdorf, J., and J. Panksepp (2006). "The Neurobiology of Positive Emotions." *Neuroscience and Biobehavioral Reviews* 30(2): 173–187.

Burleson, M. H., W. L. Gregory, et al. (1995). "Heterosexual Activity— Relationship with Ovarian-Function." *Psychoneuroendocrinology* 20(4): 405–421.

Burman, D. D., T. Bitan, et al. (2008). "Sex Differences in Neural Processing of Language Among Children." *Neuropsychologia* 46(5): 1349–1362.

Burnett, S., G. Bird, et al. (2009). "Development During Adolescence of the Neural Processing of Social Emotion." *Journal of Cognitive Neuroscience* 21(9): 1736–1750.

Burns, J. M., and R. H. Swerdlow (2003). "Right Orbitofrontal Tumor with Pedophilia Symptom and Constructional Apraxia Sign." *Archives of Neurology* 60(3): 437–440.

Burns-Cusato, M., B. M. Cusato, et al. (2005). "A New Model for Sexual Conditioning: The Ring Dove (Streptopelia Risoria)." *Journal of Comparative Psychology* 119(1): 111–116.

Burri, A. V., L. M. Cherkas, et al. (2009). "The Genetics and Epidemiology of Female Sexual Dysfunction: A Review." *Journal of Sexual Medicine* 6(3): 646–657.

Burroughs, W. S., J. Grauerholz, et al. (2003). *Naked Lunch*. New York: Grove Press.

Bush, G., P. Luu, et al. (2000). "Cognitive and Emotional Influences in Anterior Cingulate Cortex." *Trends in Cognitive Sciences* 4(6): 215–222.

Bushman, B. J., and C. A. Anderson (1999). "Can One Generalize the Results of Laboratory Aggression Studies to the 'Real World'?" *Aggressive Behavior* 25(1): 31–31.

Bushman, B. J., R. F. Baumeister, et al. (2009). "Looking Again, and Harder, for a Link Between Low Self-Esteem and Aggression." *Journal of Personality* 77(2): 427–446.

Buss, D. M. (1994). *The Evolution of Desire: Strategies of Human Mating*. New York: Basic Books.

Buss, D. M. (2002). "Human Mate Guarding." *Neuroendocrinology Letters* 23 Suppl 4: 23–29.

Buss, D. M. (2005). *The Handbook of Evolutionary Psychology*. Hoboken, NJ: Wiley.

BIBLIOGRAPHY

Buss, D. M., and D. P. Schmitt (1993). "Sexual Strategies Theory—An Evolutionary Perspective on Human Mating." *Psychological Review* 100(2): 204–232.

Byers, E. S., C. Purdon, et al. (1998). "Sexual Intrusive Thoughts of College Students." *Journal of Sex Research* 35(4): 359–369.

Byne, W., S. Tobet, et al. (2001). "The Interstitial Nuclei of the Human Anterior Hypothalamus: An Investigation of Variation with Sex, Sexual Orientation, and HIV Status." *Hormones and Behavior* 40(2): 86–92.

Cahill, L. (2006). "Why Sex Matters for Neuroscience." *Nature Reviews Neuroscience* 7(6): 477–484.

Cahill, L., M. Uncapher, et al. (2004). "Sex-Related Hemispheric Lateralization of Amygdala Function in Emotionally Influenced Memory: An fMRI Investigation." *Learning & Memory* 11(3): 261–266.

Calvo-Merino, B., C. Urgesi, et al. (2010). "Extrastriate Body Area Underlies Aesthetic Evaluation of Body Stimuli." *Experimental Brain Research* 204(3): 447–456.

Campbell, J. E. (2005). "Outing PlanetOut: Surveillance, Gay Marketing and Internet Affinity Portals." *New Media & Society* 7(5): 663–683.

Cannas, A., P. Solla, et al. (2006). "Hypersexual Behaviour, Frotteurism and Delusional Jealousy in a Young Parkinsonian Patient During Dopaminergic Therapy with Pergolide: A Rare Case of Iatrogenic Paraphilia." *Progress in Neuro-Psychopharmacology and Biological Psychiatry* 30(8): 1539–1541.

Cantor, J. M., P. E. Klassen, et al. (2005). "Handedness in Pedophilia and Hebephilia." *Archives of Sexual Behavior* 34(4): 447–459.

Capel, B., and D. Coveney (2004). "Frank Lillie's Freemartin: Illuminating the Pathway to 21(st) Century Reproductive Endocrinology." *Journal of Experimental Zoology*, Part A: Comparative Experimental Biology 301A(11): 853–856.

Carani, C., J. Bancroft, et al. (1990). "The Endocrine Effects of Visual Erotic Stimuli in Normal Men." *Psychoneuroendocrinology* 15(3): 207–216.

Carani, C., A. Scuteri, et al. (1990). "The Effects of Testosterone Administration and Visual Erotic Stimuli on Nocturnal Penile Tumescence in Normal Men." *Hormones and Behavior* 24(3): 435–441.

Carbaugh, B. T., M. W. Schein, et al. "Effects of Morphological Variations of Chicken Models on Sexual Responses of Cocks." *Animal Behaviour* 10(3–4): 235–238.

Carrel, L., and H. F. Willard (2005). "X-Inactivation Profile Reveals Extensive Variability in X-Linked Gene Expression in Females." *Nature* 434(7031): 400–404.

Carroll, J. S., L. M. Padilla-Walker, et al. (2008). "Generation XXX—Pornography Acceptance and Use Among Emerging Adults." *Journal of Adolescent Research* 23(1): 6–30.

Carter, C. S. (2007). Sex Differences in "Oxytocin and Vasopressin: Implications for Autism Spectrum Disorders?"*Behavioral Brain Research* 176(1): 170–186.

Carvalheira, A., and F. A. Gomes (2003). "Cybersex in Portuguese Chatrooms: A Study of Sexual Behaviors Related to Online Sex." *Journal of Sex & Marital Therapy* 29(5): 345–360.

Casanova, M. F., G. Mannheim, et al. (2002). "Hippocampal Pathology in Two Mentally Ill Paraphiliacs." *Psychiatry Research-Neuroimaging* 115(1–2): 79–89.

Caspi, A., E. Chajut, et al. (2008). "Participation in Class and in Online Discussions: Gender Differences." *Computers & Education* 50(3): 718–724.

Cato, M. A., D. C. Delis, et al. (2004). "Assessing the Elusive Cognitive Deficits Associated with Ventromedial Prefrontal Damage: A Case of a Modern-Day Phineas Gage." *Journal of the International Neuropsychological Society* 10(3): 453–465.

Chadha, H. K., and C. H. Hubscher (2008). "Convergence of Nociceptive Information in the Forebrain of Female Rats: Reproductive Organ Response Variations with Stage of Estrus." *Experimental Neurology* 210(2): 375–387.

Chalkley, A. J., and G. E. Powell (1983). "The Clinical Description of 48 Cases Of Sexual Fetishism." *British Journal of Psychiatry* 142(MAR): 292–295.

Chan, A. H. N. (2008). " 'Life in Happy Land': Using Virtual Space and Doing Motherhood in Hong Kong." *Gender Place and Culture* 15(2): 169–188.

Chan, A. W. Y., M. V. Peelen, et al. (2004). "The Effect of Viewpoint on Body Representation in the Extrastriate Body Area." *Neuroreport* 15(15): 2407–2410.

Charman, T., T. Ruffman, et al. (2002). "Is There a Gender Difference in False Belief Development?" *Social Development* 11(1): 1–10.

Charnov, E. L. (2002). "Reproductive Effort, Offspring Size and Benefit-Cost Ratios in the Classification of Life Histories." *Evolutionary Ecology Research* 4(5): 749–758.

Chavanne, T. J, and G. G. Gallup Jr. (1998). "Variation in Risk Taking Behavior Among Female College Students as a Function of the Menstrual Cycle." *Evolution and Human Behavior* 19(1): 27–32.

Cheng, G. H. L., D. K. S. Chan, et al. (2006). "Qualities of Online Friendships with Different Gender Compositions and Durations." *Cyberpsychology & Behavior* 9(1): 14–21.

Cheng, S. Y., K. Taravosh-Lahn, et al. (2008). "Neural Circuitry of Play Fighting in Golden Hamsters." *Neuroscience* 156(2): 247–256.

Chiao, J. Y., R. B. Adams, et al. (2008). "Knowing Who's Boss: fMRI and ERP Investigations of Social Dominance Perception." *Group Processes & Intergroup Relations* 11(2): 201–214.

Chiao, J. Y., V. A. Mathur, et al. (2009). "Neural Basis of Preference for Human Social Hierarchy Versus" *Egalitarianism. Values, Empathy, and Fairness Across Social Barriers.* 1167: 174–181.

Childress, A. R., R. N. Ehrman, et al. (2008). "Prelude to Passion: Limbic Activation by 'Unseen' Drug and Sexual Cues." *PLoS One* 3(1): 7.

Chivers, M., and R. Blanchard (1996). "Prostitution Advertisements Suggest Association of Transvestism and Masochism." *Journal of Sex & Marital Therapy* 22(2): 97–102.

BIBLIOGRAPHY

Chivers, M. L. (2005). "Clinical Management of Sex Addiction." *Archives of Sexual Behavior* 34(4): 476–478.

Chivers, M. L. (2006). "Psychophysiological and Subjective Sexual Arousal to Visual Sexual Stimuli in New Women—Lori A. Brotto et al.—J Psychosom Obstet Gynecol 2005;26(4);229–230." *Journal of Psychosomatic Obstetrics and Gynecology* 27(3): 125–125.

Chivers, M. L. (2007). "The Case of the Female Orgasm: Bias in the Science of Evolution." *Journal of Sex Research* 44(1): 104–105.

Chivers, M. L., and J. M. Bailey (2005). "A Sex Difference in Features That Elicit Genital Response." *Biological Psychology* 70(2): 115–120.

Chivers, M. L., G. Rieger, et al. (2004). "A Sex Difference in the Specificity of Sexual Arousal." *Psychological Science* 15(11): 736–744.

Chivers, M. L., M. C. Seto, et al. (2007). "Gender and Sexual Orientation Differences in Sexual Response to Sexual Activities Versus Gender of Actors in Sexual Films." *Journal of Personality and Social Psychology* 93(6): 1108–1121.

Chivers, M. L., M. C. Seto, et al. (2010). "Agreement of Self-Reported and Genital Measures of Sexual Arousal in Men and Women: A Meta-Analysis." *Archives of Sexual Behavior* 39(1): 5–56.

Choisy (abbé de), (1994). *The transvestite memoirs of the abbé de Choisy and The story of the Marquise-Marquis de Banneville*. C. Perrault, Trans; London: Peter Owen Ltd.

Chong, T. T. J., R. Cunnington, et al. (2008). "fMRI Adaptation Reveals Mirror Neurons in Human Inferior Parietal Cortex." *Current Biology* 18(20): 1576–1580.

Clancy, S. A. (2010). *The Trauma Myth: The Truth About the Sexual Abuse of Children—and Its Aftermath*. New York: Basic Books.

Clark, D. A., C. Purdon, et al. (2000). "Appraisal and Control of Sexual and Non-Sexual Intrusive Thoughts in University Students." *Behaviour Research and Therapy* 38(5): 439–455.

Clark, R. D., and E. Hatfield (1989). "Gender Differences in Receptivity to Sexual Offers." *Journal of Psychology & Human Sexuality* 2(1): 39-55.

Clark, R. D., and E. Hatfield (2003). "Love in the Afternoon." *Psychological Inquiry* 14(3-4): 227–231.

Clavel-Chapelon, F. and E. N. E. Grp (2002). "Evolution of age at menarche and at onset of regular cycling in a large cohort of French women." *Human Reproduction* 17(1): 228-232.

Cohen, A. S., R. C. Rosen, et al. (1985). "EEG Hemispheric–Asymmetry During Sexual Arousal—Psychophysiological Patterns in Responsive, Unresponsive, and Dysfunctional Men." *Journal of Abnormal Psychology* 94(4): 580–590.

Cohen, D., and J. Belsky (2008). "Individual Differences in Female Mate Preferences as a Function of Attachment and Hypothetical Ecological Conditions." *Journal of Evolutionary Psychology* 6(1): 25–42.

Cohen, P. G. (1999). "Sexual Dysfunction in the United States." *Journal of the American Medical Association* 282(13): 1229–1229.

Colapinto, J. (2001), *As Nature Made Him: The Boy Who Was Raised as a Girl*. New York: Harper Perennial.

Coles, C. D., and M. J. Shamp (1984). "Some Sexual, Personality, and Demographic Characteristics of Women Readers of Erotic Romances." *Archives of Sexual Behavior* 13(3): 187–209.

Colley, A., and J. Maltby (2008). "Impact of the Internet on Our Lives: Male and Female Personal Perspectives." *Computers in Human Behavior* 24(5): 2005–2013.

Companion, M., and R. Sambrook (2008). "The Influence of Sex on Character Attribute Preferences." *Cyberpsychology & Behavior* 11(6): 673–674.

Conaglen, H. M., and I. M. Evans (2006). "Pictorial Cues and Sexual Desire: An Experimental Approach." *Archives of Sexual Behavior* 35(2): 201–216.

Confer, J. C., J. A. Easton, et al. "Evolutionary Psychology: Controversies, Questions, Prospects, and Limitations." *American Psychologist* 65(2): 110–126.

Cooke, B. M., and C. S. Woolley (2005). "Sexually Dimorphic Synaptic Organization of the Medial Amygdala." *Journal of Neuroscience* 25(46): 10759–10767.

Coolen, L. M. (2005). "Neural Control of Ejaculation." *Journal of Comparative Neurology* 493(1): 39–45.

Cooper, A. (1998). "Sexuality and the Internet: Surfing into the New Millenium." *CyberPsychology & Behavior* 1:181–187.

Cooper, A., N. Galbreath, et al. (2004). "Sex on the Internet: Furthering Our Understanding of Men With Online Sexual Problems." *Psychology of Addictive Behaviors* 18(3): 223–230.

Cooper, A., S.-A. Mensson, et al. (2003). "Predicting the Future of Internet Sex: Online Sexual Activities in Sweden." *Sexual and Relationship Therapy* 18(3): 277–291.

Cooper, A., J. Morahan-Martin, et al. (2002). "Toward an Increased Understanding of User Demographics in Online Sexual Activities." *Journal of Sex & Marital Therapy* 28(2): 105–129.

Cornwallis, C. K. and T. R. Birkhead (2007). "Changes in Sperm Quality and Numbers in Response to Experimental Manipulation of Male Social Status and Female Attractiveness." *American Naturalist* 170(5): 758–770.

Cornwallis, C. k., and T. R. Birkhead. (2007). "Experimental Evidence that Female Ornamentation Increases the Acquisition of Sperm and Signals Fecundity." *Proceedings of the Royal Society Biological Sciences* 274(1609): 583–590.

Cornwallis, C. K., and T. R. Birkhead (2008). "Plasticity in Reproductive Phenotypes Reveals Status-Specific Correlations Between Behavioral, Morphological, and Physiological Sexual Traits." *Evolution* 62(5): 1149–1161.

Correll, S. (1995). "The Ethnography of an Electronic Bar—The Lesbian Cafe." *Journal of Contemporary Ethnography* 24(3): 270–298.

Cosans, C. E. (1998). "Aristotle's Anatomical Philosophy of Nature." *Biology & Philosophy* 13(3): 311–339.

Cosgrove, K. P., C. M. Mazure, et al. (2007). "Evolving Knowledge of Sex Differences in Brain Structure, Function, and Chemistry." *Biological Psychiatry* 62(8): 847–855.

Cosgrove, L., M. Pearrow, et al. (2008). "Toward a New Paradigm for Psychiatric Diagnoses and Clinical Research in Sexology." *Feminism & Psychology* 18(4): 457–465.

Costa, M., C. Braun, et al. (2003). "Gender Differences in Response to Pictures of Nudes: A Magnetoencephalographic Study." *Biological Psychology* 63(2): 129–147.

Costa, R. M., and F. Esteves (2008). "Skin Conductance Responses to Visual Sexual Stimuli." *International Journal of Psychophysiology* 67(1): 64–69.

Couch, D., and P. Liamputtong (2008). "Online Dating and Mating: The Use of the Internet to Meet Sexual Partners." *Qualitative Health Research* 18(2): 268–279.

Cox, A., and M. Fisher (2009). "The Texas Billionaire's Pregnant Bride: An Evolutionary Interpretation of Romance Fiction Titles." Special Issue: Proceedings of the 3rd Annual Meeting of the NorthEastern Evolutionary Psychology Society, *Journal of Social, Evolutionary and Cultural Psychology* 3(4): 386–401.

Craig, A. "Once an Island, Now the Focus of Attention." *Brain Structure and Function* 214(5): 395–396.

Crawford, C., and C. Salmon (2004). *Evolutionary Psychology, Public Policy, and Personal Decisions.* Mahwah, N.J.: Lawrence Erlbaum Associates.

Crews, D. (2005). "Evolution of Neuroendocrine Mechanisms That Regulate Sexual Behavior." *Trends in Neuroendocrinology and Metabolism* 16(8): 354–361.

Crews, D., and M. C. Moore (1986). "Evolution of Mechanisms Controlling Mating-Behavior." *Science* 231(4734): 121–125.

Critelli, J. W., and J. M. Bivona (2008). "Women's Erotic Rape Fantasies: An Evaluation of Theory and Research." *Journal of Sex Research* 45(1): 57–70.

Cromby, J. (2007). "Integrating Social Science with Neuroscience: Potentials and Problems." *BioSocieties* 2(02): 149–169.

Cronin, B., and E. Davenport (2001). "E-rogenous Zones: Positioning Pornography in the Digital Economy." *Information Society* 17(1): 33–48.

Cross, P. A., and K. Matheson (2006). "Understanding Sadomasochism: An Empirical Examination of Four Perspectives." *Journal of Homosexuality* 50(2–3): 133–166.

Crowe, M. (2007). "Sexual and Gender Diagnoses of the Diagnostic and Statistical Manual (DSM): A Reevaluation." *Australian and New Zealand Journal of Psychiatry* 41(6): 559–559.

Crowe, S. F., and J. Ponsford (1999). "The Role of Imagery in Sexual Arousal Disturbances in the Male Traumatically Brain Injured Individual." *Brain Injury* 13(5): 347–354.

Cupples, J. (2002). "The Field as a Landscape of Desire: Sex and Sexuality in Geographical Fieldwork." *Area* 34(4): 382–390.

Cushing, B. S., and K. M. Kramer (2005). "Mechanisms Underlying Epigenetic Effects of Early Social Experience: The Role of Neuropeptides and Steroids." *Neuroscience and Biobehavioral Reviews* 29(7): 1089–1105.

Dabbs, J. M., and M. F. Hargrove. (1997). "Age, testosterone, and behavior among female prison inmates." *Psychosomatic medicine* 59(5): 477–480.

Dabholkar, P. A., and X. J. Sheng (2009). "The Role of Perceived Control and Gender in Consumer Reactions to Download Delays." *Journal of Business Research* 62(7): 756–760.

Daleiden, E. L., K. L. Kaufman, et al. (1998). "The Sexual Histories and Fantasies of Youthful Males: A Comparison of Sexual Offending, Nonsexual Offending, and Nonoffending Groups." *Sexual Abuse: A Journal of Research and Treatment* 10(3): 195–209.

Dalgleish, T. (2004). "The Emotional Brain." *Nature Reviews Neuroscience* 5(7): 582–589.

Dalí, S. (2004). *Maniac Eyeball*. London: Creation Books.

Damasio, H., T. Grabowski, et al. (1994). "The Return of Gage, Phineas—Clues About the Brain from the Skull of a Famous Patient." *Science* 264(5162): 1102–1105.

D'Amato, A. (June 23, 2006). *Porn Up, Rape Down*. Northwestern Public Law Research Paper No. 913013. Available at SSRN: http://ssrn.com/abstract=913013.

Damon, W., and R. M. Lerner (2006). *Handbook of Child Psychology*. Hoboken, N.J.: John Wiley & Sons.

Daneback, K., A. Cooper, et al. (2005). "An Internet Study of Cybersex Participants." *Archives of Sexual Behavior* 34(3): 321–328.

Daneback, K., S. A. Mansson, et al. (2007). "Using the Internet to Find Offline Sex Partners." *Cyberpsychology & Behavior* 10(1): 100–107.

Darling, C. A., J. K. Davidson, et al. (1990). "Female Ejaculation—Perceived Origins, the Grafenberg Spot Area, and Sexual Responsiveness." *Archives of Sexual Behavior* 19(1): 29–47.

David, N., M. X. Cohen, et al. (2007). "The Extrastriate Cortex Distinguishes Between the Consequences of One's Own and Others' Behavior." *Neuroimage* 36(3): 1004–1014.

Davidson, J. K. (1985). "Sexual Fantasies Among Married Males—An Analysis of Sexual Satisfaction, Situational Contexts, and Functions." *Sociological Spectrum* 5(1–2): 139–153.

Davis, J. F., M. Loos, et al. (2010). "Lesions of the Medial Prefrontal Cortex Cause Maladaptive Sexual Behavior in Male Rats." *Biological Psychiatry* 67(12): 1199–1204.

Davis, M., G. Hart, et al. (2006). "Sex and the Internet: Gay Men, Risk Reduction and Serostatus." *Culture Health & Sexuality* 8(2): 161–174.

Davis, S. R. (2001). "An External Perspective on the Report of the International Consensus Development Conference on Female Sexual

Dysfunction: More Work to Be Done." *Journal of Sex & Marital Therapy* 27(2): 131–133.

Dawkins, R. (2006) [1978], *The Selfish Gene* (30th anniversary edition) Oxford; New York: Oxford University Press.

Dawood, K., K. M. Kirk, et al. (2005). "Genetic and Environmental Influences on the Frequency of Orgasm in Women." *Twin Research and Human Genetics* 8(1): 27–33.

de Jong, D. C. (2009). "The Role of Attention in Sexual Arousal: Implications for Treatment of Sexual Dysfunction." *Journal of Sex Research* 46(2–3): 237–248.

Deaner, R. O., A. V. Khera, et al. (2005). "Monkeys Pay Per View: Adaptive Valuation of Social Images by Rhesus Macaques." *Current Biology* 15(6): 543–548.

DeBruine, L. M., B. C. Jones, et al. (2006). "Correlated Preferences for Facial Masculinity and Ideal or Actual Partner's Masculinity." *Proceedings of the Royal Society B-Biological Sciences* 273(1592): 1355–1360.

Deeb, A., C. Mason, et al. (2005). "Correlation Between Genotype, Phenotype and Sex Of Rearing in 111 Patients with Partial Androgen Insensitivity Syndrome." *Clinical Endocrinology* 63(1): 56–62.

Dehkordi, M. A., B. Zarei, et al. (2008). "The Effect of Gender and Age Differences on Media Selection in Small and Medium Tourism Enterprises." *Cyberpsychology & Behavior* 11(6): 683–686.

Delacosteutamsing, C., and R. L. Holloway (1982). "Sexual Dimorphism in the Human Corpus-Callosum." *Science* 216(4553): 1431–1432.

Delfabbro, P., D. King, et al. (2009). "Is Video-Game Playing a Risk Factor for Pathological Gambling in Australian Adolescents?" *Journal of Gambling Studies* 25(3): 391–405.

Delgado, J. M. R. (1969). *Physical Control of the Mind; Toward a Psychocivilized Society*. New York: Harper & Row.

Della Marca, G., S. Dittoni, et al. (2009). "Abnormal Sexual Behavior During Sleep." *Journal of Sexual Medicine* 6(12): 3490–3495.

Devinsky, O., M. J. Morrell, et al. (1995). "Contributions of Anterior Cingulate Cortex to Behaviour." *Brain* 118: 279–306.

De Vries, G. J., E. F. Rissman, et al. (2002). "A Model System for Study of Sex Chromosome Effects on Sexually Dimorphic Neural and Behavioral Traits." *Journal of Neuroscience* 22(20): 9005–9014.

Devries, G. J., R. M. Buijs, et al. (1984). "Sex-Differences in Vasopressin and Other Neurotransmitter Systems in the Brain." *Progress in Brain Research* 61: 185–203.

Dew, B. J., and M. P. Channey (2004). "Sexual Addiction and the Internet: Implications for Gay Men." *Journal of Addictions & Offender Counseling*, American Counseling Association 24: 101–114.

DeWall, C. N., R. F. Baumeister, et al. (2008). "Evidence That Logical Reasoning Depends on Conscious Processing." *Consciousness and Cognition* 17(3): 628–645.

Dewaraja, R. (1987). "Formicophilia, an Unusual Paraphilia, Treated with Counseling and Behavior-Therapy." *American Journal of Psychotherapy* 41(4): 593–597.

Dewaraja, R., and J. Money (1986). "Transcultural Sexology—Formicophilia, A Newly Named Paraphilia in a Young Buddhist Male." *Journal of Sex & Marital Therapy* 12(2): 139–145.

Dhikav, V., K. Anand, et al. (2007). "Grossly Disinhibited Sexual Behavior in Dementia of Alzheimer's Type." *Archives of Sexual Behavior* 36(2): 133–134.

Diamond, J. (1983). "Laboratory, Field, and Natural Experiments." *Nature* 304: 586–587.

Diamond, L. M. (2004). "Emerging Perspectives on Distinctions Between Romantic Love and Sexual Desire." *Current Directions in Psychological Science* 13(3): 116–119.

Diamond, M., and H. K. Sigmundson (1997). "Sex Reassignment at Birth—Long-Term Review and Clinical Implications." *Archives of Pediatrics & Adolescent Medicine* 151(3): 298–304.

Diamond, M. and A. Uchiyama (1999). "Pornography, Rape, and Sex Crimes in Japan." *International Journal of Law and Psychiatry* 22(1): 1–22.

Dieckmann, G., B. Schneider-Jonietz, et al. (1988). "Psychiatric and Neuropsychological Findings After Stereotactic Hypothalamotomy, In Cases of Extreme Sexual Aggressivity." *Acta Neurochirurgica* Supplement (Wien) 44: 163–166.

Dimitrov, M., M. Phipps, et al. (1999). "A Thoroughly Modern Gage." *Neurocase* 5(4): 345–354.

Dixson, A. F. (1997). "Evolutionary Perspectives on Primate Mating Systems and Behavior." *Annals of the New York Academy of Sciences* 807(1): 42–61.

Dixson, A. F. (1998). *Primate Sexuality: Comparative Studies of the Prosimians, Monkeys, Apes, and Human Beings.* Oxford; New York: Oxford University Press.

Dixson, A. F. (2009). "The Evolutionary Biology of Human Female Sexuality." *Archives of Sexual Behavior* 38(6): 1067–1069.

Dixson, A. F., and C. M. Nevison (1997). "The Socioendocrinology of Adolescent Development in Male Rhesus Monkeys (Macaca Mulatta)." *Hormones and Behavior* 31(2): 126–135.

Dixson, A. F., and J. Brancroft. (1999). *Primate Sexuality: Comparative Studies of the Prosimians, Monkeys, Apes, and Human Beings.* New York: Oxford University Press.

Dixson, B., G. Grimshaw, et al. "Eye-Tracking of Men's Preferences for Waist-to-Hip Ratio and Breast Size of Women." *Archives of Sexual Behavior,* in press Epub ahead of print retrieved August 30, 2010, retrieved from http://www.ncbi.nlm.nih.gov/pubmed/20169468

Dixson, B. J., A. F. Dixson, et al. (2010). "Human Physique and Sexual Attractiveness in Men and Women: A New Zealand-US Comparative Study." *Archives of Sexual Behavior* 39(3): 798–806.

Dixson, B. J., A. F. Dixson, et al. (2007). "Human Physique and Sexual Attractiveness: Sexual Preferences of Men and Women in Bakossiland, Cameroon." *Archives of Sexual Behavior* 36(3): 369–375.

Dixson, B. J., A. F. Dixson, et al. (2007). "Studies of Human Physique and Sexual Attractiveness: Sexual Preferences of Men and Women in China." *American Journal of Human Biology* 19(1): 88–95.

Dixson, B. J., K. Sagata, et al. (2010). "Male Preferences for Female Waist-to-Hip Ratio and Body Mass Index in the Highlands of Papua New Guinea." *American Journal of Physical Anthropology* 141(4): 620–625.

Dixson, B. J., P. L. Vasey, et al. (2010). "Men's Preferences for Women's Breast Morphology in New Zealand, Samoa, and Papua New Guinea." *Archives of Sexual Behavior*, in press. Epub ahead of print retrieved August 30, 2010, from http://www.ncbi.nlm.nih.gov/pubmed/20862533.

Dobson, S. D. (2010). "Face To Face with the Social Brain: Correlated Evolution of Neocortical Structure and Facial Expression in Anthropoids." *American Journal of Physical Anthropology*: 96–96.

Doering, N. (2008). "Sexuality and the Internet. An Overview of Current Research." *Zeitschrift Fur Sexualforschung* 21(4): 291–+.

Donohoe, M. L., W. von Hippel, et al. (2009). "Beyond Waist-Hip Ratio: Experimental Multivariate Evidence That Average Women's Torsos Are Most Attractive." *Behavioral Ecology* 20(4): 716–721.

Doody, M. A. (1995). *Introduction to Samuel Richardson's Pamela*. New York: Viking Press.

Doring, N. M. (2009). "The Internet's Impact on Sexuality: A Critical Review of 15 Years of Research." *Computers in Human Behavior* 25(5): 1089–1101.

Doshi, P., and P. Bhargava (2008). "Hypersexuality Following Subthalamic Nucleus Stimulation for Parkinson's Disease." *Neurology India* 56(4): 474–476.

Downing, P. E., Y. H. Jiang, et al. (2001). "A Cortical Area Selective for Visual Processing of the Human Body." *Science* 293(5539): 2470–2473.

Dreger, A. D. (2008). "The Controversy Surrounding *The Man Who Would Be Queen*: A Case History of the Politics of Science, Identity, and Sex in the Internet Age." *Archives of Sexual Behavior* 37(3): 366–421.

Drescher, J. (2009). "Handbook of Sexual and Gender Identity Disorders." *Psychiatric Services* 60(3): 407–407.

Durndell, A., and Z. Haag (2002). "Computer Self Efficacy, Computer Anxiety, Attitudes Towards the Internet and Reported Experience with the Internet, by Gender, in an East European Sample." *Computers in Human Behavior* 18(5): 521–535.

Durston, S., H. E. H. Pol, et al. (2001). "Anatomical MRI of the Developing Human Brain: What Have We Learned?" *Journal of the American Academy of Child and Adolescent Psychiatry* 40(9): 1012–1020.

Dutton, D. G., and A. P. Aron (1974). "Some Evidence for Heightened Sexual Attraction Under Conditions of High Anxiety," *Journal of Personality and Social Psychology* 30(4): 310–317.

BIBLIOGRAPHY

Eagly, A. H. (1995). "The Science and Politics of Comparing Women and Men." *American Psychologist* 50(3): 145–158.

Earls, C. M., and M. L. Lalumiere (2002). "A Case Study of Preferential Bestiality (Zoophilia)." *Sex Abuse* 14(1): 83–88.

Earls, C. M., and M. L. Lalumiere (2009). "A Case Study of Preferential Bestiality." *Archives of Sexual Behavior* 38(4): 605–609.

East, M. L., H. Hofer, et al. (1993). "The Erect Penis Is a Flag of Submission in a Female-Dominated Society—Greetings in Serengeti Spotted Hyenas." *Behavioral Ecology and Sociobiology* 33(6): 355–370.

Easton, J. A., J. C. Confer, et al. (2010). "Reproduction Expediting: Sexual Motivations, Fantasies, and the Ticking Biological Clock." *Personality and Individual Differences* 49(5): 516–520.

Edelman, B. (2009). "Markets Red Light States: Who Buys Online Adult Entertainment?" *Journal of Economic Perspectives* 23(1): 209–220.

Edwards, R. (1997). "Evolution of the Primate Penis: New Evidence and Novel Hypotheses." *American Zoologist* 37(5): 202A.

Eghwrudjakpor, P. O., and A. A. Essien (2008). "Hypersexual Behavior Following Craniocerebral Trauma: An Experience with Five Cases." *Libyan Journal of Medicine* 3(4): 192–194.

Ehrhardt, A. A., H. F. L. Meyerbahlburg, et al. (1985). "Sexual Orientation After Prenatal Exposure to Exogenous Estrogen." *Archives of Sexual Behavior* 14(1): 57–77.

Einstein, G. (2007). *Sex and the Brain*. Cambridge, MA: MIT Press.

El-Gabalawi, F., and R. A. Johnson (2007). "Hypersexuality in Inpatient Children and Adolescents: Recognition, Differential Diagnosis, and Evaluation." *CNS Spectrums* 12(11): 821–827.

Elliott, M. L., and L. S. Biever (1996). "Head Injury and Sexual Dysfunction." *Brain Injury* 10(10): 703–717.

Ellis, B. J., and D. Symons (1990). "Sex-Differences in Sexual Fantasy—An Evolutionary Psychological Approach." *Journal of Sex Research* 27(4): 527–555.

Ellison, J. M. (1982). "Alterations of Sexual-Behavior in Temporal-Lobe Epilepsy." *Psychosomatics* 23(5): 499–+.

Ellison, P. T. (2003). "Energetics and Reproductive Effort." *American Journal of Human Biology* 15(3): 342–351.

Ellison, P. T., and P. B. Gray (2009). *Endocrinology of Social Relationships*. Cambridge, MA: Harvard University Press.

Else-Quest, N. M., J. S. Hyde, et al. (2006). "Gender Differences in Temperament: A Meta-Analysis." *Psychological Bulletin* 132(1): 33–72.

Epstein, A. W. (1975). "Fetish Object—Phylogenetic Considerations." *Archives of Sexual Behavior* 4(3): 303–311.

Escasa, M., P. B. Gray, et al. (2010). "Male Traits Associated with Attractiveness in Conambo, Ecuador." *Evolution and Human Behavior* 31(3): 193–200.

Eslinger, P. J., and A. R. Damasio (1985). "Severe Disturbance of Higher Cognition After Bilateral Frontal-Lobe Ablation: Patient EVR." *Neurology* 35(12): 1731–1741.

Evangelia, N., P. S. Kirana, et al. "Level of Bother and Treatment-Seeking Predictors Among Male and Female In-Patients with Sexual Problems: A Hospital-Based Study." *Journal of Sexual Medicine* 7(2): 700–711.

Exton, M. S., A. Bindert, et al. (1999). "Cardiovascular and Endocrine Alterations After Masturbation-Induced Orgasm in Women." *Psychosomatic Medicine* 61(3): 280–289.

Fagan, P. J. (2004). *Sexual Disorders: Perspectives on Diagnosis and Treatment.* Baltimore: Johns Hopkins University Press.

Fanous, S., R. P. Hammer, Jr., et al. (2010). "Short- and Long-Term Effects of Intermittent Social Defeat Stress on Brain-Derived Neurotrophic Factor Expression in Mesocorticolimbic Brain Regions." *Neuroscience* 167(3): 598–607.

Farmer, M. A., and Y. M. Binik (2005). "Psychology Is from Mars, Sexology Is from Venus: Can They Meet on Earth?" *Canadian Psychology—Psychologie Canadienne* 46(1): 46–51.

Farmer, M. A., P. D. Trapnell, et al. (2009). "The Relation Between Sexual Behavior and Religiosity Subtypes: A Test of the Secularization Hypothesis." *Archives of Sexual Behavior* 38(5): 852–865.

Fatel, M. (Producer) (2008). *Miniskirts and Muffins* [Audio CD]. United States: BSeenMedia.

Fausto-Sterling, A. (2000). "The Five Sexes, Revisited—The Emerging Recognition That People Come in Bewildering Sexual Varieties Is Testing Medical Values and Social Norms." *Sciences-New York* 40(4): 18–23.

Fausto-Sterling, A. (2003). "How Sexually Dimorphic Are We? Review and Synthesis—Response." *American Journal of Human Biology* 15(1): 115–116.

Federman, D. D. (2004). "Three Facets of Sexual Differentiation." *New England Journal of Medicine* 350(4): 323–324.

Feinberg, D. R., B. C. Jones, et al. (2006). "Menstrual Cycle, Trait Estrogen Level, and Masculinity Preferences in the Human Voice." *Hormones and Behavior* 49(2): 215–222.

Feldman, R. H. L. (1975). "Relationship of School, Grade, and Sex to Traditional-Modern Attitudes Among Gusii Students in Kenya." *Journal of Social Psychology* 96(1): 135–136.

Fernandez-Guasti, A., F. P. M. Kruijver, et al. (2000). "Sex Differences in the Distribution of Androgen Receptors in the Human Hypothalamus." *Journal of Comparative Neurology* 425(3): 422–435.

Ferree, M. (2003). "Women and the Web: Cybersex Activity and Implications." *Sexual and Relationship Therapy* 18(3): 385–393.

Ferretti, A., M. Caulo, et al. (2005). "Dynamics of Male Sexual Arousal: Distinct Components of Brain Activation Revealed by fMRI." *Neuroimage* 26(4): 1086–1096.

Fessler, D. M. T., and C. D. Navarrete (2003). "Domain-Specific Variation in Disgust Sensitivity Across the Menstrual Cycle." *Evolution and Human Behavior* 24(6): 406–417.

Fessler, D. M. T., and C. D. Navarrete (2004). "Third-Party Attitudes Toward Sibling Incest—Evidence for Westermarck's Hypotheses." *Evolution and Human Behavior* 25(5): 277–294.

Fessler, D. M. T., D. Nettle, et al. (2005). "A Cross-Cultural Investigation of the Role of Foot Size in Physical Attractiveness." *Archives of Sexual Behavior* 34(3): 267–276.

Fiorino, D. F., A. Coury, et al. (1997). "Dynamic Changes in Nucleus Accumbens Dopamine Efflux During the Coolidge Effect in Male Rats." *Journal of Neuroscience* 17(12): 4849–4855.

First, M. B. and A. Tasman (2010). *Clinical Guide to the Diagnosis and Treatment of Mental Disorders*. Chichester, UK; Hoboken, NJ: Wiley-Blackwell.

Fisher, H. E., A. Aron, et al. (2002). "Defining the Brain Systems of Lust, Romantic Attraction, and Attachment." *Archives of Sexual Behavior* 31(5): 413–419.

Fisher, R. A. (1930). *The Genetical Theory of Natural Selection*. Oxford: The Clarendon Press.

Fisher, T. D. (2007). "Sex of Experimenter and Social Norm Effects on Reports of Sexual Behavior in Young Men and Women." *Archives of Sexual Behavior* 36(1): 89–100.

Fisher, W. A., and A. Barak (2001). "Internet Pornography: A Social Psychological Perspective on Internet Sexuality." *Journal of Sex Research* 38(4): 312–323.

Fisher, W. A., and D. Byrne (1978). "Sex-Differences in Response to Erotica— Love Versus Lust." *Journal of Personality and Social Psychology* 36(2): 117–125.

Flood, M. (2007). "Exposure to Pornography Among Youth in Australia." *Journal of Sociology* 43(1): 45–60.

Fontenelle, L. F., I. D. Soares, et al. (2009). "Empathy and Symptoms Dimensions of Patients with Obsessive-Compulsive Disorder." *Journal of Psychiatric Research* 43(4): 455–463.

Forger, N. G., and S. M. Breedlove (1986). "Sexual Dimorphism in Human and Canine Spinal-Cord—Role of Early Androgen." *Proceedings of the National Academy of Sciences of the United States of America* 83(19): 7527–7531.

Frankfurt, M., and B. S. McEwen (1991). "5,7-Dihydroxytryptamine and Gonadal-Steroid Manipulation Alter Spine Density in Ventromedial Hypothalamic Neurons." *Neuroendocrinology* 54(6): 653–657.

Freeman, J. B., N. O. Rule, et al. (2009). "The Cultural Neuroscience of Person Perception." *Cultural Neuroscience: Cultural Influences on Brain Function.Progress in Brain Research* 178: 191–201.

Freeman, W. (1973). "Sexual-Behavior and Fertility After Frontal Lobotomy." *Biological Psychiatry* 6(1): 97–104.

Freund, K., and R. Watson (1990). "Mapping the Boundaries of Courtship Disorder." *Journal of Sex Research* 27(4): 589–606.

BIBLIOGRAPHY

Friday, N. (2009). *Beyond My Control: Forbidden Fantasies in an Uncensored Age.* Naperville, IL: Sourcebooks.

Frith, C. D., and T. Singer (2008). "The Role of Social Cognition in Decision Making." *Philosophical Transactions of the Royal Society B-Biological Sciences* 363(1511): 3875–3886.

Frohman, E. M., T. C. Frohman, et al. (2002). "Acquired Sexual Paraphilia in Patients with Multiple Sclerosis." *Archives of Neurology* 59(6): 1006–1010.

Fujii, N., S. Hihara, et al. (2009). "Social State Representation in Prefrontal Cortex." *Society for Neuroscience* 4(1): 73–84.

Fuller, J. E. (2004). *Equality in Cyberdemocracy? Gauging Gender Gaps in On-line Civic Participation. Social Science Quarterly* 85(4): 938–957.

Fumagalli, M., M. Vergari, et al. (2010). "Brain Switches Utilitarian Behavior: Does Gender Make the Difference?" *PLoS ONE* 5(1).

Furnham, A., V. Swami, et al. (2006). "Body Weight, Waist-to-Hip Ratio and Breast Size Correlates of Ratings of Attractiveness and Health." *Personality and Individual Differences* 41(3): 443–454.

Gabbard, G. O. (2001). "Musings on the Report of the International Consensus Development Conference on Female Sexual Dysfunction: Definitions and Classifications." *Journal of Sex & Marital Therapy* 27(2): 145–147.

Gaffney, G. R., S. F. Lurie, et al. (1984). "Is There Familial Transmission of Pedophilia." *Journal of Nervous and Mental Disease* 172(9): 546–548.

Gagnon, J. H. (2008). "Is This a Work of Science?" *Archives of Sexual Behavior* 37(3): 444–447.

Gailey, J. A., and A. Prohaska (2006). " 'Knocking Off a Fat Girl': An Exploration of Hogging, Male Sexuality, and Neutralizations." *Deviant Behavior* 27(1): 31–49.

Gaither, G. A. (2009). "A Representative Survey of Sexual Fantasies?: A Review of: '*Who's Been Sleeping in Your Head? The Secret World of Sexual Fantasies.* By Brett Kahr.'—New York: Basic Books, 2008, 493 pages. Paperback, $28.00." *Journal of Sex Research* 47(4): 399–401.

Gallace, A., and C. Spence (2010). "The Science of Interpersonal Touch: An Overview." *Neuroscience and Biobehavioral Reviews* 34(2): 246–259.

Gallagher, H. L., and C. D. Frith (2003). "Functional Imaging of 'Theory of Mind.' " *Trends in Cognitive Sciences* 7(2): 77–83.

Gallagher, H. L., F. Happe, et al. (2000). "Reading the Mind in Cartoons and Stories: An fMRI Study of 'Theory of Mind' in Verbal and Nonverbal Tasks." *Neuropsychologia* 38(1): 11–21.

Gallup, G. G., R. L. Burch et al. (2006). "Semen displacement as a sperm competition strategy—Multiple mating, self-semen displacement, and timing of in-pair copulations" *Human Nature—An Interdisciplinary Biosocial Perspective* 17(3): 253–264.

Gallup, G., R., Burch, et al. (2006). "Semen Displacement as a Sperm Competition Strategy." *Human Nature* 17(3): 253–264.

Gangestad, S. W. (2000). *Human Sexual Selection, Good Genes, and Special Design. Evolutionary Perspectives on Human Behavior* 907: 50–61.

Gangestad, S. W. (2006). "Adapting Minds: Evolutionary Psychology and the Persistent Quest for Human Nature." *Journal of Anthropological Research* 62(1): 138–140.

Gangestad, S. W., M. G. Haselton, et al. (2006). "Evolutionary Foundations of Cultural Variation: Evoked Culture and Mate Preferences." *Psychological Inquiry* 17(2): 75–95.

Gangestad, S. W., J. A. Simpson, et al. (2004). "Women's Preferences for Male Behavioral Displays Change Across the Menstrual Cycle." *Psychological Science* 15(3): 203–207.

Gangestad, S. W., and R. Thornhill (2008). "Human Oestrus." *Proceedings of the Royal Society B-Biological Sciences* 275(1638): 991–1000.

Gangestad, S. W., R. Thornhill, et al. (2005). "Adaptations to Ovulation— Implications for Sexual and Social Behavior." *Current Directions in Psychological Science* 14(6): 312–316.

Garavan, H., J. Pankiewicz, et al. (2000). "Cue-Induced Cocaine Craving: Neuroanatomical Specificity for Drug Users and Drug Stimuli." *American Journal of Psychiatry* 157(11): 1789–1798.

Garbarino, E., and M. Strahilevitz (2004). "Gender Differences in the Perceived Risk Oo Buying Online and the Effects of Receiving a Site Recommendation." *Journal of Business Research* 57(7): 768–775.

Garcia, L. T., K. Brennan, et al. (1984). "Sex-Differences in Sexual Arousal to Different Erotic Stories." *Journal of Sex Research* 20(4): 391–402.

Gaul, C., B. Jordan, et al. (2007). "Kluver-Bucy Syndrome in Humans." *Nervenarzt* 78(7): 821–823.

Gaulin, S. J. C., and R. W. Fitzgerald (1986). "Sex-Differences in Spatial Ability—An Evolutionary Hypothesis and Test." *American Naturalist* 127(1): 74–88.

Gauthier, D. K., and N. K. Chaudoir (2004). "Tranny Boyz: Cyber Community Support in Negotiating Sex and Gender Mobility Among Female to Male Transsexuals." *Deviant Behavior* 25(4): 375–398.

Gee, D. G., G. J. Devilly, et al. (2004). "The Content of Sexual Fantasies for Sexual Offenders." *Sexual Abuse: A Journal of Research and Treatment* 16(4): 315–331.

Geer, J. H., and H. S. Bellard (1996). "Sexual Content Induced Delays in Unprimed Lexical Decisions: Gender and Context Effects." *Archives of Sexual Behavior* 25(4): 379–395.

Gelez, H., E. Archer, et al. (2004). "Role of Experience in the Neuroendocrine Control of Ewes' Sexual Behavior." *Hormones and Behavior* 45(3): 190–200.

Georgiadis, J. R., M. J. Farrell, et al. "Dynamic Subcortical Blood Flow During Male Sexual Activity with Ecological Validity: A Perfusion NRI Study." *Neuroimage* 50(1): 208–216.

Georgiadis, J. R., M. J. Farrell, et al. (2010). "Dynamic Subcortical Blood Flow During Male Sexual Activity with Ecological Validity: A Perfusion NRI Study." *Neuroimage* 50(1): 208–216.

BIBLIOGRAPHY

Georgiadis, J. R., R. Kortekaas, et al. (2006). "Regional Cerebral Blood Flow Changes Associated with Clitorally Induced Orgasm in Healthy Women." *European Journal of Neuroscience* 24(11): 3305–3316.

Georgiadis, J. R., A. Reinders, et al. (2007). "Brain Activation During Human Male Ejaculation Revisited." *Neuroreport* 18(6): 553–557.

Georgiadis, J. R., A. Reinders, et al. (2009). "Men Versus Women on Sexual Brain Function: Prominent Differences During Tactile Genital Stimulation, but Not During Orgasm." *Human Brain Mapping* 30(10): 3089–3101.

Gergen, K. J., M. M. Gergen, et al. (1973). "Deviance in Dark." *Psychology Today* 7(5): 129–131.

Geschwind, N., and P. Behan (1982). "Left-Handedness—Association with Immune Disease, Migraine, and Developmental Learning Disorder." *Proceedings of the National Academy of Sciences of the United States of America-Biological Sciences* 79(16): 5097–5100.

Ghofrani, H. A., I. H. Osterloh, F. Grimminger. (2006). "Sildenafil: from Angina to Erectile Dysfunction to Pulmonary Hypertension and Beyond." *Nature Reviews Drug Discovery* 5(8): 689–702.

Giedd, J. N. (2008). "The Teen Brain: Insights from Neuroimaging." *Journal of Adolescent Health* 42(4): 335–343.

Gijs, L., and L. Gooren (1996). "Hormonal and Psychopharmacological Interventions in the Treatment of Paraphilias: An Update." *Journal of Sex Research* 33(4): 273–290.

Gil, V. E. (1990). "Sexual Fantasy Experiences and Guilt Among Conservative Christians—An Exploratory-Study." *Journal of Sex Research* 27(4): 629–638.

Gilbert, S. F. (2002). *The Genome in Its Ecological Context: Philosophical Perspectives on Interspecies Epigenesis*. New York Academy of Sciences.

Gillath, O., M. Mikulincer, et al. (2007). "Does Subliminal Exposure to Sexual Stimuli Have the Same Effects on Men and Women?" *Journal of Sex Research* 44(2): 111–121.

Gillies, G. E., and S. McArthur (2010). "Estrogen Actions in the Brain and the Basis for Differential Action in Men and Women: A Case for Sex-Specific Medicines." *Pharmacological Reviews* 62(2): 155–198.

Gimpl, G., and F. Fahrenholz (2001). "The Oxytocin Receptor System: Structure, Function, and Regulation." *Physiological Reviews* 81(2): 629–683.

Giraldi, A., L. Marson, et al. (2004). "Physiology of Female Sexual Function: Animal Models." *Journal of Sexual Medicine* 1(3): 237–253.

Girolami, L., and C. Bielert (1987). "Female Perineal Swelling and Its Effects on Male Sexual Arousal—An Apparent Sexual Releaser in the Chacma Baboon (Papio-Ursinus)." *International Journal of Primatology* 8(6): 651–661.

Gizewski, E. R., E. Krause, et al. (2006). "There Are Differences in Cerebral Activation Between Females in Distinct Menstrual Phases During Viewing of Erotic Stimuli: A fMRI Study." *Experimental Brain Research* 174(1): 101–108.

BIBLIOGRAPHY

Gizewski, E. R., E. Krause, et al. (2009). "Specific Cerebral Activation Due to Visual Erotic Stimuli in Male-to-Female Transsexuals Compared with Male and Female Controls: An fMRI Study." *Journal of Sexual Medicine* 6(2): 440–448.

Goldman, P. S., H. T. Crawford, et al. (1974). "Sex-Dependent Behavioral-Effects of Cerebral Cortical-Lesions in Developing Rhesus-Monkey." *Science* 186(4163): 540–542.

Goldsmith, H. H., K. S. Lemery, et al. (1999). "Genetic Analyses of Focal Aspects of Infant Temperament." *Developmental Psychology* 35(4): 972–985.

Goldstein, I. (2007). "Female Sexual Dysfunction and the Central Nervous System." *Journal of Sexual Medicine* 4: 255–256.

Goldstein, J. M., M. Jerram, et al. (2005). "Hormonal Cycle Modulates Arousal Circuitry in Women Using Functional Magnetic Resonance Imaging." *Journal of Neuroscience* 25(40): 9309–9316.

Goodson, J. L., and A. H. Bass (2001). "Social Behavior Functions and Related Anatomical Characteristics of Vasotocin/Vasopressin Systems in Vertebrates." *Brain Research Reviews* 35(3): 246–265.

Goodson, P., D. McCormick, et al. (2001). "Searching for Sexually Explicit Materials on the Internet: An Exploratory Study of College Students' Behavior and Attitudes." *Archives of Sexual Behavior* 30(2): 101–118.

Gooren, L. (2006). "The Biology of Human Psychosexual Differentiation." *Hormones and Behavior* 50(4): 589–601.

Gooren, L. J. G., B. R. Rao, et al. (1984). "Estrogen Positive Feedback on LH-Secretion in Transsexuality." *Psychoneuroendocrinology* 9(3): 249–259.

Gordon, M. E., L. A. Slade, et al. (1986). "The Science of the Sophomore Revisited—From Conjecture to Empiricism." *Academy of Management Review* 11(1): 191–207.

Gorman, D. G., and J. L. Cummings (1992). "Hypersexuality Following Septal Injury." *Archives of Neurology* 49(3): 308–310.

Gorski, R. A., J. H. Gordon, et al. (1978). "Evidence for a Morphological Sex Difference Within Medial Preoptic Area of Rat-Brain." *Brain Research* 148(2): 333–346.

Gosling, S. (2008). *Snoop : What Your Stuff Says About You.* New York: Basic Books.

Gosling, S. D., S. Vazire, et al. (2004). "Should We Trust Web-Based Studies? A Comparative Analysis of Six Preconceptions About Internet Questionnaires." *American Psychologist* 59(2): 93–104.

Gossett, J. L., and S. Byrne (2002). " 'Click Here'—A Content Analysis of Internet Rape Sites." *Gender & Society* 16(5): 689–709.

Gottlieb, L. (2010), *Marry Him: The Case for Settling for Mr. Good Enough.* New York: Dutton.

Gottschall, J. (2007) "Greater Emphasis on Female Attractiveness in Homo Sapiens: A Revised Solution to an Old Evolutionary Riddle." *Evolutionary Psychology* 5: 347.

BIBLIOGRAPHY

Gould, E., C. S. Woolley, et al. (1990). "Gonadal-Steroids Regulate Dendritic Spine Density in Hippocampal Pyramidal Cells in Adulthood." *Journal of Neuroscience* 10(4): 1286–1291.

Goy, R. W., B. S. McEwen, et al. (1980). *Sexual Differentiation of the Brain: Based on a Work Session of the Neurosciences Research Program*. Cambridge, MA: MIT Press.

Grammer, K., B. Fink, et al. (2005). "Physical Attractiveness and Health: Comment on Weeden and Sabini (2005)." *Psychological Bulletin* 131(5): 658–661.

Grammer, K., B. Fink, et al. (2003). "Darwinian Aesthetics: Sexual Selection and the Biology Of Beauty." *Biological Reviews* 78(3): 385–407.

Grasswick, L. J., and J. M. Bradford (2003). "Osteoporosis Associated with the Treatment of Paraphilias: A Clinical Review of Seven Case Reports." *Journal of Forensic Science* 48(4): 849–855.

Gray, J. (1992). *Men Are from Mars, Women Are from Venus: A Practical Guide for Improving Communication and Getting What You Want in Your Relationships*. New York: HarperCollins.

Gray, P. B., A. B. Singh, et al. (2005). "Dose-Dependent Effects of Testosterone on Sexual Function, Mood, and Visuospatial Cognition in Older Men." *Journal of Clinical Endocrinology and Metabolism* 90(7): 3838–3846.

Green, R. (2002). "Is Pedophilia a Mental Disorder?" *Archives of Sexual Behavior* 31(6): 467.

Greenberg, J. (1987). "The College Sophomore as Guinea-Pig—Setting the Record Straight." *Academy of Management Review* 12(1): 157–159.

Greenberg, M., and R. Littlewood (1995). "Post-Adoption Incest and Phenotypic Matching—Experience, Personal Meanings and Biosocial Implications." *British Journal of Medical Psychology* 68: 29–44.

Greeno, N. C., and S. Semple (2009). "Sex Differences in Vocal Communication Among Adult Rhesus Macaques." *Evolution and Human Behavior* 30(2): 141–145.

Greimel, E., M. Schulte–Ruther, et al. (2010). "Development of Neural Correlates of Empathy from Childhood to Early Adulthood: An fmri Study in Boys and Adult Men." *Journal of Neural Transmission* 117(6): 781–791.

Greitemeyer, T., S. Hengmith, et al. (2005). "Sex Differences in the Willingness to Betray and Switch Romantic Partners." *Swiss Journal of Psychology* 64(4): 265–272.

Griffiths, M. (2001). "Sex on the Internet: Observations and Implications for Internet Sex Addiction." *Journal of Sex Research* 38(4): 333–342.

Grosbras, M. H., M. Jansen, et al. (2007). "Neural Mechanisms of Resistance to Peer Influence in Early Adolescence." *Journal of Neuroscience* 27(30): 8040–8045.

Grov, C., B. Gillespie, et al. "Perceived Consequences of Casual Online Sexual Activities on Heterosexual Relationships: A U.S. Online Survey." *Archives of Sexual Behavior*, in press. Epub ahead of print, retrieved August 30, 2010 from http://www.ncbi.nlm.nih.gov/pubmed/20174862

BIBLIOGRAPHY

Guadagno, R. E., and R. B. Cialdini (2002). "Online Persuasion: An Examination of Gender Differences in Computer-Mediated Interpersonal Influence." *Group Dynamics—Theory Research and Practice* 6(1): 38–51.

Gueguen, N. (2007). "Women's Bust Size and Men's Courtship Solicitation." *Body Image* 4(4): 386–390.

Gueguen, N. (2009). "Menstrual Cycle Phases and Female Receptivity to a Courtship Solicitation: An Evaluation in a Nightclub." *Evolution and Human Behavior* 30(5): 351–355.

Guenther, F. H. (2006)"Cortical Interactions Underlying the Production of Speech Sounds." *Journal of Communication Disorders* 39(5): 350–365.

Guenther, F. H. (1995). "Speech Sound Acquisition, Coarticulation, and Rate Effects in a Neural Network Model of Speech Production." *Psychological Review* 102(3): 594–621.

Guenther, F. H., J. S. Brumberg, et al. (2009). "A Wireless Brain-Machine Interface for Real-Time Speech Synthesis." *PLoS One* 4(12).

Guenther, F. H., S. S. Ghosh, et al. (2006). "Neural Modeling and Imaging of the Cortical Interactions Underlying Syllable Production." *Brain and Language* 96(3): 280–301.

Guenther, F. H., M. Hampson, et al. (1998). "A Theoretical Investigation of Reference Frames for the Planning of Speech Movements." *Psychological Review* 105(4): 611–633.

Guillem, F., and M. Mograss (2005). "Gender Differences in Memory Processing: Evidence from Event-Related Potentials to Faces." *Brain and Cognition* 57(1): 84–92.

Gur, R. C., L. H. Mozley, et al. (1995). "Sex-Differences in Regional Cerebral Glucose-Metabolism During a Resting State." *Science* 267(5197): 528–531.

Haake, P., M. Schedlowski, et al. (2003). "Acute Neuroendocrine Response to Sexual Stimulation in Sexual Offenders." *Canadian Journal of Psychiatry—Revue Canadienne De Psychiatrie* 48(4): 265–271.

Hagen, E. H., R. J. Sullivan, et al. (2009). "Ecology and Neurobiology of Toxin Avoidance and the Paradox of Drug Reward." *Neuroscience* 160(1): 69–84.

Hald, G. M., N. M. Malamuth, et al. (2010). "Pornography and Attitudes Supporting Violence Against Women: Revisiting the Relationship in Nonexperimental Studies." *Aggressive Behavior* 36(1): 14–20.

Halpern, C. J. T., J. R. Udry, et al. (2000). "Adolescent Males' Willingness to Report Masturbation." *Journal of Sex Research* 37(4): 327–332.

Hamann, S. (2005). "Sex Differences in the Responses of the Human Amygdala." *Neuroscientist* 11(4): 288–293.

Hamann, S., R. A. Herman, et al. (2004). "Men And Women Differ in Amygdala Response to Visual Sexual Stimuli." *Nature Neuroscience* 7(4): 411–416.

Hamilton, L. D., A. H. Rellini, et al. (2008). "Cortisol, Sexual Arousal, and Affect in Response to Sexual Stimuli." *Journal of Sexual Medicine* 5(9): 2111–2118.

Haqq, C. M. (1995). "Molecular-Basis of Mammalian Sexual Determination—Activation of Mullerian-Inhibiting Substance Gene-Expression by Sry (Vol 266, PG 1494, 1994)." *Science* 267(5196): 317–317.

Hardy, S. (2008). "The Pornography of Reality." *Sexualities* 11(1–2): 60–64.

Harenski, C. L., O. Antonenko, et al. (2008), "Gender Differences in Neural Mechanisms Underlying Moral Sensitivity." *Social Cognitive and Affective Neuroscience* 3(4): 313–321.

Hargittai, E. (2007). "Whose Space? Differences Among Users and Non-Users of Social Network Sites." *Journal of Computer-Mediated Communication* 13(1): 21.

Hargittai, E. and S. Shafer (2006). "Differences in Actual and Perceived Online Skills: The Role of Gender." *Social Science Quarterly* 87(2): 432–448.

Hariri, A. G., F. Karadag, et al. (2009). "Sexual Problems in a Sample of the Turkish Psychiatric Population." *Comprehensive Psychiatry* 50(4): 353–360.

Hariton, E. B. (1973). "Sexual Fantasies of Women." *Psychology Today* 6(10): 39–44.

Hariton, E. B., and J. L. Singer (1974). "Womens Fantasies During Sexual Intercourse—Normative and Theoretical Implications." *Journal of Consulting and Clinical Psychology* 42(3): 313–322.

Harlow, J. M. (1999). "Passage of an Iron Rod Through the Head." *Journal of Neuropsychiatry and Clinical Neurosciences* 11(2): 281–283.

Harris, H. (1995). *Human Nature and the Nature of Human Love.* Unpublished doctoral dissertation, University of Santa Barbara, California, United States.

Harrison, K., and B. J. Bond (2007). "Gaming Magazines and the Drive for Muscularity in Preadolescent Boys: A Longitudinal Examination." *Body Image* 4(3): 269–277.

Haselton, M. G., and D. M. Buss (2001). "The Affective Shift Hypothesis: The Functions of Emotional Changes Following Sexual Intercourse." *Personal Relationships* 8(4): 357–369.

Haselton, M. G., and G. R. Miller (2006). "Women's Fertility Across the Cycle Increases the Short-Term Attractiveness of Creative Intelligence." *Human Nature: An Interdisciplinary Biosocial Perspective* 17(1): 50–73.

Haselton, M. G., M. Mortezaie, et al. (2007). "Ovulatory Shifts in Human Female Ornamentation: Near Ovulation, Women Dress to Impress." *Hormones and Behavior* 51(1): 40–45.

Hassett, J. M., E. R. Siebert, et al. (2004). "Sexually Differentiated Toy Preferences in Rhesus Monkeys." Academic Press Inc. Elsevier Science.

Hassett, J. M., E. R. Siebert, et al. (2008). "Sex Differences in Rhesus Monkey Toy Preferences Parallel Those of Children." *Hormones and Behavior* 54(3): 359–364.

Hatfield, E. R., R. L. (2009). *The Neuropsychology of Passionate Love and Sexual Desire.* Hauppauge, NY: Nova Science.

Hatfield, E. S. (2007) Commentary. *HBES E-Newsletter,* summer (Human Behavior and Evolution Society): 1–10.

Hawk, S. T., R. Tolman, et al. (2007). "The Effects of Target Attractiveness on Men's Sexual Arousal in Response to Erotic Auditory Stimuli." *Journal of Sex Research* 44(1): 96–103.

BIBLIOGRAPHY

Hawley, P. H., and W. A. Hensley (2009). "Social Dominance and Forceful Submission Fantasies: Feminine Pathology or Power?" *Journal of Sex Research* 46(6): 568–585.

Heaton, J. P. W., and M. A. Adams (2003). "Update on Central Function Relevant to Sex: Remodeling the Basis of Drug Treatments for Sex and the Brain." *International Journal of Impotence Research* 15: S25–S32.

Hedges, L. V., and A. Nowell (1995). "Sex-Differences in Mental Test-Scores, Variability, and Numbers Of High-Scoring Individuals." *Science* 269(5220): 41–45.

Heider, D., and D. Harp (2002). "New Hope or Old Power: Democracy, Pornography and the Internet." *Howard Journal of Communications* 13: 285–299.

Heiman, J. R. (1977). "Psychophysiological Exploration of Sexual Arousal Patterns in Females and Males." *Psychophysiology* 14(3): 266–274.

Heiman, J. R., D. L. Rowland, et al. (1991). "Psychophysiological and Endocrine Responses to Sexual Arousal in Women." *Archives of Sexual Behavior* 20(2): 171–186.

Heinzel, A., M. Walter, et al. (2006). "Self-Related Processing in the Sexual Domain: A Parametric Event-Related fMRI Study Reveals Neural Activity in Ventral Cortical Midline Structures." *Social Neuroscience* 1(1): 41–51.

Hellhammer, D. H., W. Hubert, et al. (1985). "Changes in Saliva Testosterone After Psychological Stimulation in Men." *Psychoneuroendocrinology* 10(1): 77–81.

Hellmis, E. (2008). "Sexual Problems in Males with Epilepsy—An Interdisciplinary Challenge!" *Seizure* 17(2): 136–140.

Henrich, J., S.J. Heine, and A. Norenzayan (2010). "The Weirdest People in the World?" *Behavioral and Brain Sciences* 33(2–3): 61–83.

Hensley, C., S. E. Tallichet, et al. (2006). "Exploring the Possible Link Between Childhood and Adolescent Bestiality and Interpersonal Violence." *Journal of Interpersonal Violence* 21(7): 910–923.

Herbert, J. (2008). "Who Do We Think We Are: The Brain and Gender Identity." *Brain* 131: 3115–3117.

Herdt, G. (1987). "Transitional Objects in Sambia Initiation." *Ethos* 15(1): 40–57.

Herdt, G. H. (1982). *Rituals of Manhood : Male Initiation in Papua New Guinea.* Berkeley: University of California Press.

Hernandez-Gonzalez, M., M. A. Guevara, et al. (2008). "Motivational Influences on the Degree and Direction of Sexual Attraction: Molecular and Biophysical Mechanisms of Arousal, Alertness, and Attention." *Annals of the New York Academy of Sciences* 1129: 61–87.

Hernandez-Gonzalez, M., C. A. Prieto-Beracoechea, et al. (2007). "Different functionality of the medial and orbital prefrontal cortex during a sexually motivated task in rats." *Physiology & Behavior* 90(2–3): 450–458.

Hicks, T. V. and H. Leitenberg (2001). "Sexual fantasies about one's partner versus someone else: Gender differences in incidence and frequency." *Journal of Sex Research* 38(1): 43–50.

Hill, C. A. and L. K. Preston (1996). "Individual differences in the experience of sexual motivation: Theory and measurement of dispositional sexual motives." *Journal of Sex Research* 33(1): 27–45.

Hilliard, R. B., and R. L. Spitzer (2002). "Change in Criterion for Paraphilias in DSM-IV-TR." *American Journal of Psychiatry* 159(7): 1249–1249.

Hilti, L. M., and P. Brugger (2010). "Incarnation and Animation: Physical Versus Representational Deficits of Body Integrity." *Experimental Brain Research* 204(3): 315–326.

Hinde, R. A., and C. M. Berman (1983). *Primate Social Relationships: An Integrated Approach*. Sunderland, MA: Sinauer Associates.

Hines, M., L. S. Allen, et al. (1992). "Sex-Differences in Subregions of the Medial Nucleus of the Amygdala and the Bed Nucleus of the Stria Terminalis of the Rat." *Brain Research* 579(2): 321–326.

Hodes, G. E., L. Yang, et al. (2009). "Prozac During Puberty: Distinctive Effects on Neurogenesis as a Function of Age and Sex." *Neuroscience* 163(2): 609–617.

Hoffmann, H., E. Janssen, et al. (2004). "Classical Conditioning of Sexual Arousal in Women and Men: Effects of Varying Awareness and Biological Relevance of the Conditioned Stimulus." *Archives of Sexual Behavior* 33(1): 43–53.

Holland, E. (2009). "Pornographic Actresses Are a Poor Choice for Assessing What Men Optimally Prefer in Women's Looks: Comments on Voracek and Fisher (2006)." *Archives of Sexual Behavior* 38(4): 458–459.

Holloway, K. S., and M. Domjan (1993). "Sexual Approach Conditioning—Unconditioned Stimulus Factors." *Journal of Experimental Psychology-Animal Behavior Processes* 19(1): 38–46.

Holloway, R. L., P. J. Anderson, et al. (1993). "Sexual Dimorphism of the Human Corpus-Callosum from 3 Independent Samples—Relative Size of the Corpus-Callosum." *American Journal of Physical Anthropology* 92(4): 481–498.

Holmes, M. M., B. D. Goldman, et al. (2008). "Social Status and Sex Independently Influence Androgen Receptor Expression in the Eusocial Naked Mole-Rat Brain." *Hormones and Behavior* 54(2): 278–285.

Holmes, M. M., G. J. Rosen, et al. (2007). "Social Control of Brain Morphology in a Eusocial Mammal." *Proceedings of the National Academy of Sciences of the United States of America* 104(25): 10548–10552.

Holstege, G., and J. R. Georgiadis (2004). "The Emotional Brain: Neural Correlates of Cat Sexual Behavior and Human Male Ejaculation." *Progress in Brain Research* 143: 39–45.

Holstege, G., J. R. Georgiadis, et al. (2003). "Brain Activation During Human Male Ejaculation." *Journal of Neuroscience* 23(27): 9185–9193.

Honk, J. v., D. J. Schutter, et al (2004). "Testosterone Shifts the Balance Between Sensitivity for Punishment and Reward in Healthy Young Women." *Psychoneuroendocrinology* 29(7): 937–943.

Hooper, P. L., and G. F. Miller (2008). "Mutual Mate Choice Can Drive Costly Signaling Even Under Perfect Monogamy." *Adaptive Behavior* 16(1): 53–70.

Hoshina, Y., T. Takeo, et al. (1994). "Axon-sparing lesion of the preoptic area enchances receptivity and diminshes proceptivity among components of female rat sexual behavior." *Behavioral Brain Research* 61(2): 197–204.

Hu, S. H., N. Wei, et al. (2008). "Patterns of Brain Activation During Visually Evoked Sexual Arousal Differ Between Homosexual And Heterosexual Men." *American Journal of Neuroradiology* 29(10): 1890–1896.

Hughes, S. M., and S. E. Nicholson (2008) "Sex Differences in the Assessment of Pain Versus Sexual Pleasure Facial Expressions." *Journal of Social, Evolutionary, and Cultural Psychology* 2(4): 289–298

Hupfer, M. E., and B. Detlor (2007). "Beyond Gender Differences: Self-Concept Orientation and Relationship-Building Applications on the Internet." *Journal of Business Research* 60(6): 613–619.

Hutsler, J., and R. A. W. Galuske (2003). "Hemispheric Asymmetries in Cerebral Cortical Networks." *Trends in Neurosciences* 26(8): 429–435.

Huws, R., A. P. W. Shubsachs, et al. (1991). "Hypersexuality, Fetishism and Multiple-Sclerosis." *British Journal of Psychiatry* 158: 280–281.

Hyde, J. S., and A. M. Durik (2000). "Gender Differences in Erotic Plasticity-Evolutionary or Sociocultural Forces? Comment on Baumeister (2000)." *Psychological Bulletin* 126(3): 375–379.

Imperato.J, L. Guerrero, et al. (1974). "Steroid 5alpha-Reductase Deficiency in Man—Inherited Form of Male Pseudohermaphroditism." *Science* 186(4170): 1213–1215.

Imperato-McGinley, J., M. Pichardo, et al. (1991). "Cognitive-Abilities in Androgen-Insensitive Subjects—Comparison with Control Males and Females from the Same Kindred." *Clinical Endocrinology* 34(5): 341–347.

Inglis, J., and J. S. Lawson (1981). "Sex-Differences in the Effects of Unilateral Brain-Damage on Intelligence." *Science* 212(4495): 693–695.

Insel, T. R., and R. D. Fernald (2004). "How the Brain Processes Social Information: Searching for the Social Brain." *Annual Review of Neuroscience* 27: 697–722.

Isbell, L. A., and T. P. Young (2002). "Ecological Models of Female Social Relationships in Primates: Similarities, Disparities, and Some Directions for Future Clarity." *Behavior* 139: 177–202.

Israel, E., and D. S. Strassberg (2009). "Viewing Time as an Objective Measure of Sexual Interest in Heterosexual Men and Women." *Archives of Sexual Behavior* 38(4): 551–558.

Iwahana, E., I. Karatsoreos, et al. (2008). "Gonadectomy Reveals Sex Differences in Circadian Rhythms and Suprachiasmatic Nucleus Androgen Receptors in Mice." *Hormones and Behavior* 53(3): 422–430.

Jackson, J. J., and L. A. Kirkpatrick (2007). "The Structure and Measurement of Human Mating Strategies: Toward a Multidimensional Model of Sociosexuality." *Evolution and Human Behavior* 28(6): 382–391.

BIBLIOGRAPHY

Jackson, L. A., Y. Zhao, et al. (2008). "Culture, Gender and Information Technology Use: A Comparison of Chinese and US Children." *Computers in Human Behavior* 24(6): 2817–2829.

Jacobs, G. (2000). "Applying Functional Grammar: A Discourse Analysis of Sexually Explicit Stories Written in Adult Magazines." *Social Semiotics* 10(3): 281–292.

Jameson, J., and N. Strauss (2004). *How to Make Love Like a Porn Star: A Cautionary Tale.* New York: Regan Books.

Jameson, K. A., S. M. Highnote, et al. (2001). "Richer Color Experience in Observers with Multiple Photopigment Opsin Genes." *Psychonomic Bulletin & Review* 8(2): 244–261.

Janssen, E., D. Carpenter, et al. (2003). "Selecting Films for Sex Research: Gender Differences in Erotic Film Preference." *Archives of Sexual Behavior* 32(3): 243–251.

Janssen, E., W. Everaerd, et al. (2000). "Automatic Processes and the Appraisal of Sexual Stimuli: Toward an Information Processing Model of Sexual Arousal." *Journal of Sex Research* 37(1): 8–23.

Janssen, E., D. Goodrich, et al. (2009). "Psychophysiological Response Patterns and Risky Sexual Behavior in Heterosexual and Homosexual Men." *Archives of Sexual Behavior* 38(4): 538–550.

Janssen, E., K. R. McBride, et al. (2008). "Factors That Influence Sexual Arousal in Men: A Focus Group Study." *Archives of Sexual Behavior* 37(2): 252–265.

Jasienska, G., and P. T. Ellison (2004). "Energetic Factors and Seasonal Changes in Ovarian Function in Women from Rural Poland." *American Journal of Human Biology* 16(5): 563–580.

Jasienska, G., A. Ziomkiewicz, et al. (2004). "Large Breasts and Narrow Waists Indicate High Reproductive Potential in Women." *Proceedings of the Royal Society of London Series B-Biological Sciences* 271(1545): 1213–1217.

Jasienska, G., and P. T. Ellison (2004) "Energetic Factors and Seasonal Changes in Ovarian Function in Women from Rural Poland." *American Journal of Human Biology* 16(5): 563–580.

Jaya, J., and M. J. Hindin (2009). "Premarital Romantic Partnerships: Attitudes and Sexual Experiences of Youth in Delhi, India." *International Perspectives on Sex and Reproductive Health* 35(2): 97–104.

Jenkins, W. J., and J. B. Becker (2001). "Role of the Striatum and Nucleus Accumbens in Paced Copulatory Behavior in the Female Rat." *Behavioural Brain Research* 121(1–2): 119–128.

Jes s Fern ndez-Villaverde, J. G., Nezih Guner "From Shame to Game in One Hundred Years: An Economic Model of the Rise in Premarital Sex and Its De-Stigmatization." Working paper, retrieved March 2010. http://papers .ssrn.com/sol3/papers.cfm?abstract_id=1545135

Johnson, A. M. (1994). *Sexual Attitudes and Lifestyles.* Oxford; Boston: Blackwell Scientific Publications.

Johnson, C., C. Knight, et al. (2006). "Challenges Associated with the Definition and Assessment of Inappropriate Sexual Behaviour Amongst Individuals with an Acquired Neurological Impairment." *Brain Injury* 20(7): 687–693.

Johnston, V. S., R. Hagel, et al. (2001). "Male Facial Attractiveness—Evidence for Hormone-Mediated Adaptive Design." *Evolution and Human Behavior* 22(4): 251–267.

Jokela, M. (2009). "Physical Attractiveness and Reproductive Success in Humans: Evidence from the Late 20th Century United States." *Evolution and Human Behavior* 30(5): 342–350.

Jones, B. A., and N. V. Watson (2005). "Spatial Memory Performance in Androgen Insensitive Male Rats." *Physiology & Behavior* 85(2): 135–141.

Jones, B. C., A. C. Little, et al. (2005), "Commitment to Relationships and Preferences for Femininity and Apparent Health in Faces Are Strongest on Days of the Menstrual Cycle When Progesterone Level Is High," *Hormones and Behavior* 48(3): 283–290.

Jones, J. C., and D. H. Barlow (1990). "Self-Reported Frequency of Sexual Urges, Fantasies, and Masturbatory Fantasies in Heterosexual Males And Females." *Archives of Sexual Behavior* 19(3): 269–279.

Jones, J. H. (1997). *Alfred C. Kinsey: A Public/Private Life.* New York: Norton.

Jones, K. J., D. W. Pfaff, et al. (1985). "Early Estrogen-Induced Nuclear-Changes in Rat Hypothalamic Ventromedial Neurons—An Ultrastructural and Morphometric Analysis." *Journal of Comparative Neurology* 239(3): 255–266.

Jones, S., C. Johnson-Yale, et al. (2008). "Academic Work, The Internet and US College Students." *Internet and Higher Education* 11(3–4): 165–177.

Jones, T. F. (2008). "Averting White Male (Ab)Normality: Psychiatric Representations and Treatment of 'Homosexuality' in 1960s South Africa." *Journal of Southern African Studies* 34(2): 397–410.

Joseph, R. (2000). "The Evolution of Sex Differences in Language, Sexuality, and Visual-Spatial Skills." *Archives of Sexual Behavior* 29(1): 35–66.

Jost, A. (1953). "Problems of Fetal Endocrinology—The Gonadal and Hypophyseal Hormones." *Recent Progress in Hormone Research* 8: 379–418.

Jost, A. (1970). "Hormonal Factors in Sex Differentiation of Mammalian Foetus." *Philosophical Transactions of the Royal Society of London Series B-Biological Sciences* 259(828): 119–130.

Joyal, C. C., D. N. Black, et al. (2007). "The Neuropsychology and Neurology of Sexual Deviance: A Review and Pilot Study." *Sexual Abuse: A Journal of Research and Treatment* 19(2): 155–173.

Jozifkova, E., and J. Flegr (2006). "Dominance, Submissivity (and Homosexuality) in General Population. Testing of Evolutionary Hypothesis of Sadomasochism by Internet-Trap-Method." *Neuroendocrinology Letters* 27(6): 711–718.

Jozifkova, E. and M. Konvicka (2009). "Sexual Arousal by Higher- and Lower-Ranking Partner: Manifestation of a Mating Strategy?" *Journal of Sexual Medicine* 6(12): 3327–3334.

BIBLIOGRAPHY

Kaas, J. H. (1999). "The Transformation of Association Cortex into Sensory Cortex." *Brain Research Bulletin* 50(5–6): 425–425.

Kaasinen, V., K. Nagren, et al. (2001) "Sex Differences in Extrastriatal Dopamine D-2-Like Receptors in the Human Brain," *American Journal of Psychiatry* 158(2): 308–311.

Kael, P. (1968). *Kiss Kiss Bang Bang.* Boston: Little.

Kael, P. (1970). *Kiss Kiss Bang Bang.* London: Calder & Boyars.

Kahr, B. (2008). *Who's Been Sleeping In Your Head?: The Secret World of Sexual Fantasies.* New York: Basic Books.

Kafka, M. P. (1997). "Hypersexual Desire in Males: An Operational Definition and Clinical Implications for Males with Paraphilias and Paraphilia-Related Disorders." *Archives of Sexual Behavior* 26(5): 505–526.

Kafka, M. P. (2003). "The Monoamine Hypothesis for the Pathophysiology of Paraphilic Disorders: An Update." *Annals of the New York Academy of Sciences.* 989: 86–94.

Kafka, M. P. (2003). "Sex Offending and Sexual Appetite: The Clinical and Theoretical Relevance of Hypersexual Desire." *International Journal of Offender Therapy and Comparative Criminology* 47(4): 439–451.

Kafka, M. P., and J. Hennen (1999). "The Paraphilia-Related Disorders: An Empirical Investigation of Nonparaphilic Hypersexuality Disorders in Outpatient Males." *Journal of Sex & Marital Therapy* 25(4): 305–319.

Kafka, M. P., and J. Hennen (2002). "A DSM-IV Axis I Comorbidity Study of Males (n =120) with Paraphilias and Paraphilia-Related Disorders." *Sexual Abuse: A Journal of Research and Treatment* 14(4): 349–366.

Kafka, M. P., and R. A. Prentky (1997). "Compulsive Sexual Behavior Characteristics." *American Journal of Psychiatry* 154(11): 1632–1632.

Kahr, B. (2008). *Who's Been Sleeping In Your Head?: The Secret World of Sexual Fantasies.* New York: Basic Books.

Kam, C. D., J. R. Wilking, et al. (2007). "Beyond the "Narrow Data Base": Another Convenience Sample for Experimental Research." *Political Behavior* 29(4): 415–440.

Kandel, E. R., J. H. Schwartz, et al. (2000). *Principles of Neural Science.* New York: McGraw-Hill, Health Professions Division.

Kansaku, K., A. Yamaura, et al. (2000). "Sex Differences in Lateralization Revealed in the Posterior Language Areas." *Cerebral Cortex* 10(9): 866–872.

Kaplan, H., K. Hill, et al. (2000). "A Theory of Human Life History Evolution: Diet, Intelligence, and Longevity." *Evolutionary Anthropology* 9(4): 156–185.

Karama, S., A. R. Lecours, et al. (2002). "Areas of Brain Activation in Males and Females During Viewing of Erotic Film Excerpts." *Human Brain Mapping* 16(1): 1–13.

Karasic, D. and J. Drescher (2005). "Introduction: Sexual and Gender Diagnoses of the Diagnostic and Statistical Manual (DSM): A Reevaluation." *Journal of Psychology & Human Sexuality* 17(3–4): 1–5.

BIBLIOGRAPHY

Karasic, D. and J. Drescher (2005). *Sexual and Gender Diagnoses of the Diagnostic and Statistical Manual (DSM): A Reevaluation.* New York: Haworth Press.

Karremans, J. C., W. E. Frankenhuis, et al. (2010). "Blind Men Prefer a Low Waist-to-Hip Ratio." *Evolution and Human Behavior* 31(3): 182–186.

Katz, A. (2007). "'Not Tonight, Dear': The Elusive Female Libido." *American Journal of Nursing* 107(12): 32–34.

Keegan, J. M. W. (2001). "The Neurobiology, Neuropharmacology, and Pharmacological Treatment of the Paraphilias and Compulsive Sexual Behaviour." *Canadian Journal of Psychiatry* 46(1): 26–34.

Kelly, B. C., D. S. Bimbi, et al. (2009). "Sexual Compulsivity and Sexual Behaviors Among Gay and Bisexual Men and Lesbian and Bisexual Women." *Journal of Sex Research* 46(4): 301–308.

Kempner, J. (2009). "The Chilling Effect: How Do Researchers React to Controversy?" *PLoS One* 6(1): 116.

Kendrick, K. M., M. R. Hinton, et al. (1998). "Mothers Determine Sexual Preferences." *Nature* 395(6699): 229–230.

Kennedy, E. C. (1970). "The American Psychological Association's Convention Discussed . . . The Soma-Environmental Revolution, Pornography, Synergistic Consciousness, Sex with Patients." *New York Times Magazine,* December 6, 1970.

Kenrick, D. T., and R. C. Keefe (1992). "Age Preferences in Mates Reflect Sex-Differences in Reproductive Strategies." *Behavioral and Brain Sciences* 15(1): 75–+.

Kenrick, D. T. and R. C. Keefe (1992). "Sex-Differences in Age Preference—Universal Reality or Ephemeral Construction—Authors Response." *Behavioral and Brain Sciences* 15(1): 119–133.

Kessler, D. (2009). *The End of Overeating: Taking Control of the Insatiable American Appetite.* New York: Rodale.

Keverne, E. B. (2004). "Importance of Olfactory and Vomeronasal Systems for Male Sexual Function." *Physiology & Behavior* 83(2): 177–187.

Kilgallon, S. J., and L. W. Simmons (2005). "Image Content Influences Men's Semen Quality." *Biology Letters* 1(3): 253–255.

Kim, W., B. R. Jin, et al. (2009). "Treatment with Selective Serotonin Reuptake Inhibitors and Mirtapazine Results in Differential Brain Activation by Visual Erotic Stimuli in Patients with Major Depressive Disorder." *Psychiatry Investigation* 6(2): 85–95.

Kimura, D. (1983). "Sex-Differences in Cerebral Organization for Speech and Praxic Functions." *Canadian Journal of Psychology—Revue Canadienne De Psychologie* 37(1): 19–35.

Kimura, D., and R. A. Harshman (1984). "Sex-Differences in Brain Organization for Verbal and Non-Verbal Functions." *Progress in Brain Research* 61: 423–441.

Kinzie, M. B., and D. R. D. Joseph (2008). "Gender Differences in Game Activity Preferences of Middle School Children: Implications for Educational Game Design." *Educational Technology Research and Development* 56(5–6): 643–663.

Kirenskaya-Berus, A. V., and A. A. Tkachenko (2003). "Characteristic Features of EEG Spectral Characteristics in Persons with Deviant Sexual Behavior." *Fiziologiya Cheloveka* 29(3): 22–32.

Kleiman, D. G. (1977). "Monogamy in Mammals." *Quarterly Review of Biology* 52(1): 39–69.

Kleinplatz, P. J., and C. Moser (2006). "Politics Versus Science—An Addendum and Response to Drs. Spitzer and Fink." *Journal of Psychology & Human Sexuality* 17(3): 135–139.

Klibanski, A. (2010). "Prolactinomas." *New England Journal of Medicine* 362(13): 1219–1226.

Klos, K. J., J. H. Bower, et al. (2005). "Pathological Hypersexuality Predominantly Linked to Adjuvant Dopamine Agonist Therapy in Parkinson's Disease and Multiple System Atrophy." *Parkinsonism & Related Disorders* 11(6): 381–386.

Klucken, T., J. Schweckendiek, et al. (2009). "Neural Activations of the Acquisition of Conditioned Sexual Arousal: Effects of Contingency Awareness and Sex." *Journal of Sexual Medicine* 6(11): 3071–3085.

Klusmann, D. (2002). "Sexual Motivation and the Duration Of Partnership." *Archives of Sexual Behavior* 31(3): 275–287.

Knafo, D., and Y. Jaffe (1984). "Sexual Fantasizing in Males and Females." *Journal of Research in Personality* 18(4): 451–462.

Knight, A. (2007). *Passionate Ink: A Guide to Writing Erotic Romance.* Carson City, NV: LooseID.

Knoll, J. L., and R. R. Hazelwood (2009). "Becoming the Victim: Beyond Sadism in Serial Sexual Murderers." *Aggression and Violent Behavior* 14(2): 106–114.

Ko, C.-H., J.-Y. Yen, et al. (2009). "Predictive Values of Psychiatric Symptoms for Internet Addiction in Adolescents: A 2-Year Prospective Study." *Archives of Pediatriatric and Adolescent Medicine* 163(10): 937–943.

Koechlin, E., C. Ody, et al. (2003). "The Architecture of Cognitive Control in the Human Prefrontal Cortex." *Science* 302(5648): 1181–1185.

Kokko, H., R. Brooks, et al. (2003). "The Evolution of Mate Choice and Mating Biases." *Proceedings of the Royal Society of London Series B-Biological Sciences* 270(1515): 653–664.

Koksal, F., M. Domjan, et al. (2004). "An Animal Model of Fetishism." *Behaviour Research and Therapy* 42(12): 1421–1434.

Komisaruk, B. R., and B. Whipple (2005). "Functional MRI of the Brain During Orgasm in Women." *Annual Review of Sex Research* 16: 62–86.

Koukounas, E., and M. P. McCabe (2001). "Sexual and Emotional Variables Influencing Sexual Response to Erotica: A Psychophysiological Investigation." *Archives of Sexual Behavior* 30(4): 393–408.

Koukounas, E., and R. Over (1993). "Habituation and Dishabituation of Male Sexual Arousal." *Behaviour Research and Therapy* 31(6): 575–585.

Koziol, L. (2008). *Subcortical Structures and Cognition: Implications for Neuropsychological Assessment.* New York: Springer.

Krafft-Ebing, R. v. (1887), *Psychopathia Sexualis: Mit Besonderer Berücksichtigung Der Conträren Sexualempfindung: Eine Klinisch-Forensische Studie*. Stuttgart: Ferdinand Enke.

Krafft-Ebing, R. v., and F. J. Rebman (1906), *Psychopathia Sexualis, with Especial Reference to the Antipathic Sexual Instinct: A Medico-Forensic Study*. New York: Rebman Co.

Kraus, S. W., and B. Russell (2008). "Early Sexual Experiences: The Role of Internet Access and Sexually Explicit Material." *Cyberpsychology & Behavior* 11(2): 162–168.

Krause, M. (2003). "Behavioral Mechanisms and the Neurobiology of Conditioned Sexual Responding." *International Review of Neurobiology* 56: 1–34.

Krueger, R. B. (2010). "The DSM Diagnostic Criteria for Sexual Masochism." *Archives of Sexual Behavior* 39(2): 346–356.

Krug, R., W. Plihal, et al. (2000). "Selective Influence of the Menstrual Cycle on Perception of Stimuli with Reproductive Significance: An Event-Related Potential Study." *Psychophysiology* 37(1): 111–122.

Kruger, D. J. (2010). "Female Scarcity Reduces Women's Marital Ages and Increases Variance in Men's Marital Ages." *Evolutionary Psychology* 8(3): 420–431.

Kruger, D. J. (2009). "Male Scarcity Is Differentially Related to Male Marital Likelihood Across the Life Course." *Evolutionary Psychology* 7(2): 280–287.

Kruger, D. J., and E. Schlemmer (2009). "When Men Are Scarce, Good Men Are Even Harder to Find: Life History, the Sex Ratio, and the Proportion of Men Married." *Journal of Social, Evolutionary, and Cultural Psychology* 3: 93–104.

Kruger, D. J. (2006). "Male Facial Masculinity Influences Attributions of Personality and Reproductive Strategy." *Personal Relationships* 13(4): 451–463.

Kruger, T., M. S. Exton, et al. (1998). "Neuroendocrine and Cardiovascular Response to Sexual Arousal and Orgasm in Men." *Psychoneuroendocrinology* 23(4): 401–411.

Kruijver, F. P. M., J. N. Zhou, et al. (2000). "Male-to-Female Transsexuals Have Female Neuron Numbers in a Limbic Nucleus." *Journal of Clinical Endocrinology and Metabolism* 85(5): 2034–2041.

Kudwa, A. E., C. Bodo, et al. (2005). "A Previously Uncharacterized Role for Estrogen Receptor Beta: Defeminization of Male Brain and Behavior." *Proceedings of the National Academy of Sciences of the United States of America* 102(12): 4608–4612.

Kudwa, A. E., F. J. Lopez, et al. (2010). "A Selective Androgen Receptor Modulator Enhances Male-Directed Sexual Preference, Proceptive Behavior, and Lordosis Behavior in Sexually Experienced, But Not Sexually Naive, Female Rats." *Endocrinology* 151(6): 2659–2668.

Kuipers, G. (2006). "The Social Construction of Digital Danger: Debating, Defusing and Inflating the Moral Dangers of Online Humor and

BIBLIOGRAPHY

Pornography in the Netherlands and the United States." *New Media & Society* 8(3): 379–400.

Kukkonen, T. M., Y. M. Binik, et al. (2007). "Thermography as a Physiological Measure of Sexual Arousal in Both Men and Women." *Journal of Sexual Medicine* 4(1): 93–105.

Laan, E. and S. Both (2008). "What Makes Women Experience Desire?" *Feminism & Psychology* 18(4): 505–514.

Laan, E., W. Everaerd, et al. (1993). "Performance Demand and Sexual Arousal in Women." *Behaviour Research and Therapy* 31(1): 25–35.

Laan, E., W. Everaerd, et al. (1995). "Assessment of Female Sexual Arousal— Response Specificity and Construct-Validity." *Psychophysiology* 32(5): 476–485.

Laan, E., W. Everaerd, et al. (1995). "Determinants of Subjective Experience of Sexual Arousal in Women—Feedback from Genital Arousal and Erotic Stimulus Content." *Psychophysiology* 32(5): 444–451.

Laan, E., W. Everaerd, et al. (1995). "Mood and Sexual Arousal in Women." *Behaviour Research and Therapy* 33(4): 441–443.

Laan, E., H. S. Scholte, and A. van Stegeren. (2006) "Brain Imaging of Gender Differences in Sexual Excitation and Inhibition." Invited presentation for the 12th annual World Congress of the International Society for Sexual Medicine, Cairo, Egypt.

Lachowsky, M. (2001). "After Reading the Report of the International Consensus Conference on Female Sexual Dysfunction." *Journal of Sex & Marital Therapy* 27(2): 157–158.

Lalumiere, M. L., and V. L. Quinsey (1998). "Pavlovian Conditioning of Sexual Interests in Human Males." *Archives of Sexual Behavior* 27(3): 241–252.

Lamm, C., and T. Singer (2010). "The Role of Anterior Insular Cortex in Social Emotions." *Brain Structure & Function* 214(5–6): 579–591.

Langstrom, N., and R. K. Hanson (2006). "High Rates of Sexual Behavior in the General Population: Correlates and Predictors." *Archives of Sexual Behavior* 35(1): 37–52.

Langstrom, N., and M. C. Seto (2006). "Exhibitionistic and Voyeuristic Behavior in a Swedish National Population Survey." *Archives of Sexual Behavior* 35(4): 427–435.

Langstrom, N., and K. J. Zucker (2005). "Transvestic Fetishism in the General Population: Prevalence and Correlates." *Journal of Sex & Marital Therapy* 31(2): 87–95.

Lanthier, R. P., and R. C. Windham (2004). "Internet Use and College Adjustment: The Moderating Role of Gender" *Computers in Human Behavior* 20(5): 591–606.

Larsson, K., and S. Ahlenius (1999). *Brain and Sexual Behavior.* New York Academy of Sciences.

Laumann, E. O. (1994). *The Social Organization of Sexuality: Sexual Practices in the United States.* Chicago: University of Chicago Press.

BIBLIOGRAPHY

Laumann, E. O., A. Das, et al. (2008). "Sexual Dysfunction Among Older Adults: Prevalence and Risk Factors from a Nationally Representative U.S. Probability Sample of Men and Women 57–85 Years Of Age Prevalence." *Journal of Sexual Medicine* 5(10): 2300–2311.

Laumann, E. O., D. B. Glasser, et al. (2009). "A Population-Based Survey of Sexual Activity, Sexual Problems and Associated Help-Seeking Behavior Patterns in Mature Adults in the United States of America." *International Journal of Impotence Research* 21(3): 171–178.

Laumann, E. O., R. T. Michael, et al. (1994). "A Political-History of the National Sex Survey of Adults." *Family Planning Perspectives* 26(1): 34–38.

Laumann, E. O., A. Paik, et al. (1999). "Sexual Dysfunction in the United States—Prevalence and Predictors." *Journal of the American Medical Association* 281(6): 537–544.

Laumann, E. O., A. Paik, et al. (2006). "A Cross-National Study of Subjective Sexual Well-Being Among Older Women and Men: Findings from the Global Study of Sexual Attitudes and Behaviors." *Archives of Sexual Behavior* 35(2): 145–161.

Law, S. W., E. M. Apostolakis, et al. (1994). "Hormonal-Regulation of Hypothalamic Gene-Expression—Identification of Multiple Novel Estrogen-Induced Genes." *Journal of Steroid Biochemistry and Molecular Biology* 51(3–4): 131–136.

Lawrence, A. A. (2006). "Clinical and Theoretical Parallels Between Desire for Limb Amputation and Gender Identity Disorder." *Archives of Sexual Behavior* 35(3): 263–278.

Lawrence, A. A. (2009). "Erotic Target Location Errors: An Underappreciated Paraphilic Dimension." *Journal of Sex Research* 46(2–3): 194–215.

Lawrence, A. A. and J. Love-Crowell (2008). "Psychotherapists' Experience With Clients Who Engage in Consensual Sadomasochism: A Qualitative Study." *Journal of Sex & Marital Therapy* 34(1): 63–81.

Lawrence, A. A., and J. M. Bailey (2009). "Transsexual Groups in Veale et al. (2008) Are 'Autogynephilic' and 'Even More Autogynephilic.'" *Archives of Sexual Behavior* 38(2): 173–175.

Lawrence, A. A., E. M. Latty, et al. (2005). "Measurement of Sexual Arousal in Postoperative Male-to-Female Transsexuals Using Vaginal Photoplethysmography." *Archives of Sexual Behavior* 34(2): 135–145.

Lawrence, A. A., and J. Love-Crowell (2008). "Psychotherapists' Experience with Clients Who Engage in Consensual Sadomasochism: A Qualitative Study." *Journal of Sex & Marital Therapy* 34(1): 63–81.

Lawrence, K. F., and M. C. Schraefel (2005). "Amateur Fiction Online—The Web of Community Trust: A Case Study in Community Focused Design for the SemanticWeb." 1st AKT Doctoral Colloquium. Milton Keynes.

Law-Smith, M. J., D. I. Perrett, et al. (2006). "Facial Appearance Is a Cue to Oestrogen Levels in Women." *Proceedings of the Royal Society B-Biological Sciences* 273(1583): 135–140.

BIBLIOGRAPHY

Laws, D. R., and W. T. O'Donohue. (2008) *Sexual Deviance: Theory, Assessment, and Treatment.* New York; London: Guilford Press.

Leavitt, J. W. (1982). "The Mosher Survey—Sexual Attitudes of 45 Victorian Women." *Bulletin of the History of Medicine* 56(2): 295–296.

Leckman, J. F. (2004). "Commentary: Current Evolutionary Perspectives on Adolescent Romantic Relations and Sexuality." *Journal of the American Academy of Child and Adolescent Psychiatry* 43(1): 20–23.

LeDoux, J. E. (2000). "Emotion Circuits in the Brain." *Annual Review of Neuroscience* 23: 155–184.

Lee, B. K., and R. Tamborini (2005). "Third-Person Effect and Internet Pornography: The Influence of Collectivism and Internet Self-Efficacy." *Journal of Communication* 55(2): 292–310.

Lee, J. K. P., H. J. Jackson, et al. (2002). "Developmental Risk Factors for Sexual Offending." *Child Abuse & Neglect* 26(1): 73–92.

Lee, S. J., S. Bartolic, et al. (2009). "Predicting Children's Media Use in the USA: Differences in Cross-Sectional and Longitudinal Analysis." *British Journal of Developmental Psychology* 27: 123–143.

Lehmann, J., and C. Boesch (2004). "To Fission or to Fusion: Effects of Community Size on Wild Chimpanzee (Pan Troglodytes Verus) Social Organisation." *Behavioral Ecology and Sociobiology* 56(3): 207–216.

Lehne, G. K., and J. Money (2003). "Multiplex Versus Multiple Taxonomy of Paraphilia: Case Example." *Sex Abuse* 15(1): 61–72.

Leiblum, S. R., and M. L. Chivers (2007). "Normal and Persistent Genital Arousal in Women: New Perspectives." *Journal of Sex & Marital Therapy* 33(4): 357–373.

Leibold, J. M., and A. R. McConnell (2004). "Women, Sex, Hostility, Power, and Suspicion: Sexually Aggressive Men's Cognitive Associations." *Journal of Experimental Social Psychology* 40(2): 256–263.

Leitenberg, H., M. J. Detzer, et al. (1993). "Gender Differences in Masturbation and the Relation of Masturbation Experience in Preadolescence And or Early Adolescence to Sexual-Behavior and Sexual Adjustment in Young Adulthood." *Archives of Sexual Behavior* 22(2): 87–98.

Leitenberg, H., and K. Henning (1995). "Sexual Fantasy." *Psychological Bulletin* 117(3): 469–496.

Lenroot, R. K., and J. N. Giedd "Sex Differences in the Adolescent Brain." *Brain and Cognition* 72(1): 46–55.

Leon-Carrion, J., J. F. Martin-Rodriguez, et al. (2007). "Does Dorsolateral Prefrontal Cortex (DLPFC) Activation Return to Baseline When Sexual Stimuli Cease? The role of DLPFC in Visual Sexual Stimulation." *Neuroscience Letters* 416(1): 55–60.

Leutmezer, F., W. Serles, et al. (1999). "Genital Automatisms in Complex Partial Seizures." *Neurology* 52(6): 1188–1191.

LeVay, S. (1991). "A Difference in Hypothalamic Structure Between Heterosexual and Homosexual Men." *Science* 253(5023): 1034–1037.

BIBLIOGRAPHY

LeVay, S. (2010). *Gay, Straight, and the Reason Why: The Science of Sexual Orientation.* Oxford; New York: Oxford University Press.

Lever, J., D. A. Frederick, et al. (2006). "Does Size Matter?: Men's and Women's Views on Penis Size Across the Lifespan." *Psychology of Men and Masculinity* 7(3): 129–143.

Levin, R. J. (1992). "The Mechanisms of Human Female Sexual Arousal." *Annual Review of Sex Research* 3: 1–48.

Levin, R. J. (2002). "The Physiology of Sexual Arousal in the Human Female: A Recreational and Procreational Synthesis." *Archives of Sexual Behavior* 31(5): 405–411.

Levin, R. J. (2005). "Sexual Arousal—Its Physiological Roles in Human Reproduction." *Annual Review of Sex Research* 16: 154–189.

Levin, R. J., and W. van Berlo (2004). "Sexual Arousal and Orgasm in Subjects Who Experience Forced or Non-Consensual Sexual Stimulation—A Review." *Journal of Clinical Forensic Medicine* 11(2): 82–88.

Levine, R. A. (1959). "Gusii Sex Offenses—A Study in Social-Control." *American Anthropologist* 61(6): 965–990.

Levine, S. B., C. B. Risen, et al. (2003). *Handbook of Clinical Sexuality for Mental Health Professionals.* New York: Brunner-Routledge.

Levine, S. B., C. B. Risen, et al. (2010). *Handbook of Clinical Sexuality for Mental Health Professionals.* New York: Brunner-Routledge.

Levitt, S. D. and J. A. List (2007). "What do laboratory experiments measuring social preferences reveal about the real world?" *Journal of Economic Perspectives* 21(2): 153–174.

Le Vome, S. (1982). "The Dreams of Young Gusii Kenya Women: A Content Analysis." *Ethnology* 21(1): 63–78.

Levy, A. (2006). *Female Chauvinist Pigs: Women and the Rise of Raunch Culture.* New York: Free Press.

Lewis, K. P., and R. A. Barton (2006). "Amygdala Size and Hypothalamus Size Predict Social Play Frequency in Nonhuman Primates: A Comparative Analysis Using Independent Contrasts." *Journal of Comparative Psychology* 120(1): 31–37.

Lewis, M. (2007). *The Blind Side: Evolution of a Game.* New York. London: W. W. Norton.

Lewis, R. W., K. S. Fugl-Meyer, et al. (2004). "Epidemiology/Risk Factors of Sexual Dysfunction." *Journal of Sexual Medicine* 1(1): 35–39.

Lick, J. R., and T. E. Unger (1975). "External Validity of Laboratory Fear Assessment—Implications from 2 Case Studies." *Journal of Consulting and Clinical Psychology* 43(6): 864–866.

Lieberman, D. (2007). "Inbreeding, Incest, and the Incest Taboo: The State of Knowledge at the Turn of the Century." *Evolution and Human Behavior* 28(3): 211–213.

Lieberman, D., and D. Symons (1998). "Sibling Incest Avoidance: From Westermarck to Wolf." *Quarterly Review of Biology* 73(4): 463–466.

Lieberman, D., J. Tooby, et al. (2003). "Does Morality Have A Biological Basis? An Empirical Test of the Factors Governing Moral Sentiments Relating to Incest." *Proceedings of the Royal Society of London Series B-Biological Sciences* 270(1517): 819–826.

Lieberman, D., J. Tooby, et al. (2007). "The Architecture of Human Kin Detection." *Nature* 445(7129): 727–731.

Lieberman, M. D., E. T. Berkman, et al. (2009). "Correlations in Social Neuroscience Aren't Voodoo: Commentary on Vul et al. (2009)." *Perspectives on Psychological Science* 4(3): 299–307.

Liljeros, F., C. R. Edling, et al. (2001). "The Web of Human Sexual Contacts." *Nature* 411(6840): 907–908.

Lillie, F. R. (1916). "The Theory of the Free-Martin." *Science* 43(1113): 611–613.

Link, B. G., and J. Phelan (1995). "Social Conditions as Fundamental Causes of Disease." *Journal of Health and Social Behavior*: 80–94.

Lippa, R. (2009). "Sex Differences in Sex Drive, Sociosexuality, and Height Across 53 Nations: Testing Evolutionary and Social Structural Theories." *Archives of Sexual Behavior* 38(5): 631–651.

Lippa, R. A. (2006). "Is High Sex Drive Associated with Increased Sexual Attraction to Both Sexes? It Depends on Whether You Are Male or Female." *Psychological Science* 17(1): 46–52.

Lippa, R. A. (2007). "The Preferred Traits of Mates in a Cross-National Study of Heterosexual and Homosexual Men and Women: An Examination of Biological and Cultural Influences." *Archives of Sexual Behavior* 36(2): 193–208.

Lippa, R. A. (2007). "The Relation Between Sex Drive and Sexual Attraction to Men and Women: A Cross-National Study of Heterosexual, Bisexual, and Homosexual Men And Women." *Archives of Sexual Behavior* 36(2): 209–222.

Lippa, R. A. (2008). "Sex Differences and Sexual Orientation Differences in Personality: Findings from the BBC Internet Survey." *Archives of Sexual Behavior* 37(1): 173–187.

Livingstone, M. (2002). *Vision and Art: The Biology of Seeing*. New York: Harry N. Abrams.

Lo, V. H., and R. Wei (2005). "Exposure to Internet Pornography and Taiwanese Adolescents' Sexual Attitudes and Behavior." *Journal of Broadcasting & Electronic Media* 49(2): 221–237.

Lufgren-Mertenson, L., and S.-A. Mensson (2009). "Lust, Love, and Life: A Qualitative Study of Swedish Adolescents' Perceptions and Experiences with Pornography." *Journal of Sex Research* 3: 1–12.

Loftus, D. (2002). *Watching Sex: How Men Really Respond to Pornography*. New York; Berkeley, CA: Thunder's Mouth Press.

Lombardo, M. V., B. Chakrabarti, et al. (2009). "A typical Neural Self-Representation in Autism." *Brain* 133: 611–624.

Longo, M. R., E. Azanon, et al. (2010). "More Than Skin Deep: Body Representation Beyond Primary Somatosensory Cortex." *Neuropsychologia* 48(3): 655–668.

Lorenz, K. (1935). "Der Kumpan in der Umwelt des Vogels." *Journal Ornithologie* 83: 137–213.

Louis, C. K., and Hartman, S. (Directors) (2008). *Louis C.K: Chewed Up* [DVD]. United States: Image Entertainment.

Lowenstein, L. F. (2002). "Fetishes and Their Associated Behavior." *Sexuality and Disability* 20(2): 135–147.

Lu, H. P., and K. L. Hsiao (2009). "Gender Differences in Reasons for Frequent Blog Posting." *Online Information Review* 33(1): 135–156.

Lubinski, D., and B. Camilla Persson (1992). "Gender Differences in Abilities and Preferences Among the Gifted: Implications for the Math-Science Pipeline." *Current Directions in Psychological Science* 1(2): 61–66.

Lucas, J. W. (2003). "Theory-Testing, Generalization, and the Problem of External Validity." *Sociological Theory* 21(3): 236–253.

Lukaszewski, A. W., and J. R. Roney (2009). "Estimated Hormones Predict Women's Mate Preferences for Dominant Personality Traits." *Personality and Individual Differences* 47(3): 191–196.

Lundberg, P. O., C. Ertekin, et al. (2001). "Neurosexology—Guidelines for Neurologists." *European Journal of Neurology* 8: 2–24.

Lunde, I., G. K. Larsen, et al. (1991). "Sexual Desire, Orgasm, and Sexual Fantasies: A Study of 625 Danish Women Born in 1910, 1936, and 1958." *Journal of Sex Education & Therapy* 17(2): 111–115.

Lutchmaya, S., and S. Baron-Cohen (2002). "Human Sex Differences in Social and Non-Social Looking Preferences, at 12 Months of Age." *Infant Behavior & Development* 25(3): 319–325.

Lykins, A. D., M. Meana, et al. (2006). "Detection of Differential Viewing Patterns to Erotic and Non-Erotic Stimuli Using Eye-Tracking Methodology." *Archives of Sexual Behavior* 35(5): 569–575.

Lykins, A. D., M. Meana, et al. (2008). "Sex Differences in Visual Attention to Erotic and Non-Erotic Stimuli." *Archives of Sexual Behavior* 37(2): 219–228.

Lynn, M. (2009). "Determinants and Consequences of Female Attractiveness and Sexiness: Realistic Tests with Restaurant Waitresses." *Archives of Sexual Behavior* 38(5): 737–745.

Maccoby, E. E. (2000). "Perspectives on Gender Development." *International Journal of Behavioral Development* 24(4): 398–406.

Maccoby, E. E. (2002). "Gender and Group Process: A Developmental Perspective." *Current Directions in Psychological Science* 11(2): 54–58.

Maccoby, E. E., and C. N. Jacklin (1974). "Myth, Reality and Shades of Gray—What We Know and Don't Know About Sex Differences." *Psychology Today* 8(7): 109–112.

Mackay, J. (2000). *The Penguin Atlas of Human Sexual Behavior.* New York: Penguin Press.

Maclean, P. D., and D. W. Ploog (1962). "Cerebral Representation of Penile Erection." *Journal of Neurophysiology* 25(1): 29–+.

BIBLIOGRAPHY

Maclusky, N. J., and F. Naftolin (1981). "Sexual-Differentiation of the Central Nervous-System." *Science* 211(4488): 1294–1303.

Macwilliams, M. W. (2008) *Japanese Visual Culture: Explorations in the World of Manga and Anime.* New York: M. E. Sharpe.

Maddox, A., G. Rhoades, et al. (2009) "Viewing Sexually-Explicit Materials Alone or Together: Associations with Relationship Quality." *Archives of Sexual Behavior,* in press. Epub ahead of print. Retrieved, August 2010, http://www.ncbi.nlm.nih.gov/pubmed/20039112

Magnet, S. (2007). "Feminist Sexualities, Race and the Internet: An Investigation of Suicidegirls.com." *New Media & Society* 9(4): 577–602.

Mah, K., and Y. M. Binik (2001). "The Nature of Human Orgasm: A Critical Review of Major Trends." *Clinical Psychology Review* 21(6): 823–856.

Mah, K., and Y. A. Binik (2005). "Are Orgasms in the Mind or the Body? Psychosocial Versus Physiological Correlates of Orgasmic Pleasure and Satisfaction." *Journal of Sex & Marital Therapy* 31(3): 187–200.

Majdandzic, M., and D. C. van den Boom (2007). "Multimethod Longitudinal Assessment of Temperament in Early Childhood." *Journal of Personality* 75(1): 121–167.

Malamuth, N. M. (1981). "Rape Proclivity Among Males." *Journal of Social Issues* 37(4): 138–157.

Malamuth, N. M. (1996). "Sexually Explicit Media, Gender Differences, and Evolutionary Theory." *Journal of Communication* 46(3): 8–31.

Malamuth, N. M., T. Addison, et al. (2000). "Pornography and Sexual Aggression: Are There Reliable Effects and Can We Understand Them?" *Annual Review of Sexual Research* 11: 26–91.

Malamuth, N. M., and J. Ceniti (1986). "Repeated Exposure to Violent and Nonviolent Pornography—Likelihood of Raping Ratings and Laboratory Aggression Against Women." *Aggressive Behavior* 12(2): 129–137.

Malu, M. K., R. Challenor, et al. (2004). "Seeking and Engaging in Internet Sex: A Survey of Patients Attending Genitourinary Medicine Clinics in Plymouth and in London." *International Journal of STD & AIDS* 15(11): 720–724.

Mani, S. K., J. D. Blaustein, et al. (1994). "Inhibition of Rat Sexual-Behavior by Antisense Oligonucleotides to the Progesterone–Receptor." *Endocrinology* 135(4): 1409–1414.

Maravilla, K., N. Kleinhans, et al. (2009). "fMRI Measurements of Cerebral Responses of Women with Sexual Arousal Disorder Compared with Control Subjects." *Journal of Sexual Medicine* 6: 372–373.

Maravilla, K., and C. Yang (2007). "Sex and the Brain: The Role of fMRI for Assessment of Sexual Function and Response." *International Journal of Impotence Research* 19(1): 25–29.

Marczyk, J. B., and T. K. Shackelford (2010). "A Biased, Incomplete Perspective on the Evolution of Human Mating Systems: A Review of Alan F. Dixson, Sexual Selection and the Origins of Human Mating Systems." *Evolutionary Psychology* 8(1): 31–36.

BIBLIOGRAPHY

Marin, O., W. Smeets, et al. (1998). "Evolution of the Basal Ganglia in Tetrapods: A New Perspective Based on Recent Studies in Amphibians." *Trends in Neurosciences* 21(11): 487–494.

Marlowe, F. W. (2004). "Mate Preferences Among Hadza Hunter-Gatherers." *Human Nature: An Interdisciplinary Biosocial Perspective* 15(4): 365–376.

Marner, L., J. R. Nyengaard, J. R., Y. Tang., and B. Pakkenberg. (2003). "Marked Loss of Myelinated Nerve Fibers in the Human Brain with Age." *The Journal of Comparative Neurology* 462(2): 144–152.

Marsh, A. A., K. S. Blair, et al. (2009). "Dominance and Submission: The Ventrolateral Prefrontal Cortex and Responses to Status Cues." *Journal of Cognitive Neuroscience* 21(4): 713–724.

Marshall, W. L. (2007). "Diagnostic Issues, Multiple Paraphilias, and Comorbid Disorders in Sexual Offenders: Their Incidence and Treatment." *Aggression and Violent Behavior* 12(1): 16–35.

Marshall, W. L., D. R. Laws, et al. (1989). *Handbook of Sexual Assault: Issues, Theories, and Treatment of the Offender.* New York: Plenum Press.

Marson, L., and A. Z. Murphy (2006). "Identification of Neural Circuits Involved in Female Genital Responses in the Rat: A Dual Virus and Anterograde Tracing Study." *American Journal of Physiology-Regulatory Integrative and Comparative Physiology* 291(2): R419–R428.

Marthol, H., and M. J. Hills (2004). "Female Sexual Dysfunction: A Systematic Overview of Classification, Pathophysiology, Diagnosis and Treatment." *Fortschritte der Neurologie, Psychiatrie* 72(3): 121–135.

Martin, R. P., J. Wisenbaker, et al. (1997). "Gender Differences in Temperament at Six Months and Five Years." *Infant Behavior & Development* 20(3): 339–347.

Martin-Alguacil, N., J. M. Schober, et al. (2008). "Clitoral Sexual Arousal: Neuronal Tracing Study from the Clitoris Through the Spinal Tracts." *Journal of Urology* 180(4): 1241–1248.

Marumo, K., R. Takizawa, et al. (2009). "Gender Difference in Right Lateral Prefrontal Hemodynamic Response While Viewing Fearful Faces: A Multi-Channel Near-Infrared Spectroscopy Study." *Neuroscience Research* 63(2): 89–94.

Mataro, M., M. A. Jurado, et al. (2001). "Long-Term Effects of Bilateral Frontal Brain Lesion—60 Years After Injury with an Iron Bar." *Archives of Neurology* 58(7): 1139–1142.

Mathews, R., R. D. Jeffs, et al. (1998). "Cloacal Exstrophy—Improving the Quality of Life: The Johns Hopkins Experience." *Journal of Urology* 160(6): 2452–2456.

Matsumoto, A. (2000). *Sexual Differentiation of the Brain.* Boca Raton, FL: CRC Press.

Matsumoto-Oda, A. (1999). "Female Choice in the Opportunistic Mating of Wild Chimpanzees (Pan Troglodytes Schweinfurthii) at Mahale." *Behavioral Ecology and Sociobiology* 46(4): 258–266.

Maxon, R. M. (1976). "Gusii Oral Texts and Gusii Experience Under British Rule." *International Journal of African Historical Studies* 9(1): 74–80.

Mazur, T. (2005). "Gender Dysphoria and Gender Change in Androgen Insensitivity or Micropenis." *Archives of Sexual Behavior* 34(4): 411–421.

McBride, K. R., S. A. Sanders, et al. (2007). "Turning Sexual Science into News: Sex Research and the Media." *Journal of Sex Research* 44(4): 347–358.

McCall, K., and C. Meston (2006). "Cues Resulting In Desire For Sexual Activity In Women." *Journal of Sexual Medicine* 3(5): 838–852.

McCall, K. and C. Meston (2007). "Differences between pre- and postmenopausal women in cues for sexual desire." *Journal of Sexual Medicine* 4(2): 364–371.

McCall, K. M., and C. M. Meston (2007). "The Effects of False Positive and False Negative Physiological Feedback on Sexual Arousal: A Comparison of Women With or Without Sexual Arousal Disorder." *Archives of Sexual Behavior* 36(4): 518–530.

McCarthy, M. M., and A. T. M. Konkle (2005). "When Is a Sex Difference Not a Sex Difference?" *Frontiers in Neuroendocrinology* 26(2): 85–102.

McClure, S. M., M. K. York, et al. (2004). "The Neural Substrates of Reward Processing in Humans: The Modern Role of fMRI." *Neuroscientist* 10(3): 260–268.

McConaghy, N. (1999). "Unresolved Issues in Scientific Sexology." *Archives of Sexual Behavior* 28(4): 285–318.

McConnell, L. G. (1977). "Sexual Value System." *Journal of Marriage and Family Counseling* 3(1): 55–67.

McCray, J. A., M. D. Bailly, et al. (2005). "The External Validity of MMPI-2 Research Conducted Using College Samples Disproportionately Represented by Psychology Majors." *Personality and Individual Differences* 38(5): 1097–1105.

McEwen, B. S. (1988). "Steroid-Hormones and the Brain—Linking Nature and Nurture." *Neurochemical Research* 13(7): 663–669.

McFarlane, M., R. Kachur, et al. (2004). "Women, the Internet, and Sexually Transmitted Infections." *Journal of Women's Health* 13(6): 689–694.

McIntyre, M. H. (2003). "Digit Ratios, Childhood Gender Role Behavior, and Erotic Role Preferences of Gay Men." *Archives of Sexual Behavior* 32(6): 495–497.

McIntyre, M. H. (2006). "The Use of Digit Ratios as Markers for Perinatal Androgen Action." *Reproductive Biology and Endocrinology* 4: 9.

McIntyre, M. H., E. S. Barrett, et al. (2007). "Finger Length Ratio (2D : 4D) and Sex Differences in Aggression During a Simulated War Game." *Personality and Individual Differences* 42(4): 755–764.

McIntyre, M. H., J. F. Chapman, et al. (2007). "Index-to-Ring Finger Length Ratio (2D : 4D) Predicts Levels of Salivary Estradiol, But Not Progesterone, Over the Menstrual Cycle." *American Journal of Human Biology* 19(3): 434–436.

McKee, A. (2005). "The Objectification of Women in Mainstream Pornographic Videos in Australia." *Journal of Sex Research* 42(4): 277–290.

McKenna, K. E. (2000). "The Neural Control of Female Sexual Function." *Neurorehabilitation* 15(2): 133–143.

McKenna, K. E. (2002). "The Neurophysiology of Female Sexual Function." *World Journal of Urology* 20(2): 93–100.

McKenna, K. Y. A., and J. A. Bargh (1998). *Coming Out in the Age of the Internet: Identity "Demarginalization" Through Virtual Group Participation*, American Psychological Association.

McLelland, M. (2006/2007). "Why Are Japanese Girls' Comics Full of Boys Bonking?" *Refractory: A Journal of Entertainment Media*: 10.

Mead, N. L., R. F. Baumeister, et al. (2009). "Too Tired to Tell the Truth: Self-Control Resource Depletion and Dishonesty." *Journal of Experimental Social Psychology* 45(3): 594–597.

Meana, M. (2010). "Elucidating Women's (hetero)Sexual Desire: Definitional Challenges and Content Expansion." *Journal of Sex Research* 47(2): 104–122.

Meaney, M. J., and B. S. McEwen (1986). "Testosterone Implants into the Amygdala During the Neonatal-Period Masculinize the Social Play of Juvenile Female Rats." *Brain Research* 398(2): 324–328.

Meana, M., and S. E. Nunnink (2006). "Gender Differences in the Content of Cognitive Distraction During Sex." *Journal of Sex Research* 43(1): 59–67.

Mednick, R. A. (1977). "Gender-Specific Variances in Sexual Fantasy." *Journal of Personality Assessment* 41(3): 248–254.

Meerkerk, G. J., R. Van den Eijnden, et al. (2006). "Predicting Compulsive Internet Use: It's All About Sex!" *Cyberpsychology & Behavior* 9(1): 95–103.

Mehta, M. D. (2001). "Pornography in Usenet: A Study of 9,800 Randomly Selected Images." *Cyberpsychology & Behavior* 4(6): 695–703.

Mehta, M. D., and D. Plaza (1997). "Content Analysis of Pornographic Images Available on the Internet." *Information Society* 13(2): 153–161.

Melis, M. R, and A. Argiolas (1995). "Dopamine and Sexual-Behavior." *Neuroscience and Biobehavioral Reviews* 19(1): 19–38.

Meloy, T. S., and J. P. Southern (2006). "Neurally Augmented Sexual Function in Human Females: A Preliminary Investigation." *Neuromodulation* 9(1): 34–40.

Messiah, A., P. Blin, et al. (1995). "Sexual Repertoires of Heterosexuals— Implications for HIV Sexually-Transmitted Disease Risk and Prevention." *AIDS* 9(12): 1357–1365.

Meston, C. M. (2000). "Sympathetic Nervous System Activity and Female Sexual Arousal." *American Journal of Cardiology* 86(2A): 30F–34F.

Meston, C. M., and A. Bradford (2007). "Sexual Dysfunctions in Women." *Annual Review of Clinical Psychology* 3: 233–256.

Meston, C. M., and D. M. Buss (2007). "Why Humans Have Sex." *Archives of Sexual Behavior* 36(4): 477–507.

BIBLIOGRAPHY

Meston, C. M., and B. B. Gorzalka (1995). "The Effects of Sympathetic Activation on Physiological and Subjective Sexual Arousal in Women." *Behaviour Research and Therapy* 33(6): 651–664.

Meston, C. M. and J. R. Heiman (1998), "Ephedrine-Activated Physiological Sexual Arousal in Women," *Archives of General Psychiatry* 55(7): 652–656.

Meston, C. M., and K. M. McCall (2005). "Dopamine and Norepinephrine Responses to Film-Induced Sexual Arousal in Sexually Functional and Sexually Dysfunctional Women." *Journal of Sex & Marital Therapy* 31(4): 303–317.

Meston C. M, L. D. Hamilton, & C. B. Harte (2009). "Sexual Motivation in Women as a Function of Age." *Journal of Sexual Medicine*, 6, 3305–3319.

Mikulincer, M., and P. R. Shaver (2007). *Attachment in Adulthood: Structure, Dynamics, and Change*. New York: Guilford Press.

Miletski, H. (2002). *Understanding Bestiality and Zoophil[i]a*. Bethesda, MD: Hani Miletski.

Miller, A. G. (1986), *The Obedience Experiments: A Case Study of Controversy in Social Science*. New York: Praeger.

Millar, M. G., and N. M. Ostlund (2006). "The Effects of a Parenting Prime on Sex Differences in Mate Selection Criteria." *Personality and Social Psychology Bulletin* 32(11): 1459–1468.

Miller, B. L., J. L. Cummings, et al. (1986). "Hypersexuality or Altered Sexual Preference Following Brain Injury." *Journal of Neurology Neurosurgery and Psychiatry* 49(8): 867–873.

Miller, G. M., J. Bendor, et al. (2004). "A Mu-Opioid Receptor Single Nucleotide Polymorphism in Rhesus Monkey: Association with Stress Response and Aggression." *Molecular Psychiatry* 9(1): 99–108.

Miller, G., J. M. Tybur, et al. (2007). "Ovulatory Cycle Effects on Tip Earnings by Lap Dancers: Economic Evidence for Human Estrus?" *Evolution and Human Behavior* 28(6): 375–381.

Mitchell, K. J., D. Finkelhor, et al. (2003). "The Exposure of Youth to Unwanted Sexual Material on the Internet—A National Survey of Risk, Impact, and Prevention." *Youth & Society* 34(3): 330–358.

Mitra, A., J. Willyard, et al. (2005). "Exploring Web Usage and Selection Criteria Among Male and Female Students." *Journal of Computer-Mediated Communication* 10(3): 24.

Miyagawa, Y., A. Tsujimura, et al. (2007). "Differential Brain Processing of Audiovisual Sexual Stimuli in Men: Comparative Positron Emission Tomography Study of the Initiation and Maintenance of Penile Erection During Sexual Arousal." *Neuroimage* 36(3): 830–842.

Moan, C. E., and R. G. Heath (1972). "Septal Stimulation for Initiation of Heterosexual Behavior in a Homosexual Male." *Journal of Behavior Therapy and Experimental Psychiatry* 3(1): 23–30.

Molzer, K. (June 2003). "100 Frauen eine Frage: Möchten Sie mit mir Schlafen?" [100 Women, One Question: Do You want to Sleep with Me?]. *Seitenblicke*: 66–69.

Money, J. (1993). "Intersexual Rights—Reply." *Sciences-New York* 33(4): 4–4.

Money, J., and M. Lamacz (1984). "Gynemimesis and Gynemimetophilia—Individual and Cross-Cultural Manifestations of a Gender-Coping Strategy Hitherto Unnamed." *Comprehensive Psychiatry* 25(4): 392–403.

Montagu, M. F. A. (1941). "Sex Variants. A Study of Homosexual Patterns." *Psychiatry* 4(4): 631–633.

Montorsi, F., D. Perani, et al. (2003). "Brain Activation Patterns During Video Sexual Stimulation Following the Administration of Apomorphine: Results of a Placebo-Controlled Study." *European Urology* 43(4): 405–411.

Moreault, D., and D. R. Follingstad (1978). "Sexual Fantasies of Females as a Function of Sex Guilt and Experimental Response Cues." *Journal of Consulting and Clinical Psychology* 46(6): 1385–1393.

Morgan, R. (1980), "Theory and Practice: Pornography and Rape," in L. J. Lederer (ed.), *Take Back the Night.* New York: William Morrow.

Moser, C. (2003). "DSM-IV-TR and the Paraphilias: An Argument for Removal." *Sexuality and Disability* 21(3): 076.

Mosher, D. L., and P. Macian (1994). "College Men and Women Respond to X-Rated Videos Intended for Male or Female Audiences—Gender and Sexual Scripts." *Journal of Sex Research* 31(2): 99–113.

Mosher, D. L., and P. Macian (1994). "College Men and Women Respond to X-Rated Videos Intended for Male or Female Audiences—Gender and Sexual Scripts." *Journal of Sex Research* 31(2): 99–113.

Mosher, D. L., and B. B. White (1980). "Effects of Committed or Casual Erotic Guided Imagery on Females' Subjective Sexual Arousal and Emotional Response." *Journal of Sex Research* 16(4): 273–299.

Mouras, H. (2007). "Central Role of Somatosensory Processes in Sexual Arousal as Identified by Neuroimaging Techniques." *Behavioral and Brain Sciences* 30(2): 217–217.

Mouras, H., S. Stoleru, et al. (2003). "Brain Processing of Visual Sexual Stimuli in Healthy Men: A Functional Magnetic Resonance Imaging Study." *Neuroimage* 20(2): 855–869.

Mouras, H., S. Stoleru, et al. (2008). "Activation of Mirror-Neuron System by Erotic Video Clips Predicts Degree of Induced Erection: An fMRI Study." *Neuroimage* 42(3): 1142–1150.

Muehlenhard, C. L., and S. K. Shippee (2009). "Men's and Women's Reports of Pretending Orgasm." *Journal of Sex Research*, in press. Epub ahead of print, retrieved August 2010, http://www.ncbi.nlm.nih.gov/pubmed/19707929

Munroe, R. L., and M. Gauvain (2001). "Why the Paraphilias? Domesticating Strange Sex." *Cross-Cultural Research* 35(1): 44–64.

Munroe, R. L., and A. K. Romney (2006). *Gender and Age Differences in Same-Sex Aggregation and Social Behavior—A Four-Culture Study.* Thousand Oaks, CA: Sage Publications Inc.

Murnen, S. K., and M. Stockton (1997). "Gender and Self-Reported Sexual Arousal in Response to Sexual Stimuli: A Meta-Analytic Review." *Sex Roles* 37(3–4): 135–153.

Murphy, F. (2003). "Functional Neuroanatomy of Emotions: A Meta Analysis." *Cognitive, Affective, and Behavioral Neuroscience* 3(3): 207–233.

Nappi, R., A. Salonia, et al. (2005). "Clinical Biologic Pathophysiologies Of Women's Sexual Dysfunction." *Journal of Sexual Medicine* 2(1): 4–25.

Newcomb, M., and B. Mustanski "Moderators of the Relationship Between Internalized Homophobia and Risky Sexual Behavior in Men Who Have Sex with Men: A Meta-Analysis." *Archives of Sexual Behavior*, in press. Epub ahead of print, retrieved August 2010, http://www.ncbi.nlm.nih.gov/pubmed/19888643

Newmahr, S. (2008). "Becoming a Sadomasochist—Integrating Self and Other in Ethnographic Analysis." *Journal of Contemporary Ethnography* 37(5): 619–643.

Nicholas, L. J. (2004). "The Association Between Religiosity, Sexual Fantasy, Participation in Sexual Acts, Sexual Enjoyment, Exposure, and Reaction to Sexual Materials Among Black South Africans." *Journal of Sex & Marital Therapy* 30(1): 37–42.

Nichols, M. (2006). "Psychotherapeutic Issues with "Kinky" Clients: Clinical Problems, Yours and Theirs." *Journal of Homosexuality* 50(2–3): 281–300.

Nielsen, J., and K. Pernice (2009). *Eyetracking Web Usability*. Berkeley, CA: New Riders.

Njus, D. M., and C. M. Bane (2009). "Religious Identification as a Moderator of Evolved Sexual Strategies of Men and Women." *Journal of Sexual Research* 46(6): 546–557.

Nobre, P. J. (2009). "Determinants of Sexual Desire Problems in Women: Testing a Cognitive-Emotional Model." *Journal of Sex & Marital Therapy* 35(5): 360–377.

Nobre, P. J., and J. Pinto-Gouveia (2006). "Emotions During Sexual Activity: Differences Between Sexually Functional and Dysfunctional Men And Women." *Archives of Sexual Behavior* 35(4): 491–499.

Nobre, P. J., and J. Pinto-Gouveia (2008). "Cognitions, Emotions, and Sexual Response: Analysis of the Relationship Among Automatic Thoughts, Emotional Responses, and Sexual Arousal." *Archives of Sexual Behavior* 37(4): 652–661.

Nobre, P. J., M. Wiegel, et al. (2004). "Determinants of Sexual Arousal and the Accuracy of Its Self-Estimation in Sexually Functional Males." *Journal of Sex Research* 41(4): 363–371.

Nopoulos, P., M. Flaum, et al. (2000). "Sexual Dimorphism in the Human Brain: Evaluation of Tissue Volume, Tissue Composition and Surface Anatomy Using Magnetic Resonance Imaging." *Psychiatry Research-Neuroimaging* 98(1): 1–13.

Nordling, N., N. K. Sandnabba, et al. (2006). "Differences and Similarities Between Gay and Straight Individuals Involved in the Sadomasochistic Subculture." *Journal of Homosexuality* 50(2–3): 41–57.

Norris, K. O. (2004). "Gender Stereotypes, Aggression, and Computer Games: An Online Survey of Women." *Cyberpsychology & Behavior* 7(6): 714–727.

Nottebohm, F. (1980). "Testosterone Triggers Growth of Brain Vocal Control Nuclei in Adult Female Canaries." *Brain Research* 189(2): 429–436.

Nottebohm, F., and A. P. Arnold (1976). "Sexual Dimorphism in Vocal Control Areas of Songbird Brain." *Science* 194(4261): 211–213.

O'Doherty, J., J. Winston, et al. (2003). "Beauty in a Smile: The Role of Medial Orbitofrontal Cortex in Facial Attractiveness." *Neuropsychologia* 41(2): 147–155.

Odonohue, W. T., and J. H. Geer (1985). "The Habituation of Sexual Arousal." *Archives of Sexual Behavior* 14(3): 233–246.

Ogas, O. "Spare Parts: New Information Reignites a Controversy Surrounding the Hopkins Gender Identity Clinic." *Baltimore City Paper*, March 1994, 10, 12–15.

Oguz, N., and N. Uygur (2005). "A Case of Diaper Fetishism." *Turk Psikiyatri Dergisi* 16(2): 133–138.

Okada, E., S. Aou, et al. (1991). "Electrical-Stimulation of Male Monkey's Midbrain Elicits Components Of Sexual-Behavior." *Physiology & Behavior* 50(1): 229–236.

Olds, J. (1956). "Pleasure Centers in the Brain." *Scientific American* 195(4): 105–116.

Olds, J., and P. Milner (1954). "Positive Reinforcement Produced by Electrical Stimulation of Septal Area and Other Regions of Rat Brain." *Journal of Comparative & Physiological Psychology* 47(6): 419–427.

Oliver, C. J., D. G. Watson, et al. (2009). "The Effect of Sexual Priming Cues on Emotional Recognition in Nonviolent Child Sexual Abusers: A Preliminary Study." *International Journal of Offender Therapy and Comparative Criminology* 53(3): 292–304.

Oliver, M. B., and J. S. Hyde (1993). "Gender Differences in Sexuality—A Metaanalysis." *Psychological Bulletin* 114(1): 29–51.

Ono, H., and M. Zavodny (2003). "Gender and the Internet." *Social Science Quarterly* 84(1): 111–121.

Oomura, Y., H. Yoshimatsu, et al. (1983). "Medial Preoptic and Hypothalamic Neuronal-Activity During Sexual-Behavior of the Male Monkey." *Brain Research* 266(2): 340–343.

Operario, D., J. Burton, et al. (2008). "Men Who Have Sex with Transgender Women: Challenges to Category-Based HIV Prevention." *AIDS and Behavior* 12(1): 18–26.

Oppenheim, J. S., B. C. P. Lee, et al. (1987). "No Sex-Related Differences in Human Corpus-Callosum Based on Magnetic-Resonance Imagery." *Annals of Neurology* 21(6): 604–606.

Oppenheimer, S. M., A. Gelb, et al. (1992). "Cardiovascular Effects of Human Insular Cortex Stimulation." *Neurology* 42(9): 1727–1732.

Ortega-Brena, M. (2009). "Peek-a-boo, I See You: Watching Japanese Hardcore Animation." *Sexuality & Culture* 13(1): 17–31.

Ortigue, S., and F. Bianchi-Demicheli (2008). "The Chronoarchitecture of Human Sexual Desire: A High-Density Electrical Mapping Study." *Neuroimage* 43(2): 337–345.

Ortigue, S., F. Bianchi-Demicheli, et al. (2007). "The Neural Basis of Love as a Subliminal Prime: An Event-Related Functional Magnetic Resonance Imaging Study." *Journal of Cognitive Neuroscience* 19(7): 1218–1230.

Ortigue, S., S. T. Grafton, et al. (2007). "Correlation Between Insula Activation and Self-Reported Quality of Orgasm in Women." *Neuroimage* 37(2): 551–560.

Ortigue, S., N. Patel, et al. (2009). "New Electroencephalogram (EEG) Neuroimaging Methods of Analyzing Brain Activity Applicable to the Study of Human Sexual Response." *Journal of Sexual Medicine* 6(7): 1830–1845.

Oudshoorn, N., E. Rommes, et al. (2004). "Configuring the User as Everybody: Gender and Design Cultures in Information and Communication Technologies." *Science Technology & Human Values* 29(1): 30–63.

Owens, I. P. F., and D. B. A. Thompson (1994). "Sex-Differences, Sex-Ratios and Sex-Roles." *Proceedings of the Royal Society B-Biological Sciences* 258(1352): 93–99.

Ozmen, M., A. Erdogan, et al. (2004). "Excessive Masturbation After Epilepsy Surgery." *Epilepsy & Behavior* 5(1): 133–136.

Page, D. C., L. G. Brown, et al. (1987). "Exchange of Terminal Portions of X-Chromosomal and Y-Chromosomal Short Arms in Human-Xx Males." *Nature* 328(6129): 437–440.

Palace, E. M. (1995). "A Cognitive-Physiological Process Model of Sexual Arousal and Response." *Clinical Psychology—Science and Practice* 2(4): 370–384.

Palace, E. M. (1995). "Modification of Dysfunctional Patterns of Sexual-Response Through Autonomic Arousal and False Physiological Feedback." *Journal of Consulting and Clinical Psychology* 63(4): 604–615.

Palace, E. M., and B. B. Gorzalka (1990). "The Enhancing Effects of Anxiety on Arousal in Sexually Dysfunctional and Functional Women." *Journal of Abnormal Psychology* 99(4): 403–411.

Paland, S., and M. Lynch (2006). "Transitions to Asexuality Result in Excess Amino Acid Substitutions." *Science* 311(5763): 990–992.

Palesh, O., K. Saltzman, et al. (2004). "Internet Use and Attitudes Towards Illicit Internet Use Behavior in a Sample of Russian College Students." *Cyberpsychology & Behavior* 7(5): 553–558.

Panksepp, J. (1998). *Affective Neuroscience: The Foundations of Human and Animal Emotions.* New York: Oxford University Press.

Panksepp, J. (2000). "Seven Sins of Evolutionary Psychology." *Evolution and Cognition* 6(2).

Panksepp, J. (2005). "Affective Consciousness: Core Emotional Feelings in Animals And Humans." *Consciousness and Cognition* 14(1): 30–80.

Panksepp, J. (2005). "Emotional Dynamics of the Organism and Its Parts." *Behavioral and Brain Sciences* 28(2): 212–213.

Panksepp, J. (2005). "On the Embodied Neural Nature of Core Emotional Affects." *Journal of Consciousness Studies* 12(8–10): 158–184.

Panksepp, J. (2007). "Criteria for Basic Emotions: Is DISGUST a Primary 'Emotion'?" *Cognition & Emotion* 21(8): 1819–1828.

Panksepp, J. (2007). "Emotional Feelings Originate Below the Neocortex: Toward a Neurobiology of the Soul." *Behavioral and Brain Sciences* 30(1): 101–103.

Panter-Brick, C. (2002). "Sexual Division of Labor: Energetic and Evolutionary Scenarios." *American Journal of Human Biology* 14(5): 627–640.

Parameshwaranand S. (2001). *Encyclopaedic Dictionary of Puranas.* New Delhi: Sarup & Sons.

Paredes, R. G. (2003) "Medial preoptic area/anterior hypothalamus and sexual motivation." *Scandinavian Journal of Psychology* 44(3): 203–212.

Paredes, R. G., and M. J. Baum. (1997). "Role of the medial preoptic area/anterior hypothalamus in the control of masculine sexual behavior." *Annual Review of Sex Research* 8: 68–101.

Parish, W. L., E. O. Laumann, et al. (2007). "Sexual Behavior in China: Trends and Comparisons." *Population and Development Review* 33(4): 729–756.

Parish, W. L., E. O. Laumann, et al. (2007). "Sexual Dysfunctions in Urban China: A Population-Based National Survey of Men and Women." *Journal of Sexual Medicine* 4(6): 1559–1574.

Parish, W. L., Y. Luo, et al. (2007). "Sexual Practices and Sexual Satisfaction: A Population Based Study of Chinese Urban Adults." *Archives of Sexual Behavior* 36(1): 5–20.

Park, J. H. (2008). "Is Aversion to Incest Psychologically Privileged? When Sex and Sociosexuality Do Not Predict Sexual Willingness." *Personality and Individual Differences* 45(7): 661–665.

Park, J. H., M. Schaller, et al. (2007). "Pathogen-Avoidance Mechanisms and the Stigmatization of Obese People." *Evolution and Human Behavior* 28(6): 410–414.

Park, J. H., M. Schaller, et al. (2008). "Psychology of Human Kin Recognition: Heuristic Cues, Erroneous Inferences, and Their Implications." *Review of General Psychology* 12(3): 215–235.

Park, K., J. J. Seo, et al. (2001). "A New Potential of Blood Oxygenation Level Dependent (BOLD) Functional MRI for Evaluating Cerebral Centers of Penile Erection." *International Journal of Impotence Research* 13(2): 73–81.

Park, S. (2009). "Concentration of Internet Usage and Its Relation to Exposure to Negative Content: Does the Gender Gap Differ Among Adults and Adolescents?" *Women's Studies International Forum* 32(2): 98–107.

Parker, J., and M. Burkley (2009). "Who's Chasing Whom? The Impact of Gender and Relationship Status on Mate Poaching." *Journal of Experimental Social Psychology* 45(4): 1016–1019.

Parsons, J. T., J. P. Severino, et al. (2007). "Internet Use among Gay and Bisexual Men with Compulsive Sexual Behavior." *Sexual Addiction & Compulsivity* 14: 239–256.

BIBLIOGRAPHY

Patchev, A. V., F. Gotz, W. Rohde. (2004). "Differential Role of Estrogen Receptor Isoforms in Sex-Specific Brain Organization" *The FASEB journal: official publication of Federation of American Societies for Experimental Biology* 18(11): 1568–1570.

Patterson, N., D. J. Richter, et al. (2006). "Genetic Evidence for Complex Speciation of Humans and Chimpanzees." *Nature* 441(7097): 1103–1108.

Patton, P. (2008). "One World, Many Minds." *Scientific American Mind* 19(6): 72–79.

Paul, B. (2009). "Predicting Internet Pornography Use and Arousal: The Role of Individual Difference Variables." *Journal of Sex Research* 46(4): 344–357.

Paul, B., and J. W. Shim (2008). "Gender, Sexual Affect, and Motivations for Internet Pornography Use." *International Journal of Sexual Health* 20(3): 187–199.

Paul, T., B. Schiffer, et al. (2008). "Brain Response to Visual Sexual Stimuli in Heterosexual and Homosexual Males." *Human Brain Mapping* 29(6): 726–735.

Paus, T., M. Keshavan, et al. (2008). "OPINION Why Do Many Psychiatric Disorders Emerge During Adolescence?" *Nature Reviews Neuroscience* 9(12): 947–957.

Pavlova, M., M. Guerreschi, et al. (2010). "Cortical Response to Social Interaction Is Affected by Gender." *Neuroimage* 50(3): 1327–1332.

Pawlowski, B. (2009). "The Evolutionary Biology of Human Female Sexuality." *Evolutionary Psychology* 7(2): 160–163.

Payne, K. A., Y. M. Binik, et al. (2007). "Effects of Sexual Arousal on Genital and Non-Genital Sensation: A Comparison of Women with Vulvar Vestibulitis Syndrome and Healthy Controls." *Archives of Sexual Behavior* 36(2): 289–300.

Pazol, K. (2003). "Mating in the Kakamega Forest Blue Monkeys (Cercopithecus Mitis): Does Female Sexual Behavior Function to Manipulate Paternity Assessment?" *Behaviour* 140: 473–499.

Pearson, S. E., R. H. Pollack (1997). "Female Response to Sexually Explicit Films." *Journal of Pscyhology and Human Sexuality* 9: 73–88.

Peelen, M. V., A. P. Atkinson, et al. (2007). "Emotional Modulation of Body-Selective Visual Areas." *Social Cognitive and Affective Neuroscience* 2(4): 274–283.

Peelen, M. V., and P. E. Downing (2007). "The Neural Basis of Visual Body Perception." *Nature Reviews Neuroscience* 8(8): 636–648.

Penton-Voak, I. S. and J. Y. Chen (2004). "High Salivary Testosterone Is Linked to Masculine Male Facial Appearance in Humans." *Evolution and Human Behavior* 25(4): 229–241.

Penton-Voak, I. S., and D. I. Perrett (2000). "Female Preference for Male Faces Changes Cyclically: Further Evidence." *Evolution and Human Behavior* 21(1): 39–48.

Penton-Voak, I. S., D. I. Perrett, et al. (1999). "Menstrual Cycle Alters Face Preference." *Nature* 399(6738): 741–742.

BIBLIOGRAPHY

Peplau, L. A. (2003). "Human Sexuality: How Do Men and Women Differ?" *Current Directions in Psychological Science* 12(2): 37–40.

Perachio, A. A., L. D. Marr, et al. (1979). "Sexual-Behavior in Male Rhesus-Monkeys Elicited by Electrical-Stimulation of Preoptic and Hypothalamic Areas." *Brain Research* 177(1): 127–144.

Perachio, A. A., L. D. Marr, et al. (1979). "Sexual-Behavior in Male Rhesus-Monkeys Elicited by Electrical-Stimulation of Preoptic and Hypothalamic Areas." *Brain Research* 177(1): 127–144.

Perrin, J. S., P. Y. Herve, et al. (2008). "Growth of White Matter in the Adolescent Brain: Role of Testosterone and Androgen Receptor." *Journal of Neuroscience* 28(38): 9519–9524.

Peter, J., and P. M. Valkenburg (2006). "Adolescents' Exposure to Sexually Explicit Material on the Internet." *Communication Research* 33(2): 178–204.

Peters, M., G. Rhodes, et al. (2008). "Does Attractiveness in Men Provide Clues to Semen Quality?" *Journal of Evolutionary Biology* 21(2): 572–579.

Peterson, R. A. (2001). "On the Use of College Students in Social Science Research: Insights from a Second-Order Meta-Analysis." *Journal of Consumer Research* 28(3): 450–461.

Peterson, Z., E. Janssen, et al. "Women's Sexual Responses to Heterosexual and Lesbian Erotica: The Role of Stimulus Intensity, Affective Reaction, and Sexual History." *Archives of Sexual Behavior.* 39(4): 880–897.

Peterson, Z. D., and E. Janssen (2007). "Ambivalent Affect and Sexual Response: The Impact of Co-Occurring Positive and Negative Emotions on Subjective and Physiological Sexual Responses to Erotic Stimuli." *Archives of Sexual Behavior* 36(6): 793–807.

Petralia, S. M., and G. G. Gallup Jr. (2002). "Effects of a Sexual Assault Scenario on Handgrip Strength Across the Menstrual Cycle." *Evolution and Human Behavior* 23(1): 3–10.

Pfaus, J. G. (1996). "Frank A. Beach Award—Homologies of Animal and Human Sexual Behaviors." *Hormones and Behavior* 30(3): 187–200.

Pfaus, J. G. (2009). "Pathways of Sexual Desire." *Journal of Sexual Medicine* 6(6): 1506–1533.

Pfaus, J. G., T. E. Kippin, et al. (2001). "Conditioning and Sexual Behavior: A Review." *Hormones and Behavior* 40(2): 291–321.

Pfaus, J. G., T. E. Kippin, et al. (2003). "What Can Animal Models Tell Us About Human Sexual Response?" *Annual Review of Sexual Research* 14: 1–63.

Philaretou, A. G. (2005). "Net.SeXXX: Readings on Sex, Pornography, and the Internet." *Journal of Sex Research* 42(2): 180–181.

Phoenix, C. H. (2009). "Organizing Action of Prenatally Administered Testosterone Propionate on the Tissues Mediating Mating Behavior in the Female Guinea Pig." *Hormones and Behavior* 55(5): 566–566.

Plante, R. F. (2006). "Sexual Spanking, the Self, and the Construction of Deviance." *Journal of Homosexuality* 50(2–3): 59–79.

Platek, S. M., and D. Singh (2010). "Optimal Waist-to-Hip Ratios in Women Activate Neural Reward Centers in Men." *PLoS One* 5(2).

Plaud, J. J. and J. R. Martini (1999). "The respondent conditioning of male sexual arousal." *Behavior Modification* 23(2): 254–268.

Plummer, C. A. and W. Njuguna (2009). "Cultural protective and risk factors: professional perspectives about child sexual abuse in Kenya." *Child Abuse and Neglect* 33(8): 524–532.

Poldrack, R. A. (2008). "The role of fMRI in Cognitive Neuroscience: where do we stand?" *Current Opinion in Neurobiology* 18(2): 223–226.

Poliakoff, E. (2010). "Introduction to Special Issue on Body Representation: Feeling, Seeing, Moving and Observing." *Experimental Brain Research* 204(3): 289–293.

Pollan, M. (2006). *The Omnivore's Dilemma: A Natural History of Four Meals.* New York: Penguin Press.

Ponseti, J., and H. Bosinski "Subliminal Sexual Stimuli Facilitate Genital Response in Women." *Archives of Sexual Behavior* 39(5): 1073–1079.

Ponseti, J., H. A. Bosinski, et al. (2006). "A Functional Endophenotype for Sexual Orientation in Humans." *Neuroimage* 33(3): 825–833.

Ponseti, J., O. Granert, et al. (2009). "Assessment of Sexual Orientation Using the Hemodynamic Brain Response to Visual Sexual Stimuli." *Journal of Sexual Medicine* 6(6): 1628–1634.

Poryazova, R., R. Khatami, et al. (2009). "Weak with Sex: Sexual Intercourse as a Trigger for Cataplexy." *Journal of Sexual Medicine* 6(8): 2271–2277.

Postmes, T., and R. Spears (2002). "Behavior Online: Does Anonymous Computer Communication Reduce Gender Inequality?" *Personality and Social Psychology Bulletin* 28(8): 1073–1083.

Pound, N. (2002). "Male Interest in Visual Cues of Sperm Competition Risk." *Evolution and Human Behavior* 23(6): 443–466.

Pound, N., M. H. Javed, et al. (2002). "Duration of Sexual Arousal Predicts Semen Parameters for Masturbatory Ejaculates." *Physiology & Behavior* 76(4–5): 685–689.

Pradhan, S., M. N. Singh, et al. (1998). "Kluver Bucy Syndrome in Young Children." *Clinical Neurology and Neurosurgery* 100(4): 254–258.

Prause, N., E. Janssen, et al. (2008). "Attention and Emotional Responses to Sexual Stimuli and Their Relationship to Sexual Desire." *Archives of Sexual Behavior* 37(6): 934–949.

Preston, B. T., and P. Stockley (2006). "The Prospect of Sexual Competition Stimulates Premature and Repeated Ejaculation in a Mammal." *Current Biology* 16(7): R239–R241.

Price, M., M. Kafka, et al. (2002). "Telephone Scatologia—Comorbidity with Other Paraphilias and Paraphilia-Related Disorders." *International Journal of Law and Psychiatry* 25(1): 37–49.

Provine, R. R. (1993). "Laughter Punctuates Speech—Linguistic, Social and Gender Contexts of Laughter." *Ethology* 95(4): 291–298.

Pujols Y. B. A., C. M. Meston, and B. N. Seal (2010). "The Association Between Sexual Satisfaction and Body Image in Women." *Journal of Sexual Medicine* 7: 905–916.

Puts, D. A. (2005). "Mating Context and Menstrual Phase Affect Women's Preferences for Male Voice Pitch." *Evolution and Human Behavior* 26(5): 388–397.

Puts, D. A., S. J. C. Gaulin, et al. (2006). "Dominance and the Evolution of Sexual Dimorphism in Human Voice Pitch." *Evolution and Human Behavior* 27(4): 283–296.

Quinsey, V. L. (2003). "The Etiology of Anomalous Sexual Preferences in Men." *Annals of the New York Academy of Sciences* 989: 105–117.

Rachman, S., and R. J. Hodgson (1968). "Experimentally-Induced Sexual Fetishism—Replication and Development." *Psychological Record* 18(1): 25–27.

Radway, J. A. (1984). *Reading the Romance: Women, Patriarchy, and Popular Literature.* Chapel Hill: University of North Carolina Press.

Rahman, Q. (2005). "The neurodevelopment of human sexual orientation." *Neuroscience and Biobehavioral Reviews* 29(7): 1057–1066.

Raisman, G., and P. M. Field (1971). "Sexual Dimorphism in Preoptic Area of Rat." *Science* 173(3998): 731–733.

Raisman, G., and P. M. Field (1973). "Sexual Dimorphism in Neuropil of Preoptic Area of Rat and Its Dependence on Neonatal Androgen." *Brain Research* 54: 1–29.

Rakic, P. (2001). "Neurobiology—Neurocreationism—Making New Cortical Maps." *Science* 294(5544): 1011–1012.

Raphael, C., C. Bachen, et al. (2006). "Portrayals of Information and Communication Technology on World Wide Web Sites for Girls." *Journal of Computer-Mediated Communication* 11(3): 31.

Rauch, S. L., L. M. Shin, et al. (1999). "Neural Activation During Sexual and Competitive Arousal in Healthy Men." *Psychiatry Research-Neuroimaging* 91(1): 1–10.

Redoute, J., S. Stoleru, et al. (2000). "Brain Processing of Visual Sexual Stimuli in Human Males." *Human Brain Mapping* 11(3): 162–177.

Regan, P. C., and L. Atkins (2006). "Sex Differences and Similarities in Frequency and Intensity of Sexual Desire." *Social Behavior and Personality* 34(1): 95–101.

Regan, P. C., and E. Berscheid (1996). "Beliefs About the State, Goals, and Objects of Sexual Desire." *Journal of Sex & Marital Therapy* 22(2): 110–120.

Reiersol, O., and S. Skeid (2006). "The ICD Diagnoses of Fetishism and Sadomasochism." *Journal of Homosexuality* 50(2–3): 243–262.

Reimers, S. (2007). "The BBC Internet Study: General Methodology." *Archives of Sexual Behavior* 36(2): 147–161.

Reiner, W. G. (2004). "Psychosexual Development in Genetic Males Assigned Female: The Cloacal Exstrophy Experience." *Child and Adolescent Psychiatric Clinics of North America* 13(3): 657–674.

Reiner, W. G. (2004). "A 7-Year Experience of Genetic Males with Severe Phallic Inadequacy Assigned Female." *Journal of Urology* 172: 2395–2398.

Reiner, W. G. (2005). "Gender Identity and Sex-of-Rearing in Children with Disorders of Sexual Differentiation." *Journal of Pediatric Endocrinology & Metabolism* 18(6): 549–553.

Reiner, W. G., and J. P. Gearhart (2004). "Discordant Sexual Identity in Some Genetic Males with Cloacal Exstrophy Assigned to Female Sex at Birth." *New England Journal of Medicine* 350(4): 333–341.

Reinisch, J. M., R. Beasley, et al. (1990). *The Kinsey Institute New Report on Sex: What You Must Know to Be Sexually Literate.* New York: St. Martin's Press.

Reisert, I., V. Han, et al. (1987). "Sex Steroids Promote Neurite Growth in Mesencephalic Tyrosine-Hydroxylase Immunoreactive Neurons Invitro." *International Journal of Developmental Neuroscience* 5(2): 91–+.

Rellini, A. H., K. M. McCall, et al. (2005). "The Relationship Between Women's Subjective and Physiological Sexual Arousal." *Psychophysiology* 42(1): 116–124.

Rellini, A. H., and C. M. Meston (2006). "Psychophysiological Sexual Arousal in Women with a History Of Child Sexual Abuse." *Journal of Sex & Marital Therapy* 32(1): 5–22.

Renaud, C. A., and E. S. Byers (2001). "Positive and Negative Sexual Cognitions: Subjective Experience and Relationships to Sexual Adjustment." *Journal of Sex Research* 38(3): 252–262.

Renaud, C. A., and S. E. Byers (2006). "Positive and Negative Cognitions of Sexual Submission: Relationship to Sexual Violence." *Archives of Sexual Behavior* 35(4): 483–490.

Rentzel, L. (1973). *When All the Laughter Died in Sorrow.* New York: Bantam Books.

Rhen, T. (2000). "Sex-Limited Mutations and the Evolution of Sexual Dimorphism." *Evolution* 54(1): 37–43.

Rhodes, S. D., D. A. Bowie, et al. (2003). "Collecting Behavioural Data Using the World Wide Web: Considerations for Researchers." *Journal of Epidemiology and Community Health* 57(1): 68–73.

Riahinia, N., and A. Azimi (2008). "Women and the Web—An Evaluation of Academic Iranian Women's Use of the Internet in Tarbiat Moalem University." *Electronic Library* 26(1): 75–82.

Rice, W. R. (1992). "Sexually Antagonistic Genes—Experimental-Evidence." *Science* 256(5062): 1436–1439.

Richters, J., R. de Visser, et al. (2006). "Sexual Practices at Last Heterosexual Encounter and Occurrence Of Orgasm in a National Survey." *Journal of Sex Research* 43(3): 217–226.

Richters, J., R. O. de Visser, et al. (2008). "Demographic and Psychosocial Features of Participants in Bondage and Discipline, 'Sadomasochism' or Dominance and Submission (BDSM): Data from a National Survey." *Journal of Sexual Medicine* 5(7): 1660–1668.

Riddick, N. V., P. W. Czoty, et al. (2009). "Behavioral and Neurobiological Characteristics Influencing Social Hierarchy Formation in Female Cynomolgus Monkeys." *Neuroscience* 158(4): 1257–1265.

Rideout, V., U. Foehr, and D. Roberts. (2010). *Generation M2: Media in the Lives of 8 to 18 Year Olds.* Kaiser Family Foundation Study.

Rieger, G., M. L. Chivers, et al. (2002). "Who Are Bisexual Men? Sexual Arousal and Sexual Orientation in Men." *Psychophysiology* 39: S70–S70.

Rieger, G., M. L. Chivers, et al. (2005). "Sexual Arousal Patterns of Bisexual Men." *Psychological Science* 16(8): 579–584.

Rilling, J. K., J. T. Winslow, et al. (2004). "The Neural Correlates of Mate Competition in Dominant Male Rhesus Macaques." *Biological Psychiatry* 56(5): 364–375.

Rimm, M. (1995). "Marketing Pornography on the Information Superhighway—A Survey of 917,410 Images, Descriptions, Short-Stories, and Animations Downloaded 8.5 Million Times by Consumers in Over 2000 Cities in 40 Countries, Provinces, and Territories." *Georgetown Law Journal* 83(5): 1849–1934.

Rinn, J. L., and M. Snyder (2005). "Sexual Dimorphism in Mammalian Gene Expression." *Trends in Genetics* 21(5): 298–305.

Rissman, E. F., A. L. Heck, et al. (2002). "Disruption of Estrogen Receptor Beta Gene Impairs Spatial Learning in Female Mice." *Proceedings of the National Academy of Sciences of the United States of America* 99(6): 3996–4001.

Robert, C. S. (2004). "Amputee Identity Disorder and Related Paraphilias." *Psychiatry* 3(8): 27–30.

Roberts, S. C., and A. C. Little (2008). "Good Genes, Complementary Genes and Human Mate Preferences." *Genetica* 134(1): 31–43.

Rodriguez-Girones, M. A., and M. Enquist (2001). "The Evolution of Female Sexuality." *Animal Behaviour* 61: 695–704.

Rogan, J. (Producer) (2007). *Shiny Happy Jihad* [Audio CD]. United States: Comedy Central.

Rokach, A. (1990). "Content-Analysis of Sexual Fantasies of Males And Females." *Journal of Psychology* 124(4): 427–436.

Roney, J. R., K. N. Hanson, et al. (2006). "Reading Men's Faces: Women's Mate Attractiveness Judgments Track Men's Testosterone and Interest in Infants." *Proceedings of the Royal Society B-Biological Sciences* 273(1598): 2169–2175.

Roney, J. R,. and Z. L. Simmons (2008). "Women's Estradiol Predicts Preference for Facial Cues of Men's Testosterone." *Hormones and Behavior* 53(1): 14–19.

Rose, A. J., and K. D. Rudolph (2006). "A Review of Sex Differences in Peer Relationship Processes: Potential Trade-offs for the Emotional and Behavioral Development of Girls and Boys." *Psychological Bulletin* 132(1): 98–131.

Rose, S. M., and D. Zand (2002). "Lesbian Dating and Courtship from Young Adulthood to Midlife." *Journal of Lesbian Studies* 6(1): 85–109.

Rosen, I. (1996). *Sexual Deviation.* Oxford; New York: Oxford University Press.

Rosenberg-Kima, R. B., and A. Sadeh (2010). "Attention, Response Inhibition, and Face-Information Processing in Children: The Role of Task Characteristics, Age, and Gender." *Child Neuropsychology* 16(4): 388–404.

Ross, M. W., B. R. S. Rosser, et al. (2007). "The Advantages and Limitations of Seeking Sex Online: A Comparison of Reasons Given for Online and Offline Sexual Liaisons by Men Who Have Sex with Men." *Journal of Sex Research* 44(1): 59–71.

Rossell, S. L., E. T. Bullmore, et al. (2002). "Sex Differences in Functional Brain Activation During a Lexical Visual Field Task." *Brain and Language* 80(1): 97–105.

Roughley, N. (2000). *Being Humans: Anthropological Universality and Particularity in Transdisciplinary Perspectives.* Berlin; New York: Walter de Gruyter.

Rowland, D., and L. Incrocci (2008). *Handbook of Sexual and Gender Identity Disorders.* Hoboken, N.J.: John Wiley & Sons.

Rowland, D. L. (2006). "Neurobiology of Sexual Response in Men and Women." *CNS Spectrums* 11(8): 6–12.

Rowland, D. L., S. E. Cooper, et al. (1995). "A Preliminary Investigation of Affective and Cognitive Response to Erotic Stimulation in Men Before and After Sex Therapy." *Journal of Sex & Marital Therapy* 21(1): 3–20.

Roy, S. K. (2009). "Internet Uses and Gratifications: A Survey in the Indian Context." *Computers in Human Behavior* 25(4): 878–886.

Rozin, P. (2009). "What Kind of Empirical Research Should We Publish, Fund, and Reward?" *Perspectives on Psychological Science* 4(4): 435–439.

Rucas, S. L., M. Gurven, et al. (2006). "Female Intrasexual Competition and Reputational Effects on Attractiveness Among the Tsimane of Bolivia." *Evolution and Human Behavior* 27(1): 40–52.

Rudebeck, P. H., D. M. Bannerman, et al. (2008). "The Contribution of Distinct Subregions of the Ventromedial Frontal Cortex to Emotion, Social Behavior, and Decision Making." *Cognitive Affective & Behavioral Neuroscience* 8(4): 485–497.

Rudman, L. A., and J. B. Heppen (2003). "Implicit Romantic Fantasies and Women's Interest in Personal Power: A Glass Slipper Effect?" *Personality and Social Psychology Bulletin* 29(11): 1357–1370.

Rullo, J., D. Strassberg, et al. "Category-Specificity in Sexual Interest in Gay Men and Lesbians." *Archives of Sexual Behavior.* 39(4): 874–879.

Rupp, H., G. Librach, et al. (2009). "Partner Status Influences Women's Interest in the Opposite Sex." *Human Nature* 20(1): 93–104.

Rupp, H. A., T. W. James, et al. (2009). "The Role of the Anterior Cingulate Cortex in Women's Sexual Decision Making." *Neuroscience Letters* 449(1): 42–47.

Rupp, H. A., and K. Wallen (2007). "Relationship Between Testosterone and Interest in Sexual Stimuli: The Effect of Experience." *Hormones and Behavior* 52(5): 581–589.

Rupp, H. A., and K. Wallen (2007). "Sex Differences in Viewing Sexual Stimuli: An Eye-Tracking Study in Men and Women." *Hormones and Behavior* 51(4): 524–533.

BIBLIOGRAPHY

Rupp, H. A., and K. Wallen (2008). "Sex Differences in Response to Visual Sexual Stimuli: A Review." *Archives of Sexual Behavior* 37(2): 206–218.

Rupp, H. A., and K. Wallen (2009). "Sex-Specific Content Preferences for Visual Sexual Stimuli." *Archives of Sexual Behavior* 38(3): 417–426.

Russell, R. (2009). "A Sex Difference in Facial Contrast and Its Exaggeration by Cosmetics." *Perception* 38(8): 1211–1219.

Saavedra-Castillo, E., E. I. Cortes-Gutierrez, et al. (2005). "47,XXY Female with Testicular Feminization and Positive SRY—A Case Report." *Journal of Reproductive Medicine* 50(2): 138–140.

Sacco, D. F., K. Hugenberg, et al. (2009). "Sociosexuality and Face Perception: Unrestricted Sexual Orientation Facilitates Sensitivity to Female Facial Cues." *Personality and Individual Differences* 47(7): 777–782.

Sachs, B. D. (2007). "A Contextual Definition of Male Sexual Arousal." *Hormones and Behavior* 51(5): 569–578.

Sachs, B. D. (2008). "Sometimes Less Is Just Less: Reply to Agmo." *Hormones and Behavior* 53(2): 319–322.

Safron, A., B. Barch, et al. (2007). "Neural Correlates of Sexual Arousal in Homosexual and Heterosexual Men." *Behavioral Neuroscience* 121(2): 237–248.

Salmon, C., and D. Symons (2001). *Warrior Lovers: Erotic Fiction, Evolution and Female Sexuality*. London: Weidenfeld & Nicolson.

Salmon, C., and D. Symons (2004). "Slash Fiction and Human Mating Psychology." *Journal of Sex Research* 41(1): 94–100.

Salonia, A., A. Giraldi, et al. (2010). "Physiology of Women's Sexual Function: Basic Knowledge and New Findings." *Journal of Sexual Medicine* 7(8): 2637–2660.

Sanchez-Franco, M. J., A. F. V. Ramos, et al. (2009). "The Moderating Effect of Gender on Relationship Quality and Loyalty Toward Internet Service Providers." *Information & Management* 46(3): 196–202.

Sand, M., and W. A. Fisher (2007). "Women's Endorsement of Models of Female Sexual Response: The Nurses' Sexuality Study." *Journal of Sexual Medicine* 4(3): 708–719.

Sandel, M. E., K. S. Williams, et al. (1996). "Sexual Functioning Following Traumatic Brain Injury." *Brain Injury* 10(10): 719–728.

Sar, M. and W. E. Stumpf (1977). "Distribution of Androgen Target—Cells in Rat Forebrain and Pituitary After [Dihydrotestosterone-H-3] Administration." *Journal of Steroid Biochemistry and Molecular Biology* 8(11): 1131–1135.

Sarlo, M., D. Palomba, et al. (2005). "Blood Pressure Changes Highlight Gender Differences in Emotional Reactivity to Arousing Pictures." *Biological Psychology* 70(3): 188–196.

Sauvageau, A., and S. Racette (2006). "Autoerotic Deaths in the Literature from 1954 to 2004: A Review." *Journal of Forensic Sciences* 51(1): 140–146.

Savic, I., H. Berglund, et al. (2005). "Brain Response to Putative Pheromones in Homosexual Men." *Proceedings of the National Academy of Sciences of the United States of America* 102(20): 7356–7361.

BIBLIOGRAPHY

Savic, I., and P. Lindstrom (2008). "PET and MRI Show Differences in Cerebral Asymmetry and Functional Connectivity Between Homo- and Heterosexual Subjects." *Proceedings of the National Academy of Sciences of the United States of America* 105(27): 9403–9408.

Sax, L. (2002). "How Common Is Intersex? A Response to Anne Fausto-Sterling." *Journal of Sex Research* 39(3): 174–178.

Saxe, R., and N. Kanwisher (2003). "People Thinking About Thinking People—The Role of the Temporo-Parietal Junction in 'Theory of Mind.'" *Neuroimage* 19(4): 1835–1842.

Schacter, S., and J. Singer (1962). "Cognitive, Social, and Physiological Determinants of Emotional State." *Psychological Review* 69(5): 379–399.

Schatzel-Murphy, E. A., D. A. Harris, et al. (2009). "Sexual Coercion in Men and Women: Similar Behaviors, Different Predictors." *Archives of Sexual Behavior* 38(6): 974–986.

Schein, M. W., and E. B. Hale (1957). "The Head as a Stimulus for Orientation and Arousal of Sexual Behavior of Male Turkeys." *Anatomical Record* 128(3): 617–618.

Schenck, C. H., I. Arnulf, et al. (2007). "Sleep and Sex: What Can Go Wrong? A Review of the Literature on Sleep Related Disorders and Abnormal Sexual Behaviors and Experiences." *Sleep* 30(6): 683–702.

Schiffer, B., T. Krueger, et al. (2008). "Brain Response to Visual Sexual Stimuli in Homosexual Pedophiles." *Journal of Psychiatry & Neuroscience* 33(1): 23–33.

Schiffer, B., T. Peschel, et al. (2007). "Structural Brain Abnormalities in the Frontostriatal System and Cerebellum in Pedophilia." *Journal of Psychiatric Research* 41(9): 753–762.

Schmitt, D. P. (2006) "On the Evolutionary Virtues of Temperate Orgasms and Prudent Sperm Allocation." *Evolutionary Psychology* 4: 471–473.

Schmitt, D. P. (2002). "A Meta-Analysis of Sex Differences in Romantic Attraction: Do Rating Contexts Moderate Tactic Effectiveness Judgments?" *British Journal of Social Psychology* 41: 387–402.

Schmitt, D. P. (2005). "Sociosexuality from Argentina to Zimbabwe: A 48-Nation Study of Sex, Culture, and Strategies of Human Mating." *Behavioral and Brain Sciences* 28(2): 247–275.

Schmitt, D. P., T. K. Shackleford, et al. (2001). "The Desire for Sexual Variety as a Key to Understanding Basic Human Mating Strategies." *Personal Relationships* 8(4): 425–455.

Schopp, L. H., G. E. Good, et al. (2006). "Masculine Role Adherence and Outcomes Among Men with Traumatic Brain Injury." *Brain Injury* 20(11): 1155–1162.

Schulman, A. H. (1970). "Precocial Sexual Behaviour in Imprinted Male Turkeys (Meleagris-Gallopavo)." *Animal Behaviour* 18: 758–759.

Schulte-Hostedde, A. I., M. A. Eys, et al. (2008). "Female Mate Choice Is Influenced by Male Sport Participation." *Evolutionary Psychology* 6(1): 113–124.

Schulte-Ruther, M., H. J. Markowitsch, et al. (2008). "Gender Differences in Brain Networks Supporting Empathy." *Neuroimage* 42(1): 393–403.

Schulz, A. W. "It Takes Two: Sexual Strategies and Game Theory." *Studies in History and Philosophy of Biological and Biomedical Sciences* 41(1): 41–49.

Schumacher, P., and J. Morahan-Martin (2001). "Gender, Internet and Computer Attitudes and Experiences." *Computers in Human Behavior* 17(1): 95–110.

Schutzwohl, A., A. Fuchs, et al. (2009). "How Willing Are You to Accept Sexual Requests from Slightly Unattractive to Exceptionally Attractive Imagined Requestors?" *Human Nature: An Interdisciplinary Biosocial Perspective* 20(3): 282–293.

Scorolli, C., S. Ghirlanda, et al. (2007). "Relative Prevalence of Different Fetishes." *International Journal of Impotence Research* 19(4): 432–437.

Segraves, R., R. Balon, et al. (2007). "Proposal for Changes in Diagnostic Criteria for Sexual Dysfunctions." *Journal of Sexual Medicine* 4(3): 567–580.

Selwyn, N. (2007). "Hi-Tech = Guy-Tech? An Exploration of Undergraduate Students' Gendered Perceptions of Information and Communication Technologies." *Sex Roles* 56(7–8): 525–536.

Selwyn, N., S. Gorard, et al. (2005). "Whose Internet Is It Anyway? Exploring Adults' (Non)Use of the Internet in Everyday Life." *European Journal of Communication* 20(1): 5–26.

Seo, Y., B. Jeong, et al. (2009). "Plasma Concentration of Prolactin, Testosterone Might Be Associated with Brain Response to Visual Erotic Stimuli in Healthy Heterosexual Males." *Psychiatry Investigation* 6(3): 194–203.

Seo, Y., B. Jeong, et al. (2010). "The Relationship Between Age and Brain Response to Visual Erotic Stimuli in Healthy Heterosexual Males." *International Journal of Impotence Research* 22(4): 234–239.

Shackelford, T. K., and A. T. Goetz (2006). "Comparative Evolutionary Psychology of Sperm Competition." *Journal of Comparative Psychology* 120(2): 139–146.

Shackelford, T. K., N. Pound, et al. (2005). "Psychological and Physiological Adaptations to Sperm Competition in Humans." *Review of General Psychology* 9(3): 228–248.

Shadle, B. L. (2008). "Rape in the Courts of Gusiiland, Kenya, 1940s–1960s." *African Studies Review* 51(2): 27–50.

Shallice, T. (2001). "'Theory of Mind' and the Prefrontal Cortex." *Brain* 124: 247–248.

Shaw, L. H., and L. M. Gant (2002). "Users Divided? Exploring the Gender Gap in Internet Use." *Cyberpsychology & Behavior* 5(6): 517–527.

Shaywitz, B. A., S. E. Shaywitz, et al. (1995). "Sex-Differences in the Functional-Organization of the Brain for Language." *Nature* 373(6515): 607–609.

Sherry, D. F. (2006). "Neuroecology." *Annual Review of Psychology* 57: 167–197.

Sherry, D. F., and E. Hampson (1997). "Evolution and the Hormonal Control of Sexually-Dimorphic Spatial Abilities in Humans." *Trends in Cognitive Sciences* 1(2): 50–56.

Shiah, I. S., C. Y. Chao, et al. (2006). "Treatment of Paraphilic Sexual Disorder: The Use of Topiramate in Fetishism." *International Clinical Psychopharmacology* 21(4): 241–243.

Shim, J. W., S. Lee, et al. (2007). "Who Responds to Unsolicited Sexually Explicit Materials on the Internet?: The Role of Individual Differences." *Cyberpsychology & Behavior* 10(1): 71–79.

Shirky, C. (2008). *Here Comes Everybody: The Power of Organizing Without Organizations.* New York: Penguin Press.

Shughrue, P. J., W. E. Stumpf, et al. (1990). "Developmental-Changes in Estrogen-Receptors in Mouse Cerebral-Cortex Between Birth and Postweaning—Studied by Autoradiography with 11-Beta-Methoxy-16-Alpha-[I-125]Iodoestradiol." *Endocrinology* 126(2): 1112–1124.

Shulman, J. L., and S. G. Horne (2006). "Guilty or Not? A Path Model of Women's Sexual Force Fantasies." *Journal of Sex Research* 43(4): 368–377.

Silberschmidt, M. (1992). "Have Men Become the Weaker Sex—Changing Life Situations in Kisii District, Kenya." *Journal of Modern African Studies* 30(2): 237–253.

Sills, T., G. Wunderlich, et al. (2005). "The Sexual Interest and Desire Inventory-Female (SIDI-F): Item Response Analyses of Data from Women Diagnosed with Hypoactive Sexual Desire Disorder." *Journal of Sexual Medicine* 2(6): 801–818.

Silver, J. M., T. W. McAllister, et al. (2005). *Textbook of Traumatic Brain Injury.* Washington, DC: American Psychiatric Publishing.

Simerly, R. B., L. W. Swanson, et al. (1984). "Demonstration of a Sexual Dimorphism in the Distribution of Serotonin-Immunoreactive Fibers in the Medial Preoptic Nucleus of the Rat." *Journal of Comparative Neurology* 225(2): 151–166.

Simerly, R. B., L. W. Swanson, et al. (1985). "Reversal of the Sexually Dimorphic Distribution of Serotonin-Immunoreactive Fibers in the Medial Preoptic Nucleus by Treatment with Perinatal Androgen." *Brain Research* 340(1): 91–98.

Simmons, L. W., R. C. Firman, et al. (2004). "Human Sperm Competition: Testis Size, Sperm Production and Rates of Extrapair Copulations." *Animal Behaviour* 68: 297–302.

Sims, K. E., M. Meana (2010). "Why Did Passion Wane? A Qualitative Study of Married Women's Attributions for Declines in Sexual Desire." *Journal of Sex & Marital Therapy* 36(4): 360–380.

Singh, D. (1993). "Adaptive Significance of Female Physical Attractiveness—Role of Waist-to-Hip Ratio." *Journal of Personality and Social Psychology* 65(2): 293–307.

Singh, D. (2002). "Female Mate Value at a Glance: Relationship of Waist-to-Hip Ratio to Health, Fecundity And Attractiveness." *Neuroendocrinology Letters* 23, Suppl 4: 81–91.

Singh, J. C., P. Tharyan, et al. (2009). "Prevalence and Risk Factors for Female Sexual Dysfunction in Women Attending a Medical Clinic in South India." *Journal of Postgraduate Medicine* 55(2): 113–120.

Sipski, M. L. (2001). "A Physiatrist's Views Regarding the Report of the International Consensus Conference on Female Sexual Dysfunction: Potential Concerns Regarding Women with Disabilities." *Journal of Sex & Marital Therapy* 27(2): 215–216.

Sisk, C. L., and D. L. Foster (2004). "The Neural Basis of Puberty and Adolescence." *Nature Neuroscience* 7(10): 1040–1047.

Slijper, F. M. E. (1984). "Androgens and Gender Role-Behavior in Girls with Congenital Adrenal-Hyperplasia (CAH)." *Progress in Brain Research* 61: 417–422.

Slimp, J. C., B. L. Hart, et al. (1978). "Heterosexual, Auto-Sexual and Social-Behavior of Adult Male Rhesus-Monkeys with Medial Preoptic-Anterior Hypothalamic-Lesions." *Brain Research* 142(1): 105–122.

Slob, A. K., C. M. Bax, et al. (1996). "Sexual Arousability and the Menstrual Cycle." *Psychoneuroendocrinology* 21(6): 545–558.

Smeets, W., O. Marin, et al. (2000). "Evolution of the Basal Ganglia: New Perspectives Through a Comparative Approach." *Journal of Anatomy* 196: 501–517.

Smith, D., and R. Over (1987). "Does Fantasy-Induced Sexual Arousal Habituate." *Behaviour Research and Therapy* 25(6): 477–485.

Smith, D., and R. Over (1987). "Male Sexual Arousal as a Function of the Content and the Vividness of Erotic Fantasy." *Psychophysiology* 24(3): 334–339.

Smith, D., and R. Over (1990). "Enhancement of Fantasy-Induced Sexual Arousal in Men Through Training in Sexual Imagery." *Archives of Sexual Behavior* 19(5): 477–489.

Smith, D. V., B. Y. Hayden, et al. "Distinct Value Signals in Anterior and Posterior Ventromedial Prefrontal Cortex." *Journal of Neuroscience* 30(7): 2490–2495.

Smith, E. P., J. Boyd, et al. (1994). "Estrogen Resistance Caused by a Mutation in the Estrogen-Receptor Gene in a Man." *New England Journal of Medicine* 331(16): 1056–1061.

Smith, K. S., A. J. Tindell, et al. (2009). "Ventral Pallidum Roles in Reward and Motivation." *Behavioural Brain Research* 196(2): 155–167.

Smuts, R. W. (1992). "Fat, Sex, Class, Adaptive Flexibility, and Cultural-Change." *Ethology and Sociobiology* 13(5–6): 523–542.

Southern, S. (2008). "Treatment of Compulsive Cybersex Behavior." *Psychiatric Clinics of North America* 31(4): 697–712

Spelke, E. S. (2005). "Sex Differences in Intrinsic Aptitude for Mathematics and Science? A Critical Review." *American Psychologist* 60(9): 950–958.

Spiering, M., W. Everaerd, et al. (2002). "Conscious Processing of Sexual Information: Interference Caused by Sexual Primes." *Archives of Sexual Behavior* 31(2): 159–164.

Spiering, M., W. Everaerd, et al. (2003). "Priming the Sexual System: Implicit Versus Explicit Activation." *Journal of Sex Research* 40(2): 134–145.

Spiering, M., W. Everaerd, et al. (2004). "Conscious Processing of Sexual Information: Mechanisms of Appraisal." *Archives of Sexual Behavior* 33(4): 369–380.

Spinella, M. (2004). "Hypersexuality and Dysexecutive Syndrome After a Thalamic Infarct." *International Journal of Neuroscience* 114(12): 1581–1590.

Spinella, M. (2007). "The Role of Prefrontal Systems in Sexual Behavior." *International Journal of Neuroscience* 117(3): 369–385.

Spink, A., B. J. Jansen, et al. (2002). "From E-Sex to E-Commerce: Web Search Changes." *Computer* 35(3): 107–109.

Spink, A., H. Partridge, et al. (2006). "Sexual and Pornographic Web Searching: Trends Analysis." *First Monday* 11(9).

Sprecher, S. (2002). "Sexual Satisfaction in Premarital Relationships: Associations with Satisfaction, Love, Commitment, and Stability." *Journal of Sex Research* 39(3): 190–196.

Stack, S., I. Wasserman, et al. (2004). "Adult Social Bonds and Use of Internet Pornography."*Social Science Quarterly* 85(1): 75–88.

Standen, V., and R. Foley (1989). *Comparative Socioecology: The Behavioural Ecology of Humans and Other Mammals.* Oxford; Boston; Brookline Village, MA: Blackwell Scientific Publications.

Stark, R., A. Schienle, et al. (2005). "Erotic and Disgust-Inducing Pictures— Differences in the Hemodynamic Responses of the Brain." *Biological Psychology* 70(1): 19–29.

Stern, J. M. (1990). "Multisensory Regulation of Maternal-Behavior and Masculine Sexual-Behavior—A Revised View." *Neuroscience and Biobehavioral Reviews* 14(2): 183–200.

Stern, J. M. (1991). "Mammalian Parenting—Biochemical, Neurobiological, and Behavioral Determinants—Krasnegor, NA, Bridges, RS." *Contemporary Psychology* 36(8): 678–679.

Stillwell, A. M., R. F. Baumeister, et al. (2008). "We're All Victims Here: Toward a Psychology of Revenge." *Basic and Applied Social Psychology* 30(3): 253–263.

Stoleru, S., M. C. Gregoire, et al. (1999). "Neuroanatomical Correlates of Visually Evoked Sexual Arousal in Human Males." *Archives of Sexual Behavior* 28(1): 1–21.

Stoleru, S., J. Redoute, et al. (2003). "Brain Processing of Visual Sexual Stimuli in Men with Hypoactive Sexual Desire Disorder." *Psychiatry Research: Neuroimaging* 124(2): 67–86.

Stoleru, S. G., A. Ennaji, et al. (1993). "LH Pulsatile Secretion and Testosterone Blood-Levels Are Influenced by Sexual Arousal in Human Males." *Psychoneuroendocrinology* 18(3): 205–218.

Stone, E.A., T. K. Shackelford, and D.M. Buss (2007), "Sex Ratio and Mate Preferences: A Cross-Cultural Investigation." *European Journal of Social Psychology* 37: 288–296.

Straiko, M. A. W., G. A. Gudelsky, et al. (2007). "Treatment with a Serotonin-Depleting Regimen of MDMA Prevents Conditioned Place Preference to Sex in Male Rats." *Behavioral Neuroscience* 121(3): 586–593.

Strassberg, D. S., and L. K. Lockerd (1998). "Force in Women's Sexual Fantasies." *Archives of Sexual Behavior* 27(4): 403–414.

Striar, S., and B. Bartlik (1999). "Stimulation of the Libido: The Use of Erotica in Sex Therapy." *Psychiatric Annals* 29(1): 60–62.

Stumpf, R. M., and C. Boesch (2005). "Does Promiscuous Mating Preclude Female Choice? Female Sexual Strategies in Chimpanzees (Pan Troglodytes Verus) of the Tai National Park, Cote d'Ivoire." *Behavioral Ecology and Sociobiology* 57(5): 511–524.

Sundaram, T., G. W. Jeong, et al. (2010). "Time-Course Analysis of the Neuroanatomical Correlates of Sexual Arousal Evoked by Erotic Video Stimuli in Healthy Males." *Korean Journal of Radiology* 11(3): 278–285.

Suschinsky, K. D., M. L. Lalumiere, et al. (2009). "Sex Differences in Patterns of Genital Sexual Arousal: Measurement Artifacts or True Phenomena?" *Archives of Sexual Behavior* 38(4): 559–573.

Swaab, D. F. (2004). "Sexual Differentiation of the Human Brain: Relevance for Gender Identity, Transsexualism and Sexual Orientation." *Gynecological Endocrinology* 19(6): 301–312.

Swaab, D. F., and E. Fliers (1985). "A Sexually Dimorphic Nucleus in the Human-Brain." *Science* 228(4703): 1112–1115.

Swaab, D. F., and M. A. Hofman (1990). "An Enlarged Suprachiasmatic Nucleus in Homosexual Men." *Brain Research* 537(1–2): 141–148.

Swami, V., and A. Furnham (2009). "Big and Beautiful: Attractiveness and Health Ratings of the Female Body by Male 'Fat Admirers.'" *Archives of Sexual Behavior* 38(2): 201–208.

Swami, V., D. Knight, et al. (2007). "Preferences for Female Body Size in Britain and the South Pacific." *Body Image* 4(2): 219–223.

Swami, V., N. Salem, et al. (2008). "The Influence of Feminist Ascription on Judgements of Women's Physical Attractiveness." *Body Image* 5(2): 224–229.

Swami, V., and M. Tovee (2009). "Big Beautiful Women: The Body Size Preferences of Male Fat Admirers." *Journal of Sex Research* 46(1): 89–96.

Swami, V., and M. J. Tovee (2006). "Does Hunger Influence Judgments of Female Physical Attractiveness?" *British Journal of Psychology* 97: 353–363.

Swami, V., and M. J. Tovee (2006). "The Influence of Body Mass Index on the Physical Attractiveness Preferences of Feminist and Nonfeminist Heterosexual Women and Lesbians." *Psychology of Women Quarterly* 30(3): 252–257.

Swami, V., and M. J. Tovee (2007). "Perceptions of Female Body Weight and Shape Among Indigenous and Urban Europeans." *Scandinavian Journal of Psychology* 48(1): 43–50.

Symons, D. (1979). *The Evolution of Human Sexuality*. New York: Oxford University Press.

Syngelaki, E. M., S. C. Moore, et al. (2009). "Executive Functioning and Risky Decision Making in Young Male Offenders." *Criminal Justice and Behavior* 36(11): 1213–1227.

Tanurdzic, M., and J. A. Banks (2004). "Sex-Determining Mechanisms in Land Plants." *Plant Cell* 16: S61–S71.

Targosz, C. (2008). *Dating the Younger Man: Guide to Every Woman's Sweetest Indulgence*. Massachusetts: Adams Media.

Taylor, S. E., L. C. Klein, et al. (2000). "Biobehavioral Responses to Stress in Females: Tend-and-Befriend, Not Fight-or-Flight." *Psychological Review* 107(3): 411–429.

Taylor, S. E., B. P. Lewis, et al. (2002). "Sex Differences in Biobehavioral Responses to Threat: Reply to Geary and Flinn (2002)." *Psychological Review* 109(4): 751–753.

Tazialix, M., A. Kahn, et al. (2008). "Enhanced Neural Activation in Brain Regions Mediating Sexual Responses Following Exposure to a Conditioned Stimulus That Predicts Copulation." *Neuroscience* 151(3): 644–658.

Tebes, J. K. (2000). "External Validity and Scientific Psychology." *American Psychologist* 55(12): 1508–1509.

ten Cate, C., M. N. Verzijden, et al. (2006). "Sexual Imprinting Can Induce Sexual Preferences for Exaggerated Parental Traits." *Current Biology* 16(11): 1128–1132.

Terrett, N. K., A. S. Bell, D. Brown, et al. (1996): "Sildenafil (VIAGRA(TM)), a Potent and Selective Inhibitor of Type 5 cGMP Phosphodiesterase with Utility For the Treatment of Male Erectile Dysfunction." *Bioorganic & Medicinal Chemistry Letters* 6(15): 1819–1824.

Terry, L., and P. Vasey "Feederism in a Woman." *Archives of Sexual Behavior*, in press. Epub ahead of print, retrieved April 2010, http://www.ncbi.nlm.nih.gov/pubmed/20041284

Terzian, H., and G. D. Ore (1955). "Syndrome of Kluver and Bucy—Reproduced in Man by Bilateral Removal of the Temporal Lobes." *Neurology* 5(6): 373–380.

Thompson, P. M., T. D. Cannon, et al. (2001). "Genetic Influences on Brain Structure." *Nature Neuroscience* 4(12): 1253–1258.

Thornhill, R., and C. T. Palmer. (2000). *A Natural History of Rape: Biological Bases of Sexual Coercion*. Cambridge, MA: MIT Press.

Thornhill, R., and S. W. Gangestad (2008). *The Evolutionary Biology of Human Female Sexuality*. Oxford; New York: Oxford University Press.

Timm, T. M. (2001). "Cybersex: The Dark Side of the Force." *Journal of Sex Research* 38(4): 345–346.

Toates, F. (2005). "Evolutionary Psychology—Towards a More Integrative Model." *Biology & Philosophy* 20(2–3): 305–328.

Toates, F. (2009). "An Integrative Theoretical Framework for Understanding Sexual Motivation, Arousal, and Behavior." *Journal of Sex Research* 46(2–3): 168–193.

Tokatlidis, O., and R. Over (1995). "Imagery, Fantasy, and Female Sexual Arousal." *Australian Journal of Psychology* 47(2): 81–85.

Tolman, D. L. (1994). "Doing Desire: Adolescent Girls' Struggles For/With Sexuality." *Gender & Society* 8(3): 324–342.

Tooby, J., and L. Cosmides (1990). "On the Universality of Human-Nature and the Uniqueness of the Individual—The Role of Genetics and Adaptation." *Journal of Personality* 58(1): 17–67.

Toran-allerand, C. D. (1980). "Sex Steroids and the Development of the Newborn Mouse Hypothalamus and Preoptic Area in Vitro. II. Morphological Correlates and Hormonal Specificity." *Brain Research* 189(2): 413–427.

Toran-Allerand, C. D., X. P. Guan, et al. (2002). "ER-X: A Novel, Plasma Membrane–Associated, Putative Estrogen Receptor That Is Regulated During Development and After Ischemic Brain Injury." *Journal of Neuroscience* 22(19): 8391–8401.

Toranallerand, C. D., R. C. Miranda, et al. (1992). "Estrogen-Receptors Colocalize with Low-Affinity Nerve Growth-Factor Receptors in Cholinergic Neurons of the Basal Forebrain." *Proceedings of the National Academy of Sciences of the United States of America* 89(10): 4668–4672.

Tovee, M. J., V. Swami, et al. (2006). "Changing Perceptions of Attractiveness as Observers Are Exposed to a Different Culture." *Evolution and Human Behavior* 27(6): 443–456.

Tracy, J. K., and J. Junginger (2007). "Correlates of Lesbian Sexual Functioning." *Journal of Women's Health* 16(4): 499–509.

Traeen, B., T. S. Nilsen, et al. (2006). "Use of Pornography in Traditional Media and on the Internet in Norway." *Journal of Sex Research* 43(3): 245–254.

Tranel, D., H. Damasio, et al. (2005). "Does Gender Play a Role in Functional Asymmetry of Ventromedial Prefrontal Cortex?" *Brain* 128: 2872–2881.

Trivers, R. L. (1972). "Mother-Offspring Conflict." *American Zoologist* 12(4): 648–648.

Trivers, R. L., and D. E. Willard (1973). "Natural-Selection of Parental Ability to Vary Sex-Ratio of Offspring." *Science* 179(4068): 90–92.

Troisi, A., and M. Carosi (1998). "Female Orgasm Rate Increases with Male Dominance in Japanese Macaques." *Animal Behavior* 56(5): 1261–1266.

Tsai, M. J., and B. W. Omalley (1994). "Molecular Mechanisms of Action of Steroid/Thyroid Receptor Superfamily Members." *Annual Review of Biochemistry* 63: 451–486.

Tsujimura, A., Y. Miyagawa, et al. (2009). "Sex Differences in Visual Attention to Sexually Explicit Videos: A Preliminary Study." *Journal of Sexual Medicine* 6(4): 1011–1017.

Tuiten, A., E. Laan, et al. (1996). "Discrepancies Between Genital Responses and Subjective Sexual Function During Testosterone Substitution in Women with Hypothalamic Amenorrhea." *Psychosomatic Medicine* 58(3): 234–241.

Turkheimer, E. (2000). "Three Laws of Behavior Genetics and What They Mean." *Current Directions in Psychological Science* 9(5): 160–164.

BIBLIOGRAPHY

Tybur, J. M., D. Lieberman, et al. (2009). "Microbes, Mating, and Morality: Individual Differences in Three Functional Domains of Disgust." *Journal of Personality and Social Psychology* 97(1): 103–122.

Urgesi, C., G. Berlucchi, et al. (2004). "Magnetic Stimulation of Extrastriate Body Area Impairs Visual Processing of Nonfacial Body Parts." *Current Biology* 14(23): 2130–2134.

Urgesi, C., B. Calvo-Merino, et al. (2007). "Transcranial Magnetic Stimulation Reveals Two Cortical Pathways for Visual Body Processing." *Journal of Neuroscience* 27(30): 8023–8030.

van Anders, S. M., L. Brotto, et al. (2009). "Associations Among Physiological and Subjective Sexual Response, Sexual Desire, and Salivary Steroid Hormones in Healthy Premenopausal Women." *Journal of Sexual Medicine* 6(3): 739–751.

van der Made, F., J. Bloemers, et al. (2009). "Childhood Sexual Abuse, Selective Attention for Sexual Cues and the Effects of Testosterone with or without Vardenafil on Physiological Sexual Arousal in Women with Sexual Dysfunction: A Pilot Study." *Journal of Sexual Medicine* 6(2): 429–439.

Van Hooff, J. C., H. Crawford, et al. (2009). "The Wandering Eye of Men: An Electrophysiological Investigation into Distraction by Attraction." *Psychophysiology* 46: S120–S121.

van Lankveld, J., and F. T. Y. Smulders (2008). "The Effect of Visual Sexual Content on the Event-Related Potential." *Biological Psychology* 79(2): 200–208.

Van Overwalle, F. (2009). "Social Cognition and the Brain: A Meta-Analysis." *Human Brain Mapping* 30(3): 829–858.

van Wingen, G., C. Mattern, et al. (2010). "Testosterone Reduces Amygdala-Orbitofrontal Cortex Coupling." *Psychoneuroendocrinology* 35(1): 105–113.

Van Wyk, P. H. (1995). "Biology of Biosexuality—Critique and Observations" *Journal of Homosexuality* 28(3): 357–373.

Vardi, Y., E. Sprecher, et al. (2009). "The P300 Event-Related Potential Technique for Libido Assessment in Women with Hypoactive Sexual Desire Disorder." *Journal of Sexual Medicine* 6(6): 1688–1695.

Vardi, Y., A. Volos, et al. (2006). "A P300 Event Related Potential Technique for Assessment of Sexually Oriented Interest." *Journal of Urology* 176(6): 2736–2740.

Vasey, P. L., D. Rains, et al. (2008). "Courtship Behaviour in Japanese Macaques During Heterosexual and Homosexual Consortships." *Behavioural Processes* 78(3): 401–407.

Veale, J. F. (2008). "Prevalence of Transsexualism Among New Zealand Passport Holders." *Australian and New Zealand Journal of Psychiatry* 42(10): 887–889.

Veale, J. F., D. E. Clarke, et al. (2008). "Sexuality of Male-to-Female Transsexuals." *Archives of Sexual Behavior* 37(4): 586–597.

Veale, J. F., D. E. Clarke, et al. (2009). "Reply to Lawrence and Bailey (2008)." *Archives of Sexual Behavior* 38(2): 176–177.

Vega, V., and N. M. Malamuth (2007). "Predicting Sexual Aggression: The Role of Pornography in the Context of General and Specific Risk Factors." *Aggressive Behavior* 33(2): 104–117.

Veniegas, R. C., and T. D. Conley (2000). "Biological Research on Women's Sexual Orientations: Evaluating the Scientific Evidence" *The Journal of Social Issues* 56(2): 267–282.

Venkatesh, V., and M. G. Morris (2000). "Why Don't Men Ever Stop to Ask For Directions? Gender, Social Influence, and Their Role in Technology Acceptance and Usage Behavior." *MIS Quarterly* 24(1): 115–139.

Vohs, K. D., and R. F. Baumeister (2009). "Addiction and Free Will." *Addiction Research & Theory* 17(3): 231–235.

Vohs, K. D., B. J. Schmeichel, et al. (2008). "Making Choices Impairs Subsequent Self-Control: A Limited-Resource Account of Decision Making, Self-Regulation, and Active Initiative." *Journal of Personality and Social Psychology* 94(5): 883–898.

Voracek, M., A. Hofhansl, M. L. Fisher. (2005). "Clark and Hatfield's Evidence of Women's Low Receptivity to Male Strangers' Sexual Offers Revisited." *Psychological Reports* 97(1): 11–20.

Voracek, M., and M. L. Fisher (2006). "Success Is All in the Measures: Androgenousness, Curvaceousness, and Starring Frequencies in Adult Media Actresses." *Archives of Sexual Behavior* 35(3): 297–304.

Voracek, M., and M. L. Fisher (2009). "Data Are the Natural Enemy of Hypotheses: Reply to Holland (2009)." *Archives of Sexual Behavior* 38(4): 460–462.

Voracek, M., M. L. Fisher, et al. (2007). "Sex Differences in Relative Foot Length and Perceived Attractiveness of Female Feet: Relationships Among Anthropometry, Physique, and Preference Ratings." *Perceptual and Motor Skills* 104(3): 1123–1138.

Waismann, R., P. B. C. Fenwick, et al. (2003). "EEG Responses to Visual Erotic Stimuli in Men with Normal and Paraphilic Interests." *Archives of Sexual Behavior* 32(2): 135–144.

Waitt, C., A. C. Little, et al. (2003). "Evidence from Rhesus Macaques Suggests That Male Coloration Plays a Role in Female Primate Mate Choice." *Proceedings of the Royal Society of London Series B-Biological Sciences* 270: S144–S146.

Walker, Q. D., R. Ray, et al. (2006). "Sex Differences in Neurochemical Effects of Dopaminergic Drugs in Rat Striatum." *Neuropsychopharmacology* 31(6): 1193–1202.

Wallen, K. (1996). "Nature Needs Nurture: The Interaction of Hormonal and Social Influences on the Development of Behavioral Sex Differences in Rhesus Monkeys." *Hormones and Behavior* 30(4): 364–378.

Wallen, K. (2005). "Hormonal Influences on Sexually Differentiated Behavior in Nonhuman Primates." *Frontiers in Neuroendocrinology* 26(1): 7–26.

Wallen, K., and H. A. Rupp (2010). "Women's Interest in Visual Sexual Stimuli Varies with Menstrual Cycle Phase at First Exposure and Predicts Later Interest." *Hormones and Behavior* 57(2): 263–268.

BIBLIOGRAPHY

Wallien, M. S. C., and P. T. Cohen-Kettenis (2008). "Psychosexual Outcome of Gender-Dysphoric Children." *Journal of the American Academy of Child and Adolescent Psychiatry* 47(12): 1413–1423.

Walsh, A. (1999). "Life History Theory and Female Readers of Pornography." *Personality and Individual Differences* 27(4): 779–787.

Walter, M., F. Bermpohl, et al. (2008). "Distinguishing Specific Sexual and General Emotional Effects in fMRI—Subcortical and Cortical Arousal During Erotic Picture Viewing." *Neuroimage* 40(4): 1482–1494.

Walter, M., J. Stadler, et al. (2008). "High Resolution fMRI of Subcortical Regions During Visual Erotic Stimulation at 7 T." *Magnetic Resonance Materials in Physics Biology and Medicine* 21(1–2): 103–111.

Wang, H. Y., and Y. S. Wang (2008). "Gender Differences in the Perception and Acceptance of Online Games." *British Journal of Educational Technology* 39(5): 787–806.

Wasserman, I. M., and M. Richmond-Abbott (2005). "Gender and the Internet: Causes of Variation in Access, Level, and Scope of Use." *Social Science Quarterly* 86(1): 252–270.

Weinberg, M., C. Williams, et al. "Pornography, Normalization, and Empowerment." *Archives of Sexual Behavior*, in press. Epub ahead of print, retrieved, August 2010, http://www.ncbi.nlm.nih.gov/pubmed/20127507

Weinberg, M. S., and C. J. Williams (2010). "Men Sexually Interested in Transwomen (MSTW): Gendered Embodiment and the Construction of Sexual Desire." *Journal of Sex Research* 47(4): 374–383.

Weinberg, T. S. (2006). "Sadomasochism and the Social Sciences: A Review of the Sociological and Social Psychological Literature." *Journal of Homosexuality* 50(2–3): 17–40.

Weiser, E. B. (2000). "Gender Differences in Internet Use Patterns and Internet Application Preferences: A Two-Sample Comparison." *Cyberpsychology & Behavior* 3(2): 167–178.

Weisfeld, G. E., and L. Woodward (2004). "Current Evolutionary Perspectives on Adolescent Romantic Relations and Sexuality." *Journal of the American Academy of Child and Adolescent Psychiatry* 43(1): 11–19.

Wells, J. W. (1990). "The Sexual Vocabularies of Heterosexual and Homosexual Males and Females for Communicating Erotically with a Sexual Partner." *Archives of Sexual Behavior* 19(2): 139–147.

Wendell, S., and C. Tan (2009), *Beyond Heaving Bosoms: The Smart Bitches' Guide o Romance Novels*. New York: Simon & Schuster.

Whitham, J. C., and D. Maestripieri (2003). "Primate Rituals: The Function of Greetings Between Male Guinea Baboons." *Ethology* 109(10): 847–859.

Whiting, B., and C. P. Edwards (1973). "Cross-Cultural Analysis of Sex-Differences in Behavior of Children Aged 3 Through 11." *Journal of Social Psychology* 91(2): 171–188.

BIBLIOGRAPHY

Whitty, M. T. (2002). "Liar, Liar! An Examination of How Open, Supportive and Honest People Are in Chat Rooms." *Computers in Human Behavior* 18(4): 343–352.

Wicker, B., C. Keysers, et al. (2003). "Both of Us Disgusted in My Insula: The Common Neural Basis of Seeing and Feeling Disgust." *Neuron* 40(3): 655–664.

Wiegel, M., C. Meston, et al. (2005). "The Female Sexual Function Index (FSFI): Cross-Validation and Development of Clinical Cutoff Scores." *Journal of Sex & Marital Therapy* 31(1): 1–20.

Wilcox, A. J., C. R. Weinberg, et al. (1995). "Timing of Sexual Intercourse in Relation to Ovulation—Effects on The Probability of Conception, Survival of the Pregnancy, and Sex of the Baby." *New England Journal of Medicine* 333(23): 1517–1521.

Wilkinson, E. (2009). "Perverting Visual Pleasure: Representing Sadomasochism." *Sexualities* 12(2): 181–198.

Williams, C. J., and M. S. Weinberg (2003). "Zoophilia in Men: A Study of Sexual Interest in Animals." *Archives of Sexual Behavior* 32(6): 523–535.

Williams, K. M., B. S. Cooper, et al. (2009). "Inferring Sexually Deviant Behavior from Corresponding Fantasies: The Role of Personality and Pornography Consumption." *Criminal Justice and Behavior* 36(2): 198–222.

Williams, M. J., and G. A. Mendelsohn (2008). "Gender Clues and Cues: Online Interactions as Windows into Lay Theories about Men and Women." *Basic and Applied Social Psychology* 30(3): 278–294.

Willoughby, T. (2008). "A Short-Term Longitudinal Study of Internet and Computer Game Use by Adolescent Boys and Girls: Prevalence, Frequency of Use, and Psychosocial Predictors." *Developmental Psychology* 44(1): 195–204.

Wilson, E. O. (2000). *Sociobiology: The New Synthesis.* Cambridge, MA: Harvard University Press.

Wilson, G. D., and C. Gosselin (1980). "Personality-Characteristics of Fetishists, Transvestites and Sadomasochists." *Personality and Individual Differences* 1(3): 289–295.

Wilson, G. D., and R. J. Lang (1981). "Sex-Differences in Sexual Fantasy Patterns." *Personality and Individual Differences* 2(4): 343–346.

Wilson, J. E., and K. M. Wilson (2008). "Amelioration of Sexual Fantasies to Sexual Abuse Cues in an Adult Survivor of Childhood Sexual Abuse: A Case Study." *Journal of Behavior Therapy and Experimental Psychiatry* 39(4): 417–423.

Wilson, J. R., R.E. Kuehn et al. (1963) "Modification in the Sexual Behavior of Male Rats Produced by Changing the Stimulus Female." *Journal of Comparative Physiology and Psychology* 56(3): 636–644.

Wincze, J. P., E. Venditti, et al. (1980). "The Effects of a Subjective Monitoring Task in the Physiological Measure of Genital Response to Erotic Stimulation." *Archives of Sexual Behavior* 9(6): 533–545.

Wingfield, J. C., R. E. Hegner, et al. (1990). "The Challenge Hypothesis—Theoretical Implications for Patterns of Testosterone Secretion, Mating Systems, and Breeding Strategies." *American Naturalist* 136(6): 829–846.

Winn, J. L., and C. Heeter (2009). "Gaming, Gender, and Time: Who Makes Time to Play?" *Sex Roles* 61(1–2): 1–13.

Winslow, J. T., N. Hastings, et al. (1993). "A Role for Central Vasopressin in Pair Bonding in Monogamous Prairie Voles." *Nature* 365(6446): 545–548.

Winters, J., K. Christoff, et al. (2009). "Conscious Regulation of Sexual Arousal in Men." *Journal of Sex Research* 46(4): 330–343.

Wirth, M., H. Horn, et al. (2007). "Sex Differences in Semantic Processing: Event-Related Brain Potentials Distinguish Between Lower and Higher Order Semantic Analysis During Word Reading." *Cerebral Cortex* 17(9): 1987–1997.

Wiszewska, A., B. Pawlowski, et al. (2007). "Father-Daughter Relationship as a Moderator of Sexual Imprinting: A Facialmetric Study." *Evolution and Human Behavior* 28(4): 248–252.

Witelson, S. F., Glezer, II, et al. (1995). "Women Have Greater Density of Neurons in Posterior Temporal Cortex." *Journal of Neuroscience* 15(5): 3418–3428.

Witte, K., and N. Sawka (2003). "Sexual Imprinting on a Novel Trait in the Dimorphic Zebra Finch: Sexes Differ." *Animal Behaviour* 65: 195–203.

Wobber, V., B. Hare, et al. (2010). "Differential Changes in Steroid Hormones Before Competition in Bonobos and Chimpanzees." *Proceedings of the National Academy of Sciences of the United States of America* 107(28): 12457–12462.

Wolak, J., K. Mitchell, et al. (2007). "Unwanted and Wanted Exposure to Online Pornography in a National Sample of Youth Internet Users." *Pediatrics* 119(2): 247–257.

Wolf, A. (2000). "Emotional Expression Online: Gender Differences in Emoticon Use." *Cyberpsychology & Behavior* 3(5): 827–833.

Wood, J. L., D. Heitmiller, et al. (2008). "Morphology of the Ventral Frontal Cortex: Relationship to Femininity and Social Cognition." *Cerebral Cortex* 18(3): 534–540.

Wood, J. M., P. K. Mansfield, et al. (2007). "Negotiating Sexual Agency: Postmenopausal Women's Meaning and Experience of Sexual Desire." *Qualitative Health Research* 17(2): 189–200.

Wood, W., and A. H. Eagly (2002). "A Cross-Cultural Analysis of the Behavior of Women and Men: Implications for the Origins of Sex Differences." *Psycholological Bulletin* 128(5): 699–727.

Woodson, J. C. (2002). "Including 'Learned Sexuality' in the Organization of Sexual Behavior." *Neuroscience and Biobehavioral Reviews* 26(1): 69–80.

Woodiwiss, K. E. (1972). *The Flame and the Flower*. New York: Avon.

BIBLIOGRAPHY

Woolf-King, S. E., S. Maisto, et al. (2009). "Selection of Film Clips and Development of a Video for the Investigation of Sexual Decision Making Among Men Who Have Sex with Men." *Journal of Sex Research*, in press. Epub ahead of print, retrieved, March 2010, http://www.ncbi.nlm.nih.gov/pubmed/19760530

Woolley, C. S., and B. S. McEwen (1992). "Estradiol Mediates Fluctuation in Hippocampal Synapse Density During the Estrous-Cycle in the Adult-Rat." *Journal of Neuroscience* 12(7): 2549–2554.

Wrangham, R. W., and M. L. Wilson (2004). *Collective Violence—Comparisons Between Youths and Chimpanzees*. New York Academy of Sciences.

Wrangham, R. W., M. L. Wilson, et al. (2006). *Comparative Rates of Violence in Chimpanzees and Humans*. Tokyo: Springer.

Wright, L. W., and H. E. Adams (1999). "The Effects of Stimuli That Vary in Erotic Content on Cognitive Processes." *Journal of Sex Research* 36(2): 145–151.

Wright, S. (2006). "Discrimination of SM-Identified Individuals." *Journal of Homosexuality* 50(2–3): 217–231.

Xerri, C., J. M. Stern, et al. (1994). "Alterations of the Cortical Representation of the Rat Ventrum Induced by Nursing Behavior." *Journal of Neuroscience* 14(3): 1710–1721.

Xiao, L., A. Bechara, et al. (2008). "Affective Decision-Making Deficits, Linked to a Dysfunctional Ventromedial Prefrontal Cortex, Revealed in 10th-Grade Chinese Adolescent Smokers." *Nicotine & Tobacco Research* 10(6): 1085–1097.

Yamasue, H., O. Abe, et al. (2008). "Sex-Linked Neuroanatomical Basis of Human Altruistic Cooperativeness." *Cerebral Cortex* 18(10): 2331–2340.

Yang, B. J., and D. Lester (2003). "National Character and Internet Use." *Psychological Reports* 93(3): 940–940.

Yang, B. J., and D. Lester (2003). "PC Versus Macintosh Users: A Follow-up Study." *Psychological Reports* 93(3): 954–954.

Yang, B. J., and D. Lester (2004). "Attitudes Toward Buying Online." *Cyberpsychology & Behavior* 7(1): 85–91.

Yang, B. J., and D. Lester (2004). "Sex Differences in Attitudes Toward Computers and the Internet." *Psychological Reports* 95(3): 862–862.

Yang, B. J., and D. Lester (2005). "Gender Differences in e-Commerce." *Applied Economics* 37(18): 2077–2089.

Yang, B. J., and D. Lester (2005). "Sex Differences in Purchasing Textbooks Online." *Computers in Human Behavior* 21(1): 147–152.

Yang, B. J., and D. Lester (2008). "Sex Differences in Online Shopping: An Exploratory Study." *Psychological Reports* 102(3): 723–726.

Yang, B. J., D. Lester, et al. (2006). "Some Personality Correlates of Using eBay." *Psychological Reports* 99(3): 762–762.

Yang, C., and C. C. Wu (2007). "Gender and Internet Consumers' Decision-making." *Cyberpsychology & Behavior* 10(1): 86–91.

BIBLIOGRAPHY

Youn, G. (2006). "Subjective Sexual Arousal in Response to Erotica: Effects of Gender, Guided Fantasy, Erotic Stimulus, and Duration of Exposure." *Archives of Sexual Behavior* 35(1): 87–97.

Young, W. C., R. W. Goy, et al. (1964). "Hormones + Sexual Behavior—Broad Relationships Exist Between Gonadal Hormones + Behavior." *Science* 143(360): 212–+.

Zaadstra, B. M., J. C. Seidell, et al. (1993). "Fat and Female Fecundity—Prospective-Study of Effect of Body-Fat Distribution on Conception Rates." *British Medical Journal* 306(6876): 484–487.

Zahn, R., J. Moll, et al. (2009). "The Neural Basis of Human Social Values: Evidence from Functional MRI." *Cerebral Cortex* 19(2): 276–283.

Zamboni, G., E. D. Huey, et al. (2008). "Apathy and Disinhibition in Frontotemporal Dementia—Insights into Their Neural Correlates." *Neurology* 71(10): 736–742.

Zbinden, M., C. R. Largiader, et al. (2004). "Body Size of Virtual Rivals Affects Ejaculate Size in Sticklebacks." *Behavioral Ecology* 15(1): 137–140.

Zemishlany, Z., and A. Weizman (2008). "The Impact of Mental Illness on Sexual Dysfunction." *Advances in Psychosomatic Medicine* 29: 89–106.

Zhou, J. N., M. A. Hofman, et al. (1995). "A Sex Difference in the Human Brain and Its Relation to Transsexuality." *Nature* 378(6552): 68–70.

Zhu, X., X. Y. Wang, et al. (2010). "Brain Activation Evoked by Erotic Films Varies with Different Menstrual Phases: An fMRI Study." *Behavioural Brain Research* 206(2): 279–285.

Zietsch, B. P., K. I. Morley, et al. (2008). "Genetic Factors Predisposing to Homosexuality May Increase Mating Success in Heterosexuals." *Evolution and Human Behavior* 29(6): 424–433.

Zimbardo, P. G. (2007) *The Lucifer Effect: Understanding How Good People Turn Evil*. New York, Random House.

Zink, C. F., Y. X. Tong, et al. (2008). "Know Your Place: Neural Processing of Social Hierarchy in Humans." *Neuron* 58(2): 273–283.

Zucker, K. J., and R. Green (1992). "Psychosexual Disorders in Children and Adolescents." *Journal of Child Psychology and Psychiatry and Allied Disciplines* 33(1): 107–151.

Zurbriggen, E. L., and M. R. Yost (2004). "Power, Desire, and Pleasure in Sexual Fantasies." *Journal of Sex Research* 41(3): 288–300.

INDEX

INDEX

Bait Bus, 129–30, 191
Bang Bus, 191
Baumeister, Roy, 79–80, 121, 124, 239
BBW (Big, Beautiful Women), 33, 35, 57, 136
behavioral adaptations, 183–84
Behrendt, Greg, 75
Belle de Jour (1967), 175–76
Berliner-Mauer, Eija-Riitta, 84
Berman, Laura, 112
Berscheid, Ellen, 62–63
beta males, 97
Beyond Heaving Bosoms: The Smart Bitches' Guide to Romance Novels (Wendell and Tan), 88
bicuckolds, 181
billionaires, 101
bisexuality, 168–70, *169*, 218, 292nn168–70
Black, Jack, 37
blacks in porn, 135, 181–182, 184
blindness, 142
boarding school culture, 31
Bodilis, Hervé, 226
body image and body maps, 139–43, 237
body-type/size interests, 32–35, *34*, 35–37, 54–58, 261n32, 262nn33–34
Bogard, Rebecca, 204
Boing Boing, 7
bondage and BDSM, 39, 91, 207–11, 300n208, 301n210. *See also* dominance, sexual
bonobos, 68
boobpedia, 47
Botox, 96
bottoms, 143–48, 150–51, 231, 286n144
Boyle, Elizabeth, 112
brain physiology: and body maps, 141; and female sensory cues, 163; and female sexual disorders, 272n70; gay and straight brains compared, 285n138; and gay cues, 138; and gender differences, 76–80, 273n71; and jealousy, 122;

and male arousal, 268n46; and objections to porn, 294n170; and sexual dominance/submission, 96, 143–45, 199–203, 298n192; and sexual fulfillment, 241; and social dominance, 96; and social networking, 78; and transformation fiction, 236–37; and transgression cues, 176–77; and visual cues, 46
Brazzers, 23
breasts, *35*, 35–37, 48–49, 57, 58–60, 140, 234, 263n37; large breasts, 30, 36–37
Brockmann, Suzanne, 104
Brockway, Connie, 97
bukkake, 226–27
bulimia, 113
Bullock, Sandra, 197
Burroughs, William S., 2
Buss, David, 55, 98–99
butts: and animal research, 23, 46; and anime, 44; and body-type interests, 33–34, 37; and female desire, 166; and gay desire, 136; and gay erotica, 138, 139–43; and Internet searches, 14, 16, *16*; and male visual cues, 46–49; and MILF porn, 30
Byron, George Gordon, 193

cameltoe, 166
candid porn, 190
Capilano Canyon Suspension Bridge experiment, 177–78
Casanova, Giacomo, 193
castration, 202
casual sex, 148–49, 287n149
CCBill, 24
Centers for Disease Control and Prevention, 34
CFMN (clothed female naked male), 185, 202
Chamberlain, Wilt, 193
Chandler, Rex, 146
Charlain, Harris, 222
Chat Roulette, 42, 266n42

INDEX

dominance/submission, 195–99;
and transgression cues, 176
dominance, social, 196–97, 204, 208,
278n99, 289n157

East Van Porn Collective, 79
Egan Morrissey, Tracie, 114
ejaculation, 53–54, 83, 132, 161, 183
Ellis, Bruce, 111–12, 298n192
Elmer Fudd, 61, 70, 73, 105, 119,
123–127
emotional cues, 74–77, 83–84, 190,
212, 226
environmental cues, 212
erotical illusions, 213–38; described,
213–15; and facials, 225–27; and
gay porn/romance, 227–32; and
paranormal romance, 220–25;
and T-girl porn, 215–20; and
transformation fiction, 232–37
erotic art, 43–44. *See also* anime and
animated porn
erotic writing. *See also* psychological
cues; romance writing: and
BDSM, 210, 301n210; erotic
romance (EroRom), 90–91,
93–95, 97, 106, 114, 229, 231;
and female desire, 212, 227–32;
gay erotica, 137–38, 146–47,
287n146; and gender differences,
255n19; Literotica, 115–16,
146–47, *181*, 181–82, 210,
285n139, 287n146, 301n210; and
transformation fiction, 232–37
estrogen, 56–57, 149, 164, 286n144
evolution, 55–57, 71–72, 80–81,
103–4, 125, 140, 239–40
The Evolution of Human Sexuality
(Symons), 20
exhibitionism, 42–43, 112, 266n42
exploitation, 202, 209–10
extended sexuality, 156–60
extrastriate body area (EBA),
141, 237

facesitting, 202
facials, 161, 225–27

faked orgasms, 186, 188–89, 191,
219, 296n186
fan fiction: and BDSM, 209–10;
and gay cues, *137*, 137–38; gay
erotica, 228; and popularity cues,
119–21; popularity of, 91–94; and
psychological arousal, 126; rape
fantasies, 116; sexual submission,
205–7; slash stories, 230–31,
303n230
Fantasti.cc, 42, 47, 169, 182, 187,
226, 297n187
Fatel, Mitch, 36, 52, 157
Feehan, Christine, 105
feet-related interests, 37–39, 48–49,
136, 139, 142, 264n37, 264n39
fellatio, 12–13, 129–130, 145, 147,
148
female sexuality, 62–84, 85–107,
108–27, 152–73. *See also*
psychological cues; visual cues;
and adorability cues, 121–23; and
appraisal mechanisms, 71–74; and
coercion/rape fantasies, 113–17;
and cultural information, 78–81;
and emotional information,
74–77; and extended sexuality,
156–60; and feminine intuition,
81–84; and gay porn/erotica,
227–32, 302n227; and gender
differences in porn preference,
170–73, 291n168; and
irresistibility, 108–13; and mind-
body problem, 68–71, 272n69–70;
and multi-cue thresholds,
123–27; and popularity cues,
117–21; and romance writing,
85–87, 87–94, 94–98, 98–101,
101–2, 102–4, 220–25; and
sensory cues, 162–70; and sexual
advance responses, 62–66; and
sexual dominance/submission,
203–7; and sexual dysfunction
treatments, 66–68; and social
information, 77–78; and visual
interests, 152–56, 160–62
femdom, 201, 202

387

INDEX

INDEX

INDEX

INDEX

INDEX